IRISH AND ENGLISH

Irish and English

Essays on the Irish linguistic and cultural frontier, 1600–1900

James Kelly & Ciarán Mac Murchaidh

EDITORS

FOUR COURTS PRESS

Set in 10 pt on 12.5 pt Ehrhardt for
FOUR COURTS PRESS LTD
7 Malpas Street, Dublin 8, Ireland
www.fourcourtspress.ie
and in North America by
FOUR COURTS PRESS
c/o ISBS, 920 N.E. 58th Avenue, Suite 300, Portland, OR 97213.

A catalogue record for this title
is available from the British Library.

ISBN 978–1–84682–340–4

Printed in England
by Antony Rowe Ltd, Chippenham, Wilts.

Contents

9 A journey from manuscript to print: the transmission of an elegy by
Piaras Feiritéar
Deirdre Nic Mhathúna

10 Pious miscellanies and spiritual songs: devotional publishing and
reading in Irish and Scottish Gaelic, 1760–1900
Niall Ó Ciosáin

Illustrations

Contributors

MARC CABALL is a senior lecturer in the College of Arts and Celtic Studies at University College, Dublin. He is the author of *Poets and politics: continuity and reaction in Irish poetry, 1558–1625* (1998), and co-editor (with Andrew Carpenter) of *Oral and print cultures in Ireland, 1600–1900* (2010). His recent publications include 'Gaelic and Protestant: a case-study in early modern self-fashioning, 1567–1608' in *Proceedings of the Royal Irish Academy*, 110C (2010), and 'History and politics: interpretations of early modern conquest and reformation in Victorian Ireland' in Stefan Berger and Chris Lorenz (eds), *Nationalizing the past: historians as nation builders in modern Europe* (2010).

BERNADETTE CUNNINGHAM is deputy librarian at the Royal Irish Academy. Her many publications include *The world of Geoffrey Keating: history, myth and religion in seventeenth-century Ireland* (2000); *The Annals of the Four Masters: Irish history, kingship and society in the early seventeenth century* (2010) and (with Raymond Gillespie) *Stories from Gaelic Ireland: microhistories from the sixteenth-century Irish annals* (2003). She is the editor of *Calendar of State Papers Ireland: Tudor period, 1566–1567* (2009) and *Calendar of State Papers Ireland: Tudor period, 1568–1571* (2010).

CHARLES DILLON lectures in Irish and Celtic Studies in the School of Modern Languages at Queen's University, Belfast. His research interests are the Irish language and literature of the seventeenth and eighteenth centuries, with particular emphasis on the Irish Franciscan texts of the early modern period and the poetry, prose and manuscript tradition of the south Ulster region. He also pursues the history and practice of Irish translation and is editor (with Ríona Ní Fhrighil) of *Aistriú Éireann* (2008).

RAYMOND GILLESPIE, MRIA, is associate Professor of History at NUI, Maynooth. He has published extensively in early modern Irish history, specializing in the seventeenth century. His recent publications include *Stories from Gaelic Ireland: microhistories from the sixteenth-century Irish annals* (with Bernadette Cunningham) (2003); *Reading Ireland: print, reading and social change in early modern Ireland* (2005); *Seventeenth-century Ireland: making Ireland modern* (2006); *Belfast c.1600 to c.1900: the making of the modern city* (with Stephen Royle) (2007); and *The Irish book in English, 1550–1800: the Oxford history of the Irish book*, vol. 3 (edited with Andrew Hadfield) (2006).

JAMES KELLY, MRIA, is Cregan Professor of History and head of the History Department at St Patrick's College, Drumcondra. His publications include

The Proceedings of the Irish House of Lords (3 vols, 2008); *Sir Richard Musgrave, 1746–1818, ultra-protestant ideologue* (2009); *Clubs and societies in eighteenth-century Ireland* (edited with M.J. Powell) (2010); and *The eighteenth-century composite state: representative institutions in Ireland and Europe, 1689–1800* (edited with D.W. Hayton and John Bergin) (2010).

LIAM MAC MATHÚNA is Professor of Irish and head of the School of Irish, Celtic Studies, Irish Folklore and Linguistics at University College, Dublin. His publications include *Béarla sa Ghaeilge* (2007), a study of Irish/English interaction in Irish texts, 1600–1900 and a critical edition of *Séadna* (1987), the first major creative work of the Irish revival. He is currently researching the Ó Neachtain circle in early eighteenth-century Dublin. He is chair of Coiste Léann na Gaeilge, the Royal Irish Academy's national committee for Irish, and editor of *Éigse: A Journal of Irish Studies*.

CIARÁN MAC MURCHAIDH is Dean of Research and Humanities at St Patrick's College, Drumcondra. His research interests lie in the areas of eighteenth-century religious literature in Irish, especially the sermon genre, and in language teaching. His publications include *Cruinnscríobh na Gaeilge*, an Irish-language grammar (fourth edn, 2012); *Filíocht ghrá na Gaeilge: love poems in Irish* (2008); *Lón Anama: poems for prayer from the Irish tradition* (2005); and *'Who needs Irish?' Reflections on the importance of the Irish language today* (2004).

DEIRDRE NIC MHATHÚNA is a lecturer in the Irish Department, St Patrick's College, Drumcondra. She completed her doctoral dissertation, 'Filíocht Phiarais Feiritéar: cnuasach dánta', a critical edition of Piaras Feiritéar's poetry, at University College, Cork in 2008. Her research interests include the editing of seventeenth-century verse, manuscript and print studies and the evolution of autobiographical writing in Irish. Her publications on Feiritéar and his work include 'In praise of two Margarets: two laudatory poems by Piaras Feiritéar', *Proceedings of the Harvard Celtic Colloquium*, 2010. Dr Nic Mhathúna is Treasurer of *Studia Hibernica* and Secretary of Cumann Merriman.

LESA NÍ MHUNGHAILE lectures in the Irish Department at Mary Immaculate College, University of Limerick and is former Irish-language editor of the journal *Eighteenth-Century Ireland/Iris an dá chultúr*. She has published many articles on various aspects of Gaelic scribal culture and the interaction between Protestant antiquarians and Gaelic scribes during the eighteenth century. Her annotated edition of Charlotte Brooke's *Reliques of Irish poetry* (1789) was published by the Irish Manuscripts Commission in 2009.

VINCENT MORLEY holds an M.Phil. in Irish studies from University College, Dublin and a PhD in history from the University of Liverpool. He is author of *An crann os coill: Aodh Buí Mac Cruitín, c.1680–1755* (Dublin, 1995); *Irish opinion and the American Revolution, 1760–1783* (Cambridge, 2002); *Ó Chéitinn go Raiftearaí: mar a cumadh stair na hÉireann* (Dublin, 2011). He has edited *Washington i gceannas a ríochta: cogadh Mheiriceá i litríocht na Gaeilge* (Dublin, 2005). An anthology of the poetry of Aodh Buí Mac Cruitín is in preparation.

NIALL Ó CIOSÁIN is a senior lecturer in the History Department at NUI, Galway. Specializing in the history of print, language and popular culture, his publications include *Print and popular culture in Ireland, 1750–1850* (1997, 2010), and, as editor, *Explaining change in cultural history: Historical Studies XXIII* (2005). He is the author of many articles appertaining to print and language in Ireland, including 'Oral culture, literacy and the growth of a popular readership, 1800–1850', 'Pedlars and book distribution', and 'Almanacs in the nineteenth century' in James H. Murphy (ed.), *The Oxford history of the Irish book, vol. 4: the Irish book in English, 1800–1891* (2011).

Acknowledgments

The transformation of Ireland from a primarily Irish-speaking to a primarily English-speaking country was arguably the most profound social change to take place on the island between the early sixteenth and the mid-nineteenth centuries. Yet the reasons for that transition, no less than the transformation itself, have been less closely perused and critically debated than they might. Recent work on linguistic interchange, on the history of print, on the nature and enduring character of the manuscript culture in Irish, and on the attitudes of both the English- and Irish-speaking communities in Ireland have cast new, sometimes glancing, light on this transition. Together they have expanded our understanding of the prolonged linguistic transformation that took place. This collection explores aspects of this transition from a number of disciplinary perspectives. The object is to offer new perspectives on the shifting linguistic frontier that obtained in Ireland in order better to understand the multiplicity of reasons for the language shift, and to expand and deepen our appreciation of the manner in which it took place, and the interaction of the Irish and English languages during this seminal transition.

As with any undertaking of this nature, the editors have incurred intellectual, personal, organizational and institutional debts during its preparation. It is our pleasure to thank our fellow contributors who have made the book possible, and who have responded with professional distinction and personal courtesy to various appeals and requests from the editors. Thanks are due also to the Research Committee at St Patrick's College for financial support, which has facilitated the publication, and to Professor Máirín Nic Eoin, whose counsel, learning and support for the project have contributed much to its realization. More broadly, we acknowledge the archives, archivists, trustees, custodians and copyright holders of the manuscripts and rare books consulted by the respective authors of the essays in the volume; we specifically acknowledge the British Library, the National Library of Ireland, the National Library of Wales, the National Library of Scotland, the Royal Irish Academy, Trinity College, Dublin, NUI, Maynooth, NUI, Galway, the National Archives, the National Archives of Ireland, the Public Record Office of Northern Ireland and the other repositories and libraries cited, without which the essays in this volume could not have been completed. Finally, it is appropriate also to thank all at Four Courts Press, who continue to lighten the labour of academic book production by their professionalism, good humour and commitment to academic excellence.

January 2012

Abbreviations

Add. MS	Additional Manuscript
BL	British Library
b.	born
bap.	baptised
c.	*circa*
d.	died
DIB	*Dictionary of Irish Biography* edited by James McGuire and James Quinn (9 vols, Cambridge, 2009)
edn.	edition
EHR	*English Historical Review*
ESTC	*English Short Title Catalogue* (3rd edn, London, 2003)
fasc.	fascicule/fascúl
fl.	*floruit*
Hist. Ir. Parl.	*History of the Irish parliament, 1692–1800* by E.M. Johnston-Liik
IHS	*Irish Historical Studies*
Irish Statutes	*The Statutes at large passed in the parliaments held in Ireland, 1310–1800* (20 vols, Dublin, 1789–1800)
ILD	Irish Legislation Database, 1692–1800 accessible at http://www.qub.ac.uk/ild/
ITS	Irish Texts Society
JKAHS	*Journal of the Kerry Archaeological and Historical Society*
MS(S)	Manuscript(s)
NAI	National Archives of Ireland
NLI	National Library of Ireland
NLS	National Library of Scotland
NLW	National Library of Wales
n.d.	no date
n.s.	new series
NUIG	National University of Ireland, Galway
NUIM	National University of Ireland, Maynooth
ODNB	*Oxford Dictionary of National Biography* (60 vols, Oxford, 2004)
PRO	Public Record Office
PRONI	Public Record Office of Northern Ireland
QUB	Queen's University, Belfast
rept.	reprinted
RIA	Royal Irish Academy
RIA proc.	*Proceedings of the Royal Irish Academy*

RSAI Jnl.	*Journal of the Royal Society of Antiquaries of Ireland*
TCD	Trinity College, Dublin
TNA	The National Archives, Public Record Office
trans.	translation
UCC	University College, Cork
UCD	University College, Dublin

Introduction: Establishing the context

In the introduction to his translation of Geoffrey Keating's *Foras feasa ar Éirinn* prepared in 1635, Michael Kearney observed that English was 'now the more respected language among us'.[1] Kearney's remark was so obviously disputable that had it entered the public domain, it must have been challenged by the traditional literary champions of Gaelic Ireland – the poets – who were determined, for cultural reasons as well as reasons of self interest, to uphold the aesthetic, the intellectual and the literary merits of the Irish language in the face of the increased penetration of English and English ways. However, Kearney's comment accurately attested to the fact that by the fourth decade of the seventeenth century the tide in the ongoing linguistic ebb and flow between Irish and English in Ireland was flowing strongly in favour of the latter. Yet the future linguistic map of the country could not be presumed. Speaking on behalf of the politically ascendant New English, the attorney general, Sir John Davies (1569–1626), maintained two decades earlier that it was their earnest wish that the Irish population would 'in toungue and heart, and everyway else, become English', but the linguistic conformity that was a prerequisite if the two islands were to arrive at a situation in which there was 'no difference or distinction but the Irish Sea between us' was still a long way from realization in 1635.[2] In common with most of his New English peers, Davies was so persuaded that English was a superior language and so convinced of the inferiority not only of the Irish language, but also of Irish culture, that he was unable either to acknowledge their intrinsic quality, or the depth of the attachment to the language by those who were its most eminent practitioners. He also failed fully to appreciate the lessons of Irish history. Davies was one of the more historically aware members of the administrative cadre overseeing the government of Ireland, and he might have concluded, had he looked more closely at the respective fortunes of the Irish and English languages in Ireland since the Anglo-Norman conquest, that the linguistic transformation he hoped for was unlikely either to occur within his antici-

---

1 RIA, MS 24 G 16 f. 36 cited in Bernadette Cunningham, 'Seventeenth-century constructions of the historical kingdom of Ireland' in Mark Williams and Stephen Paul Forrest (eds), *Constructing the past: writing Irish history, 1600–1800* (Woodbridge, 2010), p. 25. For Kearney see *eadem*, 'Colonised Catholics; perceptions of honour and history in Michael Kearney's reading of *Foras feasa ar Éirinn*' in V.P. Carey and Ute Lotz-Heumann (eds), *Taking sides? Colonial and confessional* mentalités *in early modern Ireland* (Dublin, 2003), pp 150–64. 2 John Davies, *A discovery of the true causes why Ireland was never entirely subdued* (London, 1612, reprint Shannon, 1969), p. 217.

pated brief time frame, or to have been as complete as his model of cultural change assumed.

From the moment English was introduced in the twelfth century, as part of the process whereby the Anglo-Normans took charge of what was denominated the lordship of Ireland, it was apparent that language lay at the heart of the complex cultural struggle that continued long after the new settlers had completed the initial military phase of their conquest. This was a consequence in the first instance of the fact that the Anglo-Normans who came to Ireland spoke a different language than the indigenous population over whom they claimed superiority. However, it was given additional, enduring, significance by the fact that from early in the history of the Irish lordships Anglo-Norman officials, local as well as national, conceived of those who spoke Irish as untrustworthy, if not inherently disloyal to the crown.[3] Still more seriously, the objections to the appointment of Irish speakers to crown offices, and the recommendation made in 1285 that members of the Gaelic Irish community should not be raised to the episcopate, demonstrated that the Irish language itself was regarded with great suspicion because it was the medium through which disloyalty was disseminated.[4] This served inevitably as a barrier to the inter-ethnic use of Irish, which informed the perception that it was an inferior language. To compound matters, the Anglo-Normans took an equally negative view of Irish culture. Guided by the descriptions of Giraldus Cambrensis, whose seminal accounts were prepared within a generation of the inauguration of the Norman conquest, they were encouraged to arrive at the conclusion that the Irish were 'so barbarous ... they cannot be said to have any culture'.[5] It so happened that Giraldus had little to say on the subject of language in his influential writings – *Topographia Hibernica* (1188) and *Expugnatio Hibernica* (1189) – on Ireland, but his reserve on this point was of minor consequence as his broader negative characterization of Irish culture both defined and encapsulated the attitude of the early generations of Norman settlers on language as well as other matters. Furthermore, it had an enduring impact, and its rediscovery by the New English in the sixteenth and early seventeenth centuries reinforced and legitimated the strong prejudices that informed their overwhelmingly negative attitude to all things Irish and particularly the Irish language.[6]

As this reference to the later history of the response to the writings of Giraldus Cambrensis suggests, the attitude of the descendants of the Anglo-

---

3 J.A. Watt, 'Gaelic polity and cultural identity' in Art Cosgrove (ed.), *A new history of Ireland*; ii: *medieval Ireland, 1169–1534* (Oxford, 1987), p. 346.   4 Tony Crowley, *Wars of words: the politics of language in Ireland, 1537–2004* (Oxford, 2005), p. 2.   5 John J. O'Meara, *Topography of Ireland by Giraldus Cambrensis* (Dundalk, 1951), p. 84.   6 Giraldus Cambrensis, *Expugnatio Hibernica*, ed. A.B. Scott and F.X. Martin (Dublin, 1978); *idem, The history and topography of Ireland*, ed., John O'Meara (Dublin, 1982); Hiram Morgan, 'Giraldus Cambrensis and the Tudor conquest of Ireland' in *idem* (ed.), *Political ideology in Ireland, 1541–1641* (Dublin, 1999), pp 22–44; Nicholas Canny, *Making Ireland British, 1580–1650* (Oxford, 2001), p. 413; Crowley, *Wars of words*, p. 3.

Norman settlers towards Irish culture and the Irish language was not unchanging. Few among the 'English of Ireland',[7] as the descendants of the Anglo-Norman settlers tellingly denominated themselves, were disposed unreservedly to recognize the Irish as ethnically, culturally or linguistically their equal, but a combination of strategic and self interest ensured that the animosity and suspicion that defined their relationship in the twelfth century yielded over time to a realization that it was mutually advantageous to interact. Intermarriage, tactical alliances, commercial co-operation and the use of Irish became so commonplace that by the mid-fourteenth century concern was openly expressed within the English community in Ireland that 'many ... [were] forsaking the English language, manners, mode of riding, laws and usages' and chose instead to 'live and govern themselves according to the manners, fashion and language of the Irish enemies'.[8] Fearful that acculturation had proceeded to such a point that the 'allegiance due our lord, the king' was endangered, the authorities famously attempted to interrupt the decay in English habits by recalling those of English ethnicity in Ireland ('the English of the said land') to English ways. To this end, as well as English manners, English dress and English 'laws and usages', the 'English of Ireland' were explicitly instructed to 'use the English language'. The Statute of Kilkenny approved by the Irish parliament in 1366, which provided that 'any English, or Irish living amongst the English [who] use the Irish language amongst themselves, contrary to this ordinance' could, if they were found guilty of same, have their property seized, represented the most noteworthy intervention of this kind.[9] Moreover, it was a clear and unambiguous statement of the determination of the authorities to arrest the backsliding they conceived was taking place and it evidently was well judged as it met with an encouraging response. The commitment required to bolster the use of English was in evidence in Waterford where the corporation determined to embrace English as the language of business from 1365, and in parliament, which decided to

---

7 See John Gillingham, 'Normanizing the English invaders of Ireland' in H. Pryce and J. A. Watts (eds), *Power and identity in the Middle Ages: essays in memory of Rees Davies* (Oxford, 2007), pp 85–97; Steven Ellis '"More Irish than the Irish themselves": the "Anglo-Irish" in Tudor Ireland', *History Ireland*, 7:1 (1999), 22–6; K.W. Nicholls, 'Worlds apart? The Ellis two-nations theory on late medieval Ireland', *History Ireland*, 7:2 (1999), 22–6; Sparky Booker, 'Intermarriage in fifteenth-century Ireland: the English and Irish in the "four obedient shires"', *RIA proc.* (forthcoming).   8 Statute of Kilkenny, 1366 cited in Crowley, *Wars of words*, p. 4. In the realm of language use, the case of Gerard, third earl of Desmond (d. 1398) can be invoked. According to Micheál Mac Craith, Irish courtly love poetry of the period 1550–1650 was influenced by English Renaissance poetry, the Gaelicized Old English being the bridge: see *Lorg na hiasachta ar na dánta grá* (Baile Átha Cliath, 1989), pp 42–61; 'Gaelic Ireland and the Renaissance' in Glanmor Williams and Robert Owen Jones (eds), *The Celts and the Renaissance: tradition and innovation* (Cardiff, 1990), pp 57–89. It must also be noted that the linguistic environment of the middle ages also accommodated Latin and Norman French: see Michael Cronin and Cormac Ó Cuilleanáin (eds), *The languages of Ireland* (Dublin, 2003).   9 Crowley, *Wars of words*, p. 4.

present its enactments in that tongue from 1472. Heartened by this show of intent, English may have consolidated its position within the heartland of the English lordship, which embraced the main towns, the Pale and the eastern littoral in Leinster.[10] This was not an exclusively English-speaking region, however; Irish was also commonly used within the Pale, particularly by those who were not of the elite, whose quotidian activity required regular contact with the Gaelic areas of the country where Irish had no rival as the language of communication. In sum, towards the end of the fifteenth century, Ireland was a bilingual society in which a proportion of the population were fluent in both Irish and English, and a majority of the population was fluent in one. Of that majority, those who were monoglot English speakers were comfortably exceeded by the larger Gaelic component of the population whose vernacular was Irish.

Had the strained social and political equilibrium that obtained in Ireland during the reign of Henry VII (1485–1509), and the first half of the reign of Henry VIII (1509–47) endured it is possible that the *de facto* linguistic accommodation that also obtained might have been perpetuated. This must have meant that the learned elite that served as the repository of learning, and whose high standing within the community was integral to Gaelic society, would have continued to serve as the guardians of a functioning linguistic and literary tradition that under-girded much that was integral to the efficient operation of Gaelic Irish society.[11] However, the early Tudors were seized by a powerful centralizing impulse, impelled by the realization, born out of the experience of the Wars of the Roses (1455–87), of just how debilitating and destructive rival sources of authority could be and by the prescient recognition that in the ultra-competitive European geo-political sphere centralized government was militarily and strategically advantageous.[12] The most signal early manifestation in Ireland of their determination not to brook rival sources of authority to that of the crown was provided by their relationship with the Fitzgeralds of Kildare, who had for several generations dominated the Irish lordship and sustained its subordination to the English crown, but whose power and predisposition to favour their own interest was a source of increasing unease.[13] The destruction of Kildare power in 1533–4 was a decisive moment in the history of the Irish lordship, and an incentive to the crown to sustain the more interventionist stance with which it was now identified, and

10 Crowley, *Wars of words*, pp 10–12.   11 James Carney, *The Irish bardic poet* (Dublin, 1947); Katharine Simms, *From kings to warlords: the changing political structures of Gaelic Ireland in the later Middle Ages* (Woodbridge, 1987); Brian Ó Cuív, *The linguistic training of the medieval Irish poet* (Dublin, 1973); James Carney (ed.), *Poems on the Butlers of Ormond, Cahir, and Dunboyne (A.D.1400–1650)* (Dublin, 1945).   12 See, *inter alia*, Philip Edwards, *The making of the modern English state, 1460–1660* (Basingstoke, 2001), chapters 1–3.   13 S.G. Ellis, *Reform and revival: English government in Ireland, 1470–1534* (Woodbridge, 1986); *DIB, sub nom* Gearóid Mór Fitzgerald.

which set the tone for the remainder of the sixteenth century.[14] It was also replete with societal consequences, as the so-called Tudor conquest was not just about enhancing the political authority of the crown. It also acquired an important religious dimension because Henry VIII's embrace of Protestantism necessarily involved the crown in an effort to absorb Ireland within the realm of reformed religion. Equally significantly in so far as the social, economic and linguistic arrangements then obtaining in Ireland were concerned, the English officials and soldiers that came to Ireland were possessed of a renewed and invigorated sense of English cultural and linguistic superiority, which committed them to an active and energetic policy of anglicization.[15]

The linguistic implications of the augmented Tudor interest in Ireland were given legislative expression in 1537 by the 'Act for the English order, habit and language'. Persuaded of the merits of a situation in which the 'English tongue ... be used by all men that will acknowledge themselves ... to be ... true and faithful subjects', and that the achievement of this desirable end required that 'the diversity that is betwixt them [his subjects] in tongue, language, order and habit' should be elided, the 1537 statute sought to provide for the enforcement of the existing regulations. To this end, it proffered the general instruction 'that all such good laws, as by wise, godly, and prudent princes ... have been heretofore made for the use of the English tongue, habit and order, within this ... land may be put in due execution'. If the wording of this clause suggested that MPs and officials believed it would suffice simply to enforce existing law on language, the practical reality was that by echoing the connection between language and loyalty previously articulated in the thirteenth century, and the thrust of the statutes approved at Kilkenny in 1366, the Irish parliament reversed the more linguistically neutral stand taken by Poynings' parliament in 1495, which omitted those regulations 'that speaketh of the Irish language'.[16] The commitment to a policy of anglicization in which language was central took concrete form in the third clause of the 1537 act, which required parents to raise their children as English speakers. It decreed that 'every person or persons, the King's true subjects, inhabiting this land of Ireland ... to the uttermost of their power, cunning, and knowl-

---

14 See Ciaran Brady, *The chief governors: the rise and fall of reform government in Tudor Ireland, 1536–1588* (Cambridge, 1994); Steven Ellis, *Ireland in the age of the Tudors, 1447–1603: English expansion and the end of Gaelic rule* (London, 1998); Nicholas Canny, *From reformation to restoration: Ireland, 1534–1660* (Dublin, 1987).   15 Jim Murray, *Enforcing the English Reformation in Ireland: clerical resistance and political conflict in the diocese of Dublin, 1534–1590* (Cambridge, 2009); Patricia Palmer, *Language and conquest in early modern Ireland: English renaissance literatures and Elizabethan expansion* (Cambridge, 2001), chapters 3 and 4.   16 28 Henry VIII, chap. 15; 10 Henry 7, chap. 8; Tony Crowley, *The politics of language in Ireland, 1366–1922* (London, 2000), pp 21–3; Crowley, *Wars of words*, pp 12–3. The relevant clause ran: 'that the said English tongue, habit and order may from henceforth continually (and without ceasing or returning at any time to Irish habit, or language) be used by all men that will acknowledge themselves according to their duties of allegiance, to be his highness's true and faithful subjects'.

edge, shall use and speak commonly the English tongue and language, and ...
bring up and keep his said child and children in such places, where they shall
or may have occasion to learn the English tongue'.[17] And in the ninth clause,
those exercising ecclesiastical authority were instructed to elicit a formal commitment from those admitted to holy orders that they would 'learn the
English language and tongue' so that they could 'instruct, teach and preach
the word of God in English'.[18]

Prompted by these directions to augment the use of English, the agents of
the Tudor state encouraged municipal and local authorities to put educational
structures in place that fostered knowledge of the language, but the surviving
documentation suggests that they did so fitfully and unsystematically.[19] Success
was certainly not facilitated by the frequent change to the personnel at the head
of the Irish administration, by significant shifts in policy,[20] or by the
increasingly confrontational relationship of the representatives of the crown and
clan leaders, which encouraged recourse to arms and more frequent and bloody
military collisions.[21] Despite this, knowledge of English expanded. The
insistence by the Tudor authorities that English was the language of
government and that business be conducted in that tongue constituted an
important marker. They certainly made no attempt to encourage officials to
learn Irish and made it clear that this was how it would remain by engaging
translators when they were required to interact with monoglot Irish speakers.
If the object was to convince chieftains and clan leaders that it was in their
interest to acquire a good working knowledge of English it succeeded. For a
time, the heads of certain clans employed Latin as a *lingua franca* in their
interactions with the state. This was generally acceded to, but the disinclination
of crown officials to facilitate its continued use, even though Latin was an
esteemed, neutral tongue, hastened its eclipse by English as the common
language of diplomatic discourse and political exchange before the end of the
century.[22] The linguistic impact of this was largely restricted to the clan leaders
and their closest allies. This elite cadre apart, the second half of the sixteenth
century witnessed no appreciable expansion in the use of English among the
Irish-speaking population. However, the language shift was manifestly in one

---

17 Crowley, *The politics of language*, p. 22.   18 Ibid.   19 See Timothy Corcoran (ed.),
State policy in Irish education, AD 1536–1816 (Dublin, 1916), pp 41–58 passim; Crowley,
The politics of language, p. 20.   20 Language policy too was not consistent; the comple-
mentary, and sometimes competing impulse to convert the Irish population to
Protestantism prompted the state to support the translation to Irish and printing of key
Protestant religious texts: see Basil Iske, *The green cockatrice* (Dublin, 1978); Nicholas
Williams, *I bprionta i leabhar: na Protastúin agus prós na Gaeilge, 1567–1727* (Baile Átha
Cliath, 1986).   21 Brady, *The chief governors: the rise and fall of reform government in Tudor
Ireland*, passim; Ellis, *Ireland in the age of the Tudors*, passim.   22 Bernadette
Cunningham, 'Loss and gain: attitudes towards the English language in early modern
Ireland in Brian Mac Cuarta (ed.), *Reshaping Ireland, 1550–1700: colonization and its con-
sequences* (Dublin, 2011), pp 165–7; Palmer, *Language and conquest*, pp 135–47.

direction – towards greater use of English. Furthermore, the foundations were incrementally being put in place for the expanded use of English. The increase in the number of New English in Ireland in the final decades of the sixteenth century, the resort to larger and more ambitious schemes of plantation and the military defeat of the remaining powerful Gaelic-Irish chieftains during the Nine Years War (1594–1603) paved the way for a marked expansion in the use of English during the early seventeenth century.

Though the 'flight of the earls' (1607) and the inauguration of the Ulster Plantation (1609), which followed rapidly on the failure of the strategy of military resistance pursued during the Nine Years War by the most resourceful leaders of Gaelic Ireland, have traditionally been identified with 'the end of the Gaelic order, and therefore, with the Irish language's decline as a cultural force', the history of its contraction as a vernacular language and its replacement by English, was more prolonged and complex, as Brendan Kane has recently properly reminded us.[23] In common with Bernadette Cunningham, who has persuasively argued that the Irish elite were prompted by 'utilitarian' (rather than ideological, or purely linguistic) considerations to embrace English in the sixteenth century, Kane accepts that English was firmly established as the language of the elite by the beginning of the seventeenth century; in his felicitous image, Irish had vacated 'the stages of elite society and politics'.[24] This did not mean that the totality of the Irish elite was fluent in the language; indicatively, a number of those selected to sit in the 1613–15 parliament could not speak English, while the willingness of anglicized Irish potentates, such as the earl of Thomond, to act as patrons of native learning and the continuing usage of Irish in the Pale demonstrates that the increased recourse to English during the sixteenth century, while a pointer to the future, did not mean that the future linguistic map of Ireland had taken firm shape.[25] Moreover, the perception that the Gaelic order had suffered such a disabling political, cultural and economic defeat during the sixteenth century

---

23 Brendan Kane, 'Languages of legitimacy? *An Ghaeilge*, the earl of Thomond and British politics in the Renaissance Pale, 1600–24' in Michael Potterton and Thomas Herron (eds), *Dublin and the Pale in the Renaissance c.1540–1660* (Dublin, 2011), p. 267. For a broader, and alternative, reading of the early seventeenth-century context see Ann Dooley 'Literature and society in early seventeenth-century Ireland: the evaluation of change' in Cyril Byrne et al. (eds), *Celtic languages and Celtic peoples: proceedings of the Second North-American Congress of Celtic Studies* (Halifax, Nova Scotia, 1992), 513–34; Joep Leerssen, *The Contention of the Bards (Iomarbhágh na bhFileadh) and its place in Irish political and literary history* (ITS subsidiary series 2, London, 1994).   24 Cunningham, 'Loss and gain', passim; Kane, 'Languages of legitimacy', p. 267. It may be observed that Kane's useful analysis of the attitude of the earl of Thomond is perhaps unduly shaped by his eagerness to disprove 'the facile notion of the near-spontaneous collapse of the Gaelic order in the wake of Kinsale', which he admits has been 'thoroughly revised in the last decade or so' (ibid., p. 278).   25 Kane, 'Languages of legitimacy', pp 267–79; John Minahane, 'Documents of spiritual resistance: a review essay' in *Dublin Review of Books*, 20 (Winter 2011–12) accessible at www.drb.ie/.

that 'the Irish language's decline as a cultural force' was preordained, once strongly argued, underestimates the literary and ideological responsiveness of the poetic order.[26]

There is no evading the fact that the collapse of the capacity of Gaelic-Irish society militarily to defend itself, which was the primary significance of the loss at Kinsale (1601) and the ill-conceived strategic retreat embarked upon in 1607, was not just ominous for the poetic elite, it was portentous for the whole Gaelic order. However, the capacity of the poets to re-imagine a functional Gaelic order – one in which they continued to possess an honoured place, of course – which proffered allegiance to a Stuart king rather than a hereditary Gaelic chieftain, which has been reconstructed so thoroughly by Breandán Ó Buachalla, was not indicative of a social order in terminal decline.[27] This conclusion is given added authority by the inherent vigour of the bardic poetry that continued to be composed and has recently been published.[28] This linguistically vigorous, aesthetically impressive and ideologically forceful corpus of over 500 poems suggests that though the Gaelic literary order was seriously weakened by the loss of the patrons with whom the poets were bound in a symbiotic relationship of power and status, it was still resilient and well capable of proffering, as John Minahane has recently argued, 'spiritual resistance' to the new economic, social and political order that was taking shape.[29] This is not an original insight; it builds on foundations laid by Ó Buachalla and others, but it is significant nonetheless, since it amplifies understanding of the Gaelic response to its incapacity to offer any practical military resistance in the wake of the flight of the earls and to the sharp surge in the number of the English-speaking settlers in the kingdom in the early seventeenth century.[30]

26 See Tom Dunne, 'The Gaelic response to conquest and colonisation: the evidence of the poetry', *Studia Hibernica*, 21 (1982), 7–30; Michelle O Riordan, *The Gaelic mind and the collapse of the Gaelic world* (Cork, 1990); Nicholas Canny, 'The formation of the Irish mind: religion, politics and Gaelic Irish literature, 1580–1750', *Past and Present*, 95 (May 1982), 91–116; Joep Th. Leerssen, *Mere Irish and fíor-Ghael: studies in the idea of Irish nationality* (Amsterdam, 1986), part 4, pp 169–289; Bernadette Cunningham, 'Native culture and political change in Ireland, 1580–1640' in Ciaran Brady and Raymond Gillespie (eds), *Natives and newcomers: essays on the making of Irish colonial society, 1534–1641* (Dublin, c.1986), pp 148–70. 27 Breandán Ó Buachalla, 'Na Stíobhartaigh agus an t-aos léinn: Cing Séamas', *RIA proc.*, 83C (1983), 81–134; *idem*, 'James our true king: the ideology of Irish royalism in the seventeenth century' in D. George Boyce et al. (eds), *Political thought in Ireland since the seventeenth century* (London, 1993), pp 7–35; *idem*, *Aisling ghéar: na Stíobhartaigh agus an t-aos léinn* (Baile Átha Cliath, 1996); *idem*, 'Ó Néill agus an t-aos léinn' in Tracey Ní Mhaonaigh and Tadhg Ó Dúshláine (eag.) *Éire agus an Eoraip sa 17ú haois: Léachtaí Cholm Cille* 38 (Maigh Nuad, 2008), pp 7–38; *idem*, 'Canóin na creille: an file ar leaba a bháis' in Máirín Ní Dhonnchadha (eag.) *Nua-léamha: gnéithe de chultúr, stair agus polaitíocht na hÉireann c.1600–c.1900* (Baile Átha Cliath, 1996), pp 149–69. 28 Damian McManus and Eoghan Ó Raghallaigh (eds), *A bardic miscellany: five hundred bardic poems from manuscripts in Irish and British libraries* (Dublin, 2010). 29 Minahane, 'Documents of a spiritual resistance', passim. 30 Raymond Gillespie, *Colonial*

As a consequence, though the outcome was never as predictable, and the configuration of the linguistic map as foreseeable as those who assigned the eclipse of the Gaelic order to the first decade of the seventeenth century may have believed, the linguistic reality of the years 1609–41 was that the amount of English spoken in Ireland increased substantially. This may be ascribed in the first instance to the influx of English speakers – soldiers, settlers, officials and religious – that took place during this time, but their presence also had the effect of encouraging Irish speakers who came into contact with them to acquire an incremental proficiency in English. Moreover, though it is not difficult to locate poets and poems that characterized this development as profoundly regressive,[31] the generality of the Irish-speaking Catholic population were more pragmatic. Since 'language had largely ceased to be the predominant cultural definer for the Catholic Irish', it was not perceived by them to possess the ideological register it was to acquire when it was re-imagined to conform to the romantic nationalist model that achieved political and intellectual ascendancy in the nineteenth century.[32] Rather the Gaelic Irish acquired the ideological armoury that helped to sustain them through the second half of the seventeenth, the eighteenth and early nineteenth centuries from counter-reformation Catholicism, as mediated by Geoffrey Keating, whose *Foras feasa ar Éirinn* skilfully and imaginatively combined history, religion and scholarship in an interpretation that answered the ideological needs of Irish society, and that constitutes one of the most successful essays in historical revision ever undertaken.[33] Keating did not operate in a vacuum, of course, or on his own; his was merely the most expansive and influential of a sequence of passionate clerical interventions that re-configured Irish history, and in so doing not only reinterpreted the past but also constructed an ideological template with which to understand the present and, potentially, to shape the future.[34]

Arising out of the more sophisticated understanding of the Gaelic order provided by recent scholarship on political thought and identity formation in the early seventeenth century, and the equally revealing examinations of the motives and ambitions and impact of the New English during the late sixteenth and early seventeenth centuries, the picture of language change that can now be painted is inherently contingent and variegated. It can also reasonably be suggested that the linguistic roots put down by the English in Ireland between the Anglo-Norman intervention in the late twelfth century and the Tudor

Ulster: the settlement of East Ulster, 1600–1641 (Cork, 1985); Canny, *Making Ireland British*, chapter 6.   **31** See Crowley, *Wars of words*, pp 57–9.   **32** Cunningham, 'Loss and gain', pp 185–6; Joep Leerssen, *National thought in Europe: a cultural history* (Amsterdam, 2006). **33** Bernadette Cunningham, *The world of Geoffrey Keating: history, myth and religion in seventeenth-century Ireland* (Dublin, 2000).   **34** Bernadette Cunningham, *The Annals of the Four Masters: Irish history, kingship and society in the early seventeenth century* (Dublin, 2010); Thomas O'Connor, 'Towards the invention of the Irish Catholic *natio*: Thomas Messingham's *Florilegium* (1624)', *Irish Theological Quarterly*, 64 (1999), 157–77.

conquest went deeper and, as a consequence, merit more attention than they are traditionally afforded in the history of the 'politics of language' in Ireland (and than they are accorded in this book). By extension, it may be that the impact and import of the legislative enactments introduced at the behest of the Tudor crown deserve less notice, since the pragmatic adoption of English in the sixteenth century was traditionally severely discounted by those who were ideologically disposed to ascribe linguistic change to compulsion rather than calculation. The implication that the conditions necessary for rapid language change did not obtain until the seventeenth century provides one of the premises upon which this collection is constructed.

The early seventeenth century thus provides the starting point for a volume that aspires to explore the moving linguistic frontier that both linked and separated Irish and English during the seventeenth, eighteenth and nine-teenth centuries. To this end, the collection seeks not only to assist, where possible, with the clarification of the disputed chronology of language change, but also to break new ground by exploring the attitudes, actions and contexts that determined which language(s) people used, the forces that shaped the type of language (the words, sentences) to which they had recourse, and where and how they accessed linguistic knowledge. The early seventeenth century was a decisive moment in this long and evolving transformation, because it was then that English emerged as a mass vernacular, built upon the foundations of the impressive inward demographic movement occasioned by plantation and by a parallel, and less readily traceable, pattern of emigration.[35] This was the period when the groundwork was laid for the substantial expan-sion in the use of English that was to occur when the economic, cultural and demographic pillars of the Protestant ascendancy were sufficiently firmly anchored to facilitate the emergence of a recognizably modern anglophone society. In order for this society to grow and to consolidate, further conflict, further plantation and further population movement had to take place. The events of the 1640s and 1650s are sufficiently familiar so as not to need other than brief rehearsal. The most salient facts are that the Cromwellian era wit-nessed the single largest transfer of land (raising the percentage in Protestant possession from 30 per cent in 1641 to 67 per cent in *c.*1675).[36] Still more important from the perspective of language use, it hastened the major demo-graphic transformation already underway and thereby not only diminished the capacity for 'spiritual resistance' manifest in the poetry of the early seven-teenth century but also prepared the way for the assumption by English of a

35 For an overview see Patrick Fitzgerald and Brian Lambkin, *Migration in Irish history, 1607–2007* (Basingstoke, 2008); and for a more specific early seventeenth-century per-spective, Michael Perceval-Maxwell, *The Scottish migration to Ulster in the reign of James I* (London, 1973).   36 Kevin McKenny, 'The restoration land settlement in Ireland: a structural interpretation' in C.A. Dennehy (ed.), *Restoration Ireland: always settling and never settled* (Aldershot, 2008), p. 39.

larger space in the public realm during the second half of the seventeenth and early eighteenth centuries. Moreover, attitudes too hardened. A constructed memory of the events of the winter of 1640–1 forged in the crucible of conflict in the 1640s was annealed by the restoration parliament and crystallized into adamantine conviction by the events of 1688–9. As a result, the negative linguistic attitudes that the Elizabethan settlers articulated were established as core convictions of the dominant Protestant interest by the 1690s.[37]

The impression cultivated during the late nineteenth and early twentieth centuries when 'de-anglicization' was identified as *the* most urgent and noble political object that the nationalist population of Ireland could pursue was that the linguistic landscape in Ireland had been ever confrontational. The blunt legal language of statute, medieval and early modern, and the curt dismissals of the Irish language and Irish culture as equally 'barbarous' by anglophone commentators encouraged such conclusions. However, the calculation with which the Gaelic ruling elite embraced English in the sixteenth and early seventeenth centuries indicates that pragmatic motives were also at play,[38] and this realization obliges us to move beyond conceiving of the relationship of Irish and English in purely confrontational terms (simply as a war or wars of words) and to acknowledge that the pragmatic considerations that animated certain chieftains in the sixteenth century were also pertinent when, as happened on occasions, settlers were prompted either to learn Irish or to avail of the printing press to assist with the task of evangelization through that medium.[39]

Such efforts as were made to evangelize through the medium of Irish in the sixteenth century were officially driven; the early seventeenth century prompted a number of heroic interventions by individuals. The contribution of William Daniel (Uilliam Ó Domhnuill), who was responsible for an Irish translation of the New Testament (1602) and the *Booke of Common Prayer* (1608), has been reconsidered recently from a theological perspective.[40] William Bedell's efforts when bishop of Kilmore, 1629–42, to organize the translation and printing of the Old Testament have attracted more notice. This may be attributed in part to his greater evidential footprint, but Bedell's life and career are also more revealing of the linguistic barriers that stood in the way of the

37 Richard Anstell, 'The 1688 Revolution in Ireland and the memory of 1641' in Mark Williams and Stephen Paul Forrest (eds), *Constructing the past: writing Irish history, 1600–1800* (Woodbridge, 2010), pp 73–93; James Kelly, 'The Glorious and immortal memory: commemoration and Protestant identity in Ireland, 1660–1800', *RIA proc.* 94C (1994), 26–9; T.C. Barnard, 'The use of 23 October 1641 and Irish Protestant celebrations', *EHR*, 106 (1991), 889–920. 38 For which see Cunningham, 'Loss and gain', passim. 39 For a perceptive modern account of the relationship of Irish with print see Niall Ó Ciosáin, 'Print and Irish, 1570–1900: an exception among the Celtic languages', *Radharc: a Journal of Irish and Irish-American studies*, 5–7 (2004–6), 75–106, at 76–81. 40 Fearghus Ó Fearghail, 'Uilliam Ó Domhnaill's Irish version of the *Booke of Common Prayer* (1608) and his Old Testament translations into Irish', *Proceedings of the Irish Bible Association*, 32 (2009), 99–130.

successful evangelization of the country through the medium of Irish. Bedell was unusual in that as well as organizing the translation into Irish of the Old Testament, he learned Irish better to acquit himself of his duties. Yet, the fact that the translated text, which was completed by 1640, was not published until 1685 is illustrative of the weighty logistical difficulties that were encountered by those who sought to bridge the chasm that separated the Irish and English languages in the early seventeenth century. It also underlines the necessity of exploring Bedell's motives clearly and it is apt therefore that a collection devoted to the exploration of the relationship of the Irish and English languages in Ireland in the early modern era should commence with an attempt by Marc Caball to establish the intellectual origins of Bedell's cultural receptivity and that locates an answer in his biography – specifically in his experiences in the ambassadorial legation in Venice (chapter 1).

Though Bedell may have been more than usually receptive both linguistically and culturally, the fact that Richard Boyle, earl of Cork, who was one of the most relentless acquirers of land in early seventeenth-century Ireland, encouraged his children to learn Irish is further evidence of the preparedness of settlers to engage with native culture when they perceived that there was good reason to do so.[41] Boyle's actions possessed an underlying economic rationale, since the survival of some legal instruments (leases and wills) in the Irish language dating from the seventeenth century indicates that knowledge of the language could be advantageous. This is not to suggest that Boyle, or the earl of Inchiquin, in whose papers the legal documents in Irish referred to are to be found,[42] were immune from the linguistic prejudices of the emerging new landed elite, but rather that they possessed a capacity not to allow sentiment to obstruct their (financial and cultural) interests. A similar pragmatism can be identified within the ranks of the small body of seventeenth- and early eighteenth-century intellectuals who sought, for a variety of reasons and motives, to understand Irish history and Irish society. Eager once they were made aware of the knowledge and learning contained in Irish manuscripts to gain access to this knowledge, they manifested the typical researcher's willingness to negotiate extant cultural and linguistic barriers in order to do so. The efforts of James Ussher, archbishop of Armagh, to scale these barriers have been excavated,[43] but the exploration of the circulation of manuscripts during the seventeenth and early eighteenth centuries by Raymond Gillespie and Bernadette Cunningham (chapter 2) demonstrates

---

41 Cunningham, 'Loss and gain', p. 174; Michael McCarthy-Morrogh, *The Munster plantation: English migration to southern Ireland, 1583–1641* (Oxford, 1986), p. 275.   42 Lesa Ní Mhunghaile, 'The legal system in Ireland and the Irish language, 1700–*c*.1843' in Michael Brown and Seán Patrick Donlon (eds), *The laws and other legalities of Ireland, 1689–1850* (Aldershot, 2011), p. 328.   43 Raymond Gillespie and Bernadette Cunningham, 'James Ussher and his Irish manuscripts', *Studia Hibernica*, 33 (2004–5), 81–100; Joep Leerssen, 'Archbishop Ussher and Gaelic culture', *Studia Hibernica*, 22 and 23 (1982–3), 50–8.

that he was not alone; James Ware and others were equally eager. The main problem was linguistic; a small number may have acquired a working knowledge of Irish sufficient for everyday purposes, but they needed assistance to negotiate the barrier posed by classical Irish. This presented an opportunity to native scholars, which some like Dubhaltach Mac Firbisigh availed of for financial reasons. Others were driven by scholarly motives. What is clear is that this was not a one-way process; Irish scholars also accessed knowledge in English-language print. As a result, the process whereby significant Irish-language manuscripts came into the possession of members of the Protestant elite in Ireland was mirrored over time by the acquisition by Gaelic scribes and men of learning of English-language texts in the areas of history, antiquity and allied realms.[44] Moreover, the frequently serpentine processes whereby manuscripts changed hands and an increasing number came into the possession of anglophone owners, was simplified by the emergence in the eighteenth century of a recognizable market in such materials. It was, of course, not as structured, or as obviously commercial, as the process whereby printed texts were issued for sale and brought into individual ownership, but the manner in which members of the industrious Ó Neachtain circle in eighteenth-century Dublin copied and sold manuscripts and the insights allowed into this practice by the reconstruction of the library of Muiris Ó Gormáin attests to its comparative vigour.[45] It attests also to the extent to which an interest in the past, which possessed obvious political implications in the eighteenth century,[46] grew over time among a strand of the Irish Protestant elite. Moreover, it indicates how important scholarly inquiry was in fostering and sustaining a sphere of interest that permitted, when it did not encourage, a degree of mutual understanding that helped to diminish the antagonism that the Protestant interest at large bore the Irish language at the outset of the eighteenth century. This is the conclusion of James Kelly's account of the evolution of Protestant attitudes to the Irish language over the course of the long eighteenth century (chapter 7).

Among the Irish-language prose manuscripts for which demand was strong within the Irish- and English-speaking communities in Ireland, Geoffrey Keating's *magnum opus*, *Foras feasa ar Éirinn*, may take pride of place.[47] Keating's reconfiguration of the course of Irish history penned in the

---

44 For a revealing case study of this in the eighteenth century, see Lesa Ní Mhunghaile, 'An eighteenth-century scribe's private library: Muiris Ó Gormáin's books', *RIA proc.*, 110C (2010), 239–76.   45 Alan Harrison, *The Dean's friend: Anthony Raymond* (Dublin, 1999), passim; M.H. Risk, 'Seán Ó Neachtain: an eighteenth-century Irish writer', *Studia Hibernica*, 15 (1975), 47–60; Ní Mhunghaile, 'Muiris Ó Gormáin's books', 251–3.   46 See Leerssen, *Mere Irish and fíor-Ghael*, pp 365–427 passim; Clare O'Halloran, *Golden ages and barbarous nations: antiquarian debate and cultural politics in Ireland, c.1750–1800* (Cork, 2004).   47 Cunningham, *The world of Geoffrey Keating*, passim; Breandán Ó Buachalla 'Annála Rioghachta Éireann agus Foras Feasa ar Éirinn: an comhthéacs comhaimseartha' *Studia Hibernica*, 22 and 23 (1982–3), 59–105.

1630s was quickly recognized as an outstanding achievement, and it is a measure of its impact and appeal that it was not only copied for circulation within Gaelic Ireland, but also sought out by members of the Protestant settler community. The response of the latter was not always positive. Sir Richard Cox, the author of the definitive Protestant history of Ireland published in the late seventeenth century, dismissed *Foras feasa* as 'an ill-digested heap of very silly fictions'. Cox also disagreed with Keating's positive characterization of the Irish language, claiming it was not 'pure and original', but rather 'the most compound language in the world'.[48] The balance of opinion was more equitable and it spurred an exceptional interest in the text that peaked in the first quarter of the eighteenth century when, as Vincent Morley's temporal analysis of the surviving manuscripts demonstrates (chapter 3), a record number of copies were made. Moreover, in keeping with the beginnings of the thaw that Kelly (chapter 7) identifies in Protestant antipathy to all things Irish, there was sufficient interest in *Foras feasa ar Éirinn* not only to prompt its translation but also to cause Dermod O'Connor to oversee the publication of a controversial (and unreliable) printed edition.[49]

The enduring popularity of *Foras feasa ar Éirinn*, to which Morley's careful mapping of the surviving copies attests, also demonstrates that the striking growth in print that took place in Ireland in the half century after the confirmation *in situ* of the Protestant ascendancy in 1690–1 did not spell the end of the manuscript as a viable cultural and literary form. Indeed, what occurred in Ireland was still more emphatically incomplete than 'the ambiguous triumph of print' that has been identified in seventeenth-century England.[50] The parallel existence of print and manuscript cultures in Ireland sustains two important historical conclusions: first, that the assumption that the invention of print signalled the end of the manuscript as a medium of creativity and communication is fundamentally misconceived; and, second, that the production of manuscripts in Ireland not only survived the marginalization of the culture that long provided its *raison d'être*, but also subsequently manifested a versatility and flexibility that permitted the emergence of a variety of demotic literary forms. Moreover, when examined closely, as is the case in both Liam Mac Mathúna's probing of the language employed in warrants and macaronic verse (chapter 4) and Charles Dillon's consideration of the writings of the poets of south Ulster (chapter 5), these forms provide particular insights into the manner in which English replaced Irish as the language of the people in the course of the eighteenth century. The precise

48 Richard Cox, *Hibernia Anglicana; or, the history of Ireland from the conquest thereof by the English to the present time* (2 vols, London, 1689–90), i, preface, quoted in Crowley, *Wars of words*, p. 63.   49 Diarmaid Ó Catháin, 'Dermot O'Connor, translator of Keating', *Eighteenth-Century Ireland*, 2 (1987), 67–87; Cunningham, *The world of Geoffrey Keating*, pp 218–25.   50 Harold Love, *Scribal publication in seventeenth-century England* (Oxford, 1993), chapter 7.

role of print in this transition has not been fully explained, but there is no gainsaying its importance.

By comparison with other jurisdictions in Europe, Ireland embraced the opportunities offered by print slowly.[51] Indeed, though the 1640s witnessed a striking surge in political print, the crushing defeat inflicted on the confederation of native Irish and Old English between 1649 and 1651 ensured that the multiple viewpoints that were then accessible in print were no longer available, and that the tight control exercised by the Irish administration (exemplified by the near monopoly permitted the King's printer) was a key factor in ensuring that the volume of print published remained small through the Restoration era.[52] This phase was brought to a conclusion by the Glorious Revolution with the result that the output of the increased number of printers working in Dublin from the 1690s embarked on an upwards trajectory that was sustained, the 1730s excepted, through the century. Since much of the impetus for this acceleration in print emanated from within the ascendancy, and Protestants perceived that there was an indivisible bond uniting the Irish language, the Catholic religion and Jacobitism, it was to be anticipated that the amount of print produced in Irish would be modest during the 1690s and early decades of the eighteenth century. This was still more likely since no Irish-language titles were published in Ireland between 1650 and 1700. Yet the paucity of Irish print is remarkable. Only four Irish-language titles are known to have been published in Ireland between 1700 and 1750, which was statistically insignificant by comparison with the *c*.9,000 titles in English published during the same period. Signally, the number of Irish-language titles was fewer than the number of surviving works in Latin (121) and French (45).[53]

Though it was long deemed legitimate to do so, it is no longer possible simply to attribute the unavailability of print in Irish to the refusal of the

---

51 Raymond Gillespie, *Reading Ireland: print, reading and social change in early modern Ireland* (Manchester, 2005); Andrew Hadfield and Raymond Gillespie (eds), *The Oxford history of the Irish book, vol 3: The Irish book in English, 1550–1800* (Oxford, 2006). The picture is complicated, of course, by the fact that some key Irish texts (religious in the main) were printed under the aegis of the Franciscans at Louvain. These texts were obviously not without ideological or religious import for Ireland, but military and political developments in the 1640s and 1650s ensured that the environment in Ireland was less than receptive: see generally Nollaig Ó Muraíle (ed.), *Mícheál Ó Cléirigh, his associates and St Anthony's College, Louvain* (Dublin, 2008); Edel Bhreathnach and Bernadette Cunningham (eds), *Writing Irish history: the Four Masters and their world* (Dublin, 2007); Mícheál Mac Craith 'An onóir do Dhia, a cclú dár násion agus d'Ord san Froinsias' in Tracey Ní Mhaonaigh and Tadhg Ó Dúshláine (eds), *Éire agus an Eoraip sa 17ú haois: Léachtaí Cholm Cille* 38 (Maigh Nuad, 2008), pp 100–50.   52 James Kelly, 'Political publishing, 1550–1700' in Hadfield and Gillespie (eds), *The Irish book in English, 1550–1800*, pp 199–209; Paul Pollard, 'Control of the press in Ireland through the king's printer patent, 1600–1800', *Irish Booklore*, 4 (1980), 79–95.   53 These figures are derived from the *English Short Title Catalogue* (3rd ed. London, 2003) and Suzanne Forbes, 'Assessing the size of the Irish print trade in the early eighteenth century: some comparisons with Scotland' (unpublished paper, 2009). I wish to thank Ms Forbes for a copy of her paper.

Protestant authorities to permit it. It is improbable, given the suspicion with which Irish was regarded in the aftermath of the Jacobite wars (see chapter 7), that the authorities would have countenanced the emergence of a flourishing trade in Irish-language print during the 1690s or early years of the eighteenth century, but printing in Irish was never proscribed. Moreover, the authorities did not target Catholic print *per se*; they were only entitled legally to intercept and to interdict seditious print.[54] Suspicious revenue officials did on occasion seize 'Popish books' in Latin, French and Spanish at their point of entry, but their superiors – the revenue commissioners – only approved these actions when duty was owing. Indeed, in one such instance, the commissioners endorsed the decision of a regional collector 'to sell ... a box of Popish books' which were 'lately seized, and condemn'd for want of claim'.[55] In the light of this, the reminder offered by the commissioners in 1750 that 'there is no law here for seizing Popish books', and the emergence from the 1720s of locally published Catholic devotional print in English, there is no escaping the conclusion that Irish-language print was not produced in any volume during the eighteenth century because there was insufficient demand.[56] If the situation had been otherwise, the enterprising retail printers who were ever on the lookout for a commercial niche must have discovered and supplied it.[57]

One cannot conclude of course that Irish speakers did not sustain a culture of print because the community was illiterate. Literacy was a requirement to read the sizeable volume of manuscripts that was produced.[58] However, since the number of people with access to information in this form must have been modest because manuscripts by definition were more exclusive than all but the smallest circulation printed titles, it can safely be concluded that the proportion of the population that could, and did, read Irish regularly, was small. Moreover, since the growth in civil society that took place in the second quarter of the eighteenth century registered but faintly in Irish-speaking Ireland, and the societies that took an interest in antiquarian and economic matters subscribed to an improving agenda, whose devotees were disposed to regard speaking Irish as regressive, there were no civic insti-

---

54 James Kelly, 'Regulating print: the state and the control of print in eighteenth-century Ireland', *Eighteenth-Century Ireland*, 23 (2008), 142–74.   55 Kelly, 'Regulating print', pp 147–9; Minutes of the revenue commissioners, 17 June 1722, 3 Jan. 1732 (TNA, CUST1/16 f. 104, 1/24 f. 7).   56 Minutes of the revenue commissioners, 16 Nov. 1750 (TNA, CUST1/49 f. 86); Hugh Fenning, 'Dublin imprints of Catholic interest, 1701–39', *Collectanea Hibernica*, 39 and 40 (1997–8), 106–54.   57 For an insight into the character of the Irish print trade see M. Pollard, *A dictionary of members of the Dublin book trade, 1550–1800: based on the records of the Guild of St Luke the Evangelist* (London, 2000); *eadem*, *Dublin's trade in books, 1550–1800* (Oxford, 1989).   58 Ó Cuív maintained that over 4,000 manuscripts date from the eighteenth and nineteenth centuries; this compares with *c*. 250 from the seventeenth century and *c*.100 from the sixteenth century: see Crowley, *Wars of words*, p. 87.

tutions or societies to assume the responsibility of printing in Irish.[59] This did not augur well for the language, which commenced the century as the vernacular of the majority of the population. Indeed, it intensified the trend, already well underway, which identified Irish with the past and with economic practices that were increasingly perceived as *passé* rather than of the moment and wealth generating. Had modernization and improvement taken root in an environment where literacy was not an economically profitable or socially desirable skill the language-use implications of this trend might not have been profound given the social, economic and political chasms that separated anglophone and Gaelic-speaking Ireland. However, literacy was an increasingly valuable skill in an economy and society in which the capacity to speak, write and read English allowed one to function at a higher, more efficient and more successful level. One must not, at the same time, adopt an economically and socially deterministic model, which involves inflexibly compartmentalizing Irish and English usage. It is striking that the centres of greatest scribal activity (Dublin, Cork, Waterford, Kilkenny, Limerick, Belfast) were also the centres of greatest print activity, though there is much about the manner in which they intersected and interacted and the implications for both print and scribal cultures that remains opaque.[60]

The social and economic benefits of literacy did not emerge *de novo* in the eighteenth century; they had long been manifested by the opportunities provided by the common law legal system, to which increasing appeal was made. The introduction of a common law legal system in Ireland, which employed English as its language of business, can be traced back to the arrival of the Anglo-Normans, but this was far from complete. The establishment of a network of assize courts that embraced the full kingdom was delayed until the

59 For the rise of sociability in Ireland, and its development in the eighteenth century, see James Kelly and Martyn Powell (eds), *Clubs and societies in eighteenth-century Ireland* (Dublin, 2010). It has been suggested (by D.F. Fleming in the same volume, p. 445) that the courts of poetry may have performed this role within Gaelic-speaking Ireland (see also Meidhbhín Ní Úrdail, *The scribe in eighteenth and nineteenth-century Ireland* (Münster, 2000), pp 33–4), but while they obviously served to bring people together, possessed clear rules, and employed legal terminology, it is not apparent that they assembled with sufficient regularity or that they possessed the indicative formal structures. This is a subject that deserves closer scrutiny: see Breandán Ó Conchúir, 'Na cúirteanna éigse i gCúige Mumhan' and L.P. Ó Murchú, 'Cúlra "Chúirt" Mherriman' both in Pádraigín Riggs et al. (eag.) *Saoi na héigse: aistí in ómós do Sheán Ó Tuama* (Baile Átha Cliath, 2000), pp 55–82, 169–95. The antipathy of improvers to the Irish language can be deduced from Samuel Madden's welcome for the displacement of the 'great partition wall' that was Irish with English: see Samuel Madden, *Reflections and resolutions proper for the gentlemen of Ireland* (Dublin, 1738, 1816), p. 78 (1816 ed.).   60 For local scribal cultures, see, *inter alia*, Breandán Ó Madagáin, *An Ghaeilge i Luimneach 1700–1900* (Baile Átha Cliath, 1974); Breandán Ó Conchúir, *Scríobhaithe Chorcaí, 1700–1850* (Baile Átha Cliath, 1982); Eoghan Ó Súilleabháin, 'Scríobhaithe Phort Láirge' in William Nolan and Thomas Power (eds), *Waterford: history and society* (Dublin, 1992), pp 265–308; Breandán Ó Buachalla, *I mBéal Feirste Cois Cuain* (Baile Átha Cliath, 1968).

completion of the Tudor conquest, while the emergence of a more uneven
network of local manor courts was dependent on the formal apportioning of
the country into estates.[61] Though it would be presumptuous to claim that
the law was administered with scrupulous impartiality, the willingness of the
native population to appeal to the courts in cases of dispute suggests that it
was perceived to possess strong merits. Indicatively, its officers were sufficiently committed to the principle of impartial justice to permit the use and
to pay the costs of employing translators as long as they were needed. This
remained the case at an incrementally smaller range of locations well into the
nineteenth century, and while it is significant that this was so, it is still more
striking that the majority of legal business was conducted in English.[62]
Moreover, while the paucity of legal documents produced in Irish during the
seventeenth century is consistent with the 'utilitarian' attitude towards
English identified by Cunningham among the Irish-speaking elite, the capacity of the courts to function in the eighteenth century without an extensive
network of translators and other linguistic supports suggests that the disposition to be pragmatic was a feature of other social levels also. What is apparent is that as Ireland was slowly absorbed during the course of the eighteenth
century into an economy whose language was English, into a cultural milieu
which deemed English the superior language, into an administrative (including a legal) system which conducted itself through English, and into a political world whose discourse was conducted in English, the incentives to
acquire English to converse, and to learn to read and to write English to
function effectively in an increasingly literate world became compelling.

It was thus highly significant, as Niall Ó Ciosáin has noted, that literacy
was a skill 'usually acquired in English'.[63] Ó Ciosáin's observation was offered
with reference to the situation at the end of the eighteenth and beginning of
the nineteenth century when the shift from Irish to English was proceeding
apace, but it also aptly describes the position a half-century earlier when the
kingdom embarked on a sustained phase of economic and commercial expansion.[64] Since the ability to speak and, increasingly, to read and write in
English were crucial to one's capacity to function optimally in a literate

---

61 Geoffrey Hand, *English law in Ireland 1290–1324* (Cambridge, 1967); John McCavitt,
'"Good planets in their several spheres": the establishment of the assize circuits in early
seventeenth-century Ireland', *Irish Jurist*, n.s., 24 (1989), 248–78.   62 Ní Mhunghaile,
'The legal system in Ireland and the Irish language, 1700–*c*.1843' provides an excellent
modern account of this subject. This is not to suggest that there were not problems. The
estate agent on Viscount Carleton's Bandon estate reported in 1718 that because he could
not always 'find a jury of Protestants to serve' in the local court leet, he was 'forced to take
Irish men who cannot speak one word of English': cited in David Dickson, *Old world
colony: Cork and south Munster, 1630–1830* (Cork, 2005), pp 198–9.   63 Niall Ó Ciosáin,
Print and popular culture in Ireland, 1750–1850 (Basingstoke, 1997), p. 154.   64 L.M.
Cullen, 'Economic development, 1750–1800' in T.W. Moody and W.E. Vaughan (eds), *A
new history of Ireland*; iv, *eighteenth-century Ireland, 1690–1800* (Oxford, 1986), pp 159–95.

world, it was inevitable that the large, if uneven network of private ('hedge') schools that was established throughout the country, but in greatest number in those areas most impacted by commercialization, prioritized the teaching of English.[65] Indeed, it may reasonably be surmised that the desire to learn English was one of the most important vectors in the accelerated formation of such schools in the second half of the eighteenth century. Certainly, the recognition that English was not only the language of the elite, but also the language of opportunity, was a prerequisite for the accelerated displacement of Irish that most commentators date to the second half of the eighteenth century. Complex back projections based on early nineteenth-century censal data, which suggest that as much as 50 per cent of males born between 1766 and 1775, and 55 per cent of those born between 1786 and 1795 were literate in English provide some perspective on the pace of change then underway and, by extension, on the pace of change that preceded if one accepts Windele's oft-cited estimate that two-thirds of the population were Irish speakers in 1730. Whatever the precise figures, there is a broad consensus that the Irish language, which had manifested resilience as a vernacular and as a medium of literary expression since the Tudors had inaugurated a new phase in Ireland's language history, had reached a critical moment.[66]

In contrast to the English in medieval Ireland who had succumbed to a greater or lesser extent to hibernicization, the Protestant community in the eighteenth century showed no signs of doing likewise. They were not under the same pressure to be sure. Their command of the levers of political, economic and social influence was more secure; they possessed substantial and secure demographic concentrations in Ulster and Dublin; and they were, by the mid-1740s, embarked on a sustained period of economic growth that generated cultural as well as economic confidence. Furthermore, they were fixedly determined not only to continue to speak English, but also eager to ensure that others would do likewise and, as a community, they manifested little interest in learning Irish (chapter 7). These were circumstances tailor-made to accelerate the language transition that was already underway, and this is what occurred. It is appropriate therefore that the examination of the process whereby the Irish language yielded to English is the theme in several essays in the volume.

65 L.M. Cullen, 'Patrons, teachers and literacy in Irish, 1707–1850' in Mary Daly and David Dickson (eds), *The origins of popular literacy in Ireland: language change and educational development, 1700–1920* (Dublin, 1990), pp 15–44; 'Report on the state of Popery in Ireland, 1731', *Archivium Hibernicum*, 3 (1914), 124–59. 66 Ó Ciosáin, *Print and popular culture*, p. 38; Garret Fitzgerald, 'Estimates for baronies of minimum level of Irish speaking amongst successive decennial cohorts 1771–81 to 1861–71', *RIA proc.* 84C (1984), 117–55; Brian Ó Cuív, *Irish dialects and Irish speaking districts* (Dublin, 1980), appendix, pp 77–94; *idem*, 'Irish language and literature, 1691–1845' in Moody and Vaughan (eds), *A new history of Ireland*; iv, *eighteenth-century Ireland*, p. 383; J[ohn] W[indele], 'Present extent of the Irish language', *Ulster Journal of Archaeology*, 5 (1857), 243–5; Crowley, *Wars of words*, p. 72; Reg Hindley, *The death of the Irish language* (London, 1990), p. 8.

Though it has only recently elicited the attention it plainly deserves in explaining the replacement of Irish by English as the primary vernacular on the island,[67] the history of linguistic borrowing and exchange provides a window into the manner in which language use changed in the course of the seventeenth, eighteenth and nineteenth centuries. Language exchange was not unidirectional of course; certain Irish words were anglicized and absorbed not only into everyday conversation, but also into official print.[68] However, in keeping with the direction in which the pendulum of language use was swinging, and the balance of political and economic power, it is clear that Irish speakers and writers borrowed more liberally from English than their English-speaking neighbours did from Irish. In his essay in this collection, Liam Mac Mathúna expands on his larger path-breaking work on this subject to engage specifically with the employment of English in selected warrants and macaronic verse in the eighteenth century. These popular poetic forms constitute a sensitive barometer of the nature of the linguistic exchange, and of the penetration of Irish by English that was ongoing (chapter 4). Though it is apparent that the order of English linguistic penetration was uneven, and that there were communities and regions in which English registered but modestly, the facility with which many Irish-language poets integrated English into their compositions and the openness with which they commented on the displacement of Irish by English was indicative of the accelerated pace with which it was now taking place. This was a matter of acute concern for Art Mac Cumhaigh, one of the most capable versifiers from south Ulster and, as Charles Dillon's examination of linguistic interaction in this region attests, Mac Cumhaigh's biography provides a vivid personal illustration of impact of the language shift in one of the Irish language's heartlands (chapter 5).

Mac Cumhaigh clearly found the transition difficult personally, though his ability to write in both languages and his reputed involvement in the infamous Armagh bye-election of 1753 would suggest that he was possessed of the required language skills to function successfully in this bilingual society. He was, moreover, following a by now established tradition. The early eighteenth-century poet and historian Aodh 'Buí' Mac Cruitín (Hugh MacCurtin) not only wrote in both languages, he also published in English.[69] Mícheál Ó Coimín (Michael Comyn), who was also from county Clare, composed poems in Irish and translated Irish poetry into English.[70] Most members of the

---

67 Liam Mac Mathúna, *Béarla sa Ghaeilge – cabhair choigríche: an códmheascadh Gaeilge/Béarla i litríocht na Gaeilge 1600–1900* (Baile Átha Cliath, 2007).   **68** See, generally, Alan Bliss, *The English language in Ireland* (Dublin, 1976); *idem, Spoken English in Ireland, 1600–1740: twenty-seven representative texts* (Dublin, 1979).   **69** Vincent Morley, *An crann os coill: Aodh Buí Mac Cruitín, c.1680–1755* (Baile Átha Cliath, 1995), passim; James Mitchell, 'Laurence Niehell (1726–1795): bishop of Kilfenora and Kilmacduagh', *Journal of the Galway Archaeological and Historical Society*, 34 (1974–5), 59.   **70** Brian Ó Dálaigh, 'Mícheál Ó Coimín: Jacobite, Protestant and Gaelic poet, 1676–1760', *Studia Hibernica*, 34 (2006–7), 135–9.

sprawling Ó Neachtain circle were also diglossic, but what is still more significant is that a bilingual facility penetrated increasingly deeply through society at large. The increase in the number of private schools was crucial in permitting this. William Shaw Mason's observation in 1819 that 'English alone' was taught in the 'hedge' schools of Tullaroan, county Kilkenny reflected a wider reality; indicatively, the monoglot Irish-speaking parents of Valentia Island sent their children to the local Erasmus Smith school in the 1790s in order to learn English.[71] The increasing range and depth of the penetration of English can be exemplified further by the fact that all of the known threatening letters conveyed to landlords, land agents, tithe proctors, and posted for the attention of the generality of the rural community in both the eighteenth and early nineteenth centuries were written in English. The grammar and syntax typically ranges from the sophisticated to the crude, but their orthographical in-exactitude is less pertinent than their language of choice.[72] Moreover, it echoes and reinforces the broader linguistic and social trend described by Lesa Ní Mhunghaile (chapter 8), which informs the story of the linguistic transition through the eighteenth into the nineteenth century.

As the end of the eighteenth century approached, it was manifest that English had replaced Irish as the vernacular of choice over much of the country. The observations of the English visitor John Bush in 1769 that 'very few of the lowest classes' could not speak English was echoed by Horace Twiss in 1775, but while this was true of much of the east and north of the country, and was evidently true of the popular destinations to which travel writers were disproportionately drawn, both men exaggerated the real permeation of English.[73] This is the implication, certainly, of the language use survey published by Whitley Stokes in 1799. His inquiries led him to the conclusion that more than 40 per cent of the population could speak Irish, but the more striking, and pertinent, statistic he produced was that 800,000, or 15 per cent, of the total were monoglot Irish speakers, since this would suggest not only that the proportion of the population that was firmly anchored in an Irish-speaking milieu had contracted sharply since 1730 but also that Irish was in rapid retreat.[74] This is not to suggest that monoglot Irish speakers were only to be encountered in the more remote parts of the country, and that it was

---

71 William Shaw Mason, *A survey of Tullaroan* (Dublin, 1819); Pádraig de Brún, 'Some documents concerning Valentia Erasmus Smith schools, 1776–95', *JKAHS*, 15–16 (1982–3), 70–81.   72 For a sample of threatening letters from the eighteenth century, see the proclamations dated 6 June 1769, 29 Aug., 30 Nov. 1786 in Kelly and Lyons (eds), *The proclamations of Ireland, 1660–1820* (forthcoming); Stephen Gibbons (ed.), *Captain Rock, knight errant: the threatening letters of pre-Famine Ireland* (Dublin, 2004).   73 John Bush, *Hibernia curiosa* (Dublin, 1769); Horace Twiss, *A tour in Ireland in 1775* (Dublin, 1775).   74 Whitley Stokes, *Projects for re-establishing the internal peace and tranquillity of Ireland* (Dublin, 1799); Crowley, *Wars of words*, pp 74, 78–9; Hindley, *Death of the Irish language*, p. 15. These percentages are based on the calculation that the population of the country was 5.4 million in 1799.

now the vernacular of the less socially and economically mobile, but this clearly was the trend. It certainly was the import of the observation offered by Charles, twelfth viscount Dillon in the House of Lords in 1793 that in order to promote the dissemination of their 'doctrines' 'in the remoter parts of the kingdom' the Society of United Irishmen 'paid interpreters to translate them to the ignorant'.[75] The account of a Whiteboy outrage near Clonmel in 1775 in which it was noted that those responsible 'were decently dressed and spoke the English language very well' is still more indicative of the link between language, social status and education that informed the attitudinal change that hastened the decline in the use of Irish across the island.[76]

This certainly was the impression garnered by Coquebert De Montbret, the percipient French visitor who noted that though the Irish language could readily be encountered, it was in full retreat in the 1790s. De Montbret was puzzled by the fact that 'nobody was able to read or write the language', but his still more pertinent observation that 'no notices appeared in it; ... it was not even used for epitaphs' seemed to suggest it was simply not to be encountered in the public sphere.[77] This was to exaggerate. The decision of Patrick Wogan (c.1740–1816), the leading Catholic printer of the day, to publish an Irish edition, albeit one fifth the size of the English-language edition he published at the same time, of the popular chapbook *Seven champions* in 1781 indicates that there was a market for popular Irish print, but that it was a fraction of the size of its English equivalent.[78] Moreover, despite the impact, symbolic and real, of the seminal bilingual edition of a selection of Irish poems published by Charlotte Brooke later the same decade, the use of Irish continued to decline across the island.[79] Thus Coquebert de Montbret noted pertinently that the Sullivans of Nedeen (Kenmare), county Kerry, 'have their children taught English', though the position of Irish as the primary vernacular in the area was acknowledged by the clergy who continued to preach and teach catechism in the Irish language.[80]

De Montbret ascribed the Sullivans' language choice to vanity. Doubtlessly, this was a factor in the calculations of those like John August O'Neill Geoghegan, later MP for Kingston-on-Hull in the imperial parliament, who changed his name in order that it should appear less 'barbarous'.[81]

---

75 James Kelly (ed.), *Proceedings of the House of Lords, 1771–1800* (3 vols, Dublin, 2008), ii, 339. 76 *Finn's Leinster Journal*, 2 Aug. 1775; Brendan Hoban, 'Dominick Bellew: parish priest of Dundalk and bishop of Killala', *Seanchas Ard Mhacha*, 6 (1972), 352. 77 S. Kennedy, 'Coquebert de Montbret in search of the hidden Ireland', *RSAI Jnl.* 82 (1952), 64–5. 78 *DIB, sub nom.* The full edition of the chapbook was 3,500, which suggests an English to Irish ratio of 6:1. 79 Charlotte Brooke, *Reliques of Irish poetry* (1789) ed. Lesa Ní Mhunghaile (Dublin, 2009). 80 Síle Ní Chinnéide, 'New view of eighteenth-century Kerry', *JKAHS*, 6 (1973), 87, 92, 93; W.H.A. Williams, *Tourism, landscape and the Irish character* (Madison, WI, 2008), pp 64, 65. 81 *Ordnance survey letters, county Galway*, ed. Michael Herity (Dublin, 2009), p. 359.

However, it is inadequate as an explanation of the multiplicity of individual decisions made across the country chronicled in the various county, baronial and parish surveys taken in the early nineteenth century that provide a near island-wide perspective on the rapid anglicization that was taking place. The use of Irish continued to be recorded in much of the country, but the perception that Irish was the 'language of the poor and ignorant' was crucial in fuelling the language shift that informed observations, such as that made of the parish of Bailieborough, county Cavan in 1815, that 'the English language is in general use'.[82] There were plenty of comparable locations. Laurence Parsons, second earl of Rosse, observed anxiously in 1822 that 'the lowest orders' in the neighbourhood of Ballylin, county Offaly, were sufficiently literate to read incendiary texts such as Pastorini's prophecies.[83] Indeed, no part of the country escaped the effects of linguistic anglicization in the early nineteenth century, but it diminished the closer one moved towards the western, southern and north-western periphery. It is notable, for example, that though the doughty Dean John Lyons of Killala recalled in 1827 that it was 'a crime' to speak Irish in the 'hedge school where we received the first rudiments of knowledge', and that his father would not employ Irish-speaking servants when he was growing up 'for fear his children would learn this vulgar tongue', Irish was the dominant language in the areas of Erris and the Mullet, county Mayo, into the 1830s and beyond.[84] John O'Donovan made a similar observation as to the situation in county Galway in 1838; commenting on the language preferences of the population of the parish of Annaghdown on the eastern shore of Lough Corrib, he noted of the inhabitants that 'Irish is the only language they wish to speak'.[85] Such attitudes were readily encountered in remote and peripheral areas across much of the country,[86] and they served to ensure, when taken together with the disproportionate rise in the number of poor revealed by the 1821 and 1841 censes, that the statistical impact of language shift was less severe than it might have been. Various contemporary estimates made between 1812 and 1842 place the number of Irish speakers at anywhere between 1.5 and 4.1 million, but the most revealing statistic (calcu-

---

82 Sean Connolly, 'Approaches to the history of popular culture', *Bullán*, 2:2 (1995–6), 94–5; B.S. Ó hAodha, 'Aspects of the linguistic geography of Ireland in the early nineteenth century', *Studia Celtica*, 20 and 21 (1985–6), 208–9; Gerard O'Brien, 'The strange death of the Irish language, 1780–1800' in *idem* (ed.), *Parliament, politics and people* (Dublin, 1989), pp 149–70; *Freeman's Journal*, 26 Jan. 1815; Máirín Nic Eoin, 'Irish language and literature in county Kilkenny in the nineteenth century' in William Nolan and Kevin Whelan (eds), *Kilkenny: history and society* (Dublin, 1990) pp 65–80. 83 A.P.W. Malcomson (ed.), *Calendar of the Rosse papers* (Dublin, 2008), pp 393–4. 84 S[éamus] Ó C[asaide], 'Dean Lyons', *Irish Book Lover*, 20 (May–June 1932), 62–3; Brendan Hoban, *Turbulent diocese: the Killala troubles, 1798–1848* (Dublin, 2011), pp 43–4, 100 note 4, 364; *idem*, 'Dominick Bellew', p. 356. 85 Herity (ed.), *Ordnance survey letters: county Galway*, p. 66. 86 See Jack Burtchaell, 'The south Kilkenny farm villages' and P.J. O'Connor, 'The maturation of town and village in county Limerick' in Kevin Whelan (ed.), *Common ground: essays on the historical geography of Ireland* (Cork, 1988), pp 117–18, 157–60.

lated by Garret FitzGerald) is that only 28 per cent of the children born in the 1830s grew up with a knowledge of Irish.[87] As a result, when the Great Famine took its disproportionate toll of the poor of the country, it precipitated a dramatic decline in the number of monoglot Irish speakers, and hastened the arrival of the moment when most of those who were raised in Irish-speaking areas were bilingual, which was increasingly the trend in the second half of the nineteenth century.[88]

Because of the speed with which the relative fortunes of the Irish and English languages were transformed in the century 1750–1850, and the expanded range of factors that must be brought into play when it comes to explaining the profound language shift that took place, it is vital that the role and impact of major institutions is scrutinized. Of these, religious institutions deserve particular attention because, since the Reformation, the printed word has been central to their evangelizing activities. Moreover, as Niall Ó Ciosáin points out (chapter 10), 'literacy in a language not the language of the state or the language of trade and commerce is rooted in religious usage'.[89] Certainly, Brian Ó Cuív's terse summation that the Catholic Church 'made little positive contribution towards maintaining the language' begs more questions than it provides answers.[90] It must be acknowledged at the same time that the church of the people was not in a powerful or privileged position throughout the period spanned by this collection. The fortunes of the Catholic Church in Ireland rose and fell sharply, but, even when they were at a low ebb, the church was still one of the most powerful, enterprising and independent institutions in the jurisdiction, with direct access to and influence over the majority of the population. Moreover, during the period covered by Dr Ó Ciosáin's essay in the collection, it was fast emerging as the most powerful institution on the island. It is this fact that makes Ó Ciosáin's comparative exploration of the relative fortunes of three devotional texts from Scotland, Ireland and Brittany so useful; it facilitates the isolation and examination of the institutional strategies pursued in a variety of congruent jurisdictions and the identification of their effects. The implications in the Irish context are not only that the Catholic Church failed to have other than the occasional recourse to print when the penal laws were still on the statute book (chapter 8), but also that it pursued a similar approach in the nineteenth century (chapter 10). According to Ciarán Mac Murchaidh, the church was not unconscious of the

87 Hindley, *The death of the Irish language*, p. 15; Connolly, 'Approaches to the history of popular culture', p. 94; FitzGerald, 'Estimates for baronies of minimum level of Irish speaking', 117–55. 88 See Seán de Fréine, *The great silence* (Dublin, 1965); Hindley, *The death of the Irish language*, pp 15–20. The accepted estimates for the proportion of Irish speakers in 1851 is 32.6 per cent; this fell to 21–2 per cent in 1871 and to 14.5 per cent in 1891: see N.M. Wolf, 'Irish speaking clergy in the nineteenth century: education, trends, and timing', *New Hibernia Review*, 12:4 (Winter 2008), p. 67. 89 Below p. 270. 90 Ó Cuiv, 'Irish language and literature, 1691–1845', p. 380; Crowley, *Wars of words*, p. 66.

consequences of relying on clergy who were linguistically unprepared to preach in the vernacular of their congregation. However, a combination of a difficult environment, structural weaknesses and a largely neutral view of language (it was simply a means of conveying the word of God) ensured that the Irish mission did not present a significant obstacle to the spread of English (chapter 6). Together, these two essays assist us to explain why the amount of Catholic devotional print in English greatly exceeded that in Irish in both the eighteenth and nineteenth centuries, and why the volume of Irish-language print produced in Ireland failed even to amount to one per cent of that in English during the crucial century, 1750–1850.[91] Moreover, when read with his other work on this subject, Ó Ciosáin's essay extends and deepens the comparison with Wales, Scotland and Brittany that reinforces the case in favour of perceiving the history of language in Ireland as unique and particular.[92]

It could be countered that print did not flourish in Irish in the eighteenth and early nineteenth centuries, though there were no overwhelming technological or regulatory barriers, because the Irish reading community was adequately catered for by literary, historical and spiritual texts in manuscript. The problem with this argument is, first, that for all its evident vigour the manuscript tradition was contracting not expanding,[93] and, second, that it patently did not meet the demand for spiritual print. Yet the failure of clerical or other authors to respond to the invitation made in 1824 by the publisher of Timothy O'Sullivan's *Pious miscellany*, which was by some margin the most popular Irish-language religious text in the nineteenth century, meant that those who could do so were unwilling to assist with the development of this market.[94] This is remarkable since English-language Catholic print not only exceeded that in Irish, but also expanded appreciably in the course of the eighteenth and early nineteenth centuries.[95] Moreover, based on those cases brought to the notice of the commissioners of the revenue, there

91 A modest 19 Irish-language titles were published in Ireland between 1751 and 1800 (ESTC), and only 150 between 1801 and 1850; this approximated to 10–15 per cent of the number of titles produced in Scottish Gaelic and Breton, and 1.5 per cent of the total in Welsh (Ó Ciosáin, 'Language, print and the Catholic Church in Ireland 1700–1900' in Donald McNamara (ed.), *Which direction Ireland?* (Newcastle, 2007), pp 125–38). By comparison the number of known English-language titles published in Ireland between 1751 and 1800 exceeded 16,000. I wish to acknowledge Suzanne Forbes' assistance with these figures.   92 Ó Ciosáin, 'Print and Irish, 1570–1900: an exception among the Celtic languages', passim; *idem*, 'Language, print and the Catholic Church in Ireland 1700–1900'; *idem*, 'Gaelic culture and language shift' in Laurence Geary and Margaret Kelleher (eds), *Nineteenth-century Ireland: a guide to recent research* (Dublin, 2005), pp 136–52.   93 Ní Úrdail, *The scribe in eighteenth and nineteenth-century Ireland*, passim, provides the most insightful account of this.   94 Ó Ciosáin, 'Language, print and the Catholic Church in Ireland', p. 127.   95 Hugh Fenning, 'Dublin imprints of Catholic interest, 1701–39', *Collectanea Hibernica*, 39 and 40 (1997–8), 106–54; *idem*, 'Dublin imprints of Catholic interest, 1740–59', *Collectanea Hibernica*, 41 (1999), 65–226; *idem*, 'Dublin imprints of Catholic interest, 1760–69', *Collectanea Hibernica*, 42 (2000), 85–119; *idem*, 'Dublin imprints of Catholic interest, 1770–82', *Collectanea Hibernica*, 43 (2001), 115–208.

is evidence to suggest that Catholic print (in Latin and other languages) was imported in significant, if unquantifiable, amounts from the continent. Indicatively, in 1749 'a great number of volumes and other Popish books' were intercepted at Baltimore, county Cork, on three priests who had embarked at Le Harve. Other consignments of 'Popish books' were regarded suspiciously by officials, but when it was established that they contained no politically seditious matter they were invariably returned to their owners.[96] The use to which such collections of print were put in Ireland remains to be established, but when taken together with Patrick Wogan's printing of parallel English and Irish-language editions of popular texts such as *Seven champions* (1787), it demands the modification of Joep Leerssen's thesis that Irish and English functioned in two separate spheres.

Leerssen maintained in 2002 that because Gaelic 'literature functioned in an oral, or at best handwritten form ... native Ireland had no public space' and that the 'hidden Ireland was a culture without a public sphere'.[97] While one may choose to modify rather than to deny Leerssen's contention that 'pamphlets, papers and debates were by and for Protestants', it is manifest from the activities of the network of Irish scribes that lived in Dublin, from the capacity of many Irish-language authors to write in English and from the interchange of printed and manuscripts texts that Leerssen's perception of Gaelic Ireland as an exclusively oral and manuscript culture is as untenable as the characterization of anglophone Ireland as exclusively print bound (see chapter 8). This is not, of course, to suggest that these linguistic realms were not in a constant state of redefinition. The detailed comparison Ní Mhunghaile has completed of the library lists of Muiris Ó Gormáin indicates that over time print assumed a more prominent place in his collection. This was in keeping with the expansion of the public sphere, and indeed of the penetration of English.[98] However, it also serves to underline the point that instead of conceiving of Ireland in terms of separate spheres, we might usefully conceptualize a linguistic world in which exchange and interchange were normative, and that as that developed, and develop it did, exchange and interchange expanded outwards from the comparatively rarefied realm of the intellectual elite through and across society in a manner and fashion that elicited different patterns of interaction, most of which remain to be delineated. This reconstruction sits more easily with the politicized impression of the Gaelic world proffered by Vincent Morley, Éamonn Ó Ciardha, Breandán Ó Buachalla and Cornelius Buttimer, based on the coverage afforded current affairs in Irish-language texts, and on the contemporary political resonances in the corpus of political poetry.[99] The suggestion that the Irish-speaking population was politicized, which has

96 Above p. 30; TNA, CUST1/47 ff 48–9.   97 Joep Leerssen, *Hidden Ireland, public sphere* (Galway, 2002), pp 31, 36.   98 Ní Mhunghaile, 'An eighteenth-century scribe's private library', 268.   99 See, *inter alia*, Vincent Morley, *Irish opinion and the American Revolution, 1760–1783* (Cambridge, 2002); Éamonn Ó Ciardha, *Ireland and the Jacobite*

been advanced by O Buachalla, Morley and O Ciardha, certainly sits uneasily with Leerssen's conclusion that 'Gaelic Ireland was atomized into many separate small-scale communities without the wherewithal to form a society, without the joint continuum of a public sphere'.[1]

If this more dynamic interactive model finds acceptance, it will be possible finally to dispense with the image of the 'hidden Ireland' famously articulated by Daniel Corkery, to which Leerssen's 2002 intervention can be seen to have given a lease of life.[2] In practice, as Liam Mac Mathúna convincingly argues in this volume (chapter 4) the situation in Ireland demands particular explanation in a manner that is not beholden to an explanatory model which presumes that the Irish and English languages were pitted in an antagonistic relationship (Corkery), and that the emergence of print consigned them to separate spheres in a world in which what happened in the public (print) sphere shaped the present and laid the ideological and cultural foundations for the future (Leerssen). To choose otherwise involves drawing too sharp a distinction between the anglophone and Irish-speaking worlds, between orality and literacy, and between print and manuscript, which the essays in this collection have sought to transcend, thereby overcoming what is, arguably, the most limiting legacy of Daniel Corkery's seminal study of the poetry of Munster – his conception of Ireland's cultural worlds as hermetically sealed one from the other, when what we know of language use, print culture, commercial activity, and the legal system, all suggest the contrary.

In sum, the relationship in which Irish and English were bound in the seventeenth, eighteenth and nineteenth centuries was more complex, more contingent and more intertwined than has been habitually portrayed prior to the recent surge in scholarship into language, print and culture. The decline of Irish both as a language of scholarship and as a vernacular and its replacement by English was prolonged partly because this is the nature of language change, but it was also a consequence of the fact that the attachment that the Irish population demonstrated for their language was deep and abiding. Indeed, though it might be suggested that the eventual outcome was inevitable by the second quarter of the nineteenth century, the fact that it was at this very moment that the foundations of scholarly enquiry into Irish culture was beginning to assume something of its modern character indicates that whatever the fate of the language as a vernacular, the intellectual, emotional and academic merits of the language were being recognized in an

---

cause, 1685–1766: a fatal attachment (Dublin, 2002); Ó Buachalla, *Aisling ghéar: na Stíobhartaigh agus an t-aos léinn.* **1** Leerssen, *Hidden Ireland, public sphere*, p. 37; Brendán Ó Buachalla, 'Seacaibíteachas Thaidhg Uí Neachtain', *Studia Hibernica* 26 (1992), 31–64; C.G. Buttimer, 'Gaelic literature and contemporary life in Cork, 1700–1840' in *idem* and Patrick O'Flanagan (eds), *Cork: history and society* (Dublin, 1993), pp 585–654; *idem*, 'An Irish text on the "War of Jenkins' Ear"', *Celtica*, 21 (1990), 75–98. **2** Daniel Corkery, *The hidden Ireland: a study of Gaelic Munster in the eighteenth century* (Dublin, 1924).

increasingly anglophone world. This is the broader cultural implication of
Thomas Crofton Croker's sometimes problematical engagement with the
poetry of Piaras Feiritéar (chapter 9). Croker was not a textual editor of particular skill, but he built upon and expanded on the achievements of
Charlotte Brooke a generation earlier. More generally, he was perpetuating
and extending the patriot interest in the Irish language and in the Irish past,
and, by demonstrating that the quality of Irish poetry and the artistic capac-
ities of the finest of its poets were of a standard deserving of notice, provided
firmer foundations upon which others were to continue to build. By comparison with the contemporary scholarly activities of John O'Donovan and John
Curry, Croker was a minor player in the history of Irish learning, but his
openness to Irish linguistic and cultural issues mirrored the permeability of
the cultural frontier that connected as well as separated the Irish and English
languages. His openness, certainly, echoes the approach that this collection
seeks to employ in order better to understand the variety of factors that are
integral to the transition of Ireland from a polity which in 1600 was largely
Irish speaking to one which in 1900 was predominantly English speaking.

I

'Solid divine and worthy scholar':[1]
William Bedell, Venice and Gaelic culture

MARC CABALL

In May 1627 the English diplomat and writer, Sir Henry Wotton (1568–1639) wrote to Charles II recommending the appointment of a scholarly Essex clergyman to the provostship of Trinity College, Dublin. Acknowledging the support of the archbishop of Armagh for the candidacy of William Bedell for the position of head of house in Ireland's Protestant seminary, Wotton made clear his esteem for the East Anglian divine. Remarkably, considering the typical social, professional and religious experience of clergymen in England and Ireland in the early decades of the seventeenth century, William Bedell had lived in Venice during the years 1607–10 when he had served as Wotton's chaplain in the Adriatic city republic. In commending Bedell to the monarch, Wotton highlighted his 'singular erudition and piety, conformity to the rites of your Church, and zeal to advance the cause of God', and emphasized his impeccable evangelical credentials during his time in Venice:

> For it may please your Majesty to know that this is the man whom Padre Paolo took, I may say, into his very soul; with whom he did communicate the inwardest thoughts of his heart; from whom he professed to have received more knowledge in all divinity, both scholastical and positive, than from any that he had ever practised in his days ...[2]

Ussher's and Wotton's efforts in favour of the self-effacing Bedell were successful and the one-time *confidante* of Paolo Sarpi, Servite friar and Venice's official theologian, was admitted provost of TCD in August 1627.

---

1 The English traveller Thomas Coryat who visited Venice in 1608 in his description of the English ambassador to Venice, Sir Henry Wotton, referred to his chaplain as follows: '... that solid divine and worthy scholar Mr. William Bedel being his preacher at the time of my being in Venice will be very forcible motives (I doubt not) to win many souls to Jesus Christ, and to draw divers of the famous papists of the city to the true reformed religion, and profession of the gospel': Thomas Coryat, *Coryats crudities* (London, 1611), p. 241.   2 Logan Pearsall Smith (ed.), *The life and letters of Sir Henry Wotton* (2 vols, Oxford, 1907), ii, 301–2.

43

William Bedell's modern reputation is pithily encapsulated in Hugh Trevor-Roper's hagiographic description of him as the 'saintly Dr Bedell' who battled against the latent and often overt hostility of a largely anglicized established church in Ireland to evangelize the Gaelic population through the medium of the Irish language.[3] During his time in Ireland, Bedell crossed both linguistic and cultural frontiers in his efforts to disseminate the message of reform among the Gaelic Irish. Animated by deep-seated religious belief and concomitant evangelical zeal, Bedell was an atypical member of the Anglican episcopate in Ireland in his commitment to negotiating beneficial interchange between English and Gaelic cultures in the early seventeenth century. It is arguable that Bedell's academic and spiritual formation at Cambridge and his subsequent seminal Venetian experience equipped him with a degree of cultural discernment and sensibility unique among English clerics and officials in Ireland at this period. If he is exceptional in an Irish episcopal context, Bedell's mindset is reflective generally of the experience of a cohort of English travellers in the Mediterranean in the late sixteenth and seventeenth centuries who were characterized by their capacity for cultural exchange and accommodation.[4] William Bedell is remembered historically for enabling the translation of the Old Testament to Irish, and it remains both his great legacy and a remarkable monument to an extraordinary episode in early modern Gaelic and English cultural interchange.

If Bedell is best known today, and arguably not entirely accurately, as an iconic and engagingly sympathetic, but contemporaneously maligned, advocate of religious and cultural dialogue in an otherwise bleakly sectarian and culturally polarized early seventeenth-century Ireland, it is necessary to explore his time in Venice to understand fully his Irish career as provost of Trinity College and subsequently as bishop of the north-eastern rural diocese of Kilmore.[5] Notwithstanding his sojourn in cosmopolitan Venice and his pivotal years in Ireland when the island's mounting ethnic and religious tensions culminated in the murderous fury of the 1641 rebellion, Bedell was first and foremost an Englishman and a loyal conformist to the rites, rituals and teaching of the Church of England.

William Bedell was born in Essex around the year 1572 and was deeply influenced throughout his life and career by his education at the newly founded Emmanuel College at Cambridge, which he entered in 1584. In the

---

3 Hugh Trevor-Roper, *Catholics, Anglicans and Puritans: seventeenth century essays* (London, 1987), p. 141.   4 Alison Games, *The web of empire: English cosmopolitans in an age of expansion 1560–1660* (New York and Oxford, 2008), p. 51.   5 K.S. Bottigheimer and Vivienne Larminie, 'Bedell, William (*bap.* 1572, *d.* 1642)' in *ODNB*, iv, 765–8. See also John Richardson, *A short history of the attempts that have been made to convert the popish natives of Ireland* (London, 1712), pp 20–6; H.J. Monck Mason, *The life of William Bedell, D.D., lord bishop of Kilmore* (London, 1843); Deasún Breathnach, *Bedell and the Irish version of the Old Testament* (Dublin, 1971); Gordon Rupp, *William Bedell, 1571–1642* (Cambridge, 1972); Aidan Clarke, 'Bishop William Bedell (1572–1642) and the Irish reformation' in Ciaran Brady (ed.), *Worsted in the game: losers in Irish history* (Dublin, 1989), pp 61–70.

previous year, the land and buildings of a former Dominican priory had been acquired by Laurence Chaderton, a fellow of Christ's College, Cambridge, and conveyed to Sir Walter Mildmay, chancellor of the exchequer and a member of Elizabeth's Privy Council. Mildmay's plans for a new college informed by a puritan ethos culminated in the grant of a royal charter of foundation in January 1584.[6] Significantly, the young Bedell was reinforced in his puritan inclinations by the influence of Chaderton, who was master of Emmanuel from 1584 until he stepped down from the post in 1602, and by the teaching of the famous William Perkins, a fellow of Christ's College.[7] The Calvinist leaning of these mentors was a critical influence on Bedell's theological formation.[8] It was at Emmanuel also that Bedell may have first come in contact with the Gaelic world in the person of Uilliam Ó Domhnuill (1570–1628) who entered the college as a student in 1586 and who was designated a scholar on the nomination of the college founder.[9] Ó Domhnuill, who graduated from the university with an MA in 1593, must surely have been Bedell's first source of detailed information on Ireland and on Gaelic society and culture. Ó Domhnuill, who was appointed archbishop of Tuam in 1609, published the Gaelic New Testament in 1602/3 and the Gaelic translation of the *Book of Common Prayer* in 1608/9. It is possible also that Bedell followed Ó Domhnuill's progress subsequent to his return to Ireland around 1593/4 through the Emmanuel nexus. The presence of Ó Domhnuill's translation of the New Testament (*Tiomna Nuadh*) in the library of Emmanuel relatively shortly after its publication suggests both pride and an interest in the achievements of the college's Irish student.[10] Bedell maintained a life-long interest in his old college and was a generous donor to its library.[11] Mildmay had been explicit in his intention that Emmanuel should serve as a seminary to supply clerics to minister to the world at large, and the original college statutes also stipulated that no fellow could remain in the college more than 10 years after taking his MA degree.[12] With a view to embarking on his pastoral mission, Bedell, who was elected a fellow of Emmanuel in 1593, was ordained to the ministry at Colchester in 1597.

The basis of Bedell's saintly reputation was articulated early by means of two highly favourable manuscript biographies compiled in the 1660s and

---

6 Sargent Bush and Carl J. Rasmussen, *The library of Emmanuel College, Cambridge, 1584–1637* (Cambridge, 1986), p. 2; Sarah Bendall, Christopher Brooke and Patrick Collinson, *A history of Emmanuel College, Cambridge* (Woodbridge, 1999), pp 13–90.   7 For Chaderton see Arnold Hunt, 'Laurence Chaderton and the Hampton Court conference' in Susan Wabuda and Caroline Litzenberger (eds), *Belief and practice in reformation England: a tribute to Patrick Collinson from his students* (Aldershot, 1998), pp 207–28. I am grateful to Dr Hunt for drawing my attention to his article.   8 In regard to Bedell's theology see Anthony Milton, *Catholic and reformed: the Roman and Protestant churches in English Protestant thought, 1600–1640* (Cambridge, 1995).   9 John Venn and J.A. Venn, *Alumni Cantabrigienses,* part 1 (4 vols, Cambridge, 1922–7), ii, 8.   10 Bush and Rasmussen, *The library of Emmanuel College,* p. 55.   11 Ibid., pp 23–4.   12 Ibid., p. 2.

1670s. The first was written by the bishop's son William (1613–70) and the second, and longer work, was composed by his son-in-law, Alexander Clogie (1614–98). The accounts of both men benefited in the first instance from proximity to their subject, and from the fact that they had witnessed Bedell's final days and funeral in 1642 in the midst of cataclysmic rebellion and dispossession. Previously, in 1659, Bedell's former dean in Kilmore, Nicholas Bernard, published a brief but laudatory account of the bishop appended to a work by the late James Ussher.[13] A biography of Bedell, largely based on Clogie's account, which was possibly written in 1675, was published by Gilbert Burnet in 1685.[14] A second edition of Burnet's work was published in 1692, five years after a French translation appeared in Amsterdam in 1687, and this biography provided the basis for continued interest in Bedell during the eighteenth century.[15] Burnet's biography seems to have circulated reasonably widely. For instance, John Evelyn owned a copy of the 1685 edition. The 1736 Dublin reprint contained additional material garnered from 'Mr Bedell Stanford, a near relation of the Bishop's'.[16] An edition of his Venetian letters was published by the printer George Faulkner in Dublin in 1742.[17] A manuscript prefatory note on Bedell in George III's copy of the 1685 edition by Richard Farmer (1735–97), literary scholar and master of Emmanuel College, is remarkably informative.[18] Possibly written in 1781, Farmer's note provides biographical and bibliographical details of Bedell.[19] Farmer refers to the entry on Bedell in Daniel Gerdes' *Florilegium historico-criticum* and this

13 K.S. Bottigheimer, 'The hagiography of William Bedell' in Toby Barnard, Dáibhí Ó Cróinín and Katharine Simms (eds), *'A miracle of learning': studies in manuscripts and Irish learning: essays in honour of William O'Sullivan* (Aldershot, 1998), pp 201–8, at p. 203.   14 Gilbert Burnet, *The life of William Bedell, D.D., lord bishop of Kilmore in Ireland* (London, 1685): 'I had a great collection of memorials put in my hands by a worthy and learned divine, Mr. Clogy, who as he lived long in this Bishop's House, so being afterwards minister at Cavan, had occasion to know him well', unpaginated preface.   15 *La vie de Guilme Bedell, eveque de Kilmore en Irlande, traduite de l'Anglois de M. le Docteur Burnet par L.D.M.* (Amsterdam, 1687).   16 Gilbert Burnet, *The life of William Bedell D.D. Bishop of Kilmore in Ireland: the second edition, with additions* (Dublin, 1736). John Evelyn's copy of the 1685 edition is now in the British Library (BL Eve.a.85). A National Library of Ireland copy of the 1685 edition (IR 92 B 14) containing the bookplate of Carton House library suggests the work may also have featured in Irish country house book collections in the eighteenth century. Holt White's gift of a copy of the 1685 edition to Mary White in July 1740 indicates that the work was also considered edifying reading for women: see White's inscription in the copy held at the Newberry Library, Chicago (Case E5.B3915).   17 Edward Hudson (ed.), *Some original letters of Bishop Bedell, concerning the steps taken toward a reformation of the religion of Venice, upon occasion of the quarrel between that state, and the pope Paul V* (Dublin, 1742).   18 This copy is now in the British Library (BL 295 i 4). When Farmer's library was auctioned in 1798, material was acquired for the King's Library, presumably including this 1685 edition of Burnet's biography: P.R. Harris, 'The King's Library' in Giles Mandelbrote and Barry Taylor (eds), *Libraries within the library: the origins of the British Library's printed collections* (London, 2009), pp 296–317, at pp 300–1.   19 The date 'Feb: 14th 1781' is written on page 260 of the King's Library copy of the 1685 edition (BL 295 i 4).

latter compendium served to maintain a degree of awareness of Bedell beyond the British Isles.[20]

Bedell left Cambridge in 1602 to minister to the congregation of the church of St Mary in Bury St Edmunds. Quickly recognized for the quality of his preaching, his son William wrote that he had not been long in the town 'ere he had gain'd a great reverence, as well from all that savoured of the power of godliness as from the gallants, knights and gentlemen, who reverenced him for his impartial, grave and holy preaching and conversation, and heard him gladly'.[21] It may have been at Bury St Edmunds that Bedell met Sir Thomas Jermyn who in 1616 presented him as rector of Horningsheath in Suffolk.[22] The pastoral sensitivity that characterized Bedell's ministry in Kilmore is evident also at this early stage in his career. In the prefatory epistle to a theological treatise written by Bedell in Bury in 1604, he displays his concern for courtesy and respect in the conduct of religious controversy. In this work, intended as a response to the criticisms of the legitimacy of the established church by the Suffolk-born William Alabaster, sometime Church of England clergyman and convert to Roman Catholicism, Bedell is insistent on the need for decorum and propriety in the conduct of polemical debate between opponents.[23] Anxious to avoid personalized and vituperative encounters, Bedell declares emolliently to the work's dedicatee Ambrose Jermyn that 'neither let it offend you if other whiles I call some of ye doctrine I write against anti-Christian &c. I write according to my perswasion &c as an accuser must of necessity, without any tooth to any person, without any gall to those, that are otherwise minded'.[24] While never deviating from his Protestant beliefs, Bedell's pastoral empathy enabled him to transcend the corrosive limitations of sectarian conflict in his personal relations with opponents.

Bedell's ministry in Suffolk was short-lived, as he was invited to travel to Venice in 1607 as chaplain to Sir Henry Wotton, English ambassador to the city. Wotton, a witty and urbane diplomat and a gifted linguist, had assumed his post in Venice at a time of political and religious ferment in the city. Tensions between Rome and the Venetian republic in regard to questions of jurisdiction dated back to the 1590s. Paul V, who had been elected pope in 1605, was embroiled in a quarrel with Leonardo Donà, appointed doge in 1606. In the same year, the Venetian authorities arrested and placed two priests on

20 Daniel Gerdes, *Florilegium historico-criticum librorum rariorum* (3rd edn, Groningen and Bremen, 1763), p. 36.   21 E.S. Shuckburgh, *Two biographies of William Bedell* (Cambridge, 1902), p. 8.   22 Diarmaid MacCulloch, 'Jermyn, Sir Thomas (bap. 1573, d. 1644/5)' in *ODNB*, xxx, 49.   23 'A defence of the answer to Mr Alablaster's four demands against a treatise intituled the Catholic's reply upon Bedell's answer to Mr Alablaster's four demands' (Lambeth Palace Library, MS 772).   24 Lambeth Palace Library, MS 772, f. 3. Ambrose Jermyn was possibly a son of Sir Ambrose Jermyn (d. 1577) of Rushbrooke south of Bury St Edmunds. The Jermyns were a leading gentry family in Suffolk: Diarmaid MacCulloch, *Suffolk and the Tudors: politics and religion in an English county, 1500–1600* (Oxford, 1986), p. 137.

trial in the republic's civic courts. The pontiff was outraged. He demanded their release, and the repeal of laws that banned the building of new churches without secular permission and that forbade the alienation of property to the church. In April 1606, Paul V, with the support of Philip III of Spain, placed Venice under an interdict that entailed the suspension of the administration of the sacraments to the city's inhabitants. Venice's state theologian and a distinguished scholar, Paolo Sarpi, argued the case for the city's autonomy. The city authorities ordered the clergy to disregard the interdict and expelled orders who refused to do so, including the Jesuits. Although the interdict was revoked a year after its first proclamation, the dispute between Rome and the Venetian republic raised the hopes of Protestants throughout Europe, and those of the English ambassador in particular, that the city might be enticed from its allegiance to the Roman faith to embrace Protestantism. Therefore, Bedell arrived in Venice in the summer of 1607 at a time of considerable ecclesiastical flux, uncertainty and potential opportunity. Venetian law prohibited unauthorized or private contact between ambassadors and senators and other senior state officials. Unaffected by these restrictions, Bedell quickly got to know Sarpi and acted as an intermediary between Wotton and him.[25]

In recent years, scholars have begun to accord closer attention to the impact of Venice on Bedell's scholarly and religious evolution. Karl Bottigheimer has written that his arrival in the city republic inaugurated a 'rich and formative interlude in his life', while Terence McCaughey has stressed how Bedell's access to the city's Jewish community, and in particular his friendship with the Talmudic scholar Leon Modena, enriched his Hebrew scholarship.[26] John McCafferty has argued that Venice was a period of unparalleled intellectual richness and fulfilment in Bedell's life. In this regard, McCafferty maintains that Bedell viewed Venice as an opportunity to act as 'an agent of the working-out of divine providence in history'.[27] In this essay, it is proposed to complement this emphasis on the influence of Venice on Bedell's intellectual and theological formation by suggesting that his Venetian experience provided him with the skills to negotiate cultural difference and alterity that were to prove so critical to his evangelical programme in Ireland from his arrival there in 1627 to his death in 1642. Bedell's intellectual curiosity acquired an anthropological dimension in Venice. Arguably, it was this capacity for cultural interpretation and observation that made him a unique figure among his fellow clerics and prelates in Ireland in the 1630s.

25 John Leon Lievsay, *Venetian Phoenix: Paolo Sarpi and some of his English friends (1606–1700)* (Lawrence, Ka., 1973), pp 19–21.   26 Bottigheimer and Larminie, 'Bedell, William', p. 766; Terence McCaughey, *Dr Bedell and Mr King: the making of the Irish Bible* (Dublin, 2001), pp 14–19. However, John McCafferty has questioned the extent of Bedell's Hebrew studies in Venice: see *idem*, 'Venice in Cavan: the career of William Bedell, 1572–1642' in Brendan Scott (ed.), *Culture and society in early modern Breifne/Cavan* (Dublin, 2009), pp 173–87, at p. 185.   27 McCafferty, 'Venice in Cavan', p. 173.

However, the tendency to anachronism must be avoided in any such emphasis on Bedell's putative cultural relativism in the same way as his depiction as an ecumenist *avant la lettre* reveals more of modern priorities than the historicity of his experience. William Bedell was a godly servant of the Almighty whose actions and aspirations, and indeed disappointments, were carefully calibrated against the inexorable call to salvation. Although Bedell displayed an undoubted inclination for anthropological observation and engagement, he was certainly not a disinterested anthropologist in the modern sense of the term.

Bedell's ability to transcend his immediate points of cultural and religious reference is apparent in a letter from Venice written in January 1608 to Adam Newton (d. 1630), former tutor to Prince Henry, the eldest son of James VI, and later a royal official under Charles I. In describing the preaching of the Franciscans that he had heard in Venice, Bedell observed dismissively that their 'whole intentions seem to be either to delight or to move: as for teaching they know not what it means'. If Bedell condemns the preaching of the friars from the reflexive oppositional viewpoint of the reformed, his unfavourable comparison of the Franciscan sermons with Jewish preaching is surely startling: '... and for my part I have found myself better satisfied (at least wise less cloy'd) with the sermons of the Jews'. Predictably, Bedell was shocked by pervasive material manifestations of Catholic faith and belief: 'Such a multitude of idolatrous statues, pictures, reliques in every corner, not of their churches onely, but houses, chambers, shopps, yea the very streets, and in the country the high wayes and hedges swarme with them'. However, Bedell goes beyond simple rhetorical condemnation and dismay and engages in frank appraisal. He informs Newton of Italian liturgical largesse and of the lavish ornamentation of churches. Indeed, he has heard it said that these 'glittering churches and monasteries of Italy', as he calls them, have resulted in 'noe small cause of the perversion of soe many of our young Gentlemen that come into these parts'.[28] In fact, such apostasy had personally touched Bedell when his friend from Emmanuel, James Wadsworth, had converted to Catholicism in Madrid where he had gone in 1605 to serve as chaplain to the English ambassador.[29] Although a devout and convinced Protestant, Bedell was not indifferent to the aesthetic appeal of Catholic church art and architecture to some of his co-religionists. He was also realistic as to the prospect of religious change in Venice. In his account to Newton of the lifting of the

28 Shuckburgh, *Two biographies*, pp 228–9.   29 Bedell's son was also alert to the dangers of seductive heresy in Italy when he wrote that his father avoided such a dire fate by means of his piety and learning: 'It might indeed have been a dangerous thing to him (then a young man) to be in such a place; as some others then and since, by travelling and converse among the Italians, have shew'd by their sad example; but by God's mercy he was better grounded in piety and good learning than to be easily subverted' (Shuckburgh, *Two biographies*, p. 9). Bedell's correspondence with Wadsworth in regard to the latter's apostasy was published as *The copies of certaine letters which have passed between Spaine and England in matter of religion* (London, 1624).

papal interdict against Venice shortly before his arrival, Bedell hardly concealed his disappointment that a *rapprochement* had been established with
Rome. Nonetheless, a precedent had been set and papal authority was now
'irrecoverably broken here, and long it will not be ere some change follow'.[30]

Aside from some letters written by Bedell himself, it is necessary to turn
to the accounts of his Venetian sojourn by his son and son-in-law for a fuller
picture of his time as chaplain to Wotton. While acknowledging the encomi-
astic nature of these biographies, there is no obvious reason to assume that
either biographer exaggerated or distorted his account of Bedell's intellectual
receptivity or capacity for cultural interchange while in the city. William
Bedell describes his father's gift for languages as a student at Cambridge. In
addition to his proficiency in the scholarly staples of Greek and Latin, Bedell
acquired knowledge of Syriac, Arabic, Aramaic and Hebrew.[31] It was during
his time in Venice that he deepened his knowledge of these languages.[32] In
view of Bedell's reputation for linguistic accomplishment, it is evident that he
developed the foundations for his capacity for engagement with foreign languages and cultures during his years of study at Cambridge, and that his
Venetian experience enhanced his linguistic ability. However, Bedell the
younger is clear in his opinion that his father benefited not only in respect of
scholarship and knowledge of languages while in Venice but also in terms of
personal development. Meeting individuals of different outlooks and religious
persuasion, Bedell refined and moderated his sense of cultural encounter and
exchange.[33] Moreover, a tantalizing reference to Bedell visiting Constantinople
suggests he may also have used Venice as a base from which to explore more
widely the eastern Mediterranean area.[34] Bedell the younger foregrounds his
father's friendship with Paolo Sarpi, which enabled him both to deepen his
knowledge of Catholicism and to become what he terms 'more polite in all his
other learning'. His father engaged with Jewish scholars in order to improve
his knowledge of Hebrew while concurrently hoping, though unsuccessfully,
to effect their conversion to Christianity.[35] Bedell befriended Jasper

---

30 Shuckburgh, *Two biographies*, p. 231.   **31** For the emphasis placed on Hebrew at
Emmanuel and Bedell's linguistic attainments see G. Lloyd Jones, *The discovery of Hebrew
in Tudor England: a third language* (Manchester, 1983), pp 145–6.   **32** Shuckburgh, *Two
biographies*, p. 3.   **33** 'He was there also much improv'd in point of prudence and moder-
ation; meeting there with men, tho' of another persuasion from himself in many points of
religion, yet very conscientious and unblameable in life and conversation, and no less
detesting the tyranny of the papacy and the gross points of popery, than the protestants
themselves': Shuckburgh, *Two biographies*, p. 13.   **34** Bedell, *The copies of certaine letters*,
p. 1.   **35** Bedell acquired a medieval manuscript Torah in Venice that he bequeathed to
Emmanuel College and which, having survived the conflagration of 1641, is extant today
in Cambridge. In 1621, Bedell presented the College with a collection of pamphlets relating to the dispute between Paul V and Venice (Bush and Rasmussen, *The library of
Emmanuel College*, pp 24, 33; McCaughey, *Dr Bedell and Mr King*, pp 17–19). A copy of
Bedell's will is reproduced in Thomas Wharton Jones (ed.), *A true relation of the life and
death of the right reverend father in God William Bedell* (London, 1872), pp 192–5.

Despontine, a Venetian physician who converted to Protestantism under his instruction. They became close friends and the Italian accompanied Bedell back to Bury St Edmunds where he settled permanently. Of course, Bedell also learned to speak Italian and in a letter written in 1613 to his friend from university days and long-time correspondent, Samuel Ward, master of Cambridge's Sidney Sussex College and a member of the second Cambridge company of translators of the King James Bible, he mentions, among other works undertaken by him in Venice, his Italian translation of the *Book of Common Prayer*.[36]

Alexander Clogie's account of Bedell in Venice is different in tone and content. Detailed and focused, Clogie's reprise of the Venetian period seems self-consciously aimed at a broader readership while his brother-in-law's somewhat terse narrative appears less considered by comparison. However, Clogie also emphasized his father-in-law's cultural openness and concomitant evangelical zeal. For instance, he depicts Bedell as immediately setting about learning Italian with the help of Paolo Sarpi and, supposedly, he was soon competent enough in Italian to deliver sermons in that language as well as in Latin. In return for Sarpi's assistance, he composed a grammar of English for the Italian priest.[37] Additionally, Clogie is more expansive in his account of Bedell's networks of friendship and sociability. Particularly close to Sarpi, Bedell was also friendly with others disposed to Protestantism such as the Servite friar Fulgenzio Micanzio, the Franciscan friar Fulgentio, and Marco Antonio de Dominis, archbishop of Spalato (Split).[38] Micanzio was a close associate of Sarpi, who assisted with his correspondence and later wrote his biography.[39] De Dominis had taken the side of Venice in its confrontation

---

36 Additionally, Bedell claimed that he translated King James' *Triplici nodo triplex cuneus* (London, 1607); Edwin Sandy's *Speculum Europae* (London, 1605), and the 'third homily of Chrysostome touching Lazarus, and some other thinges into the Italian toung' (Shuckburgh, *Two biographies*, p. 254). Nicholas Williams has noted that the Italian translation of the *Book of Common Prayer* published in London in 1685 was not Bedell's version as is sometimes assumed (N.J.A. Williams, 'William Bedell: piúratánach, easpag, aistritheoir', *Léachtaí Cholm Cille: an Bíobla in Éirinn*, 20 (1990), 72–97 at p. 96). For his correspondence with Ward see Margo Todd, 'The Samuel Ward papers at Sidney Sussex College, Cambridge', *Transactions of the Cambridge Bibliographical Society*, 8 (1981–5), 582–92 at p. 586.   37 Nicholas Bernard claimed to have seen the manuscript grammar Bedell composed for Sarpi: *Certain discourses ... unto which is added a character of Bishop Bedel* (London, 1659), pp 348–9.   38 Bedell in a letter to Newton wrote of Micanzio: 'There passeth allmost noe day, wherein we are not for an hour together: and under pretence of reading English to him (as indeed this last summer I made some entrance therein to him, and Mᵣₒ Paulo, and haveing given some rules of our language we read over the Acts of the Apostles together) under this colour, we read, and conferrd about the whole course of the Gospells, on which he is to preach every day this Lent: and I perswade myself, Christ is present with us, and am assured, that the end shall not be without some profitt' (Shuckburgh, *Two biographies*, pp 230, 250). For Fulgentio, see Edward Brown (trans.), *The letters of the renowned Father Paul* (London, 1693), pp 155, 173, 180–3.   39 For Micanzio see the various references in David Wootton, *Paolo Sarpi: between renaissance and*

with Rome in 1606–7 and he was assiduously cultivated by Wotton and his
successor Sir Dudley Carleton, in their efforts to wean the city and its terri-
tories from their allegiance to Catholicism. In the case of de Dominis, their
hopes were realized when in 1616 the archbishop fled to England where he
converted to Anglicanism and enjoyed the patronage of King James.
Ultimately disillusioned by his experience, he returned to the Continent and
the Roman church in 1622.[40]

Bedell the younger mentions his father's encounters with Venice's Jewish
community and his progress in Hebrew. Clogie provides more details and
writes of Bedell's friendship with Leon Modena who 'taught him the Oriental
pronunciation of the Hebrew tongue'. Born to two wealthy Italian Jewish
families in 1571, Leon was a noted rabbinic authority, teacher and musician
who was ordained a rabbi in 1609.[41] In the seventeenth century, Leon
Modena's reputation extended beyond the confines of the Venetian ghetto on
the basis of his description in Italian of Jewish ritual expressly written for a
gentile audience.[42] This work of ethnography, published in English translation in London in 1650, was long an important source of information on the
Jews for Christian readers.[43] Apparently, both men learned much from each
other in their discussions of the Hebrew Old Testament and Modena enabled
Bedell to acquire a medieval manuscript of the Torah. The influence of these
Venetian friendships continued on his return to England through a series of
translations he made of texts deriving from or related to this period. Among
his translations to Latin were his versions of Sarpi's histories of the Venetian
interdict and of the inquisition, and his Latin translation of the first two
books of Sarpi's history of the Council of Trent.[44] It is known from a second
Venetian letter written in 1609 from Bedell to Newton that he became
acquainted also with Giovanni Diodati, who published an Italian translation

---

enlightenment (Cambridge, 1983).   **40** W.B. Patterson, 'Dominis, Marco Antonio de
(1560–1624)' in *ODNB*, xvi, 487–9.   **41** Mark R. Cohen (ed.), *The autobiography of a seventeenth-century Venetian rabbi: Leon Modena's life of Judah* (Princeton, 1988), p. 214. Most
recently on Leon Modena see Yaacob Dweck, *The scandal of Kabbalah: Leon Modena,
Jewish mysticism, early modern Venice* (Princeton, 2011).   **42** Howard E. Adelman, 'Leon
Modena: the autobiography and the man' in Cohen (ed.), *The autobiography of a seventeenth-century Venetian rabbi*, pp 19–49, p. 29.   **43** Leo Modena, *The history of the rites,
customes, and manner of life, of the present Jews, throughout the world* (London, 1650), translated to English by Edmund Chilmead.   **44** Graham Rees and Maria Wakely have recently
proposed that the Latin translation of Sarpi's history of the Council of Trent was a collaborative affair 'undertaken by people close to the government and to Venetian affairs'.
They have suggested that Bedell translated the first two books of the history, that the next
four were by Marco Antonio de Dominis and the last two by Sir Adam Newton: G. Rees
and M. Wakely, *Publishing, politics, and culture: the king's printers in the reign of James I and
VI* (Oxford, 2009), pp 110–11; William Bedell (trans.), *Interdicti Veneti historia de motu
Italiae sub initia pontificatus Pauli V commentarius* (Cambridge, 1626); Shuckburgh, *Two
biographies*, pp 81–8; Stuart Handley, 'Newton, Sir Adam, first baronet (d. 1630)' in
ODNB, xl, 689. See also Charles McNeill (ed.), *The Tanner letters, original documents and
notices of Irish affairs in the sixteenth and seventeenth centuries* (Dublin, 1943), p. 82.

of the Bible in Geneva in 1603. Diodati had previously visited Venice in 1605 and on the occasion of his second visit in 1608, he brought with him copies of his translation and he preached in Wotton's residence.[45] Later, Bedell brought his copy of Diodati's Bible with him to Dublin and Kilmore and he used it for comparative purposes during the translation of the Irish Old Testament.[46]

Evidently, William Bedell's service as chaplain to Sir Henry Wotton in Venice during the years 1607 to 1610 was an unusually rich and stimulating experience for a modest and unassuming clergyman who might reasonably have expected to spend his life in quiet but worthy obscurity in East Anglia. It is somewhat ironic, therefore, that Bedell is remembered by posterity for his admittedly dramatic Irish career, and that his crucial and formative Venetian experience has until recently been largely overlooked. In the remainder of this essay, it is proposed that Bedell's time in Venice equipped him with cultural and linguistic skills that were key to his evangelical mission to the Gaelic Irish. In essence, it is arguable that both Venice and Ireland represent a seamless continuum in Bedell's career in terms of his cultural experience and are inaccurately characterized as discrete and mutually exclusive episodes. While Gaelic Ireland and the renaissance city-state of Venice constituted significantly distinct cultural spheres in early modern Europe, Bedell developed a capacity for interpretation and engagement in Venice which in many respects was generic and applicable in the context of Gaelic society and culture. Moreover, Bedell was also an adept linguist whose interest in the creation of a universal language underlines his commitment to ongoing engagement with and interchange between cultures.[47]

On hearing initially of his possible preferment to a position in Dublin, Bedell was cautious and somewhat reluctant to exchange his settled appointment as rector of Horningsheath for a new life in Ireland. Ultimately however, Bedell was prepared to surrender convenience and stability should an alternative fate have been ordained for him by God. Tellingly, he admitted he would travel not just to Ireland but to Virginia should the Almighty so determine.[48] On his arrival, his capacity for intercultural contact was immediately evident in his determination to learn Irish: '... my endeavour shall be

45 Shuckburgh, *Two biographies*, p. 248. **46** According to Clogie, such was the obscurity of his father-in-law in the 1620s that when Diodati visited London in 1627 and enquired of his old English friend among bishops and clergy, no one had heard of him. Fortuitously, Diodati encountered Bedell by chance in Cheapside (Shuckburgh, *Two biographies*, p. 92). Nicholas Williams has confirmed the influence of Diodati's text on the Irish Old Testament in *I bprionta i leabhar: na Protastúin agus prós na Gaeilge, 1567–1724* (Dublin, 1986), p. 54. **47** Vivian Salmon, 'William Bedell and the universal language movement in seventeenth-century Ireland', *Essays and studies*, n.s. 36 (1983), 27–39. See also *eadem*, 'Missionary linguistics in seventeenth-century Ireland and a north American analogy', *Historiagraphia Linguistica*, 12:3 (1985), 321–49. **48** Bedell to Ward, 15 March 1627 in McNeill (ed.), *The Tanner letters*, p. 75.

to understand the tongue of this country which I see (although it be accounted otherwise) is a learned and exact language and full of difficulty. I have taken a little Irish boy, a minister's son, of whom I hope to make good use to the purpose when I shall have a little more leisure'.[49] This decision at the outset of his Irish career reveals a great deal of Bedell's versatility in matters of cultural interpretation and discernment.[50] His reading of Gaelic cultural politics indicates that he judged both the expertise and *imprimatur* of the learned elite as highly important to the success of his broader programme of engagement with the Gaelic Irish, and, more particularly, his Old Testament translation project.[51]

The reformation in Ireland, like its counterpart in England, was fundamentally informed by political imperatives. As the religious ancillary of the Tudor and Stuart programmes of political consolidation in Ireland, the established church acquired a progressively colonial and anglicized focus. During the course of the late sixteenth and early seventeenth centuries, efforts to evangelize the island's Gaelic-speaking population were limited and largely ineffectual. Typically during this period, evangelical engagement with Irish-speakers was undertaken by Cambridge-educated Gaelic Irish or Irish-born clergymen such as Seaán Ó Cearnaigh, Nicholas Walsh, Fearganaimn Ó Domhnalláin and Uilliam Ó Domhnuill.[52] Accordingly, Bedell's commitment to the use of Irish for purposes of evangelical outreach was exceptional in a state church whose episcopate was largely drawn from Britain. Although Bedell has been hailed for his patronage of the Old Testament translation, finally published as late as 1685, his real contemporary achievements are perhaps less tangible because they were more evidentially elusive. His more-or-less immediate employment of the Gaelic scholar Muircheartach Ó Cionga, a member of a midlands hereditary bardic family, indicates the acuity of Bedell's anthropological sense of cultural discernment.[53] Praise poets were pivotal agents of cultural and political legitimation in Gaelic Ireland in the late medieval and early modern periods. The poets' deployment of a generic and linguistically standardized repertoire of motifs and conceits enabled them to articulate a vision of elite Gaelic society which was highly potent in political and dynastic terms.

---

49 Bedell to Ward, 16 July 1628 in ibid., p. 86.   **50** Bedell's acute awareness of the cultural dimension to conversion is evident in his remarks on the Jesuit mission to China in a letter in Latin to Jasper Despontine. A copy of this letter is preserved in the papers of William Sancroft (1617–93), archbishop of Canterbury and a former master of Emmanuel: Lambeth Palace Library, MS 595, pp 55–6.   **51** The Old Testament translation project is discussed in Williams, *I bprionta i leabhar*, pp 48–55. More generally see Breandán Ó Madagáin, 'An Bíobla i nGaeilge (1600–1981)' in Máirtín Mac Conmara (ed.), *An léann eaglasta in Éirinn, 1200–1900* (Dublin, 1988), 176–86.   **52** Marc Caball, 'Gaelic and Protestant: a case study in early modern self-fashioning, 1567–1608', *RIA proc.*, 110C (2010), 191–215.   **53** Thomas F. O'Rahilly, 'Irish poets, historians, and judges in English documents, 1558–1615', *RIA proc.*, 36C (1921–4), 86–120 at 89; McCaughey, *Dr Bedell and Mr King*, pp 36–41.

All previous Gaelic evangelicals who used the new technology of print to communicate the message of Protestant reform, namely John Carswell, Seaán Ó Cearnaigh and Uilliam Ó Domhnuill, publicly acknowledged the superior cultural authority of the praise poets. It is remarkable that within months of arriving in Ireland, Bedell grasped the importance of the learned elite to the presentation of the message of reform in a guise that complemented Gaelic culture. Carswell in his Gaelic translation of *The Book of Common Order*, published in Edinburgh in 1567, as *Foirm na n-urrnuidheadh*, sought the indulgence of the learned elite in regard to his supposedly imperfect written command of classical Irish. He claimed that in Scotland and in Ireland only a handful of professional scholars were fully adept in the written language ('Agas is tearc neach agá bfuil ceart canamhna na Gaoidheilge ... acht mara bfuil sé ag beagán d'aois ealadhna mhaith ré dán agas ré seanchus.') In a charming prefatory poem addressed to his printed book, Carswell commands it to travel around Gaelic Scotland and Ireland and commends it to the attention of the learned elite.[54] Seaán Ó Cearnaigh's Irish primer and catechism published in Dublin in 1571 as *Aibidil Gaoidheilge & Caiticiosma* also deferred to the cultural authority of the Gaelic learned orders. In a section on the Gaelic alphabet, Ó Cearnaigh advises readers who might wish for more information to consult the praise poets as such matters fell within their professional remit ('& gebé lé nab áil lórgaireachd do dhénamh orrtha so nó a bhfios d'fhághbháil, fághbhadh fóghluim óna fileaghuibh').[55] Uilliam Ó Domhnaill, Bedell's contemporary at Emmanuel, availed substantially of the expertise and advice of praise poets in the Irish translation of the New Testament. In a short account of the translation project in an address in Irish to the reader, Ó Domhnuill mentions the contribution of previous clerical translators Ó Cearnaigh, Nicholas Walsh and Fearganainm Ó Domhnalláin. While Ó Domhnuill mentioned his fellow divines in the preceding epistle dedicatory in English to King James, he made no reference to the contribution of two praise poets to the project. However, in the Irish address to the reader he noted that both he and Ó Domhnalláin were assisted by two poets, Maoilín Óg Mac Bruaideadha and Domhnall Óg Ó hUiginn. Their expertise in the Irish language is specifically acknowledged. In the case of Mac Bruaideadha, he is described as an expert in the Irish language at Trinity College, while Ó hUiginn assisted Ó Domhnuill with transcription, correct usage and grammar.[56] The absence of reference to both these Gaelic scholars in the English epistle dedicatory probably reflects the contested status of praise poets in Tudor Ireland where this influential Gaelic caste was periodically condemned

---

54 R.L. Thomson (ed.), *Foirm na n-urrnuidheadh: John Carswell's Gaelic translation of the Book of Common Order* (Edinburgh, 1970), pp 12–13. **55** Brian Ó Cuív (ed.), *Aibidil Gaoidheilge & caiticiosma: Seaán Ó Cearnaigh's Irish primer of religion published in 1571* (Dublin, 1994), p. 67. **56** Uilliam Ó Domhnuill (trans.), *Tiomna nuadh ar dtighearna agus ar slanaightheora Iosa Criosd* (Dublin, 1602), 'Do chum an leughthora'.

by the English authorities as agents of dissension and resistance. Unlike previous translators who worked from within the Gaelic tradition and who would have immediately recognized the social and intellectual prestige of the learned elite, such an appreciation would not have been axiomatic in Bedell's case. In terms of early seventeenth-century settlers in Ireland who acquired a sophisticated knowledge of Gaelic culture and scholarship, Bedell is best compared to Sir Matthew de Renzy (1577–1634). Of German birth, Matthew de Renzy settled in Ireland in 1606 having worked as a merchant in Antwerp and London. Skilled in languages, he was taught Irish by the Mac Bruaideadha bardic family of Thomond. Unusually, he learned to write Irish and is reputed to have composed a grammar, dictionary and chronicle in Irish. None of these is now extant.[57] Conchubhar Mac Bruaideadha described how, having mastered spoken Irish, de Renzy sought out the company of scholars to deepen his knowledge of the language.[58] It surely is no coincidence that de Renzy, like Bedell, had lived on the Continent and knew several languages including German and Dutch. The cosmopolitan outlook of both men differentiated them from the great majority of contemporary New English immigrants in Ireland and explains their readiness to engage proactively with Gaelic scholarship for instrumentalist and cultural reasons.

In his first Venetian letter to Adam Newton, Bedell observed, presciently in view of his later experience in Ireland, that 'all changes in religion seem to me to come from reasons of conscience, or of state'.[59] Manifestly, the state had failed, even by the standards of its limited ambitions in this respect, to secure the adherence of the Gaelic population in any meaningful sense to the established church. Where coercive legislation proved futile, Bedell clearly envisaged an appeal to conscience. In the case of the Gaelic Irish, a process of persuasion could only be effected fruitfully through the medium of the indigenous language and culture. Writing to Primate Ussher in July 1628, Bedell apprised him of his progress in relation to the advancement of the gospel among speakers of the Irish language. He noted that he had arranged for Ó Cionga to read from the Irish Book of Common Prayer every day for an hour to a group of students.[60] Already, Bedell was attentive to the need to

---

57 Brian Mac Cuarta, 'A planter's interaction with Gaelic culture: Sir Matthew de Renzy, 1577–1634', *Irish Economic and Social History*, 20 (1993), 1–17.   58 Brian Mac Cuarta (ed.), 'Conchubhar Mac Bruaideadha and Sir Matthew de Renzy (1577–1634)', *Éigse*, 27 (1993), 122–6.   59 Shuckburgh, *Two biographies*, p. 231.   60 'Propounded Mr Burton's son for a native's place, and we have chosen him thereto with condition that he shall have allowance when he can read the tongue. We have brought Mr King to read an hour every day to those that are already chosen to frame them to the right pronunciation and exercise of the language; to which purpose we have gotten a few copies of the Book of Common Prayer, and do begin with the catechism which is therein. I hope this course will not be unfruitful': Bedell to Ussher, 30 July 1628 in McNeill (ed.), *The Tanner letters*, p. 87. See Alan Ford (ed.), 'Correspondence between archbishops Ussher and Laud', *Archivium Hibernicum*, 46 (1991–2), 5–21 at 10.

provide a Gaelic translation of the psalms – a core component of the Anglican liturgy – which had not been translated in their entirety previously. Ó Cionga had undertaken a trial translation of the first psalm, which had elicited the approval of Gaelic-speakers. But again, Bedell was well informed and he was made aware that a manuscript translation of the psalms was in the possession of the widow of the late archbishop of Tuam, Uilliam Ó Domhnuill. Anxious to secure this translation, Bedell dispatched an intermediary to Connaught to secure the text.[61] It is arguable that Bedell's identification of Ó Cionga as his assistant, his immediate move to teach clerical students how to read Irish, and his plans for the translation of the psalms reveal a shrewd and practical cultural interlocutor at work in a new and, in many respects, alien environment.

If Bedell's Protestant faith was nurtured in Cambridge and in East Anglia, his remarkable and atypical capacity for cultural interpretation surely derived from his time in Venice. Bedell became a cosmopolitan in Venice. It is arguable that Bedell's intellectual and cultural formation in the richly diverse environs of the Adriatic city republic is enduringly exemplified in his Irish Old Testament. In the short term, Bedell's achievements were swept away by the sectarian enmity and dissension of 1641. The burning of Bibles early in the rebellion by the Gaelic Irish at the market cross of Belturbet in Bedell's diocese of Kilmore signalled a furious explosion of ethnic and religious rancour.[62] Ironically, over three hundred years later when in the wake of the Second Vatican Council, the vernacular replaced Latin as the medium of the Catholic liturgy, it was Bedell's Old Testament which was used for daily mass in the Gaeltacht areas in the absence of a Roman Catholic Irish-language Bible.[63] Bedell the seventeenth-century moderate puritan had turned full circle to become Bedell the twentieth-century ecumenist.

61 'The translation of the psalms into prose and verse whereof I spake to your grace would be a good work, and Mr King hath given us an assay in the first psalm which doth not dislike Mr Fitzgerald and Mr Lisiagh. Yet I do forbear to urge it yet, because I hear that there is a translation made of the psalms already in the hands of the late archbishop of Tuam's wife, which I also put in hope to obtain by means of one Mr Birmingham sometimes of this house. I beseech your grace to help what you may to the obtaining of this copy, and in this and all other attempts direct us with your advice' (Bedell to Ussher, 30 July 1628 in McNeill (ed.), *The Tanner letters*, p. 87). However, the translation of the psalms continued in Dublin: see Richard Parr, *The life of the most reverend father in God, James Ussher, late lord arch-bishop of Armagh* (London, 1686), p. 403.   62 Raymond Gillespie, 'Faith, family and fortune: the structures of everyday life in early modern Cavan' in R. Gillespie (ed.), *Cavan: essays on the history of an Irish county* (Dublin, 1995), pp 99–114, at p. 104.   63 Breathnach, *Bedell and the Irish version of the Old Testament*, p. 24.

I am indebted to the Irish Research Council for the Humanities and Social Sciences and the Department of the Taoiseach for a Project Grant in Theology and Religious Studies, which has enabled me to undertake research for this essay.

2

Cultural frontiers and the circulation of manuscripts in Ireland, 1625–1725

BERNADETTE CUNNINGHAM & RAYMOND GILLESPIE

In 1709 the young scientist and future astronomer Samuel Molyneux travelled to Connacht. He noted in his record of the journey that on Wednesday 21 April 'I went to visit old Flaherty who lives, very old, in a miserable condition at Park ... in Hiar or west Connaught. I expected to have seen there some old Irish manuscripts but his ill fortune has stripped him of these as well as his other goods so that he has nothing now left but some few of his own writing, and a few old rummish books of history printed.' On the surface the encounter between Samuel Molyneux (1689–1728) and Roderic O'Flaherty (1629–1718) might be represented as a meeting of two contrasting cultures, involving a modern man of science (Molyneux) educated at Trinity College and instrumental in the early eighteenth-century revival of the Dublin Philosophical Society, which had brought modern ways of thinking to Dublin; and a man from an earlier time (O'Flaherty), who lived among the 'multitudes of barbarous uncivilized Irish', who defied the laws of the country and lived 'in so open a state of nature' against the 'wholly civilised' world of the rest of Ireland.[1]

In this world of apparent contrasts, Molyneux's quest for Irish manuscripts – relics of the old scribal world gradually being eroded by the modern world of print – in a language that he probably could not read, might simply be dismissed as a quest for the exotic and curious. In a complex society where contrasting cultures were perceived to coexist, cultural frontiers often attracted those in search of diversion or entertainment rather than those interested in engaging with what lay beyond the frontiers they were so curiously intent on crossing. Yet this meeting between Samuel Molyneux and O'Flaherty is not as clear-cut as it first appears, since it is manifest from other sources that O'Flaherty was not an isolated survivor of a disappearing world. He had certainly owned or had access to a number of Irish-language

---

1 Aquilla Smith (ed.), 'Journey to Connaught – April 1709' in *Miscellany of the Irish Archaeological Society*, 1 (Dublin, 1846), 171. The Connacht journey was made by Samuel Molyneux but was wrongly attributed to Thomas Molyneux in Smith's edition: see J.G. Simms, *William Molyneux of Dublin* (Dublin, 1982), p. 140, note 15.

manuscripts, including a set of the Annals of the Four Masters and a transcript made in 1660 of Conall MacGeoghegan's English rendering of the Annals of Clonmacnoise, which he annotated.[2] He both annotated and referred to the autograph set of Annals of the Four Masters to which he had access in his two-volume history of Ireland, *Ogygia*, which was published in 1685.[3] However, by the time he met Samuel Molyneux he no longer possessed the Irish manuscripts that might be regarded as relics of an older society and an older technology. Instead, and in their place, he owned the very symbol of scholarly modernity: the printed book. Moreover, he was well versed in how print worked and, as Molyneux well knew, O'Flaherty was personally active in the cultural networks of print. In 1685, O'Flaherty's two-volume history of Ireland, *Ogygia*, had been published in Latin. The work was printed in London and achieved a satisfactory circulation outside Ireland.[4] It was deployed by Bishop Stillingfleet in his response to the Scottish propagandist Sir George Mackenzie – a debate in print in which O'Flaherty was keen to participate. O'Flaherty's reply to Mackenzie, entitled 'Ogygia vindicated', did not find a publisher at the time but was eventually issued in print in 1775 through the mediation of Charles O'Conor (1710–91).[5] O'Flaherty's *Ogygia*, which surveyed early Irish history, was the fruit of reading printed books as well as manuscripts. The *Ogygia* included references not only from historians such as Bede, but also from such seminal classical authorities as Ovid's *Metamorphosis*, Tertullian's *Against the Jews*, Virgil's *Aeneid*, Caesar's *Gallic wars* and the *Annals* of Tacitus, among many others. He also used Augustine's *City of God*, Bernard's Life of Malachy, the works of Thomas Aquinas, and the more contemporary multi-volume Catholic church history of Caesar Baronius. Closer to home, he drew on the standard range of six-

2 Robinson Library, Armagh, 1660 transcript of Annals of Clonmacnoise containing O'Flaherty's annotations; Bernadette Cunningham, *The annals of the Four Masters: Irish history, kingship and society in the early seventeenth century* (Dublin, 2010), p. 59. For other manuscripts with O'Flaherty's annotations, see RIA, MSS B iv 2, E iv 4, C ii 1, TCD, MS 1292, f. 164 ff.   3 For example of citations, Roderic O'Flaherty, *Ogygia: seu, rerum Hibernicarum chronologia* (London, 1685), pp 10, 12, 42, 86, 89, 90, 94, 95, 117, 129, 138 and for annotations TCD, MS 1301. For identification of the hands of the annotators, as well as an edition of the annotations, see Kenneth Nicholls' introduction to the reprint of John O'Donovan (ed.), *Annals of the kingdom of Ireland by the Four Masters* (Dublin, 1848–51, rept. Dublin, 1990). On the nature of the annotations, see Cunningham, *Annals of the Four Masters*, pp 59–60.   4 On the publication and reception of *Ogygia*, see Toby Barnard, *Improving Ireland: projectors, prophets and profiteers, 1641–1786* (Dublin, 2008), pp 98–100.   5 Sir George Mackenzie, *A defence of the antiquity of the royal-line of Scotland; with a true account when the Scots were govern'd by kings in the isle of Britain* (London, 1685); Edward Stillingfleet, *Origines Britannicae; or, The antiquities of the British churches* (London, 1685); Roderic O'Flaherty, *The Ogygia vindicated against the objections of Sir George Mac Kenzie* (Dublin, 1775). On this debate, see Bernadette Cunningham and Raymond Gillespie, 'Patrick Logan and *Foras feasa ar Éirinn*, 1696', *Éigse*, 32 (2000), 146–52 at 147–9. For the late eighteenth-century publishing context, see Barnard, *Improving Ireland*, pp 98–100.

teenth-century printed works in Latin by Scottish historians such as George Buchanan, John Mair and Hector Boece. In addition, he had read William Camden's *Britannia* in either Latin or English, and John Selden's *Titles of honor*, the third edition of which had been published in London in 1672, as well as several authors on the history of France. Predictably, O'Flaherty was also familiar with the printed works in English and Latin by seventeenth-century Irish-based authors, notably Sir John Davies, Archbishop James Ussher and Sir James Ware. Although the notes to O'Flaherty's *Ogygia* usually give page numbers when referring to printed works it is possible that some of his references were obtained second-hand, at one remove from the texts cited. Even if this was sometimes the case, it cannot be concluded that O'Flaherty was not immersed in a world of print culture. He was a sophisticated reader of print. He was well aware that John Mair's history of Scotland was perceived by contemporaries to contain 'illfounded, desultory, and fabulous invention' and, although Thomas Dempster's work on saints was available in print, that 'Catholics are positively interdicted the reading of Dempster's menology'.[6] Indeed, so absorbed was O'Flaherty in the world of printed books and libraries that his correspondence with Edward Lhuyd (1660–1709) between 1702 and 1708 was peppered with references to printed works, and works being prepared for print. In writing to Edward Lhuyd at Oxford in November 1702, for instance, he assumed Lhuyd's access to Thomas Bodley's library would mean he automatically had available to him the two folio volumes of Irish saints' lives edited by John Colgan in the 1640s, and indeed any printed work that O'Flaherty might care to name.[7] O'Flaherty was also aware of the activities of the Dublin Philosophical Society in shaping modern science. He contributed a substantial essay on west Connacht for an ambitious project coordinated in Ireland by William Molyneux.[8] The scheme was planned by the London bookseller Moses Pitt in co-operation with the Royal Society in London, the secretary of which, Robert Hooke, was among Molyneux's correspondents. When seeking to make contact with the revived Dublin Philosophical Society in 1708, O'Flaherty resorted first to his own family network in this regard. He asked a relative – Francis Lynch[9] – who was a merchant in Dublin, to contact the Society concerning information he had gathered on natural history, and he subsequently corresponded with the Society's secretary, the young Samuel Molyneux.[10]

---

6 Roderic O'Flaherty, *Ogygia; or, a chronological account of Irish events, collected from very ancient documents*, trans. James Hely (Dublin, 1793), p. lxv.   7 O'Flaherty to Lhuyd, 6 Nov. 1702 (Bodleian Library, Ashmole MS 1817). We are grateful to Richard Sharpe for a transcript of this letter.   8 Roderic O'Flaherty, *A chorographical description of west or h-Iar Connaught*, ed. James Hardiman (Dublin, 1846); the original manuscripts collected by William Molyneux for this abortive project are now in TCD, MS 888 (copies in TCD, MS 883).   9 O'Flaherty to S. Molyneux, 9 Apr. 1708 in K. Theodore Hoppen (ed.), *Papers of the Dublin Philosophical Society, 1683–1709* (2 vols, Dublin, 2008), ii, 826.   10 Correspondence between O'Flaherty and Samuel Molyneux in 1708 and 1709 is preserved

If the characterization from one side of the presumed cultural frontier of O'Flaherty as a relic of a bygone age is misleading so too is the perception of Molyneux as a thoroughly modern man. As well as science, Samuel Molyneux displayed an interest in Irish antiquity and, to judge from his visit to O'Flaherty, he was interested also in collecting older Irish manuscripts.[11] In addition to O'Flaherty he sought out Arthur Brownlow during his tour to Ulster in 1708 to inspect his collection of Irish manuscripts.[12] He was also eager to acquire manuscripts for himself. In 1708 Christopher Ussher notified Molyneux that 'I am told there are some Irish manuscripts in the hands of Mr Keough, a relation of your acquaintance near me, which I will enquire after and if you think fit will make some proposals about the purchase of them'.[13] Molyneux's 1709 visit to O'Flaherty was certainly not undertaken on a whim. O'Flaherty and the Molyneux family were well acquainted. In 1699 Thomas Molyneux, uncle to Samuel, wrote to Lhuyd that 'I very rarely hear from O'Flaherty and cannot [tell real]ly whether he be now alive; but if he be, I canno[t tell] you that you would receive much satisfaction in a cor[respondence] with him, for he seems to have busied himself little in [the] real antiquities of this country, but has chiefly spe[culated] in the enquiry into their fabulous history and gene[alogy]'.[14] As two generations of the Molyneux family were well aware, O'Flaherty had long shown interest in a wider range of scholarly endeavours, as his contribution to the projected Irish section of the *New English atlas* coordinated by Samuel's father, William, indicates. It is clear that William Molyneux thought highly of Roderic O'Flaherty, describing him as the 'man most learned of any of the native Irish that yet undertook the Irish antiquities'. William also acted as an intermediary between O'Flaherty and the London bookseller who published the *Ogygia* in 1685. While the book had been virtually complete some twenty years earlier, O'Flaherty only succeeded in having it published when Molyneux facilitated his access to print.[15] A manuscript copy of the *Ogygia* in the hand of William

in Molyneux's letter book, which is in Southampton City Archives, D/M, 2/1. It is printed in volume two of Hoppen (ed.), *Papers of the Dublin Philosophical Society*. 11 For an overview of the range of Samuel Molyneux's interests, see *A catalogue of the library of the hon. Samuel Molyneux, deceas'd ... with several curious manuscripts, and all his mathematical, optical and mechanical instruments* (1730). 12 Samuel Molyneux, 'Journey to the north, August 1708' (TCD, MS 888/2, ff 183–8v) in R.M. Young, *Historical notices of old Belfast and its vicinity* (Belfast, 1896), pp 152–60, at p. 154. Young wrongly ascribes this narrative to Thomas Molyneux, but the original manuscript is in the hand of Samuel Molyneux, and internal references to his cousin Samuel Dopping, and to his estate at Castle Dillon (which Samuel inherited from his father, William) confirm Samuel as the author. For the relevant biographical details on Dopping, see *DIB sub nom.* 13 C. Ussher to S. Molyneux, 15 Aug. 1708 in Hoppen (ed.), *Papers of the Dublin Philosophical Society*, ii, 849. 14 T. Molyneux to Lhuyd, 4 May 1699 in Hoppen (ed.), *Papers of the Dublin Philosophical Society*, ii, 699. 15 Letter from O'Flaherty to John Lynch, printed among the preliminaries in *Ogygia* (1685), pp 1–24; Capel Molyneux, *An account of the family and descendants of Thomas Molyneux, kt* (Evesham, 1820), pp 61–2.

Molyneux survives as an indication of the enthusiasm of Molyneux for the text.[16] Moreover, the relationship did not end there; William Molyneux and O'Flaherty maintained an occasional correspondence through the 1690s.[17] Some years after William's death, his son, Samuel revived the correspondence and was keen to arrange for the publication of O'Flaherty's unpublished researches.[18]

I

The interaction of Roderic O'Flaherty and two generations of the Molyneux family demonstrates that the problem of negotiating cultural frontiers between the older world of Gaelic Ireland and the ostensibly more modern settler world represented by, for example, the members of the Dublin Philosophical Society from the 1680s, was more complex than it appears at first glance.[19] Cultural frontiers were far more fluid than they might seem, and more difficult to grasp than they appear on the surface. Culture in this context is a process rather than a fixed entity. Contrasting cultural zones cannot be delineated as neat lines on a map, in the manner of the Pale ditch in the late Middle Ages, because there is too much evidence of cross-cultural activity. There are various ways of measuring this cultural interaction and permeability, and identifying the networks that these activities created. Perhaps most obvious is a consideration of the ways in which the Irish and English languages were used by the inhabitants of late seventeenth-century Ireland. A number of recent studies have explored some of the possibilities in this regard.[20] There are some basic methodological difficulties, however, in employing language use and language change as precise indicators of cultural interaction and cultural change. Everyday linguistic interactions are rarely

---

16 Southampton City Archives, Molyneux MSS, microfilm copy in NLI, P1527.   17 Mícheál Ó Duigeannáin (ed.), 'A letter from Roderic O'Flaherty to William Molyneux, 29 Jan. 1697', *Journal of the Galway Archaeological and Historical Society*, 18 (1938–9), 183– 5.   18 Barnard, *Improving Ireland*, p. 99.   19 David Berman and Patricia O'Riordan (eds), *The Irish enlightenment and counter enlightenment* (6 vols, Bristol, 2002), i, introduction, pp vii–xxiii.   20 For recent explorations of language as a cultural indicator in sixteenth, seventeenth and early eighteenth-century Ireland see Toby Barnard, 'Protestants and the Irish language, c.1675–1725', *Journal of Ecclesiastical History*, 44 (1993), 243–72'; Michael Cronin, *Translating Ireland: translation, languages, cultures* (Cork, 1996), pp 47–71; Vincent Carey, 'Bi-lingualism and identity formation in sixteenth-century Ireland' in Hiram Morgan (ed.), *Political ideology in Ireland, 1541–1641* (Dublin, 1999), pp 45–61; Patricia Palmer, *Language and conquest in early modern Ireland* (Cambridge, 2001); Liam Mac Mathúna, *Béarla sa Ghaeilge* (Baile Átha Cliath, 2007); Marie-Louise Coolahan, *Women, writing and language in early modern Ireland* (Oxford, 2010), pp 69–77; Bernadette Cunningham, 'Loss and gain: attitudes towards the English language in early modern Ireland' in Brian Mac Cuarta (ed.), *Reshaping Ireland, 1550–1700: colonization and its consequences* (Dublin, 2011), pp 163–86.

recorded and the evidence that survives often says more about official attitudes to languages than about the everyday realities of bilingualism and linguistic interaction. The large number of English loan words in Richard Plunkett's Latin-Irish dictionary (*c.*1662) not found in the literature of the period, hints at significant divergence between the spoken and written languages.[21] It is clear that increasing levels of bilingualism among the learned and the wealthy in seventeenth-century Ireland were such that concerns were already being expressed as early as the 1620s and 1630s about the cultural need to preserve the Irish language.[22] While it is clear that bilingualism, by definition, facilitates cultural contact and interaction across cultural frontiers, the precise nature of that cultural interaction remains rather elusive.

Within the scholarly community, at least, there is an alternative, more tangible, way of exploring how cultural frontiers were crossed and re-crossed, and establishing what impact that movement may have had. The study of the circulation of Irish manuscripts among the learned can be illuminating in this regard, yet it has been little exploited. It was, after all, an interest in Irish manuscripts that brought O'Flaherty and the Molyneux family together, which raises questions about the nature of the encounters between them.

Manuscripts are important for the exploration of cultural interaction because they have a number of attributes. First, they were items that could cross language boundaries since they could be valued on purely aesthetic grounds, as distinct from the meaning and significance of their contents. Thus in the 1680s when Narcissus Marsh as provost of Trinity College, Dublin, had sight of the Book of Durrow he so esteemed the decorated capital letters in the manuscript that he copied some of them in one of his letters. Earlier in the century, the antiquarian James Ware copied letters from the Book of Kells presumably because he also found them pleasing.[23] The ability to read medieval Irish-language manuscripts, even among fluent speakers of Irish, was a specialist skill.[24] Apart from the recurring challenge posed by obsolete words, in a world lacking adequate dictionaries, medieval scribes were never consistent in matters of orthography, and they made extensive use of contractions. Their recourse to a kind of shorthand was originally prompted by a desire to save space on expensive vellum pages, but may have been appealed to later 'to confine their works to the initiated'.[25]

---

21 Tomás de Bhaldraithe, 'Risteard Pluincéad (fl.1662) – a neglected pioneer Irish lexicographer', *Studia Celtica Japonica*, 3 (1990), 1–8, at p. 7. 22 Cunningham, 'Loss and gain', pp 178–80; *eadem*, 'Colonised Catholics: perceptions of honour and history in Michael Kearney's reading of *Foras feasa ar Éirinn*' in V.P. Carey and Ute Lotz-Heumann (eds), *Taking sides?: colonial and confessional* mentalités *in early modern Ireland* (Dublin, 2002), pp 150–64. 23 Narcissus Marsh to Dr Charlett, 30 Nov. 1699, cited in Muriel McCarthy, *Marsh's Library, Dublin: all graduates and gentlemen* (new ed., Dublin, 2003), p. 66; BL, Add. MS 4791, ff 119–22v. 24 J.H. Todd (ed.), 'Autograph letter of Thady O'Roddy', *Miscellany of the Irish Archaeological Society*, 1 (Dublin, 1846), 123. 25 De Bhaldraithe, 'Risteard Pluincéad', 5.

However, manuscripts did not rely on comprehension to make a cultural statement, and ownership and exchange of such manuscripts, of itself, was an important way in which cultural frontiers were negotiated. Second, manuscripts are physical objects whose travels can be tracked. As the older learned schools which were the traditional keepers of manuscripts broke up in the late sixteenth and early seventeenth centuries – for want of patrons as Tadhg Ó Rodaighe explained in the late seventeenth century – manuscripts left their traditional homes and began to circulate more freely.[26] As the lineage-dominated society of the sixteenth century, in which genealogy and history formed the basis of social power, gave way to a new society, in which land and its ownership became central to social definition, the uses to which manuscripts were put changed with the emergence of altered ideas about learning and social organization. The rise of new networks shaped by these transformed social relationships meant, for instance, that manuscripts began to circulate in different ways than hitherto. The changes became most apparent in the years after 1660, even though there were still some members of the older learned families who did retain their manuscripts. A case in point is Cú Choigcríche Ó Cléirigh, one of the 'Four Masters', who was the owner of a personal library that he used as the basis of his work as a professional scholar in the older tradition.[27] In his will of 1664 he left his books to Diarmaid and Seaán Ó Cléirigh, and the family still retained their manuscripts into the nineteenth century.[28] However, the uses to which they were now put were rather different. Whereas Cú Choigcríche Ó Cléirigh had the benefit of a bardic education and generally enjoyed the patronage necessary to make a living as a professional historian, as his ancestors had done, his sons did not. Similarly, his sons' contemporary, Roderic O'Flaherty, was a new type of gentleman scholar in that he was not from a traditional learned family. He had enjoyed a classical education in Galway, and his scholarly activities were funded from his own resources. As Katharine Simms has pointed out, the emergence of a literate elite outside of the hereditary learned families accelerated the decline in demand for the services of a professional learned class, since learning was no longer confined to this hereditary, professional class.[29] The move from the practice of *seanchas*, through traditional families such as Ó Maoilchonaire or Ó Duibhgeannáin, to antiquarianism, whether by the native Irish (such as

---

26 Todd (ed.), 'Autograph letter of Thady O'Roddy', 123.   **27** Pádraig A. Breatnach, 'The methodology of *seanchas*: the redaction by Cú Choigcríche Ó Cléirigh of the chronicle poem *Leanam croinic Clann nDálaigh*', *Éigse*, 29 (1996), 14–16.   **28** RIA, MS 23 D 17, p. 271; Nessa Ní Shéaghdha, *Catalogue of Irish manuscripts in the National Library of Ireland*, fasc. 2 (Dublin, 1961), p. 67. For other families who continued as keepers of manuscripts, see *eadem*, *Catalogue of Irish manuscripts in the National Library of Ireland*, fasc. 1 (Dublin, 1967), pp 13–14.   **29** Katharine Simms, 'Literacy and the Irish bards' in Huw Price (ed.), *Literacy in medieval Celtic societies* (Cambridge, 1998), pp 238–58, at p. 252.

O'Flaherty or MacGeoghegan), New English (such as Ware or Brownlow) or Old English (such as Ussher) was, by definition, an exercise in crossing cultural frontiers.

One significant factor in this process was the increasing importance of the market in manuscripts.[30] While manuscripts had previously been the property of learned families, as that order collapsed those manuscripts came onto the open market for the curious and those interested in Irish antiquity. Thus, probably in the 1650s, Seafraidh Ó Donnchadha, possibly the Kerry poet of that name, could buy a seventeenth-century copy of an older grammatical tract in Dublin rather than acquire it through traditional means.[31] The tour of the Welsh manuscript collector Edward Lhuyd in Scotland and Ireland between August 1699 and July 1700 reveals what might be acquired from the remnants of the learned families by those with money. At Larne, county Antrim, Lhuyd purchased 'about a dozen ancient manuscripts on parchment', from Eoin Ó Gnímh, a member of the learned family who had been hereditary poets to the O'Neills of Clandeboy.[32] Having travelled westwards, Lhuyd bought a number of law manuscripts from the Ó Cuirnín family in county Sligo, including one of fourteenth-century date. The Ó Cuirnín family had been hereditary *ollamhna* to the O'Donnells until the fourteenth century. William O'Sullivan has established that most of the Irish law manuscripts acquired by Lhuyd had previously been in the possession of Dubhaltach Mac Fhirbhisigh (*c*.1600–71).[33] Among them were a significant number of relatively 'modern' law manuscripts that had originated at the MacEgan law school at Park, near Tuam, county Galway, mostly written in the 1560s and 1570s. The most valuable of Lhuyd's acquisitions was probably the manuscript now known as the Book of Leinster, a large compilation of texts that had been used extensively by the learned class when producing new manuscript compilations in the fourteenth century.[34] Lhuyd also acquired the Yellow Book of Lecan, a fourteenth-century compilation, which the O'Sullivans have suggested he may have acquired somewhere in the midlands.[35] Lhuyd's manuscript acquisitions also included annals of Munster,

30 Raymond Gillespie, 'The problems of plantations: material culture and social change in early modern Ireland' in James Littleton and Colin Rynne (eds), *Plantation Ireland: settlement and material culture, c.1550–c.1700* (Dublin, 2009), pp 43–60, at pp 57–8.   31 RIA, MS 24 P 28, p. 1.   32 Many of Lhuyd's Irish purchases were acquired by Trinity College, Dublin, in 1786. For a detailed account of where and how Lhuyd acquired them, see Anne O'Sullivan and William O'Sullivan, 'Edward Lhuyd's collection of Irish manuscripts', *Transactions of the Honourable Society of Cymmrodorion* (1962), 57–76; see also, William O'Sullivan, 'The book of Domhnall Ó Duibhdábhoireann, provenance and codicology', *Celtica*, 23 (1999), 276–99. Further Lhuyd manuscripts are preserved in the National Library of Ireland: MSS G 4, G 5–6.   33 O'Sullivan, 'The book of Domhnall Ó Duibhdábhoireann', p. 277.   34 William O'Sullivan, 'Notes on the scripts and make-up of the Book of Leinster', *Celtica*, 7 (1966), 1–31, at 3–4.   35 O'Sullivan and O'Sullivan, 'Edward Lhuyd's collection of Irish manuscripts', 66. The Yellow Book of Lecan is now TCD, MS 1318, while a fragment from the same compilation is now NLI, MS G 4.

some saints' lives and a Book of Rights.[36] Anxious to have a copy of Geoffrey
Keating's history of Ireland, Lhuyd succeeded in purchasing a manuscript
containing an English translation of *Foras feasa* from Thomas Moynihan, near
Killarney, county Kerry, in 1700.[37] In all, some forty-six Irish manuscripts
from Lhuyd's collection are now preserved in the library of Trinity College,
Dublin, alone, almost all of them purchased from their hereditary owners in
1699 and 1700. Willingness to sell was not universal. Lhuyd negotiated with
Tadhg Ó Rodaighe, in county Leitrim, over the sale of manuscripts but,
unlike others, Ó Rodaighe was not prepared to part with his substantial collection. As Ó Rodaighe explained, the manuscripts were still valued for what
they represented: 'as poor as wee are, wee have a greate value for those
descended from the said antiquaryes, etc., who preserved and recorded our
descents, feates, relation, titles, etc., and left it to us in weather-beaten parch-
ments standing for thousands of yeares'.[38] His perception of the manuscripts
in his possession was that they were 'the very bookes that the Milesian antiquaryes brought into Ireland, tho' transcribed since by other able hands'.[39]
Previously, the east Ulster poet Fear Flatha Ó Gnímh, writing in defence of
his profession and of Irish-language scholarship in the early seventeenth century, insisted in a poem addressed to Art Óg Ó Néill that 'information about
the descendants of Gaoidheal Glas is not in English or Welsh, and it is not
available in Latin books to be researched as we research it'.[40] The same mind-
set was articulated by Dubhaltach Mac Fhirbhisigh in 1656 when compiling
the 'Writers of Ireland'. Mac Fhirbhisigh asserted that the *Gaeil* had been
writing down their history before they ever came to Ireland, while still in
Scythia, Egypt and Spain.[41] Mac Fhirbhisigh retained ownership of his manuscripts and, according to O'Flaherty, they stayed within the traditional
Gaelic milieu after his death.[42] In contrast, Roderic O'Flaherty lost possession
of most of his own manuscripts in the 1690s, but they appear to have
remained in the west of Ireland and some of them were later acquired by
Charles O'Conor of Belanagare in the mid-eighteenth century.[43] However,

36 Now NLI, MS G 5–6; for description and provenance, see Ní Shéaghdha, *Cat. Ir. Mss
in NLI*, fasc. 1, pp 31–6. **37** The manuscript translation of Keating's history purchased
by Lhuyd is now TCD, MS 1443. Other copies of what is essentially the same translation
also survive: Bernadette Cunningham, *The world of Geoffrey Keating: history, myth and religion in seventeenth-century Ireland* (Dublin, 2000), pp 190–1. **38** Todd (ed.), 'Autograph
letter of Thady O'Roddy', 122. **39** Ibid., 121. **40** Tadhg Ó Donnchadha (ed.), *Leabhar
Cloinne Aodha Buidhe* (Dublin, 1931), p. 227, translated in Simms, 'Literacy and the Irish
bards', p. 252. **41** Mac Fhirbhisigh's text is edited from Bodleian Library, Rawlinson MS
B 480, ff 55–62v in James Carney (ed.), '*De scriptoribus Hibernicis*', *Celtica*, 1:1 (1946), 86–
110, at 88. **42** Bodleian Library, Ashmole MS 1817a, f. 30r, cited in Nollaig Ó Muraíle,
The celebrated antiquary (Maynooth, 1996), p. 303. **43** RIA, MS B iv 2 is one such manuscript. It was acquired by Charles O'Conor having been formerly in the possession of
O'Flaherty: Elizabeth FitzPatrick, *Catalogue of Irish manuscripts in the Royal Irish Academy*,
fasc. 24 (Dublin, 1940), p. 3023. On O'Conor, see Diarmaid Ó Catháin, 'Charles O'Conor
of Belanagare: antiquary and Irish scholar', *RSAI Jnl.*, 119 (1989), 136–63.

O'Sullivan has suggested that Lhuyd may have obtained some manuscripts from O'Flaherty that had formerly been owned by Mac Fhirbhisigh.[44] In Munster, the poet, Dáibhí Ó Bruadair also lost possession of his manuscripts towards the end of his life, much to his regret.[45]

Others were also in the manuscript market. In the early 1720s, when assembling materials for his proposed history of Ireland, Anthony Raymond went so far as to advertise publicly a list of manuscripts he sought to locate and purchase, having engaged the Dublin bookseller, Luke Dowling of High Street, as his agent in the matter.

> Mr Dowling is commissioned to purchase the following books, or any other valuable Irish manuscripts that should be offered to him. Leabhar Ardmacha, remains of Psaltair Chaisil, Leabhar na Huachongmhala, Psaltair na Rann, Uidhir Chiarain, Leabhar buidhe Moling, Leabhar Gearr na Pailisi, Catha Cluana Tarbh, Cath Muighe Tarbh, Cath Muighe Mucroimhe, The Blacc Book of Hoath for which will be given Ten Pounds … N.B. These manuscripts are in publick libraries but there are in the hands of private gentlemen of this country, a great number.[46]

Raymond was correct in his assumption that many manuscripts remained in private hands. From the 1730s, John Fergus and Charles O'Conor emerged as prominent collectors of Irish manuscripts. They, too, made contact with the descendants of hereditary learned families. Thus, for example, about 1732 Fergus bought part of the Annals of the Four Masters from the collection of one John Conry, a descendant of Fearfeasa Ó Maoilchonaire. The contact, in this instance, was Charles O'Neal, Conry either having died or sold his manuscripts about 1730–1.[47] John Conry was described by William Nicolson in 1724 as owning 'the most valuable collection of Irish MSS that I have met with, in any private hand, here in Dublin, next to that of [John Stearne,] the Lord Bishop of Clogher'. Although Fergus was born in county Mayo, he spent his professional life in Dublin, where through his interest in manuscript collecting, he became well known to the Dublin scribal circle. They were able

44 William O'Sullivan, 'The manuscript collection of Dubhaltach Mac Fhirbhisigh' in Alfred P. Smyth (ed.), *Seanchas: studies in early and medieval Irish archaeology, history and literature in honour of Francis J. Byrne* (Dublin, 2000), pp 439–47, at p. 447.   45 John Mac Erlean (ed.), *Duanaire Dhaibhidh Uí Bhruadair: the poems of David Ó Bruadair* (3 vols, ITS, London, 1910–17), iii, poem 31; Bernadette Cunningham and Raymond Gillespie, 'Lost worlds: history and religion in the poetry of Dáibhí Ó Bruadair' in Pádraigín Riggs (ed.), *Dáibhí Ó Bruadair: his historical and literary context*, ITS subsidiary series eleven (London, 2001), pp 18–45, at pp 42–3.   46 Cited in Alan Harrison, 'Who wrote to Edward Lhwyd', *Celtica*, 16 (1984), 175–8 at 177.   47 Diarmaid Ó Catháin, 'John Fergus MD: eighteenth-century doctor, book-collector and Irish scholar', *RSAI Jnl.*, 118 (1988), 139–62, at 139–44.

to borrow manuscripts from his collection and he also borrowed from them.[48]
In 1766, when John Fergus' library was auctioned in Dublin, the collection
was described as including 'a rare collection of Irish history both print and
manuscript, some of them not to be met elsewhere'.[49] In another development
associated with the cultural economy that sustained the creation of a market for
manuscripts, a new type of scribe emerged in commercial centres, such as
Dublin, previously not associated with Gaelic manuscript culture.[50] These
responded to commercial opportunity by copying manuscripts that both
English and Irish speakers wanted rather than prioritizing texts that the learned
traditionally esteemed. In addition, new bodies such as the institutional or
university library were emerging, which gathered manuscripts together in new
settings.[51] In these ways the circulation of Irish manuscripts was gradually
transformed through changing demand created, in part, by the permeability of
cultural frontiers. The pattern of manuscript use can be an indicator of cultural
contact and its limitations in a politically divided society. It must also be
recognized that those manuscript exchanges took place in a world that was
being increasingly permeated by a print culture. The functions served by
manuscript and print among scholars evolved in tandem with each other.

II

It is possible to trace in some detail the processes by which the manuscript
collections of the hereditary learned class within Gaelic Ireland were redis-
tributed as a result of the undermining of that class during the 1620s and
1630s by political developments and the rise of a market economy.[52] When
the Four Masters and Geoffrey Keating – each working independently in different parts of Ireland – began assembling source material for their major histories of Ireland in the late 1620s and early 1630s, they were able to assemble
substantial collections of manuscripts in the Irish language by extending their
search beyond the usual contexts of the learned families and their schools.[53]
In the case of the Four Masters, they were able to bring together in one place
a range of materials drawn from various parts of the country that they used
as the basis of their new compilations. They clearly had access to annals com-

---

48 Ó Catháin, 'John Fergus MD', 141; Alan Harrison, *The dean's friend: Anthony
Raymond, 1675–1726, Jonathan Swift and the Irish language* (Dublin, 1999), pp 46–8.   49
Advertisement for the sale, cited in Ó Catháin, 'John Fergus MD', p. 140.   50 Harrison,
The dean's friend, pp 19–66; Nessa Ní Shéaghdha, 'Irish scholars and scribes in eighteenth-
century Dublin', *Eighteenth-Century Ireland*, 4 (1989), 41–54.   51 Raymond Gillespie,
'Manuscript collectors in the age of Marsh' in Muriel McCarthy and Ann Simmons (eds),
Marsh's Library: a mirror on the world (Dublin, 2009), pp 234–50.   52 Raymond Gillespie,
The transformation of the Irish economy, 1550–1700 ([Dundalk], 1991), pp 12–29.   53 Anne
Cronin, 'Sources of Keating's *Foras feasa ar Éirinn*: 2, manuscript sources', *Éigse*, 5 (1945–
7), 122–35.

piled by or under the auspices of their own learned families: Ó Duibhgeannáin, Ó Maoil Chonaire and, of course, Ó Cléirigh, and in that sense they drew on an older tradition of manuscript accumulation.[54] They also had access to the eleventh-century manuscript known as *Leabhar na hUidhre* (Book of the Dun Cow),[55] which was in the possession of the O'Donnells in the sixteenth century.[56] The team also prepared new recensions of older texts to meet new circumstances, and compiled new listings of kings and saints – utilizing older sources for this purpose.[57] These works, in turn, were copied and entered the corpus of manuscripts available to others in new cultural contexts.[58] Thus, for example, included with the original manuscript of Downing's account of the natural history and antiquities of county Mayo prepared in the 1680s was a note on the name 'Britannia' provided by Tadhg Ó Rodaighe from the Ó Cléirigh recension of the *Leabhar Gabhála*, then in his possession.[59] In the midlands, Conall MacGeoghegan, though not a member of a hereditary learned family, assembled a collection of historical manuscripts from which he compiled a set of Irish annals in English translation. Among the more important manuscripts he consulted was an Ó Maoilchonaire chronicle and the book of Calloch O'More, which is to be identified with the Book of Leinster.[60]

It is no coincidence that the decades in which new historical writing in Irish flourished coincided with the period when Irish manuscripts were being acquired by English and Old English antiquarian collectors. The gradual decline of the hereditary learned families made older manuscripts available to native Irish and Old English and settler families. Indeed, some of the exemplars that the Four Masters and Geoffrey Keating wished to use had already left the hands of the traditional families and had made their way into the ownership of antiquarian collectors by the 1620s. Yet, this did not pose an

54 *AFM*, I, pp xliv, xlvi. **55** RIA, MS 23 E 25, a manuscript written before 1106 and associated with Clonmacnoise. **56** Cunningham, *Annals of the Four Masters*, ch. 3. **57** Cunningham, *Annals of the Four Masters*, pp 63–73; Eugene O'Curry, *Lectures on the manuscript materials of ancient Irish history* (Dublin, 1861), pp 162–80. For adaptation, see Breandán Ó Buachalla, *The crown of Ireland* (Galway, 2006), pp 38–40. **58** Transcripts of the Four Masters' Genealogies of kings and saints, for example, are found in a number of seventeenth and eighteenth-century manuscripts including RIA, MS 24 P 33, pp 43–98, MS 23 A 40, pp 66–127; MS 23 D 9, pp 16–64, MS C vi 1, pp 185–284, and TCD, MS 1348. From the mid seventeenth century, one set of the Annals of the Four Masters was in Louvain where they were used mainly by John Colgan; another set was available to Galway scholars including Roderic O'Flaherty. TCD, MS 1301 is part of the autograph manuscript of AFM complete with O'Flaherty's annotations. Transcripts and translations of Keating's *Foras feasa* circulated much more widely. **59** TCD, MS 888/2, f.109. Ó Rodaighe explained the source of his information, noting: 'These out of the Leabhar Gabhála, the prime book of the kingdom mentioning all the conquests of Ireland refined by the five prime antiquaries of Ireland, anno 1631, which I have here'. **60** Denis Murphy (ed.), *The annals of Clonmacnoise, being annals of Ireland from the earliest period to AD 1408* (Dublin, 1896), p. 10; D.P. Mc Carthy, *The Irish annals: their genesis, evolution and history* (Dublin, 2008), pp 292–3.

insurmountable obstacle. The antiquarian James Ussher, archbishop of Armagh (1581–1656), acquired the Book of Ballymote before 1620, but he shared information about it with the Ossory priest David Rothe and later cited it in his ecclesiastical history, *Britannicarum ecclesiarum antiquitates* (1639).[61] A small portion of the Book of Leinster containing the Martyrology of Tallaght appears to have been in Ussher's library at Drogheda in the late 1620s.[62] In fact, Ussher might have had access to more of the Book of Leinster than just this portion. The Book was borrowed by Conall MacGeoghegan from its traditional keepers, the O'Mores, before 1627, and MacGeoghegan and Ussher are known to have exchanged other manuscripts so that it is possible that Ussher borrowed the Book of Leinster from this source. A clearer instance of exchange of manuscripts between Ussher and MacGeoghegan is provided by the Book of Lecan. This was in the possession of Henry Perse by 1612 and was subsequently acquired by Ussher.[63] Some years afterwards, the Book of Lecan was on loan to the Westmeath landowner Conall MacGeoghegan in the 1630s, and, while it is difficult to prove conclusively, it is certainly likely that both Geoffrey Keating and Mícheál Ó Cléirigh had access to this manuscript through MacGeoghegan in the mid-1630s. MacGeoghegan was a man who straddled two worlds, native Irish yet literate in English. He was a new landowner who had connections with the old order and this ensured that he was well placed to act as a conduit between two traditions of manuscript use and to facilitate the circulation of manuscripts and printed books among different cultural groups.[64] What is more certain is that Ó Cléirigh was able to obtain access to the Martyrology of Tallaght, from the Book of Leinster, in 1627, when that portion of the manuscript appears to have been in Ussher's library at Drogheda. Indeed, Ó Cléirigh retained that section of the Book of Leinster thereafter, bringing it to Louvain for the use of the Franciscan hagiographers there.[65]

In Munster, the government official Sir George Carew (1555–1629) assembled his own collection of manuscript materials of Irish interest, including much Irish-language material. Carew's early seventeenth-century interest

---

61 RIA, MS 23 P 12; William O'Sullivan, 'Correspondence of David Rothe and James Ussher, 1619–23', *Collectanea Hibernica*, 36–37 (1994–5), 7–49 at 16, 18, 34; C.R. Elrington and J.H. Todd (eds), *The whole works of James Ussher* (17 vols, Dublin, 1847–64), vi, 230, 336, 344, 536.   62 The Book of Leinster is now TCD, MS 1339; for the movements of this manuscript in the seventeenth century, see O'Sullivan, 'Notes on the scripts and make-up of the Book of Leinster', 4. For the suggestion that the section of the Book of Leinster containing the Martyrology of Tallaght was in Ussher's possession at Drogheda by 1627, see Paul Walsh, *Irish leaders and learning through the ages*, ed. Nollaig Ó Muraíle (Dublin, 2003), pp 353–4.   63 RIA, MS 23 P 2; Ó Muraíle, *Celebrated antiquary*, pp 193–4; Bernadette Cunningham and Raymond Gillespie, 'James Ussher and his Irish manuscripts', *Studia Hibernica*, 33 (2004–5), 81–99, at 92–3.   64 Cunningham and Gillespie, 'James Ussher and his Irish manuscripts'.   65 The Martyrology of Tallaght remained in Franciscan hands thereafter, and is now UCD-OFM, MS A 3; Walsh, *Irish leaders and learning*, pp 353–4.

in Irish historical manuscripts may have originated in a desire to document his own military and political career as lord president of Munster. He was also keen to reclaim the Carew estates in the province and possibly sought out historical evidence that would support his case.[66] In any event, his antiquarian pursuits soon broadened out and he purchased manuscripts containing Irish annals and other historical material. In the latter years of his life in London, Carew discussed Gaelic genealogical matters with Florence MacCarthy Reagh, then imprisoned in the Tower. MacCarthy Reagh, who had acted as historian for the earl of Thomond, had been among Carew's military opponents in Munster.[67] MacCarthy Reagh's work was also known to the antiquarian James Ware, who had a copy of his letter to Thomond on the history of Ireland among his papers.[68] In turn, Carew's manuscript collection was passed to others with an interest in this material. Some items from Carew's collection, including three Irish-language manuscripts, were acquired by James Ussher.[69] Still further items found their way to the Bodleian Library at Oxford having been passed to Archbishop William Laud (1573–1645) by Thomas Stafford to whom Carew bequeathed them.[70] Laud was not the only English scholar with an interest in Irish material. Ussher was certainly in touch with a number of prominent English antiquarians, including Robert Cotton (1586–1631), in London, and promised Cotton at least one manuscript of Irish saints' lives.[71] Cotton himself acquired a number of Irish-language manuscripts. Cotton's Irish collection was eclectic, and included west of Ireland manuscripts such as the 'Annals of Boyle', compiled in the early fourteenth century,[72] a life of St Caillín written in 1535,[73] and miscellaneous late-sixteenth century items.[74] Other English administrators also

66 For Carew, see Jason Dorsett, 'Sir George Carew: the study and conquest of Ireland' (D.Phil thesis, Oxford University, 2000); see also Anne O'Sullivan, 'Tadhg O'Daly and Sir George Carew', *Éigse*, 14:1 (1971), 27–38, for a poem addressed to Carew by one of the learned class in the area in which he settled in county Cork.   67 Terry Clavin, 'MacCarthy Reagh, Florence (Finian, Finghín)' in *DIB*.   68 BL, Add. MS 4796, ff 3–17. 69 William O'Sullivan, 'Ussher as a collector of manuscripts', *Hermathena*, 88 (1956), 34–42; Carew was probably Ussher's source for TCD, MSS 1432–7; Toby Barnard, 'The purchase of Archbishop Ussher's library in 1657', *Long Room*, 4 (1971), 9–14.   70 The most significant of Laud's Irish manuscripts were Bodleian Library, MSS Laud Misc. 610 and Laud Misc. 615. For the ownership history of these two compilations, see Brian Ó Cuív, *Catalogue of Irish language manuscripts in the Bodleian Library at Oxford and Oxford College libraries* (2 vols, Dublin, 2001–3), i, pp xx–xxii.   71 O'Sullivan, 'Ussher as a collector of manuscripts', 34–9; BL, Cotton, Julius C III, ff 380, 381. For an overview of Cotton's manuscript collection, see C.G.C. Tite, *The manuscript library of Sir Robert Cotton*. The Panizzi Lectures, 1993 (London, 1994).   72 BL, Cotton, Titus A. XXV.   73 BL, Cotton, Vespasian E. II, ff 108–120.   74 BL, Cotton, Nero A. VII, ff 132–57 a law manuscript written by Matha Ó Luinín in 1571; and Cotton, Appendix LI, a computus or ecclesiastical calendar written by Tomás Ó hIcidhe in 1589. For descriptions of these Irish manuscripts from the Cotton library see S.H. O'Grady and Robin Flower, *Catalogue of Irish manuscripts in the British Library [formerly British Museum]* (3 vols, rept, Dublin, 1992), i, 141, 285–327.

acquired Irish manuscripts, possibly while visiting the country, most notably Henry Spelman who owned what is now British Library Harley MS 5280.[75] This was not an isolated example, and other Irish manuscripts were also taken to England. The antiquary Charles Fairfax had acquired a seventeenth-century Irish manuscript containing an historical tract and poetry by 1665,[76] while Isaac Voss obtained an Irish manuscript containing sagas and tales in England sometime between 1670 and 1689.[77] Part of William Bedell's Irish translation of the Old Testament was taken to England by Revd Robert Huntington, probably in 1688 or 1690–1.[78]

Sir James Ware, a second-generation settler and a close associate of Archbishop Ussher in terms of their antiquarian pursuits, also collected Irish-language manuscripts. After his death, Ware's library was dispersed, but much of his manuscript collection can be reconstructed.[79] Items acquired by Ware have been identified in a range of modern archives, including the British Library, Trinity College, Dublin and in the Bodleian Library at Oxford, where there are thirteen Irish language items formerly owned by Ware, together with a selection of items in English or Latin. One copy of the Annals of Ulster, now Rawl B. 489, was in Ware's library by 1620.[80] The Annals of Ulster were cited extensively by James Ussher in his *Britannicarum*,[81] though he may have possessed his own copy acquired independently of that owned by Ware[82] By 1648, Ware also owned the major medieval miscellany now known as Bodleian Library, Rawlinson MS B. 502.[83] This latter manuscript was available to Geoffrey Keating in the early 1630s by which time it may already have passed into Ware's possession. The same manuscript, described as 'Psalter Narrane' (Saltair na Rann), is included in a list of manuscripts loaned by Sir James Ware between 1627 and 1636, though

75 O'Grady and Flower, *Cat. Ir. mss in BL*, ii, 300. For other examples, ibid, 231, 255. 76 Bodleian Library, Rawlinson B 475; Ó Cuiv, *Catalogue of Irish manuscripts in Oxford*, i, 101–3. 77 L.C. Stern, 'Le manuscrit Irlandais de Leide', *Revue Celtique*, 13 (1982), 1. 78 Cambridge University Library, MS Dd.9.7; Pádraig de Brún and Máire Herbert, *Catalogue of Irish manuscripts in Cambridge libraries* (Cambridge, 1986), p. 123. 79 William O'Sullivan, 'A finding list of Sir James Ware's manuscripts', *RIA proc.*, 97C (1997), 69–99. 80 Ó Cuiv, *Catalogue of Irish manuscripts in Oxford*, i, pp xxiii, 161–2; James Ware to James Ussher, 10 July 1620 (TCD, MS 582, f. 81r) cited in Elizabethanne Boran, 'Writing history in seventeenth-century Ireland: Dudley Loftus' annals' in McCarthy and Simmons (eds), *Marsh's Library: a mirror on the world*, p. 215. 81 Elrington and Todd (eds), *Whole works of James Ussher*, vi, 146, 252–3, 256, 262–3, 278. 82 Ussher's references to this source indicate that he was using the copy now preserved in TCD 1282, rather than the Rawlinson set of the Annals of Ulster that had been owned by Ware. Ussher appears to have acquired a set of the Annals of Ulster by 1619, as in his correspondence with David Rothe he described the manuscript he was using as his own: O'Sullivan (ed.), 'Correspondence of David Rothe and James Ussher', 7–49. 83 Ó Cuiv, *Catalogue of Irish manuscripts in Oxford*, i, 163. For discussion of the discontinuities that could following the transition into antiquarian hands, see Pádraig Ó Riain, 'The Book of Glendalough: a continuing investigation', *Zeitschrift für Celtische Philologie*, 56 (2008), 71–88.

the name of the borrower is not stated.[84] O Cuív has suggested that Keating may have found this manuscript in the Drogheda library of James Ussher, though it is possible that access was arranged through an intermediary.[85] Ware had his own contacts in county Tipperary also, and appears to have acquired the Irish-language portions of Bodleian Library, Rawlinson MS B. 486 as a gift from the Conway family in that county in 1625.[86] Ware's contacts, like those of Ussher extended into English antiquarian circles and he certainly borrowed Irish-language materials from both Carew and Cotton.[87] Ware's historical interests were extensive. His publications indicate that he was particularly interested in large-scale compilations, including annals of the sixteenth century, and prosopographies of Irish writers and Irish bishops.[88] Such eclectic compilations necessitated access to a broad range of source material in a variety of languages, and Ware actively cultivated the full range of scholarly networks necessary to achieve his objectives.

While James Ussher, likewise, assiduously pursued the Irish manuscript materials he required for his ecclesiastical history of Ireland, he was circumspect in his dealings with those who owned them.[89] In addition to sourcing manuscripts from Catholic contacts, Ussher employed specialists to translate extracts from his Irish-language manuscript collection into Latin for his use.[90] Thus, an impressive if discreet scholarly network was constructed that gave Ussher and Ware access to Irish manuscript sources, and facilitated their interpretation. Some individuals, of whom Conall MacGeoghegan may be the best example, acted as brokers through whom those who sought to consult Irish manuscripts could be facilitated.[91] An important example of how such manuscripts moved across cultural frontiers is provided by BL, Cotton, Vespasian MS E II. This shortened version of the life of St Caillín, written in Irish in Donegal in the 1530s, was in the hands of Sir Robert Cotton in London by 1621.[92] To make such a move it would have required a mediator.

84 BL, Add. MS 4821, ff 239r, 242r. We are grateful to Mark Empey for providing a transcript of these lists.   85 Ó Cuív, *Catalogue of Irish manuscripts in Oxford*, i, 177.   86 Ó Cuív, *Catalogue of Irish manuscripts in Oxford*, i, 123.   87 BL, Cotton, Julius C III, ff 388, 386.   88 *The whole works of Sir James Ware concerning Ireland ... revised and improved by Walter Harris* (2 vols, Dublin, 1739–64).   89 O'Sullivan, 'Correspondence of David Rothe and James Ussher', 7–49; Cathaldus Giblin, 'Aegidus Chaissy, OFM, and James Ussher, Protestant archbishop of Armagh', *Irish Ecclesiastical Record*, 85:6 (1956), 393–405; Cunningham and Gillespie, 'James Ussher and his Irish manuscripts', 81–99. While Ussher was fearful of openly acknowledging his Catholic contacts, he had no difficulty in revealing his dealings with Sir Robert Cotton concerning access to manuscripts: Elrington and Todd (eds), *Whole works of James Ussher*, xv, 5, 15.   90 TCD, MS 574 contains historical notes prepared by and for Ussher, including a partial copy of the Annals of Ulster in Irish with a Latin translation on facing pages, beginning at p. 446. For an acknowledgment by Ussher of assistance received from a translator, see Elrington and Todd (eds), *Whole works of James Ussher*, vi, 428.   91 Cunningham and Gillespie, 'James Ussher and his Irish manuscripts', passim.   92 Raymond Gillespie, 'Relics, reliquaries and hagiography in south Ulster, 1450–1550' in Rachel Moss, Colmán Ó Clabaigh and Salvador Ryan

By the time Cotton had acquired the manuscript it had been provided with
an English summary that ensured that Cotton knew the contents of what he
owned; for the learned a note of the contents was also provided in Latin.[93]
While this permitted intellectual access, the channel by which it came to
Cotton is less clear. A reasonable guess is that the link was the Donegal settler Sir Basil Brooke. Brooke and Cotton were on book-borrowing terms and
exchanged items on a number of occasions.[94] Thus the Donegal planter may
well have been the means by which an Irish-language manuscript crossed the
physical space from Ulster to London. Crossing the cultural space from the
Irish language to the English summary placed at the start of the work may
have required the services of another broker.

Through the activities of such mediators, important medieval manuscripts
that passed into the ownership of antiquaries such as Ussher or Ware became
accessible to others outside their immediate circle of contacts.[95] The
Franciscan community in Ireland, which transcended Old English and native
Irish divisions, and also sustained a network within which manuscripts could
circulate, was part of the wider scholarly circle that shared an interest in spe-
cific medieval manuscripts. Francis Matthews, for example, was among the
Irish Franciscan historians permitted to make transcripts of manuscripts from
Ussher's collection.[96] In another instance, it appears that the version of the
Liber hymnorum used by the Donegal Franciscans may have been the same
one that was known to Sir James Ware and James Ussher.[97] That Sir James
Ware was able to access and cite this rare late eleventh-century source in his
De scriptoribus Hiberniae (1639),[98] and again in his *S. Patricio ... adscripta
opuscula* (1656), is just one by-product of the cultural interaction represented
by manuscript exchanges.[99] Ussher, too, compared the copy he owned of the
Hymn to St Patrick by Secundius with that found in the Franciscan copy of
the *Liber hymnorum*.[1]

(eds), *Art and devotion in late medieval Ireland* (Dublin, 2006), pp 197–8; BL, Harley MS
6018, f. 15.   93 BL, Cotton MS Vespasian E II, ff 106, 108–8v, partly printed in O'Grady
and Flower, *Cat. Ir. mss in BL*, ii, 465–6.   94 BL, Harley MS 6018, ff 149v, 179v.   95
Cunningham and Gillespie, 'James Ussher and his Irish manuscripts', passim.   96 Richard
Sharpe, *Medieval Irish saints' lives: an introduction to vita sanctorum Hiberniae* (Oxford,
1991), pp 99–100. For the Franciscan network, see Cunningham, *Annals of the Four
Masters*, pp 282–93; Raymond Gillespie, 'The Ó Cléirigh manuscripts in context' in Edel
Bhreathnach and Bernadette Cunningham (eds), *Writing Irish history: the Four Masters and
their world* (Dublin, 2007), pp 43–8.   97 J.H. Bernard and R. Atkinson (eds), *The Irish
Liber hymnorum* (2 vols, London, 1898), i, pp xiv–xv; Caoimhín Breatnach, 'Foinsí an lea-
gain de Bheatha Cholaim Chille a scríobhadh faoi stiúradh Mhaghnuis Uí Dhomhnaill', in
P.A. Breatnach, C. Breatnach and M. Ní Úrdail (eds), *Léann lámhscríbhinní Lobháin: the
Louvain manuscript heritage* (*Éigse* Publications, Occasional supplementary series, 1)
(Dublin, 2007), pp 137–8.   98 James Ware, *De scriptoribus Hiberniae, libri duo* (Dublin,
1639), p. 15.   99 James Ware, *S. Patricio ... adscripta opuscula, quorum aliqua nunc primum
ex antiquis MSS, codicibus in lucem emissa sunt* (London, 1656), p. 150.   1 Bodleian
Library, Rawlinson MS B. 480, ff 83r–84v; Ó Cuív, *Catalogue of Irish manuscripts in
Oxford*, i, 112.

Not being educated within the Gaelic tradition, both Ussher and Ware needed translators to interpret the Irish-language content of some of the medieval manuscripts they acquired. This dependence on scholars from the Gaelic tradition for specialist expertise probably strengthened links across the religious and cultural divides, although attitudes to translation could be mixed. While many early seventeenth-century Irish translators did not mask their concern that their native language was regarded as inferior to English, and were aware that changing political and social circumstances created the demand for their work, they nonetheless lent their linguistic expertise to the negotiation of cultural boundaries that their work of translation encouraged.[2] Translators were necessarily intermediaries between cultures. The best known of the Gaelic scholars who prepared translations for James Ware was Dubhaltach Mac Fhirbhisigh. The autograph copy of part of his 1666 English translation of a set of Annals of Lecan survives in the British Library.[3] In the course of Mac Fhirbhisigh's dealings with Ware in 1665, he referred specifically to the Book of Lecan in the library of Trinity College, Dublin, but he did not imply that this great manuscript compilation was beyond his reach.[4] Mac Fhirbhisigh's collaborations with Sir James Ware were not exclusively for Ware's benefit. At least one of Ware's books ended up in Mac Fhirbhisigh's possession, having apparently been presented to him after Ware's death.[5]

III

The movement of manuscripts in early seventeenth-century Ireland certainly transcended cultural frontiers among a well-defined group of antiquarians and the curious. However, the process of Irish-language manuscripts moving across cultural boundaries was not confined to Ireland. A programme of collecting manuscripts and the compilation and translation of texts from Irish manuscript sources was embarked on by Irish scholars overseas in the early

2 For the view of Conall MacGeoghegan, translator of the Annals of Clonmacnoise (1627), see Murphy (ed.), *The Annals of Clonmacnoise*, p. 8. For the view of Michael Kearney, translator of Keating's *Foras feasa ar Éirinn* (1635), see RIA, MS 24 G 16, f. 34; the view of Francis Walsh (1713) is given in his preface to *Grammatica Anglo-Hibernica*, cited in Harrison, *The dean's friend*, p. 38. 3 BL, Add. MS 4799; John O'Donovan (ed.), 'The annals of Ireland, from the year 1443 to 1468, translated from the Irish by Dudley Firbisse ... for Sir James Ware, in the year 1666' in *Miscellany of the Irish Archaeological Society*, 1 (Dublin, 1846), 198–302. A partial extract from the Annals of the Four Masters, in Irish, can also be found among Ware's notebooks: BL, Add MS 4784, ff 36–86. For an analysis of this item, see Cunningham, *Annals of the Four Masters*, pp 291–2. Ware also acquired a Latin translation of portions of the same work: TCD, MS 804, pp 283–94. 4 Ó Muráile, *The celebrated antiquary*, p. 209, n. 170. 5 Ware's *De Praesulibus Hiberniae*, TCD, shelfmark C.2.12A; for identification of Mac Fhirbhisigh's annotations, mostly in Irish, in this printed book, see Ó Muráile, *The celebrated antiquary*, pp 257–8.

seventeenth century providing an interface between Gaelic Ireland and a
wider world. Most successful were the endeavours of Patrick Fleming, Hugh
Ward and John Colgan at St Anthony's College, Louvain, whose scholarship
was directed towards the collection of the lives of Irish saints in Latin and
Irish and translating them into the European *lingua franca* of Latin.[6] The
experience of encountering new cultures in European university towns
fomented a desire to promote a positive image of Ireland and Irishness among
students and clergy there. This ambition, coupled with an interest in history
as a polemical tool of the Counter Reformation, prompted much new research
among the circle of Franciscan scholars linked to the Irish College at
Louvain.[7] At a higher political level, aspirations to seek assistance from the
Spanish and Roman authorities, for what was presented as the Irish Catholic
cause, gave rise to further propagandist writing on Irish historical topics.
Political tracts produced by leading clergy such as Peter Lombard (*c*.1554–
1625) at Rome had a strong historical perspective, drawing on a familiar historical corpus.[8] Philip O'Sullivan Beare's polemical history, *Historiae
Catholicae Iberniae compendium*, published at Lisbon in 1621, evoked the
image of Ireland as an island of saints and scholars. Dedicated to the new
Spanish king, Philip IV, it also attempted to use Irish history to make a case
for Spanish military support for the Irish Catholic cause. In doing so, it
attempted to bridge cultural frontiers between Ireland and Spain by stressing
supposed historical connections between Ireland and the Iberian Peninsula,
notably the concluding element of the traditional Book of Invasions origin
myth for Ireland which linked Milesius, the legendary ancestor of the Gaeil,
with Spain.[9]

Such writings were based on manuscripts from Ireland sometimes – as in
the case of the Irish Franciscans – deliberately collected, and sometimes
chanced upon. However they were encountered, such manuscripts represented yet another instance of movements across cultural frontiers in the seventeenth century.[10] Those in Europe who engaged in the use of this material

6 Sharpe, *Medieval Irish saints' lives: an introduction*, passim; Pádraig Breatnach, 'An Irish
Bollandus: Fr Hugh Ward and the Louvain hagiographical enterprise, *Éigse*, 31 (1999), 1–
30; Canice Mooney, 'Father John Colgan, OFM, his work and times and literary milieu'
in Terence O'Donnell (ed.), *Father John Colgan OFM* (Dublin, 1959), pp 7–40.   7
Cunningham, *Annals of the Four Masters*, pp 26–40; Bernadette Cunningham, 'The culture
and ideology of Irish Franciscan historians at Louvain, 1607–1650' in Ciaran Brady (ed.),
Ideology and the historians: Historical Studies 17 (Dublin, 1991), pp 11–30, 223–7.   8
Thomas O'Connor, 'An argument for European intervention in early modern Ireland:
Peter Lombard's *Commentarius*' in Thomas O'Connor and Mary Ann Lyons (eds), *Irish
migration to Europe after Kinsale, 1602–1820* (Dublin, 2003), pp 14–31; Tadhg Ó
hAnnracháin, 'Lombard, Peter' in *DIB*.   9 Clare Carroll, 'Irish and Spanish cultural and
political relations in the work of O'Sullivan Beare' in Hiram Morgan (ed.), *Political ideology in Ireland, 1541–1641* (Dublin, 1999), pp 229–53; Hiram Morgan, 'O'Sullivan Beare,
Philip' in *DIB*.   10 Medieval manuscripts collected by the Franciscans at Louvain include
the Psalter of St Caimín (UCD-OFM, MS A 1) (11th–12th century); the *Liber hymnorum*

in a scholarly way gave detailed attention to the most highly regarded vernacular manuscript sources. Thus, in tandem with the preparation of editions of saints' lives, attention was also directed towards the preparation of traditional secular sources for dissemination among continental audiences. Far from being conceived as a rescue mission for manuscripts in danger of destruction or loss, one key aim of these ambitious historical enterprises was to transmit contemporary Catholic interpretations of the Irish Christian past across cultural frontiers in early modern Europe.[11] Much of this work was done by the team referred to by John Colgan as the 'Four Masters', just one of whom, Mícheál Ó Cléirigh, is known to have spent time on the Continent.[12] A comprehensive new chronicle of the kingdom of Ireland was compiled; a new recension of the Book of Invasions origin legend was prepared; a new martyrology of Irish saints was edited and chronological lists of Irish kings and saints were drawn up.[13] Among the many revisions to older sources characteristic of these endeavours, one of the most consistent was the omission of non-Irish content. Thus, for example, all biblical allusions were removed from the Book of Invasions; non-Irish saints were omitted from the Martyrology of Donegal; and stray references in the older Irish annals to events abroad were generally omitted from the Annals of the Four Masters. This 'purification' of the Irish sources may have been intended to make the contents of older manuscripts more acceptable to readers outside Ireland, reducing the likelihood of embarrassing discrepancies emerging between Irish and European sources.[14] All of these compilations may have been intended for publication in Latin translation.[15] Financial constraints on the publishing enterprise meant that not all that was planned came to fruit. The publication in 1645 and 1647 of two very substantial volumes of Irish saints' lives was a high point in the public achievements of the Louvain scholars. These hefty

(Book of hymns) (UCD-OFM, MS A 2) (11th–12th century); and the Martyrology of Tallaght (UCD-OFM, MS A 3), which had formed part of the twelfth-century Book of Leinster.   11 Breandán Ó Buachalla, '*Annála ríoghachta Éireann* is *Foras feasa ar Éirinn*: an comhtheacs comhaimseartha', *Studia Hibernica*, 22–3 (1982–3), 59–105; Bernadette Cunningham, 'Writing the Annals of the Four Masters' in Bhreathnach and Cunningham (eds), *Writing Irish history*, pp 26–30. For the nineteenth-century context in which the myth of a rescue mission emerged, see Bernadette Cunningham, 'John O'Donovan's edition of the Annals of the Four Masters: an Irish classic?' in Dirk Van Hulle and Joep Leerssen (eds), *Editing the nation's memory: textual scholarship and nation-building in nineteenth-century Europe*. European Studies, 26 (Amsterdam, 2008), pp 129–49.   12 Cunningham, *Annals of the Four Masters*, pp 260–2, 270–4.   13 Brendan Jennings, *Michael Ó Cléirigh, chief of the Four Masters and his associates* (Dublin, 1936); Cunningham, *Annals of the Four Masters*, pp 64–72.   14 For one instance of a discrepancy between Irish and European sources in the Annals of the Four Masters that had to be rectified later, see Cunningham, *Annals of the Four Masters*, pp 159–68.   15 Paul Walsh (ed.), *Genealogiae regum et sanctorum Hiberniae by the Four Masters* (Dublin, 1918), pp 131, 147; Cuthbert Mhág Craith (eag.), *Dán na mBráthar Mionúr* (2 vols, Baile Átha Cliath, 1967), poem 39, stanza 19; Breatnach, 'On the Ó Cléirigh recension of *Leabhar Gabhála*', p. 31.

tomes, edited by John Colgan, were intended for institutional libraries where
they would serve as key reference points for those interested in the story of
the Christian church in early Ireland. Colgan meticulously recorded his manuscript sources in his extensive notes to his published editions of texts. The
fruits of Colgan's labours were drawn on by later writers addressing quite different audiences. Thus, in their writings on Irish subjects for English readers
of Latin, Roderic O'Flaherty's *Ogygia* (1685)[16] used Colgan's books as a
source of reference, as did John Stevens in his reworking of the *Monasticon
Hibernicum* (1722).[17]

    Irish cultural links with continental Europe continued to be important
throughout the seventeenth and eighteenth centuries. While the magnitude of
the scholarly achievements of the Irish Franciscans in the early seventeenth
century was not repeated subsequently, Irish manuscripts continued to move
between Ireland and the Continent. Some prestige manuscripts, such as the
Cathach and the Book of Lecan left Ireland in the late seventeenth century.[18]
When Peadar Ó Neachtain, son of Tadhg, brought one of his father's Irish
manuscripts to Santiago in the late 1730s, it was probably just one among
many instances in which individual Irish manuscripts were taken abroad for
personal use.[19] This constant movement of Irish manuscripts is an indicator
of the permeability of the cultural boundaries that surrounded the Irish in
Europe in these years.

IV

For many, the principal barrier in the way of their engagement with the content of the manuscripts they owned or chanced upon was linguistic; they did
not possess an adequate knowledge of the sometimes archaic language in
which medieval manuscripts were written. This was a problem that those on
continental Europe had to face in understanding the manuscripts that they
brought there. Bonaventure Ó hEodhasa's *Rudimenta grammaticae Hibernicae*,[20]
compiled at Louvain earlier in the seventeenth century, provided an explanation of the grammar of classical modern Irish to readers of Latin. It circulated
on the Continent in manuscript only, but copies soon made their way back to
Ireland. Significantly, two of the earliest surviving manuscript copies were in
Marsh's Library before 1707, and were seen there by the Welsh manuscript
collector, Edward Lhuyd.[21] Mícheál Ó Cléirigh's *Foclóir no sanasain nua*, pub-

---

16 O'Flaherty, *Ogygia* (1685), pp 3, 63, 170, 190, 322, 409, 411.   17 On Stevens, see
Barnard, *Improving Ireland*, pp 100–1.   18 Harrison, *The dean's friend*, p. 29.   19
Harrison, *The dean's friend*, p. 31; for other examples, see O'Grady and Flower, *Cat. Ir mss
in BL*, ii, 161, 323, 429.   20 Parthalán Mac Aogáin (ed.), *Graiméir Ghaeilge na mBráthar
Mionúr* (Dublin, 1968); Giolla Bríde Ó hEodhasa, *Comhréir agus gramadach Ghaeilge Uladh
i 1600: rudimenta grammaticae Hibernicae*, ed. and trans. Séamus de Napier (Dublin, 2001).
21 Marsh's Library, MSS Z3.5.3 and Z3.4.19; Edward Lhuyd, *Archaeologia Britannica*

lished at Louvain in 1643, was intended to assist scholars to interpret diffi-cult Irish words encountered in older manuscripts. Printed copies of this work are very scarce, but yet numerous manuscript transcripts of the printed text survive.[22] Interestingly, as Tomás de Bhaldraithe pointed out, all major Irish-language dictionaries since Ó Cléirigh's 1643 *Foclóir* have been bilingual, involving explanation of Irish words by means of translations.[23] This is a clear indication of the essentially bilingual nature of the cultural world that has underpinned the use of Irish-language manuscripts since the mid-seventeenth century. In 1713, Francis Walsh, OFM, produced an Irish grammar written in English, which he may have intended to publish under the title *Grammatica Anglo-Hibernica*, but in the event it, too, circulated in manuscript only.[24] This work was intended to assist in interpreting historical sources, 'the most ancient monuments of this Kingdom'.[25] In a decided blurring of cultural boundaries, facilitated by print, Walsh indicated that his work was derived in part from Edward Lhuyd's 'Brief introduction to the Irish or ancient Scotish language' (1707),[26] Francis O'Molloy's *Grammatica Latino-Hibernica* published at Rome in 1677 and from a manuscript grammar dated 1637, which was the work of student named Philip Ó Cléirigh, at the Irish college of St Isidore in Rome.[27] Some years earlier, in 1706, Walsh compiled a modern Irish–Old Irish glossary derivative of Ó Cléirigh's 1643 work, with the same objective in mind. One later transcript of Francis Walsh's glossary included some explanations in English also.[28] A major step forward came in Paris in 1732 with the publication of Hugh McCurtin and Conor Begley's English–Irish dictionary.[29] This followed on from McCurtin's earlier publication, *The ele-ments of the Irish language, grammatically explained in English*, published at Louvain in 1728.

Understanding the language and script in which older Irish manuscripts were written was not just a problem that those on continental Europe faced; it was equally a problem for those at home, and this influenced the way in which manuscripts circulated both within and across cultural groups. As the Irish manuscript collector Tadhg Ó Rodaighe commented in the 1690s. 'I have several volumes that none in the world now can peruse', the reason

---

(Oxford, 1707), p. 436.   **22** The only printed copy of the 1643 text identified in an Irish library is in the NLI. Seventeen manuscript copies, derivatives of the printed text, are extant in the Royal Irish Academy collection alone.   **23** De Bhaldraithe, 'Irish dictionar-ies' in Foclóir na Nua-Ghaeilge, *Corpas na Gaeilge, 1600–1882: the Irish language corpus* (Dublin, 2004), p. 76.   **24** Copies survive in BL, Egerton MS 143; King's Inns, Gaelic MS 24; and NLI, MS G 332. See also, Harrison, *The dean's friend*, pp 38–9.   **25** Cited from Walsh's preface in Harrison, *The dean's friend*, p. 38.   **26** Lhuyd, *Archaeologia Britannica*, pp 299–309.   **27** Mac Aogáin (ed.), *Graiméar Ghaeilge na mBráthar Mionúr*, pp xv–xvi.   **28** RIA, MS 23 D 21 is a 1739 transcript of Walsh's dictionary, in the hand of John Heyden, with additions in another hand: RIA, MS 23 O 5 is a nineteenth-century transcript of RIA, MS 23 D 21.   **29** *The English Irish dictionary: an focloir Bearla Gaoidheilge*, ed. Conchubhar Ó Beaglaoich and Aodh Buidhe Mac Cruitín (Paris, 1732).

being the number of archaic words and the complex system of contractions used by the scribes.[30] This situation was confirmed by Edward Lhuyd in 1700, when he observed that 'the ignorance of their criticks is such, that tho' I consulted the chiefest of them, as O'Flaherty ... and several others, they could scarce interpret one page of all my manuscripts'.[31] Even among the learned in Trinity College in 1702, Thomas Molyneux reported regretfully to Edward Lhuyd that 'there is not any of the youth in our college that I can hear of that understands writing the Irish character, so that I fear you must not expect any assistance towards forwarding your work from copying passages out of those Irish mss that belong in our library.'[32] Because of this, late seventeenth-century writers of histories of Ireland often contented themselves with deploying a narrow range of manuscripts, mostly of recent origin, through which the older primary sources were selectively mediated. The Franciscan, Peter Walsh's narrative history was one of the first lengthy histories of Ireland to become available in print. Published in London in 1682, his *A prospect of the state of Ireland from the year of the world 1756 to the year of Christ 1652* was a work of more than 500 octavo pages. It was largely derivative of Geoffrey Keating's *Foras feasa ar Éirinn*, then only available in manuscript, and to a lesser extent of John Lynch's *Cambrensis eversus*, published in Latin at St Malo in 1662. John Lynch's major polemical history, *Cambrensis eversus*, itself owed much to Keating's work. Yet, it is clear that Lynch had a number of manuscripts from various sources at his disposal when preparing his book in Galway in the late 1650s. He had access to the recently compiled genealogies of Dubhaltach Mac Fhirbhisigh for his chapter linking the Stuart kings to the various Irish royal lines.[33] Mac Fhirbhisigh was probably also his source for early Irish law tracts, the appearance of which Lynch could describe in detail:

> I saw a great number of thick volumes of Irish laws, with the text written in large characters, and a large space between the lines, to admit more conveniently in smaller letters a glossary on the meaning of the words. The page was covered over with copious commentaries, inserted between the text, as are usually seen in compilations of canon or civil law.[34]

---

30 Todd (ed.), 'Autograph letter of Thady O'Roddy', 123.   31 E. Lhuyd to Tancred Robinson, 25 Aug. 1700, cited in O'Sullivan and O'Sullivan, 'Edward Lhuyd's collection of Irish manuscripts', 65.   32 T. Molyneux to E. Lhuyd, 10 Aug. 1702 in Hoppen (ed.), *Papers of the Dublin Philosophical Society*, ii, 716.   33 John Lynch, *Cambrensis eversus, seu potius historica fides in rebus Hibernicis Giraldo Cambrensi abbrogata*, ed. and trans. Matthew Kelly (3 vols, Dublin, 1848–52), iii, 32–143; see Nollaig Ó Muraíle, 'Aspects of the intellectual life of seventeenth-century Galway' in Gerard Moran (ed.), *Galway: history and society* (Dublin, 1996), pp 158–9.   34 Lynch, *Cambrensis eversus*, ii, 374–5, cited in Ó Muraíle, 'Aspects of the intellectual life', p. 159.

(Vidi ego plura e pergameno spissa legume Hibernicarum volumina, et in illis textum character grandiori conscriptum lineis modice disjunctis faciliori vocum interpretione minutioribus literis inserta. Uberiora commentaria per paginam diffusa textum obibant eadem omnino ratione qua textum et glossam in libris utriusque juris aspicimus.)

Lynch acknowledged that he used transcripts of material Mac Fhirbhisigh had earlier extracted from these sources. He then went on to explain that

> As the laws themselves have been long since excluded from the courts, they would have fallen into oblivion, if a small number of persons, inspired by an innate zeal to save their native language from ruin, had not resolved to study them, and thus by their voluntary exertions, rescue from the fate to which the English so often attempted to consign it by their prohibitory and penal enactments.

> (Leges illae jampridem tribunalibus exclusae in desuetudinem penitus abiissent nisi pauci admodum innato quodam linguae patriae ab interitu vendicandae studio capti iis addiscendis incubuissent; operam ultro impendentes ad illam ruinae subducendam, quam illi multoties Angli intentabant, eam comprimere lata lege saepius aggressi.)[35]

Conscious of the importance of consulting older vernacular manuscripts when engaged in historical research, Lynch praised William Camden's methodology, noting:

> It affords great confidence to his reader, and reflects great renown on himself, that Camden had diligently studied both the English and Saxon languages. It enabled him to draw his writings not from the streamlets, but from the fountain head, and thus impart to his narrative that high authenticity which can only be found in those venerable documents, written in the vernacular language of the country, whose ancient history is to be published.

> (Magnam certudinem lectori et memorabilem commendationem sibi Camdenus peperit: quod linguae Britannicae, et Saxonicae sedulo incubuerit. Hinc enim ea quae literis mandavit, non e rivulis, sed e fontibus illum hausisse perspectum habemus, si quidem nulla est exploratior narration, quam quae veteris memoriae monumentis vernacular patriae cujus rei priscae in lucem producuntur lingua exaratis eruitur.)[36]

---

35 Lynch, *Cambrensis eversus*, ii, 374–5. 36 Ibid., 376–7.

John Lynch strove to emulate Camden in his use of vernacular manuscripts. In this context, Ó Muraíle has observed that Lynch displayed a thorough knowledge of Seán Mór Ó Dubhagáin's topographical poem, 'Triallam
timcheall na Fódla',[37] and was able to outline in detail the succession of early
Irish kings. Lynch also drew extensively on the Book of Uí Mháine, a late
fourteenth-century compilation of historical lore, which was then in the hands
of the Ó Ceallaigh family of Tonalig, county Roscommon.[38] Clearly, Lynch
and his circle, which included the renowned genealogist Dubhaltach Mac
Fhirbhisigh, had access to a significant collection of manuscripts in Galway
in the 1650s that he had acquired from hereditary learned families.[39] In all
probability, it was through Mac Fhirbhisigh that Lynch was able to access
such manuscript materials and, in that sense, Mac Fhirbhisigh probably
played a similar role to that of Conall MacGeoghegan in the early seventeenth
century.[40] While such transactions between Lynch and Mac Fhirbhisigh could
be interpreted as crossing a cultural frontier between Lynch, the Old English
classically educated priest, and Mac Fhirbhisigh, the representative of a
hereditary Gaelic learned family, it might equally be seen as a collaboration
between Galway-based Catholic scholars with a shared interest in how the
Irish past was portrayed.

V

While manuscripts certainly circulated and were used within a combined Old
English–Gaelic Irish context there is compelling evidence also that over time

---

37 James Carney (ed.), *Topographical poems by Seán Mór Ó Dubhagáin and Giola-na Naomh
Ó hUidhrín* (Dublin, 1943). More than 35 transcripts of this renowned poem survive in the
manuscript collection of the Royal Irish Academy. A version containing prose prefaces to
each section also existed in the seventeenth century (RIA, MS 23 N 28, in the hand of Cú
Choigcríche Ó Cléirigh). For an edition of this text that includes the prose, see John
O'Donovan (ed.), *The topographical poems of John O'Dubhagain and Giolla na naomh
O'Huidhrin* (Dublin, 1862). **38** RIA, MS D ii 1. Éamonn Ó Ceallaigh of Tonalig also had
the Leabhar Breac and a number of other Connacht manuscripts in the early eighteenth
century: see RIA, MS 23 P 16, p. 221, MS 23 O 35, p. 197 and possibly the copy of
Keating in RIA, MS 24 P 23. The passages cited by Lynch from Book of Uí Mháine are
itemised in detail in Nollaig Ó Muraíle, 'Leabhar ua Maine alias Leabhar uí Dhubhagáin',
Éigse, 23 (1989), 168–73. **39** On Lynch as historian, see P.J. Corish, 'Two contemporary
historians of the Confederation of Kilkenny: John Lynch and Richard O'Ferrall', *IHS*, 8
(1952–3), 217–36; Bernadette Cunningham, 'Representations of king, parliament and the
Irish people in Geoffrey Keating's *Foras feasa ar Éirinn* and John Lynch's *Cambrensis
Eversus* (1662)' in J.H. Ohlmeyer (ed.), *Political thought in seventeenth-century Ireland: kingdom or colony* (Cambridge, 2000), pp 131–54. **40** A letter from O'Flaherty to Lynch,
dated September 1665, which was printed as an introduction to the *Ogygia*, 1685, at pp 1–
24, discussed a range of sources for the chronology of Irish history, including the Annals
of the Four Masters, the Book of Lecan, and the Book of Uí Mháine, which he described
as 'a parchment book of O'Duvegan, antiquarian to the O'Kellys'.

New English settlers assumed a greater interest in the relics of an older Ireland for a number of reasons. The interest of Narcissus Marsh, provost of Trinity College in the 1680s and later archbishop of Dublin, in Irish manuscripts was probably linguistic, given his background as a scholar of Near Eastern languages. He certainly acquired a large Latin–Irish dictionary compiled by Richard Plunkett, OFM, comprising over 840 pages of closely written text in double columns. This work he deemed so valuable that he required a surety of £10 before lending it.[41] Marsh was not the only one to interest himself in this manuscript since it also attracted the attention of Thomas Molyneux and Edward Lhuyd.[42] Lhuyd arranged to have the dictionary copied, although the copyist made numerous transcription errors.[43] Dudley Loftus (1618–95), the oriental linguist and member of the Dublin Philosophical Society, was another who probably collected Irish-language manuscripts for their linguistic interest rather than their substantive content although it is notable that he also owned a copy of Keating's history in Irish, and made notes from it.[44] Loftus also had at least some contacts in the world of Irish learning, and he was fondly remembered by Roderic O'Flaherty as 'my great friend, Dr Loftus' more than ten years after his death.[45]

However, there were those who showed an interest in Irish-language manuscripts, sometimes in translation, for other reasons. The Cork-born lawyer and administrator, Sir Richard Cox (1650–1733), had access to an English translation of Keating, in manuscript, although in his own history of Ireland Cox referred to Keating's work mainly to dismiss it.[46] The transcript of Keating to which he had access is now preserved as NLI, MS G 293. It contains a note by Sir Robert Southwell to the effect that 'This book was lent by Sir John Percivale to Mr Cox. And returned to Sir R. Southwell in London March 1689/90' suggesting the borrowing and lending of such manuscripts was commonplace.[47] While Cox's history of Ireland, which he compiled in 1690, does not suggest any active engagement with the manuscript materials for early Irish history, he was at least curious about manuscripts. When he was on circuit in Connacht in 1699, he encountered the antiquary Tadhg Ó Rodaighe (1614–1706). Owner of some thirty Irish-language law books, Ó Rodaighe displayed them to his legal colleague, noting of the encounter: 'Sir

41 Marsh's Library, MS Z4.2.5; Thomas Molyneux to Edward Lhuyd, 10 Aug., 10 Nov. 1702, in Hoppen (ed.), *Papers of the Dublin Philosophical Society*, ii, 716, 719. 42 O'Sullivan and O'Sullivan, 'Edward Lhuyd's collection of Irish manuscripts', 70. 43 De Bhaldraithe, 'Risteard Pluincéad', 7; An extract from the copy of Plunkett's dictionary in Marsh's Library is extant in TCD, MS 1320. 44 Marsh's Library, MS Z4.2.5 (*Foras feasa*); MS Z4.2.11 (Loftus' Commonplace book); see Boran, 'Writing history in seventeenth-century Ireland', pp 216–17. 45 O'Flaherty to S. Molyneux, 9 Apr. 1708 in Hoppen (ed.), *Papers of the Dublin Philosophical Society*, ii, 825. O'Flaherty's *Ogygia* had included a printed approbation from Dudley Loftus when published in 1685, sig. B[3v]. 46 Richard Cox, *Hibernia Anglicana* (London, 1689–90), 'To the reader', sig. b1–1v. 47 NLI, MS G 293, 2nd flyleaf.

Richard Cox was once of opinion that our law was arbitrary, and not fixed
nor written, till I satisfied him to the contrary in summer 1699, by shewing
him some of the said lawe books.'[48] It appears that Ó Rodaighe may have
acquired these Irish legal manuscripts from the collection of the genealogist
Dubhaltach Mac Fhirbhisigh, and thus they were mostly the same manuscripts that had earlier been available to John Lynch.[49] Ó Rodaighe was proud
of his eclectic collection, boasting that he owned 'as many Irish books of philosophy, physicke, poetry, genealogys, mathematicke, invasions, law,
romances, etc., and as ancient as any in Ireland'.[50] Encounters such as that
between the manuscript collector, Ó Rodaighe, and Cox probably heightened
the consciousness of those who did not read Irish that the language barriers
to antiquarian research could be significant; they may have been marginally
less conscious of the way in which perceptions of cultural difference could
exacerbate the technical limitations that restricted access to these works. Cox's
intellectual home was among the members of the Dublin Philosophical
Society, many of whose active participants would have shared his dilemma of
simultaneous fascination with and dislike of aspects of the complex Irish cultural world he inhabited. The tension between perceptions of barbarity and
reality are clearly articulated in Edward Lhuyd's comments to Thomas
Molyneux in January 1700, in respect of his Scottish travels:

> though the highlanders be represented both in England and Ireland
> barbarous and inhospitable, we found 'em quite otherwise; the gentle-
> men, men of good sense and breeding, and the commons a subtle
> inquisitive people and more civil to strangers in directing them the way
> (the mean occasion we had of their kindness) than in most other coun-
> ties. The main cause of their being reputed barbarous I take to be not
> other than the roughness of their country, as consisting very much of
> barren mountains and loughs, and their retaining their ancient habits,
> custom, and language, on which very account many gentlemen of good
> sense in England esteem the the [sic] Welsh at this day barbarous and
> talk so much of wild Irish in this kingdom.[51]

Of such ambiguities were the early eighteenth-century world made.

Cox was not alone at either elite or popular level in his inquisitiveness
about Irish-language manuscripts. At the upper social level William King
(1650–1729), Antrim-born son of a Scottish settler, who became archbishop
of Dublin in 1703, began to engage seriously with Irish manuscript material

48 Ó Rodaighe to [Lhuyd], n.d., in *Miscellany of the Irish Archaeological Society*, i, 123.
49 O'Sullivan, 'The manuscript collection of Dubhaltach Mac Fhirbhisigh' in Smyth (ed.),
Seanchas: studies in early and medieval Irish archaeology, history and literature, 444.   50 Ó
Rodaighe to [Lhuyd], n.d., in *Miscellany of the Irish Archaeological Society*, i, p. 122.   51
Lhuyd to T. Molyneux, 29 Jan. 1699/1700 in Hoppen (ed.), *Papers of the Dublin
Philosophical Society*, ii, 700–1.

from about 1718. His account books show that in the following three years he regularly paid for transcripts of 'old records' and 'old manuscripts'. King was hoping to write an ecclesiastical history of Ireland, and as might be expected, some of the transcripts he commissioned were ecclesiastical sources in Latin.[52] It is noteworthy, however, that in April 1721 he paid £3 9s. 0d. for a transcript of the Psalter of Cashel, an investment that indicates that by then he was taking a serious interest in Irish-language material.[53] Lower in the social hierarchy Patrick Logan, a Quaker schoolmaster in county Armagh, commissioned a transcript of Keating's work from an Irish tenant on the Brownlow estate for the Advocates' Library at Edinburgh. He was confident that the language of the text would not be a problem, since 'these that have the Irish language will explain it'.[54] Among the Protestant intellectuals who most actively engaged with Irish manuscripts was Anthony Raymond (1675–1726), the Kerry-born son of an English settler. He was a graduate of Trinity College, Dublin, and served as vicar of Trim, county Meath, from 1705 until his death. Raymond was among those who claimed to have learned Irish using a grammar and a dictionary.[55] By the late 1710s he had studied the language to a level to be a competent and ambitious translator.[56] Towards the end of his life, he prepared an English translation of Keating's *Foras feasa*, but was beaten by Dermod O'Connor in the race into print.[57] The well-documented row that ensued between Raymond and O'Connor was particularly bitter precisely because their ambitions and interests were so similar despite their differing cultural backgrounds.

Anthony Raymond's interest in Irish manuscripts may have been inspired by Edward Lhuyd's *Archaeologia Britannica*.[58] His translation of Lhuyd's Irish preface to that work was later published by William Nicolson.[59] Raymond established close contacts from about 1718 with the Dublin circle of scribes centred on Tadhg Ó Neachtain, and he commissioned copies of manuscripts from them. The Dublin scribes used an Irish version of his name, 'Uaine Raimon',[60] and Tadhg Ó Neachtain corresponded with him in Irish. To aid his various researches, Raymond sought to buy Irish manuscripts in the

---

52 Gillespie, 'Manuscript collectors in the age of Marsh', p. 247.   **53** TCD, MS 751/3, f. 143. For the identity and contents of the 'Psalter of Cashel', see Pádraig Ó Riain, 'The psalter of Cashel: a provisional list of contents', *Éigse*, 23 (1989), 107–30.   **54** NLS, Advocates MS 33.4.11, f. vi. See also Cunningham and Gillespie, 'Patrick Logan', 146–52. **55** RIA, MS 24 G 11, p. 369. **56** Harrison, *The dean's friend*, p. 90. **57** For the detail of the dispute over the publication of an English translation of Keating's *Foras feasa*, see Diarmuid Ó Catháin, 'Dermot O'Connor, translator of Keating', *Eighteenth-century Ireland*, 2 (1987), 67–87; Harrison, *The dean's friend*, pp 105–48. **58** Harrison, *The dean's friend*, pp 92–3; Alan Harrison, 'Who wrote to Edward Lhuyd', *Celtica*, 16 (1984), 269–72. **59** Nicolson, *Irish historical library*, pp 191–215. **60** RIA, MS 24 P 41, part C, p. 300, contains the poem beginning with the line 'Éire oll i gcaoch-cheo atá', addressed by Tadhg Ó Neachtain to Anthony Raymond. The poem is published in Alan Harrison, *Ag cruinniú meala: Anthony Raymond (1675–1726): ministéir Protastúnach agus léann na Gaeilge i*

rapidly commercializing world, and he used the Dublin scribes to establish contacts with owners. Where owners were unwilling to sell, he commissioned transcripts.[61] His aim to acquire a full transcript of the Book of Lecan foundered when he was quoted a price of £1,000.[62] However, he did succeed in borrowing the similar compilation known as the Book of Ballymote from the library of Trinity College, Dublin, in 1719, apparently with the assistance of his former tutor, Owen Lloyd (1664–1738). Indeed, the Book of Ballymote appears to have remained in the possession of the Dublin scribal circle for some years after Raymond's sudden death in London in 1726. As well as facilitating access to manuscripts in Trinity College, through men such as Owen Lloyd, Raymond was also a link in the chain between the group of provincial-born Dublin-based Irish scholars most of whom were Catholics and the Anglo-Irish and predominantly protestant world of the Dublin Philosophical Society.[63] Owen Lloyd was serving as Professor of Divinity in Trinity College in 1700 when he assisted Edward Lhuyd in his enquiries about the work of the ninth-century writer known as 'Nennius'. He was able to relate that the relevant text was contained in the 'Book of Sligo', the manuscript better known as the Book of Lecan. However, he also had to admit that the manuscript was then missing from the college: 'we had the misfortune to lose ours in the late troubles and I cannot direct you where to find another'. Nor was Lloyd optimistic about finding Irish scholars locally, advising the Welshman that 'The county of Leitrim is as likely a place as any where you may meet with men that are able to write and read Irish.'[64] Owen Lloyd also took an interest in an early medieval gospel book, probably to be identified as the Book of Durrow, which Marsh had apparently borrowed from the College, and Lloyd was able to offer his own opinion as to its likely antiquity.[65]

Sufficient overlaps developed to ensure a fruitful collaboration between the networks of the Dublin scribes working with Irish-language manuscripts and the networks of the scholars who associated themselves with the Dublin Philosophical Society. Borrowing and lending of manuscripts became routine, and Dublin-based scribes, many of whom had rural roots, became a pivotal point of contact between hereditary owners and potential antiquarian collectors.[66] Thus, the Church of Ireland minister, John Keogh of Strokestown, county Roscommon, though no longer an active participant in the work of the Dublin Philosophical Society, was identified as one source of Irish manuscript

mBaile Átha Cliath (Baile Átha Cliath, 1988), pp 58–60. See also, Harrison, *The dean's friend*, pp 68–9. **61** Harrison, *The dean's friend*, p. 95. **62** RIA, MS 24 G 11, p. 122, cited in Harrison, *The dean's friend*, p. 94. **63** Hoppen (ed.), *Papers of the Dublin Philosophical Society*, ii, 952. **64** O. Lloyd to Lhuyd, 17 Feb. 1700 in Hoppen (ed.), *Papers of the Dublin Philosophical Society*, ii, 707. **65** O. Lloyd to Lhuyd, 23 Mar. 1700 in Hoppen (ed.), *Papers of the Dublin Philosophical Society*, ii, 708. For the identification of this gospel book as the Book of Durrow, see William O'Sullivan, 'The donor of the Book of Kells', *IHS*, 11 (1958–9), 5–7. **66** Harrison, *The dean's friend*, pp 51–3.

material.[67] In Keogh's earlier contribution on county Roscommon, written for William Molyneux's natural history project, he had made explicit reference to one of his own circle of contacts through whom Irish manuscripts could be accessed:

> There are in this county some Irish chroniclers, my neighbours, and one among the rest, the best of them all, who, if he pleased, might give a most exact account of any part of Ireland, for matter of antiquities and rarities, with the names and etymologies mentioned in the queries by the help of Irish records in manuscripts, many of which he is admirably well acquainted withal. Expecting his resolves, and willing to give you the most exact account of some topics, I therefore hitherto delayed writing to you; but finding him slack of performance, and all because he expected some hire (for he says he cannot procure some necessary books without going far for them and something to bear his charges) and not knowing what hire to proportion, I thought good herein to expect your advice'.[68]

The activities of Anthony Raymond, Owen Lloyd and the Dublin Philosophical Society point to the importance of institutional activity in identifying and gathering Irish manuscripts in the late seventeenth century. In particular, the collection held in Trinity College, Dublin was vital to manuscript scholars. The college had acquired Archbishop Ussher's collection in the 1650s and others deemed it an appropriate place to deposit Irish manuscripts.[69] Bishop Jones of Meath, for instance, donated both the Book of Kells and the Book of Durrow. The late seventeenth-century provosts, Narcissus Marsh and his successor Robert Huntington, both promoted the acquisition of manuscripts, whether Irish or Oriental, as part of the scholarly study of language and theology.[70] This absorption of Irish manuscripts into institutional repositories in the late seventeenth century effectively restricted access to them for their hereditary owners, though as already seen channels did exist through which access to particular manuscripts could be arranged for selected individuals.

The engagement with this new group of settler scholars in an institutional context reshaped the canon of authoritative Irish manuscripts. In the early seventeenth century traditional learned families canonized a group of texts (some of which, such as the Psalter of Tara, were wholly fictional) that were part of the cultural power of that group.[71] As such, manuscripts derived their importance from being part of this canon, which formed the core of the cul-

67 C. Ussher to S. Molyneux, 15 Aug. 1708 in Hoppen (ed.), *Papers of the Dublin Philosophical Society*, ii, 849. 68 John Keogh's account of Roscommon (TCD, MS 883/1, p. 159). 69 Barnard, 'The purchase of Archbishop Ussher's library', 9–14. 70 Barnard, *Improving Ireland*, pp 95–6; O'Sullivan, 'Donor of the Book of Kells', 5–6. 71 For the canon as articulated by the learned class, see Lambert McKenna (ed.), *Iomarbhádh na*

tural literacy of those who arbitrated on the past and made it relevant to the present. With the shifts in sources of cultural authority that subsequently took place, this canon became less relevant to contemporary needs and new principles emerged for selecting which manuscripts one might aspire to read or copy. This process of defining a canon of Irish-language manuscripts for English-language readers within a new institutional setting is clear from William Nicolson's *Irish historical library*, published in Dublin in 1724. This followed the pattern of his successful *English historical library* first published in parts between 1696 and 1699 and reissued in an enlarged edition in 1714. Nicolson's work proved enduring, and his combined *English, Scotch and Irish historical libraries*, was published posthumously in 1736 and reissued in yet another edition forty years later. Nicolson's work on Ireland aimed to highlight 'the authors and records in print or manuscript, which may be serviceable to the compilers of a general history of Ireland'.[72] For there to be a market for his work presupposed an environment in which there were scholars keen to write just such a history and a structure to support their work. Nicolson judged that this was indeed the case. Nicolson's readers would also have known Lhuyd's *Archaeologia Britannia* (1707), a highly influential work that may have broadened people's perception of what constituted research on Irish affairs.

When compiling his *Irish historical library* (1724), William Nicolson claimed that he sourced his information 'out of the publick and private libraries of both kingdoms'.[73] The network that Nicolson drew on was that created by seventeenth-century antiquarian collectors including Robert Cotton, James Ussher, James Ware and later Robert Harley (1661–1724) and his son Edward Harley (1689–1741), and the institutional libraries that eventually absorbed their collections.[74] He also had access to the library of John Stearne, bishop of Clogher (1660–1745), which was based on collections assembled by John Madden[75] and by James Brydges, duke of Chandos (1674–1744), who had acquired some manuscripts assembled by James Ware, comprising 'old annals, chronicles, laws, synodical constitutions, register-books, lives of saints, etc'.[76] Nicolson was well aware that his account of source materials for Irish history should include sources in the Irish language as well as

bhfileadh: the contention of the bards (2 vols, ITS, London, 1918), i, poems 15 and 21; O'Donovan (ed.), *Annals of the Four Masters*, i, prelims, pp lxiv–lxvii; David Comyn and P.S. Dinneen (eds), *Foras feasa ar Éirinn: the history of Ireland, by Geoffrey Keating* (4 vols, ITS, London, 1902–14), i, 78–81; Cecile O'Rahilly (ed.), *Five seventeenth-century political poems* (Dublin, 1977), pp 42–3.   **72** Title page (1724 ed.).   **73** William Nicolson, *Irish historical library: pointing at most of the authors in print or manuscript which may be serviceable to the compilers of a general history of Ireland* (Dublin, 1724), p. x.   **74** Nicolson, *Irish historical library*, pp x–xi.   **75** William O'Sullivan, 'John Madden's manuscripts' in Vincent Kinane and Anne Walsh (eds), *Essays on the history of Trinity College Library* (Dublin, 2000), pp 104–15.   **76** Nicolson, *Irish historical library*, p. xii. For the identification of Chandos manuscripts formerly owned by Ware, see O'Sullivan, 'A finding list of Sir James

in English.[77] Relying primarily on Keating and O'Flaherty as his authorities, Nicolson noted the existence of the Book of Armagh, the Psalter of Cashel and Book of Glendalough, and reiterated Keating's assertions about Irish attention to the historical record in a manuscript known as the 'Psalter of Tara'.[78] Adopting a systematic approach to the recording of manuscripts, Nicolson classified Irish historical evidence into eight categories: geography and natural history; general history; ecclesiastical history; lives of saints; register books of cathedrals and monasteries; other Irish biographers, Irish records and law books; and, finally, antiquarian artefacts such as coins and medals. Having devoted a chapter to each of these categories of sources, he was conscious that his treatment of Irish-language manuscript sources was still incomplete. To compensate for this Nicolson inserted an appendix comprising 'an alphabetical account of several ancient Irish historians, annals, etc., mention'd and referr'd by Dr Keating; which are either barely nam'd, or wholly omitted in the foregoing chapters'.[79] In compiling this list, Nicolson explained that he drew upon the Dublin edition of the newly published translation of Keating's work, issued the previous year.[80] This admission is a further indication that Nicolson's world was essentially the world of print, which provided a restricted, mediated access to the manuscript world. It is also an early acknowledgment of the attractiveness of the printed edition of Keating's work as a guide to the nature of Irish-language manuscripts. It was an illustration of the way in which the public sphere of Irish scholarship relied on the mediation of a print culture that, for commercial reasons, was necessarily in Latin or English.

In Nicolson's guide to Irish historical writing, printed works were prioritized over manuscript sources, but he was aware of the importance of the extant Irish annals, and of medieval compilations such as the Book of Lecan, which he termed 'Arch-bishop Usher's and Mr Flaherty's great oracle'.[81] There was greater focus on manuscript sources in Nicolson's chapter on saints' lives – necessarily so – but his footnotes indicate that much of his discussion on saints, too, was derived from the published works of James Ussher, James Ware and John Colgan.[82] Given the resources at his disposal,

Ware's manuscripts'. **77** Nicolson, *Irish historical library*, p. xii. **78** Nicolson, *Irish historical library*, pp xviii–xix. For Keating's traditional view of the Psalter of Tara, see Comyn and Dinneen (eds), *Foras feasa ar Éirinn*, ii, 250; iii, 32–3. Eighteenth-century commentators cast doubt on the existence of this manuscript and ridiculed Dermot O'Connor's claims that he had consulted it when preparing his translation of Keating's history (Cunningham, *World of Geoffrey Keating*, pp 221, 224). However, some scholars clung to the belief that the 'Psalter of Tara' was contained within the Book of Ballymote, and a manuscript written by Tadhg Ó Neachtain contains a list of contents of the Book of Ballymote and extracts from it under the title 'The Psalter of Tara rewritten by Tadhg Ó Neachtain': Harrison, *The dean's friend*, pp 137–8, citing TCD, MS 1361 [H. 4. 20], p. 1. **79** Nicolson, *Irish historical library*, pp 179–90. **80** Geoffrey Keating, *The general history of Ireland ... collected by the learned Jeoffry Keating ... faithfully translated from the Irish ... by Dermo'd O'Connor* (Dublin, 1723). **81** Nicolson, *Irish historical library*, p. 38.

Nicolson's was a very creditable effort at itemizing an 'Irish historical library', and one that clearly demonstrated an awareness of the extent to which historical investigation necessarily transcended linguistic and cultural boundaries. He did not make an issue of the point; his work simply reflected the outcome of a process of cultural exchange through the loan and purchase of Irish manuscripts that had been a routine feature of Irish historical scholarship over the previous hundred years.

VI

By the end of the seventeenth century contemporaries were aware that many manuscripts had recently been lost or destroyed. Thus, Edward Lhuyd noted in 1700 that 'the Irish have many more ancient manuscripts than we in Wales but since the late revolution they are much lessened'.[83] However a good deal survived outside an institutional context in the private hands of settlers and some native Irish. Nicholson, for instance, was only too well aware that some of the more significant Irish-language sources still existed outside institutions. Among private collectors, for example, Arthur Brownlow, the third-generation settler who had made his home in county Armagh and whose family had married into all the ethnic groups in Irish society, engaged in a process of manuscript acquisition as part of his attempt to understand the world in which he lived.[84] Brownlow, a member of successive Dublin parliaments from 1692 until his death in 1710, was deemed by Samuel Molyneux to be unusual in that he was able to read the Irish manuscripts in his possession.[85] His knowledge of Irish was sufficient to allow him translate a poetic elegy on Eoghan Ruadh Ó Néill from Irish to English.[86]

For Brownlow to gain an understanding of the world of Armagh that existed before his family had made their home there, it was necessary to extend his interests beyond the cultural world of his own family into that of the Gaelic families who had lived in the region in earlier generations. His particular interest in Eoghan Ruadh Ó Néill apparently stemmed from the fact

---

82 Ibid., pp 84–107.   83 R.T. Gunter (ed.), *Early science in Oxford, XIV: life and letters of Edward Lhuyd* (Oxford, 1945), p. 430.   84 Bernadette Cunningham and Raymond Gillespie, 'An Ulster settler and his Irish manuscripts' *Éigse*, 21 (1986), 27–36; Breandán Ó Buachalla, 'Arthur Brownlow, a gentleman more curious than ordinary', *Ulster Local Studies*, 7:2 (1982), 24–8; Éamonn Ó Tuathail, 'Arthur Brownlow and his MSS', *Irish Book Lover*, 24 (1936), 26–8.   85 Molyneux, 'Journey to ye north' in Young, *Historical notices of old Belfast*, p. 154.   86 For an edition of Brownlow's translation of 'Do chaill Éire a céile fircheart', see Ó Buachalla, 'Arthur Brownlow', pp 24–8. Brownlow's grandmother, Elinor O'Doherty, was an Irish woman from Derry, and it seems that both his mother and grandmother were Irish speakers. Brownlow himself spent his youth in an Irish-speaking region in Louth, moving to Armagh only when he inherited property there: Cunningham and Gillespie, 'An Ulster settler', p. 28.

that Brownlow's estate comprised part of Eoghan Ruadh's former lands.[87] In 1707 Edward Lhuyd, fresh from a manuscript collecting tour of Ireland, published lists of manuscripts that he had seen and identified their owners.[88] Lhuyd recorded twelve Irish manuscripts in Brownlow's collection, omitting an Irish grammar, which he also saw, and the Book of Armagh, presumably because it was in Latin.[89] Among the items in Brownlow's possession were Keating's *Foras feasa ar Éirinn* and Mícheál Ó Cléirigh's recension of the *Leabhar gabhála* (Book of invasions). Also in his possession was the *Leabhar Eoghanach* which largely consisted of genealogies of the Uí Néill who were Brownlow's predecessors on his Armagh lands. Now preserved in that same manuscript are poems addressed to the O'Neills of Clandeboy, and the manuscript bears an inscription in Irish indicating that it was in the possession of Arthur Brownlow on 1 August 1689.[90]

In instances where Brownlow commissioned particular manuscripts, we get a glimpse into the world of his cultural networks. A number of the Irish tenants on his estates were competent if not expert scribes. Séamás Ó Gruibín, for instance, made a copy of Keating's *Foras feasa* in 1696 and he also provided a manuscript for the friars in Armagh.[91] In 1685, Brownlow commissioned Pádraig Mac Óghanáin to transcribe a copy of *Cath Maighe Léana* (the Battle of Magh Lena),[92] an initiative that suggests direct contact with the world of Gaelic scribes. Brownlow also acquired one medieval Ulster manuscript of major importance, the ninth-century Patrician compilation now known as the 'Book of Armagh'.[93] This was the manuscript cited by Ussher a generation earlier as '*Codex Ecclesiae Armachanae*'.[94] The Book of Armagh was sold in the late seventeenth century by its hereditary keepers, to pay for expenses arising out of the 'Popish Plot', and it appears to have found its way into Brownlow's possession about that time.[95] It may simply be that Brownlow was in the right place at the right time, but he clearly had already established the contacts necessary to make this very significant acquisition.

Just a few years later than Brownlow, another Ulsterman, Brian Maguire of Knockninny, was actively assembling another collection of Irish historical, literary and devotional manuscripts for his own use in county Fermanagh. In the 1710s and 1720s Brian Maguire commissioned some 2,000 pages of Irish manuscript text that shed light on his ancestry, the history of his family and his locality. His most significant act of cultural patronage may have been the commissioning of a new 'Book of Knockninny' a compilation of historical lore that claimed to be derived from the Book of Lecan, the Psalter of Cashel, the

87 Cunningham and Gillespie, 'An Ulster settler', 34. 88 O'Sullivan and O'Sullivan, 'Edward Lhuyd's collection of Irish manuscripts', 57–76. 89 Lhuyd, *Archaeologia Britannica*, p. 436. 90 RIA, MS 24 P 22, f. 25. 91 Cunningham and Gillespie, 'Patrick Logan', p. 146; RIA, MS 24 L 17. 92 RIA, MS 24 L 36. 93 John Gwynn (ed.), *Liber Ardmachanus: the Book of Armagh* (Dublin, 1913). 94 Elrington and Todd (eds), *Whole works of James Ussher*, iv, 318, 330. 95 Gwynn (ed.), *Liber Ardmachanus*, pp xiii–xiv, cxix.

Book of Clonmacnoise, Keating's *Foras feasa* and other such traditional historical sources.[96] But just as Arthur Brownlow's interest in local and family history encouraged him to cross cultural boundaries in search of historical evidence, so Brian Maguire's resort to history for justification of his current social status prompted him to cross cultural boundaries also. Thus it was that Captain Brian Maguire 'erected a stately tomb over his [father's] body with his achievements and ensigne armorial engravened thereon'.[97] This action indicates that this branch of the Maguires had assumed a coat of arms to enhance their gentry status within late seventeenth-century Fermanagh society. The arms are still clearly visible on the tombstone, which survives at the east wall of Callowhill graveyard, at Derrylin, county Fermanagh, though the stone carving appears to have been the work of an amateur.[98] Although Brian Maguire commissioned an extensive collection of manuscript material in the Irish language on his local and family history, the inscription on the tombstone he erected in memory of his father was in English and it used English heraldic devices.[99] The world within which Brian Maguire sought advancement was clearly a transitional one, and he embraced elements of both native and settler culture in his quest for enhanced status and respect. In terms of the historical manuscripts he valued most highly, it is clear that for him the canon of authoritative texts consisted of those that had been deemed important by the Four Masters and Geoffrey Keating almost a century earlier:

> They brought together from every quarter the chief books of Conquest and the histories of the kingdom to Knockninny, so that house is the source and dwelling-place of the best Knowledge to be found in Ireland. No one need henceforth search for more perfect or more reliable authorities than the books of Knockninny, if he is prepared to trust The Book of Lecan Mic Firbhisigh, the books of O Clérigh, of O Duigenan and of O Maelconaire, the Psalter of Cashel, the books of Clonmacnois, the Poem of Ua Dubhagáin, and Doctor Keating, with many other compilations approved by different authorities.[1]
>
> (cruinniughadh leó as gach aird priomhleabhair ghabhála agus dheadheólais na ríghtheachta go Cnoc Ninne, ionnas gurab é sin tiobraid agus áras deadh-eólais as oirdheirce a meastar a bheith a nÉirinn re cían d'aimsir ionnas nach righthar a leas, eólas as foirfe nó as barántamhla nó

---

96 RIA, MS C vi 1; The preface to this manuscript is edited and translated in Paul Walsh, *Irish men of learning*, pp 241–5; see also, Bernadette Cunningham and Raymond Gillespie, 'The purposes of patronage': Brian Maguire of Knockninny and his manuscripts', *Clogher Record*, 13:1 (1988), 38–49 at 44–5.   97 P. Ó Maolagáin (ed.), 'An early history of Fermanagh', *Clogher Record*, 2 (1957–9), 291.   98 Personal visit to site, Summer 1988. 99 The inscription is no longer fully legible but part of it reads 'This monument was erected / by Brien Maguire for his be / loved father Knogher Mo / Doerre Maguire and his / posterity who lyeth hereunder / and dyed in February'.   1 Translation of the

Leabhar Chnuic Ninne d'iarraidh ó so amach, más firinneach Leabhar
Leacáin Mic Firbhisigh, Leabhar Uí Chléirigh agus Uí Dhuibhgeannáin
agus Uí Mhaoilchonaire, Saltair Chaisil, Leabhair Chluana mic Nóis,
Duain Uí Dhubhagán agus Doctúir Kéatinn mar aon re morán
collections oile atá ar na ndearbadh ó dheadh-ughdaraibh oile).[2]

The books of Ó Cléirigh, Ó Duibhgeannáin and Ó Maoilchonaire mentioned
here echo the sources cited by the Four Masters while the 'poem of Ua
Dubhagáin' was Seán Mór Ó Dubhagáin's (d.1372) historical poem, 'Triallam
timcheall na Fódla', a work well known to the learned.[3] Brian Maguire of
Knockninny continued as a patron throughout his life, commissioning copies
of a wide range of manuscripts, including Mac Fhirbhisigh's genealogies,
Keating's *Trí biorghaoithe an bháis* (Three shafts of death), and the *Leabhar
Gabhála*.[4] He also acquired a fifteenth-century medical manuscript which he
arranged to have rebound, c.1700. This significant acquisition has been
described as 'a representative medical library', and is the largest known medical compilation from medieval Ireland.[5] Maguire was not alone in his interests for in 1721 the descendants of the MacNamaras in Clare were engaged
in a similar exercise employing Aindrias Mac Cruitín to transcribe the late
medieval text *Caithréim Thoirdhealbhaigh* which recounted events in Thomond
in the later Middle Ages.[6] The canon of key manuscripts was slow to change,
but they now existed in a bilingual world and, through the work of scribes
and translators, those texts were made available to new audiences.

VII

For multi-lingual Irish Catholic writers such as Geoffrey Keating, Roderic
O'Flaherty and Hugh McCurtin, the English and Latin languages were channels through which they accessed the wider world of print. Their works
incorporated material from printed works in these languages without difficulty. Indeed, those who were bilingual in Irish and English and who also
knew Latin had an advantage over those educated in English and Latin only,
and Irish scholars did not tire of pointing this out. Keating had been

scribe's testimonial preserved in RIA, MS C vi 1, printed in Paul Walsh, *Irish men of
learning*, pp 244–5. 2 RIA, MS C vi 1, p. i, extract printed in Elizabeth FitzPatrick,
Catalogue of Irish manuscripts in the Royal Irish Academy, fasc. 21 (Dublin, 1940), p. 2700.
3 Carney (ed.), *Topographical poems*. See above, p. 82. 4 Cambridge University Library,
Add. MS 4205 (Keating); RIA, MS C vi 2 (Mac Fhirbhisigh); RIA, MS 23 K 45 (*Leabhar
Gabhála*). 5 NLI, MS G11. For a detailed description of this manuscript and its contents, see Ní Shéaghdha, *Cat. Ir. Mss in NLI*, fasc. 1, pp 63–93. 6 Mac Cruitín's transcript (TCD, MS 1292) was used in the edition of this text: Seán Mac Craith, *Caithréim
Thoirdhealbhaigh: the triumphs of Turlough*, ed. Standish Hayes O'Grady (2 vols, Dublin,
1929), i, 1.

emphatic on this point in the 1630s in his criticism of Richard Stanihurst and other writers. He rejected Stanihurst's qualifications to write history largely on the grounds that 'he was blindly ignorant in the language of the country in which were the ancient records and transactions of the territory, and of every people who had inhabited it; and, therefore, he could not know these things'.[7] Two generations later, O'Flaherty's review of the historical writing of Edmund Borlase[8] was similarly insistent on the need for a proper comprehension of manuscripts in the Irish language. In refuting Borlase's version of Irish history he observed 'the Dark side of the cloud was still towards the author as to the original of the Irish and their Chronicles of which he could not participate'.[9] Yet, such point scoring on the matter of the language of the manuscripts was not an argument for the centrality of the Irish language to the transmission of historical matter to new audiences. Rather, insofar as the technology of print was necessary for the dissemination of their ideas outside Ireland, printing in English or Latin was the chosen medium. Yet, for Keating and McCurtin, for example, though they lived a century apart, many aspects of their scholarship could be disseminated effectively to their core local readership in Irish and in manuscript.[10] Given the extraordinary influence of such transitional writers, the assumed canon of Irish history was slow to change. It still had a traditional audience, though one with increasingly eclectic interests, inspired by contacts across linguistic and cultural boundaries. Through the work of translators and synthesizers, the essence of the work of these Irish scholars also reached new audiences in other languages. Thus, the public sphere of historians writing in Irish in the seventeenth and early eighteenth centuries was never a monoglot Irish one. Rather it was a multi-lingual public sphere that embraced manuscript and print in a variety of languages and for diverse audiences. While the scope of historical writing was constrained by partisan religious and political allegiances, the underlying interest in manuscript sources, and the consequent interaction over exchange of manuscript materials, was more catholic. The pursuit of documentary research into Irish history and antiquities necessitated the repeated crossing of cultural frontiers. The ensuing encounters, exemplified by the exchange of manuscript materials, did not always imply a meeting of minds, but it did alert the participants to the nuances and complexities of cultural worlds beyond their own. As with the learned in Europe since the beginnings of the Renaissance, an awareness of cultural difference and a willingness to pursue research even when it led to engagement with unfamiliar or problematic

7 Comyn and Dinneen (eds), *Foras feasa ar Éirinn*, i, 42–3. (Do bhí sé dall aineolach i dteangaidh na tíre i n-a raibhe seanchus agus seandála na críche, agus gach foirne d'ár áitigh innte; agus mar sin, níor bh'fhéidir dó a bhfios do bheith aige.)   8 Edmund Borlase, *The history of the execrable Irish rebellion, trac'd from many preceding acts to the grand eruption, 23 October 1641* (London, 1680).   9 TCD, MS 883/2, p. 332.   10 Vincent Morley, *An crann os coill: Aodh Buí Mac Cruitín, c.1680–1755* (Baile Átha Cliath, 1995); Cunningham, *World of Geoffrey Keating*, pp 201–25.

sources from other cultures was an essential feature of scholarship in the humanities.[11] It was sometimes a problematic position. Ussher's hostile attitude to Catholicism in his writings was at odds with his known collaboration with individual Franciscans in his pursuit of manuscript sources he needed for his research.[12] The manuscript collector and New English administrator Sir George Carew, likewise, has been portrayed as being 'simultaneously repelled and fascinated by Irish culture and society'.[13] Scholars interested in Ireland's past, from all cultural backgrounds, embraced the culture of print in English and Latin for both their reading and publishing endeavours. While not all made the commercial move into print with their own writings, enough did so to demonstrate that by the early eighteenth century the public sphere of Irish-language scholarship was one that transcended the supposed cultural boundaries as defined by language or religious allegiance or as defined by any dichotomy between manuscript and print.

11 For instances among scholars working with classical texts, see Anthony Grafton, *Defenders of the text* (Harvard, 1991), pp 23–46.   12 O'Sullivan, 'Correspondence of David Rothe and James Ussher', passim; Cunningham and Gillespie, 'James Ussher and his Irish manuscripts', 83–5.   13 Terry Clavin, 'Carew, Sir George' in *DIB*.

3

The popular influence of *Foras feasa ar Éirinn* from the seventeenth to the nineteenth century

VINCENT MORLEY

In 1725 Seán Ó Murchú na Ráithíneach, a poet from county Cork, addressed a poem to one Dónall Mac Cairteáin in which he asked to borrow a manuscript copy of Geoffrey Keating's *Foras feasa ar Éirinn* ('a foundation of knowledge about Ireland') for the purpose of transcribing it. Ó Murchú praised his correspondent's generosity, acknowledged the inadequacies of his own education ('is anbhfann riamh me i ndiaidh na bhfáidh ag rith') and pledged his undying gratitude should Mac Cairteáin agree to lend him the book. Recognizing the value of the manuscript, Ó Murchú concluded his appeal by offering two *moidores* – a sum then equivalent to £3 Irish or £2 14*s*. sterling – as a deposit that would be forfeit if he failed to return the volume to its owner in good condition:

> I ngá an leighis sin ós deimhneach me i ngalar tar fóir,
> is ráim foilseach gur shaibhreas liom a amharc ar ló,
> d'fháil radhairc air bead foighneach á bhreacadh fám dhóid
> dá *mhoidore* go bhfaighirse nó an leabhar i gcló.[1]

> (As I am certainly in need of that medicine in a grievous illness, I declare openly that viewing it for a day would be wealth in my opinion, to have sight of it I will patiently give it under my hand that you will receive two *moidores* or the book in good shape.)

Assuming that the amount of the deposit reflected the replacement value of the manuscript, and given that Keating's history runs to some 140,000 words, this suggests a scribal tariff at the time of about 1*d*. per two hundred words. In any event, the poem had the desired effect and Ó Murchú noted that he

---

This material has previously appeared in chapter 3 of Vincent Morley, *Ó Chéitinn go Raiftearaí: mar a cumadh stair na hÉireann* (Baile Átha Cliath, 2011), a study of the formation of the vernacular historical tradition. 1 'Torna' [Tadhg Ó Donnchadha] (eag.), *Seán na Ráithíneach* (Baile Átha Cliath, 1954), p. 63. I have normalized the orthography and punctuation of Irish quotations in verse; all translations are mine.

received Mac Cairteáin's copy of Keating's history on 8 July 1725 and retained it until his transcription was finished.[2]

Nearly a century later, in 1816, Maoileachlainn Ó Comhraí, a Clare-born poet and elder brother of the distinguished scholar Eoghan Ó Comhraí, addressed a similar request to Philip Ó Leidhin of Croom, county Limerick. Like Ó Murchú, Ó Comhraí wished to make a copy of *Foras feasa ar Éirinn* for his own use. He too praised his correspondent's generosity and admitted that he needed a copy of the text in order to improve his knowledge of Irish history to a standard befitting a man of letters ('seanchas Gael ba mhéin liom a thaithí, de réir mar chleachtaíodh dáimhe'). Ó Comhraí did not offer a deposit, but he promised to handle the manuscript carefully and to protect it from the gaze of unsympathetic eyes while it remained in his possession:

> Aitim an leabhar so a thafann uait chugam gan mhoill,
> is ní heagal duit salachar ná sracadh ar bith dó, go deimhin,
> masla ná amharc súl fleascaigh de dhúrshliocht Gaill,
> go gcasad gan easpa é faoi mhaise chugat féin, Uí Leidhin.[3]

> (I beg for this book to be sent from you to me without delay, and you need have no fear of its being soiled or torn, nor indeed of any insult or scrutiny by a rascal of boorish English descent, until I return it in good condition to yourself, Ó Leidhin.)

Although the poet did not record the result of his appeal on this occasion, it would also appear to have been successful because a copy of *Foras feasa ar Éirinn* penned by Ó Comhraí in 1816 is extant.[4]

The similarity between the episodes described above conveys a strong impression of cultural continuity between the early eighteenth and early nineteenth centuries. This impression is reinforced when one considers the number of recognized authors from widely dispersed localities who are known to have transcribed Keating's history during the eighteenth and nineteenth centuries. In addition to those already mentioned, the list includes Aindrias Mac Cruitín (*c.*1650–1738), a native of west Clare; Eoghan Ó Caoimh (1656–1726) from county Cork; Aogán Ó Rathaille (*c.*1670–1729) from county Kerry; Tadhg Ó Neachtain (*c.*1671–*c.*1749), a resident of Dublin city; Seán Clárach Mac Dónaill (1691–1745) from north Cork; Peadar Ó Doirnín (*c.*1700–69) from county Louth; Seán Ó Tuama (1707/8–75) from east Limerick; Seán Ó Muláin (*c.*1750–1826), a resident of Cork city; and Art Mac Bionaid (1793–1879) from south Armagh.[5] This list refers only to manuscripts that have survived; many others must have been lost.

---

2 This manuscript appears to be lost: I have identified two copies of *Foras feasa ar Éirinn* written by Ó Murchú (Cambridge Add. 3095 and UCC 61) but both date from the 1750s. 3 NUIM C 15, pp 94–5. 4 RIA 23 Q 17. 5 Mac Cruitín copied RIA 23 O 10, 23 G 9, 23 E 10; BL Add. 27,910; NLI G.599; and Mount Mellaray 1. Ó Caoimh copied RIA 23

Furthermore, the literature of the period is littered with references that show the high regard in which *Foras feasa ar Éirinn* was held as an authoritative account of Ireland's early history, as a vindication of the country's status as an ancient Christian kingdom, and as a work of considerable literary merit. Writing in 1682, Dáibhí Ó Bruadair (1625–98), a Cork-born and Limerick-based poet, praised Keating's defence of the Irish past against the calumnies perpetrated by malicious authors of published histories:

> D'fhág Séathra fál scéithe ar cháil chlé gach údair
> dár éilnigh clár Fhéilim d'áirc bréag i bprionta.[6]

(Geoffrey left a protective barrier against the evil character of every author who besmirched Féilim's plain [Ireland] from a voracity for lies in print.)

When the Sligo-based poet Seán Ó Gadhra (1648–*c.*1720) commended Peter Walsh for his *A prospect of the state of Ireland* (London, 1682) – the earliest publication in English to draw substantially on Keating's history – he noted Walsh's faithfulness to his principal source with approval:

> Do scríobh go cumhra an t-údar céanna
> beatha na ríthe síos gan chlaonadh,
> a heaspaig is ceannas a cléire
> ó Phádraig anall gus an aimsir dhéanaigh;
> is do-bheir 'Oileán na Naomh' ar Éirinn;
> is do lean a stíl mar Dhochtúir Céitinn.[7]

(The same author elegantly wrote down the lives of the kings without distortion, her [Ireland's] bishops and clerical leadership from Patrick as far as recent times, and he calls Ireland the 'Isle of Saints', and his style followed that of Doctor Keating.)

Ó Gadhra's reference to Keating as '*dochtúir*' lent further credibility and prestige to his history, and his academic credentials were frequently cited by later authors. The practice of invoking Keating's authority in support of historical arguments can be seen in an elegy for Fr Philip Ó Raghallaigh (d.1722), which has been plausibly attributed to the county Louth poet Séamas Dall Mac Cuarta (*c.*1647–1733). The elegist validated his account of his subject's ancestry by invoking an unimpeachable authority:

E 23, 23 H 14; NLI G 17, G.117; UCC 62; and Limerick O. Ó Rathaille copied NLI G.226 and G.598. Ó Neachtain copied NLI G.192. Mac Domhnaill copied Fermoy 20. Ó Doirnín copied NLI G.190. Ó Tuama copied NLI G. 56. Ó Muláin copied NLI G.112. Mac Bionaid copied NLI G.536.   6 John MacErlean (ed.), *Duanaire Dháibhidh Uí Bhruadair*, ii (London, 1913), p. 280.   7 An tAthair Mac Domhnaill (eag.), *Dánta is amhráin Sheáin Uí Ghadhra* (Baile Átha Cliath, 1955), p. 14.

> Atá fianaise ag Céitinn céillí stuama
> i gcroinic na nGael cibé léifeas suas í,
> gurb ag Eochaidh na gcéimeann, an tréin-rí suaithní,
> scaras síol Néill le Raghallaigh is Ruarcaigh.[8]

> (Sensible prudent Keating has evidence in the chronicle of the Gaels, whoever will read it, that it is with Eochaidh of the dignities, the illustrious mighty king, that the progeny of Niall [Naoighiallach] separates from the O'Reillys and O'Rourkes.)

Although Keating noted that Eochaidh Muighmheadhon fathered both Niall Naoighiallach and Brian mac Eochaidh, he did not mention that the O'Reillys descended from the latter.[9] Nonetheless, the above quotation illustrates the status which *Foras feasa ar Éirinn* had achieved by the early eighteenth century as 'croinic na nGael' – a codified recital of the orthodox version of early Irish history. Keating's history was a yardstick against which other accounts of the past could be assessed. This is how Tadhg Gaelach Ó Súilleabháin (1715–95) – an author whose devotional verse was posthumously published under the title *Timothy Sullivan's Pious miscellany* – praised the intellectual accomplishments of the *spéirbhean* who appeared to him in a Jacobite *aisling* composed around the middle of the century:

> Is eagnach, éasca a léifeadh an Bíobla,
> starthacha Chéitinn, is tréithe na ndraoithe
> i Laidin, 's i nGréigis, i dtéacsanna díochta,
> le seanchas tréanmhar na Traoi thoir go líofa.[10]

> (Intelligently and readily she would read the Bible, Keating's tales, and the works of the poets in Latin, Greek and religious texts, and fluently the valiant history of Troy to the east.)

Evidently, the authority and prestige attaching to Keating's history in the field of native learning bore comparison with that enjoyed by sacred scripture in relation to religion, or the epics of Homer and Virgil in the classics. Similarly, when the county Armagh poet Art Mac Cumhaigh (*c.*1738–73) composed an elegy for one of the O'Neills of the Fews who died in 1769, he supported his assertions concerning the importance of the dead man's ancestors by citing three authorities – an important historical compilation prepared for the Clandeboy O'Neills which has been edited under the title *Leabhar Cloinne Aodha Buí*, a renowned but long-lost codex known as the 'Psaltar of Cashel', and *Foras feasa ar Éirinn*:

8 The poem beginning 'Is brúite atá Múrtún an uairse' in Seán S. Ó Gallchóir, 'Filíocht Shéamais Dhaill Mhic Cuarta' (MA thesis, Maynooth, 1967), p. 176.   9 Patrick Dineen (ed.), *Foras feasa ar Éirinn*, ii (London, 1908), p. 366.   10 Úna Nic Éinrí (eag.), *An cantaire siúlach: Tadhg Gaelach* (An Daingean, 2001), p. 167.

Tá an Leabhar Eoghanach fós dá mhíniú,
is Saltair Chaisil ag Cuileannán caoimh-ghlan,
is Dochtúir Céitinn 'na ndéidh dá scríobhadh,
gurbh iad Síol Néill thug an chéim 's an chraobh leo.[11]

(The *Leabhar Eoghanach* expounds it moreover, and the Psaltar of
Cashel by dear honest Cuileannán, and Doctor Keating after them
records it, that the dignity and the laurels were won by the progeny of
Niall [Naoighiallach].)

Keating continued to be cited as a historical authority in the nineteenth century, although not always accurately. For example, his name was invoked in
a metrical survey of Irish history that the county Kerry poet Tomás Rua Ó
Súilleabháin (1785–1848) composed to the popular air 'Síle Ní Ghadhra':

Féach-sa Cluain Tarbh mar ar cailleadh Brian Bóirmhe
an tréanfhear breá, calma, gaisceamhail, cróga;
tiarna Maighe Life is ar mhair ann dá chomhlacht,
Mac Baodáin, is ógshliocht Chinnéide mhic Lórcain.
    Bheir Céitinn ina chroinic dúinn cruinnfhios go deimhin
    gur cúig mhíle is fiche acu thit insan bhfeidhm:
    Ó Failghe ó Mhaigh Life, Ó Ceallaigh, Ó hEidhin,
aon mhac Rí Uladh, Murchadh, Toirdhéalbhach,
is Cian maol modhmhilis de chine Mhaolraonaidh.[12]

(Consider Clontarf where Brian Bóirmhe died, the fine brave heroic
courageous champion; the lord of the Liffey's plain and all his company who lived there, Mac Baodáin and the youthful progeny of
Cinnéide mac Lórcain. Keating gives us exact information in his
chronicle with certainty – that twenty-five thousand of them fell in the
action: Ó Failghe from the Liffey's plain, Ó Ceallaigh, Ó hEidhin, the
only son of the king of Ulster, Murchadh, Toirdhealbhach, and bare-
headed gracious Cian from the kindred of Maolraonaidh.)

In reality, the figure of 25,000 fatalities at the battle of Clontarf is not supported by Keating, who estimated the number of those killed at 17,800,
comprising 6,700 from the Norse expedition, 4,000 from among the Norse of
Dublin and the fleet, 3,100 of their Irish allies from Leinster, and 4,000 from
Brian's army.[13] Among the casualties named above, only Brian himself, his
son Murchadh, his grandson Toirdhealbhach, Tadhg Ó Ceallaigh, and
Maolruanaidh Ó hEidhin are mentioned by name in *Foras feasa ar Éirinn*.[14]

11 Tomás Ó Fiaich (eag.), *Art Mac Cumhaigh: dánta* (Baile Átha Cliath, 1973), p. 122.   12
Máire Ní Shúilleabháin (eag.), *Amhráin Thomáis Rua Uí Shúilleabháin* (Má Nuad, 1985), p.
53.   13 Patrick Dineen (ed.), *Foras feasa ar Éirinn*, iii (London, 1908), p. 274.   14 Ibid., pp

His careless citation of sources notwithstanding, it is known that Ó Súilleabháin was familiar with Keating's history: another of his songs describes a mishap in which he lost his entire library, including a copy of *Foras feasa ar Éirinn*, when a boat overturned.[15] By chance, a contemporary of Ó Súilleabháin, the county Galway poet Antaine Raiftearaí (1779–1835), also quoted Keating on the number of casualties suffered by the Norse at the battle of Clontarf in his 'Seanchas na Sceiche', a long poem summarizing the course of Irish history which was composed in the 1820s:

> Bhí dhá mhíle dhéag, dúirt Dochtúir Céitinn,
> de Lochlannaigh leagtha i gcoinne a chéile,
> ach an méid acu a rith agus nár fhan le scéala,
> i mBaile Átha Cliath a thit tubaiste an lae orthu.[16]

(There were twelve thousand, said Doctor Keating, of the Norse felled together, apart from those who fled and didn't wait for news, it was in Dublin that the day's disaster befell them.)

This was reasonably close to Keating's estimate of total Norse casualties; moreover, he actually states that twelve thousand Norsemen came from overseas to fight at Clontarf.[17] This ability of a blind poet from the province of Connacht – a region which lacked an active culture of manuscript production – to cite *Foras feasa ar Éirinn* in support of his account of the Irish past is eloquent testimony to the continuing importance of Keating's history in the early nineteenth century.

In the light of the evidence presented above, it is hardly possible to disagree with Bernadette Cunningham that *Foras feasa ar Éirinn* 'deserves particular attention because of its prolonged and profound influence on perceptions of Irishness'.[18] Successive generations of *literati* actively engaged with Keating's history, from the conservative writers of the late seventeenth century who still looked to the syllabic verse of the professional bardic poets of previous centuries for literary models, to the bilingual authors of the eighteenth century who embraced the metres of popular song, to the folk poets of the nineteenth century whose compositions have been recovered from the oral tradition. Such a sustained engagement over a period of two hundred years provides a factual basis for the claim concerning Keating's influence advanced by Pádraig Ó Fiannachta:

> Nuair a chuaigh an saol Gaelach faoi thalamh dála Thuatha Dé
> Danann sa seachtú haois déag, thugadar lón anama leo – *Foras Feasa*

274, 276. 15 See 'Amhrán na Leabhar' in Ní Shúilleabháin, *Amhráin Thomáis Rua*, p. 22. 16 Ciarán Ó Coigligh (eag.), *Raiftearaí: amhráin agus dánta* (Baile Átha Cliath, 1987), p. 145. 17 Dineen, *Foras feasa*, iii, p. 270. 18 Bernadette Cunningham, *The world of Geoffrey Keating: history, myth and religion in seventeenth-century Ireland* (Dublin, 2000), p. 226.

ar Éirinn. Ba é seo an saothar a choimeád an spiorad beo. Scaip sé ó cheann ceann na tíre, ó theach mór go bothán, ó bhothán go scairt.[19]

(When the Gaelic population went underground like the Tuatha Dé Danann in the seventeenth century, they took sustenance for the soul with them – *Foras feasa ar Éirinn*. This was the work that kept the spirit alive. It spread from one end of the country to the other, from big house to cabin, from cabin to shelter.)

Ó Fiannachta's assessment was echoed by Pádraig de Brún:

Níl aon saothar is mó ar thug na scríobhaithe gean dó ná Foras Feasa an Chéitinnigh, agus tá an-chuid cóipeanna go léir de le fáil fós againn. B'é seo insint na nGael ar a stair féin, an stair a choimeád spioraid agus misneach iontu le linn gach aon ní dár bhain leo a bheith fé tháir agus fé tharcaisne ag daoine a bhí 'éirithe i rachmas an tsaoil'.[20]

(There is no work that won more favour with the scribes than Keating's *Foras feasa*, and we still have a very large number of extant copies. This was the Gaels' account of their own history, the history which kept their spirit and courage alive when everything associated with them was treated with contempt and scorn by those who had 'prospered in worldly wealth'.)

More recently, Breandán Ó Doibhlin has summarized Keating's achievement as follows:

Rinne sé gnéithe scaipthe an tseanchais sin, idir dhinnseanchas, naomhsheanchas, mhiotaseolaíocht agus stair, a dhíleá ina n-aon arsú leanúnach amháin. Ní miste a rá gur chruthaigh an Céitinneach miotas náisiúnta a dhéanfadh dúshraith shíceolaíoch do mhuintir na hÉireann go cionn trí chéad bliain.[21]

(He digested the scattered elements of that *seanchas* [historical lore] – including toponymy, hagiography, mythology and history – into a single continuous narrative. It is fair to say that Keating created a national myth that would serve as a psychological foundation for the Irish people for three hundred years.)

The importance of Keating's history in helping to shape Irish views of the past at a formative period in the country's history cannot be denied: his vision

---

19 Pádraig Ó Fiannachta, 'Stair finnscéal agus annála', *Léachtaí Cholm Cille*, 2 (1971), 5.
20 Pádraig de Brún, 'Gan teannta buird ná binse; scríobhaithe na Gaeilge, *c.*1650–1850', *Comhar*, Nov. 1972, p. 19.   21 Breandán Ó Doibhlin, *Manuail de litríocht na Gaeilge*, iii (Baile Átha Cliath, 2007), p. 42.

of Ireland as a distinct and ancient kingdom ('do bhí Éire 'na ríoghacht ar leith léi féin, amhail domhan mbeag') whose people were unswerving in their allegiance to the faith brought by Patrick ('is follus nach ndeachaidh báthadh ar an gcreideamh tug Pádraig i nÉirinn') and were now governed by a royal house of Milesian descent ('táinig de Chineadh Scoit, mar atá, do shliocht Mháine mic Chuirc mic Luighdheach, táinig ó Eibhear mac Míleadh Easpáinne') coincided perfectly with the perspective of the Catholic political nation at the time of its composition and for long afterwards.[22]

Yet if *Foras feasa ar Éirinn* was accorded a position of honour in the Irish literary canon, it never achieved a monopoly in the field of native historiography. Several of the texts utilized by Keating in the 1630s continued to be copied and to circulate in manuscript during the following two centuries: notable examples include *Leabhar gabhála Éireann,* an account of the mythological invasions of Ireland on which Keating relied for the first part of his history; the *Réim ríoghraidhe* ('dynastic succession') or roll of kings which provided the narrative backbone for most of his history; and *Caithréim Cheallacháin Chaisil* which was an important source for the Norse wars. Historical compositions in verse were especially popular with scribes. For example, modernized versions of two poems from the *Leabhar gabhála* – 'Éire ard, inis na rí' ('noble Ireland, isle of the kings'), which lists the pagan kings of Ireland from its first settlement to Niall Naoighiallach, and 'Éire ógh, inis na naomh' ('chaste Ireland, isle of the saints'), which lists the Christian kings from Laoghaire to Maoilsheachlainn II – continued to be copied frequently during the eighteenth and nineteenth centuries: the manuscript collection of the Royal Irish Academy alone contains at least 14 eighteenth-century and 15 nineteenth-century copies of the former,[23] as well as 11 eighteenth-century and 15 nineteenth-century copies of the latter.[24] Similarly, a poem quoted by Keating which begins 'Fuaras i Saltair Chaisil' ('I found in the Psaltar of Cashel') and describes the several invasions of Ireland from its first settlement to the coming of the English (and which concludes by predicting their eventual expulsion) was popular and is found in at least seven eighteenth-century and twenty nineteenth-century manuscripts in the RIA collection.[25] Further-

---

22 David Comyn (ed.), *Foras feasa ar Éirinn,* i (London, 1902), p. 38; Dinneen, *Foras feasa,* iii, p. 350; Comyn, *Foras feasa,* i, p. 208 respectively.   23 For the eighteenth-century copies, see RIA 23 F 14, 23 D 9, 23 A 40, 23 M 18, 23 D 5, 23 C 35, 23 Q 1, D iii 2, 23 H 18, 23 H 25, 23 H 28, 23 G 8, C vi 1 and 23 G 1; for the nineteenth-century copies, see RIA 23 G 12, 23 O 28, 24 M 26, 24 C 8, 24 C 24, 23 B 24, 23 N 4, 23 N 33, 24 C 3, 3 B 26, 23 K 1, 12 E 14, 23 C 33, 12 K 8 and 24 A 25.   24 For the eighteenth-century copies, see RIA 23 D 9, 23 A 40, 23 M 18, 23 C 35, D iii 2, 23 H 18, 23 H 28, C i 3, 23 G 8, C vi 1 and 23 G 1; for the nineteenth-century copies, see RIA 23 G 12, 23 O 28, 24 M 26, 24 C 8, 23 C 18, 23 B 24, 23 N 4, 23 N 33, 23 Q 2, 24 C 3, 3 B 26, 23 K 1, 12 B 8, 12 K 8 and 24 A 25.   25 For the text of the poem, see Morley, *Ó Chéitinn go Raiftearaí,* pp 23–8. For Keating's references to the poem, see Comyn, *Foras feasa,* i, pp 138 and 154. For the eighteenth-century copies, see RIA F v 5, 23 E 7,

more, the native tradition of historiography did not terminate with Keating's history, as will be seen below.

* * *

The evidence for cultural continuity between the seventeenth and nineteenth centuries is strong; but continuity is not synonymous with stasis and the literary tradition continued to evolve throughout the period. Indeed, the concept of evolution requires the coexistence of continuity and change – two aspects of history that complement rather than negate each other. If the qualitative evidence presented in the previous section has conveyed an over-riding impression of continuity, the quantitative approach adopted below will highlight the extent to which the place of Keating's text in Irish literary culture changed over time.

A survey of the catalogues of the principal collections of Irish manuscripts has identified 144 manuscripts that contain copies of *Foras feasa ar Éirinn* – fragments of what may once have been full copies were counted, but the numerous manuscripts that contain only selected passages from the history were excluded from the survey.[26] Although published catalogues are now available for most of the major collections of Irish manuscripts, this is not universally the case; publication of the catalogues of some important repositories is still in progress or has yet to commence. The number of extant

---

23 K 24, 23 N 15, 23 E 16, 23 D 32, 23 G 5; for the nineteenth-century copies, see RIA 23 G 12, 3 B 5, F vi 2, 23 G 24, 24 C 8, 24 C 20, 23 A 38, 23 B 24, 23 N 33, 24 B 34, 24 C 3, 3 B 26, 23 K 1, 23 N 7, 12 E 14, 3 C 10, 24 L 23, 12 E 23, 12 K 8 and 24 P 19.

26 For details of the manuscripts see the following published sources: *Catalogue of the Irish manuscripts in the library of Trinity College, Dublin* (Dublin, 1921) for TCD; *Catalogue of Irish manuscripts in the British Museum* (3 vols, Oxford, 1926–53) for BL; *Catalogue of Irish manuscripts in the Royal Irish Academy*, fascicules 1–27 (Dublin, 1926–70) for RIA; *Lámhscríbhinní Gaeilge Choláiste Phádraig, Má Nuad*, fascicules 1–7 (Maynooth, 1943–1972) for NUIM; *Celtica* 4 (1958) for Liverpool MSS; *Catalogue of Irish manuscripts in the National Library of Ireland*, fascicules 1–13 (Dublin, 1961–96) for NLI; *Clár na lamhscríbhinní Gaeilge i Leabharlann Phoiblí Bhéal Feirste* (Dublin, 1962) (for Belfast Public Library); *Manuscript sources for the history of Irish civilisation* (Boston, 1965) for BN, Cashel, Chicago, Donovan, Kett, Killarney, Manchester, Marsh's, Mazarine, NLI, NLS, NLW, Ring, and UCD Morris, and *Supplement* (Boston, 1979) for Hess and PRONI; *Éigse* 12 (1967–8) for Limerick MSS; *Catalogue of Irish manuscripts in the Franciscan Library, Killiney* (Dublin, 1969) for UCD Franciscans; *Catalogue of Irish manuscripts in King's Inns Library Dublin* (Dublin, 1972) for King's Inns; *Éigse* 17 (1977–9) for Roscrea MSS; *Clár lámhscríbhinní Gaeilge: leabharlanna na cléire agus mionchnuasaigh* (2 vols, Baile Átha Cliath, 1978–80) for Fermoy, Leeson St, Clonakilty; *Catalogue of Irish manuscripts in the Cambridge libraries* (Cambridge, 1986) for Cambridge; *Catalogue of Irish manuscripts in Mount Melleray Abbey Co. Waterford* (Baile Átha Cliath, 1991) for Mount Melleray; *Clár lámhscríbhinní Gaeilge Choláiste Ollscoile Chorcaí: cnuasach Uí Mhurchú* (Dublin, 1991) for UCC; *Catalogue of Irish language manuscripts in the Bodleian Library at Oxford and Oxford college libraries*, part 1 (Dublin, 2001) for Oxford. In addition, see the unpublished catalogues of the Hyde collection in NUIG compiled by Áine de Búrca (henceforth NUIG Hyde) and of the UCC collection compiled by Máire Eibhlín Ní Dhonnchadha (henceforth UCC).

copies of Keating's history must exceed 144, but the sample is sufficiently large for the findings detailed below to be broadly representative. In several instances, the date and place of transcription was not recorded in a scribal colophon, but it was possible to ascertain the scribe's *floruit* and home district from other sources and the manuscript was assigned accordingly. Likewise, when watermarks provided the only means of dating a manuscript, the date of the most recent watermark was accepted as the date of transcription. By the use of such approximations it was possible to assign all but 17 of the 144 manuscripts to a twenty-five-year interval. Of the 17 exceptions, 3 would appear to date from the seventeenth century,[27] 9 from the eighteenth century,[28] and 3 from the nineteenth century,[29] while the information available was insufficient to suggest any date for 2 manuscripts.[30] Of the copies of *Foras feasa ar Éirinn* that could be assigned to a twenty-five-year period, it was also possible to assign a large majority (90 out of 127) to a particular region, as is shown in the tables below.

Keating's history was completed around the year 1634 and the survival of at least eleven copies dating from 1650 or earlier indicates that the appearance of the work generated an initial flurry of scribal activity (see Table 1). As Bernadette Cunningham has pointed out, much of this was associated with the Ó Maolchonaire and Ó Duibhgeannáin families in counties Clare and Leitrim respectively, as well as with members of the Franciscan order.[31]

Table 1: *Foras feasa ar Éirinn* – origin of known manuscripts,
1650 or before

Place of origin	Number	Manuscripts
Clare	4 copies	RIA 23 O 19; TCD H.5.26, H.5.32; Hess MS
Leitrim	2 copies	BL Egerton 107; BN Fonds Celtique 66
Kildare	1 copy	UCD Franciscans A14
Wexford	1 copy	TCD H.5.22
Unknown	3 copies	RIA 24 P 23; Oxford Fairfax 29; UCD Franciscans A15
Total	11 copies	

The number of extant copies that can be assigned to the years 1651–75 is significantly fewer than that for the preceding period (see Table 2). This may

27 NUIM C 2, TCD F.3.21, and NLS Gaelic XLIII. 28 RIA 23 I 42, 23 Q 15, 3 A 11; NUIM C 20; NLI G.190, G.331; PRONI T2738; Cambridge Add. 6,557; and Chicago Ms. 29 RIA 23 E 19, UCC Gaelic 104 Y, and Waterford 3. 30 NLI G.832 and Belfast Public Library XLI. 31 Cunningham, *The world of Geoffrey Keating*, pp 174–8.

reflect the disruption of traditional centres of manuscript production and networks of dissemination, as well as the suppression of Catholic religious orders,
resulting from the Cromwellian conquest.

Table 2: *Foras feasa ar Éirinn* – origin of known manuscripts, 1651–75

Place of origin	Number	Manuscripts
Bohemia	1 copy	NUIM R 68
Laois	1 copy	King's Inns 2
Leitrim	1 copy	RIA 24 N 3
Tipperary	1 copy	RIA 23 Q 14
Unknown	2 copies	RIA 24 P 43; Marsh's Z3.1.7
Total	6 copies	

The data for the final quarter of the seventeenth century are indicative of the
fact that the more settled conditions following the Restoration facilitated a
modest recovery in manuscript production, notwithstanding the renewed disruption attendant on the Williamite conquest (see Table 3).

Table 3: *Foras feasa ar Éirinn* – origin of known manuscripts, 1676–1700

Place of origin	Number	Manuscripts
Cork	2 copies	NLI G.17, G.117
Dublin	1 copy	UCD Gaelic 15
Tipperary	1 copy	BL Add. 4,779
Unknown	8 copies	RIA C iv 1, 23 F 20; NLI G. 999; UCC 91 M^2; NLW Add. 413D; TCD H.3.13; Marsh's Z4.5.6; NLS Advocates 33.4.11
Total	12 copies	

It is only in the period 1701–25 that evidence can be found for the extensive
copying of Keating's history (see Table 4). It is true, of course, that the risk
of a manuscript being lost increases with the passage of time, but it is hardly
conceivable that the elapse of twenty-five years could account for a three-fold
increase in the number of extant manuscripts – from 12 in 1676–1700 to 37
in 1701–25. The conclusion would seem to be unavoidable that the first quarter of the eighteenth century witnessed a striking increase in the production
of copies of Keating's history. This increase is more likely to reflect the gen-

eral growth in scribal activity at the time – especially in Munster, where a burgeoning Irish-speaking middle class existed – rather than an intensified interest in Keating's history *per se*: it has been estimated that approximately 4,000 Irish manuscripts are extant from the eighteenth and nineteenth centuries, compared with only 250 from the seventeenth.[32]

Table 4: *Foras feasa ar Éirinn* – origin of known manuscripts, 1701–25

Place of origin	Number	Manuscripts
Cork	7 copies	RIA 23 E 23, 23 G 1, 23 H 14; Cambridge Add. 4,181; UCC 62; Limerick O; Fermoy 20
Clare	5 copies	RIA 23 O 10, 23 G 9; BL Add. 27,910; NLI G.599; Mount Melleray 1
Dublin	3 copies	NLI G.192, G.465; Manchester Irish 123
Kerry	3 copies	NLI G.18, G.226, G.598
Limerick	3 copies	RIA 23 G 3; NUIM SF 4; Cashel 4,729
Meath	3 copies	RIA 23 C 1, 23 C 34; NLI G.54
Kildare	1 copy	BL Egerton 109
London, England	1 copy	BL Add. 18,745
Unknown	11 copies	RIA 23 E 8, 23 Q 8, 24 H 10; NUIM R 67; BL Egerton 108, Sloane 3806–7, Add. 31,873; NLW Add. 415D; TCD H.4.13; Manchester Irish 101; Donovan MS (NLI Pos. 1,947)
Total	37 copies	

However, the most remarkable finding to emerge from this survey is the abrupt decline in the copying of Keating's history that took place after 1725 (see Table 5). Only ten manuscripts can be assigned with confidence to the second quarter of the eighteenth century. Although the figures show a modest increase in production during the following twenty-five years, production fell back again in the last quarter of the century (see Tables 6 and 7).

The results of the survey provide little indication that the copying of *Foras feasa ar Éirinn* increased in the first half of the nineteenth century (see Tables 8 and 9) – the small apparent increase for the first quarter of the century may reflect nothing more than the better survival rate of later manuscripts.

32 Brian Ó Cuív, 'Irish language and literature, 1691–1845' in T.W. Moody and W.E. Vaughan (eds), *A new history of Ireland*, iv: *eighteenth-century Ireland, 1691–1800* (Oxford, 1986), p. 391.

Manuscript production virtually ceased after the middle of the century when famine-related mortality dealt a severe blow to the poor of the south and west, the demographic group that was most strongly Irish speaking (see Table 10).

Table 5: *Foras feasa ar Éirinn* – origin of known manuscripts, 1726–50

Place of origin	Number	Manuscripts
Cork	2 copies	NLI G.334, G.347
Dublin	2 copies	TCD H.6.3; NUIG Hyde 26
Clare	1 copy	RIA 23 E 10
Waterford	1 copy	UCC 91 M
Unknown	4 copies	RIA 23 E 22; NLI G.191; Fermoy 22(a); NLS Gaelic LVIII
Total	10 copies	

Table 6: *Foras feasa ar Éirinn* – origin of known manuscripts, 1751–75

Place of origin	Number	Manuscripts
Cork	9 copies	RIA 24 N 4; NLI G.112, G.534; NUIM M 102; UCC 61, 86 I; Leeson St 1; Cambridge Add. 3,095; Mazarine 4470
Limerick	4 copies	NLI G.56, G.294, G.338; Cambridge Add. 619
Kerry	2 copies	UCD Ó Lochlainn 15; Liverpool 12029M
Tipperary	1 copy	BL Add. 31,872
Unknown	2 copy	NLI G.115, G.1,132
Total	18 copies	

Table 7: *Foras feasa ar Éirinn* – origin of known manuscripts, 1776–1800

Place of origin	Number	Manuscripts
Cork	5 copies	RIA 23 H 29, 24 C 58; BL Egerton 112; NLI G.291; Clonakilty MS
Limerick	2 copies	RIA 23 H 16, 23 G 7
Clare	1 copy	RIA 23 G 16
Kilkenny	1 copy	King's Inns 41
Unknown	1 copy	RIA 24 M 12
Total	10 copies	

Table 8: *Foras feasa ar Éirinn* – origin of known manuscripts, 1801–25

Place of origin	Number	Manuscripts
Cork	5 copies	RIA 23 K 35, 24 B 21; NUIM M61–62; Franciscans A52; Killarney MS
Limerick	3 copies	RIA 23 Q 17, 23 Q 20; UCC 110
Armagh	1 copy	NLI G.536
Down	1 copy	UCD Morris 12
Dublin	1 copy	King's Inns 1
Tipperary	1 copy	NLI G.830
Unknown	1 copy	Kett MS
Total	13 copies	

Table 9: *Foras feasa ar Éirinn* – origin of known manuscripts, 1826–50

Place of origin	Number	Manuscripts
Armagh	1 copy	RIA 23 G 11
Clare	1 copy	NLW Add. 421D
Cork	1 copy	NLI G.438
Galway	1 copy	RIA 12 E 13–14
Tipperary	1 copy	NLI G.640
Unknown	1 copy	Roscrea 1
Total	6 copies	

Table 10: *Foras feasa ar Éirinn* – origin of known manuscripts, 1851–1900

Place of origin	Number	Manuscripts
Waterford	2 copies	Ring MSS 4–5
Cork	1 copy	Fermoy 19
Dublin	1 copy	G.189
Total	4 copies	

It is evident from the manuscript record that scribal production of *Foras feasa ar Éirinn* peaked in the first quarter of the eighteenth century and declined sharply thereafter. While there are signs that a modest revival took place later in the century, the level of production never again approached the level achieved in the 1701–25 period. The question must be posed: why did the interest of scribes in Keating's history decline so sharply in the period after 1725?

* * *

An obvious possibility that must be considered is that the interest of the
Irish-speaking population in Irish history may have declined in the later eighteenth century. This suggestion can be safely rejected. I have elsewhere surveyed the temporal and regional distribution of manuscript copies of the long
historical poem entitled 'Tuireamh na hÉireann' ('Ireland's dirge') which was
composed by Seán Ó Conaill in county Kerry around 1655.[33] This composition presents an account of Irish history that closely resembles that in *Foras
feasa ar Éirinn*: the migration of the Milesians from Spain; their victory over
the Tuatha Dé Danaan; the descent of the principal Irish lineages from
Milesius; Fionn mac Cumhail, and his Fianna; the arrival of Saint Patrick on
a mission mandated by Pope Celestine; the sanctity of early Christian Ireland
which earned it the name *'oileán na naomh'*; the depredations of the Norse
and their ultimate defeat by King Brian at Clontarf; the sexual immorality of
Diarmait Mac Murchadha and his introduction of the Anglo-Normans –
many of whom interbred with the native Irish. So strong is the similarity
between the representations of the Irish past found in Ó Conaill's poem and
in Keating's history that Pádraig Ó Fiannachta has likened 'Tuireamh na
hÉireann' to a précis of *Foras feasa ar Éirinn* ('ba gheall le cuimre ar an
bhForas Feasa an dán seo').[34] What is most remarkable in the present context
is that the copying of Ó Conaill's poem began much later than Keating's history (the earliest extant copy, in BL Egerton 187, was written some three
decades after the poem was composed), and that the rate of manuscript production continued to increase steadily throughout the eighteenth century and
into the early nineteenth century. Given that it required less effort to copy a
poem – even a long poem of 496 lines in its standard edition – than to copy
a prose text of some 140,000 words, the absolute number of manuscripts is
less important than the trends revealed in the figure below.[35]

In the light of the data for 'Tuireamh na hÉireann', the reduced scribal
interest in Keating after 1725 cannot be attributed to a lack of interest in Irish
history on the part of either the scribes themselves or their clients. However,
one significant difference between the scope of the two works must be noted:
with the exception of an historiographic preface in which he took issue with
the arguments of earlier writers who had criticized the native Irish, Keating

33 For the text of the poem, see Cecile O'Rahilly (ed.), *Five seventeenth-century political
poems* (Dublin, 1952), pp 59–82; for a version in modernized orthography, see Morley, *Ó
Chéitinn go Raiftearaí*, pp 69–83. For the survey of manuscript copies, see Morley, *Ó
Chéitinn go Raiftearaí*, pp 127–38; for an earlier English version with less complete
statistics, see Vincent Morley, 'Views of the past in Irish vernacular literature, 1650–1850',
Proceedings of the British Academy, 134 (2006), 171–98.   34 Ó Fiannachta, 'Stair finnscéal
agus annála', p. 5.   35 *Foras feasa ar Éirinn* could take months to transcribe: King's Inns
2 was written by Seán Ó Maolchonaire between 3 June and 23 July 1657; NLI G.17 was
written by Eoghan Ó Caoimh between 24 June and 22 Sept. 1696; NLI G.54 was written
by Seon Mac Solaidh between 19 Jan. and 15 Apr. 1713.

Figure 3.1: Extant copies of *Foras feasa* (left) and of 'Tuireamh na hÉireann'

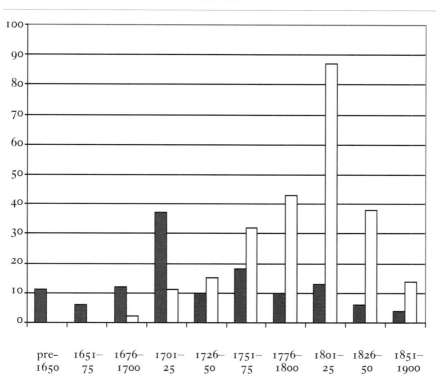

discussed no event more recent than the arrival of the Anglo-Normans in the twelfth century. Seán Ó Conaill, by contrast, carried the narrative down to his own lifetime and gave a strongly anti-English and anti-Protestant account of the Reformation, the Nine Years War, and the Cromwellian conquest. In most circumstances, recent events arouse more interest than the events of the remote past, and the possibility that the lower level of scribal interest in *Foras feasa* owed something to Keating's decision to conclude his narrative as early as the twelfth century cannot be entirely excluded.

One other difference between 'Tuireamh na hÉireann' and *Foras feasa ar Éirinn* should be mentioned. While Keating's Irish was modern in comparison with previous writing on historical subjects – the extravagant archaism of Lughaidh Ó Cléirigh's *Beatha Aodha Ruaidh Uí Dhomhnaill*, for example, or the more conventional conservatism of Mícheál Ó Cléirigh and his collaborators – it still exhibited features of the classical literary language that was used by the professional learned class for hundreds of years until the early seventeenth century.[36] While the obsolescent grammatical forms used by Keating did not constitute a serious barrier to comprehension, they may have been off-putting for those who had no training in the older literary language; in the words of one twentieth-century critic, Keating's use of such forms represented 'an unevenness in the fabric of his language'.[37] 'Tuireamh na hÉireann', by contrast, was entirely modern in idiom. It is therefore likely to have spoken more immediately to a popular audience in the eighteenth and nineteenth centuries. Indeed, its primary method of transmission was probably oral. Yet this factor can hardly account for the reduced scribal interest in *Foras feasa ar Éirinn* after 1725: had Keating's linguistic register posed a significant problem for potential readers, the scribes would surely have responded by modernizing its more conservative features.

Another possible explanation for the reduced scribal interest in *Foras feasa ar Éirinn* after 1725 is that demand for copies of the text may have been substantially satisfied by the appearance in print of a loose English translation by Dermod O'Connor, a scribe from Limerick who is known to have penned four copies of the history.[38] O'Connor's book was published under the title *The general history of Ireland* at London in 1723 and the appearance of a Dublin edition later in the same year confirms that there was a market for an English translation in Ireland. Indeed, even those authors and scribes who worked primarily in Irish displayed an interest in English-language publications on the subject of Irish history. Seán Ó Gadhra's favourable assessment of Peter Walsh's *A prospect of the state of Ireland* has been noted above. Likewise, a quatrain survives in which the county Clare poet Seon Ó hUaithnín (b. *c*.1688) asked to borrow a copy of Walsh's book from Aodh Buí Mac Cruitín (*c*.1680–1755), a fellow Clareman and poet.[39] Mac Cruitín himself published a history of early Ireland in English that drew copiously on Keating.[40] Mac Cruitín's book, in turn, also attracted sufficient interest for it to be translated into Irish before the end of the eighteenth century.[41] It is clear, therefore, that many of those who were interested in Irish letters and antiquities were bilingual and literate in English. None the less, it is difficult to believe that many readers of Irish would have preferred an English translation of Keating's history – even a full and accurate translation of the work – to the original text. Not only would Keating's prose have been lost in translation, but readers of the translation would also have been deprived of the original versions of the many quotations

36 For examples see Osborn Bergin (ed.), *Sgéalaigheacht Chéitinn: stories from Keating's history of Ireland*, 3rd edn. (Dublin, 1981), pp xii–xxvii, and Gerald O'Nolan, *Studies in modern Irish*, iv (Dublin, 1922), pp 11–18.   37 O'Nolan, *Studies*, p. 9.   38 RIA 23 G 3, MN SF 4, BL Add. 18,745 and Cashel 4,729. For O'Connor, see Diarmaid Ó Catháin, 'Dermot O'Connor, translator of Keating', *Eighteenth-Century Ireland*, 2 (1987), 67–87.   39 Eoghan Ó hAnluain, *Seon Ó hUaithnín* (Baile Átha Cliath, 1973), p. 61.   40 Hugh Mac Curtin, *A brief discourse in vindication of the antiquity of Ireland* (Dublin, 1717); see Vincent Morley, *An crann os coill: Aodh Buí Mac Cruitín, c.1688–1755* (Baile Átha Cliath, 1995), pp 47–61.   41 'Seanreacht na hÉireann' in NLI G.81, a manuscript written by S. de

from older texts with which the work abounds. Nor was the printed book much cheaper than a manuscript copy: the first London edition cost either two or four guineas (42*s.* or 84*s.* sterling) depending on the quality of the paper.[42] This can be compared with the two *moidores* (54*s.* sterling) pledged by Seán Ó Murchú for a manuscript copy around the same time; later in the century, the Dublin-based scribe Muiris Ó Gormáin valued two manuscript copies in his possession at 3 guineas 'at the least' and 5 guineas (63*s.* or 105*s.* sterling).[43] Furthermore, the book published by O'Connor was neither a full nor an accurate translation of Keating's text. The title page itself contained a contradictory notice that must have alerted all but the most unwary:

> Faithfully translated from the Original Irish Language, By Dermo'd O Connor.
>   With many curious Amendments taken from the Psalters of Tara and Cashel, and other authentick records.[44]

The idea of a faithful translation incorporating changes is an absurdity. The nature and purpose of O'Connor's 'curious amendments' quickly became a source of controversy, with the Revd Anthony Raymond, a minister of the established church, alleging in print that the notorious deist John Toland had assisted the project for the purpose of introducing material intended to undermine belief in revealed religion.[45] More importantly in the present context, the translation was condemned by those who were competent to compare it with the original text. Writing in 1753, the antiquary Charles O'Conor of Belanagare characterized the work as 'the grossest imposition that has been ever yet obtruded on a learned age'.[46] As late as the 1780s Peadar Ó Conaill (1755–1826), a prolific county Clare scribe, wrote the following scathing assessment:

> I am sure, if the said Keating would now live to see how his history has been murdered & basely abused, Intirely Corrupted & so ill handled by the dull dunce & plagy plagarian & in short the foolish fanatick fantastical fellow he'd no longer own it his own work.[47]

It is unclear whether Ó Conaill's comments on the translation were original or merely copied from an earlier source, but in either event they testify to the

Róiste in 1785.   **42** Alan Harrison, *Ag cruinniú meala: Anthony Raymond (1675–1726), ministéir Protastúnach, agus léann na Gaeilge i mBaile Átha Cliath* (Baile Átha Cliath, 1988), p. 98.   **43** Lesa Ní Mhunghaile, 'An eighteenth-century Gaelic scribe's private library: Muiris Ó Gormáin's books', *RIA proc.* 110C (2010), 248.   **44** Dermo'd O'Connor, *The general history of Ireland ... collected by the learned Jeoffry Keating D.D.*, second edition (London, 1726), title page.   **45** See Ó Catháin, 'Dermot O'Connor, translator of Keating', pp 80–5; Alan Harrison, *Ag cruinniú meala*, chapter 4; Alan Harrison, *Béal eiriciúil as Inis Eoghain: John Toland (1670–1722)* (Baile Átha Cliath, 1994), pp 72–7.   **46** Quoted in Ó Catháin, 'Dermot O'Connor, translator of Keating', pp 84–5.   **47** NUIM C 95, p. 27.

longevity of the hostility aroused by O'Connor's book. On the other hand, it is clear that the book satisfied a demand among a less discriminating anglophone readership: the first edition of 1723 was followed by a second London (or Westminster) edition in 1726 which was reprinted in 1732, and a third London edition followed in 1738. Interestingly, however, the publishers of the Dublin edition of 1723 were not encouraged to repeat the exercise. Had O'Connor's *General history* never appeared, those who were either ignorant of Irish, or who spoke the language without being able to read it, would have had no interest in owning a copy of Keating's text – except perhaps as a curio. It seems safe to conclude that, although O'Connor's book would have reduced the demand for the English and Latin translations of *Foras feasa*, which had previously circulated in manuscript, it is unlikely to have had a significant impact on the demand for copies of Keating's text from those who were literate in Irish.[48] It is even possible that the controversy it aroused may have stimulated interest in the original.

Given the absence of a convincing explanation for the precipitate decline in the copying of Keating's history after 1725 that is specific to the work itself, a more general explanation must be sought in the culture of the period as a whole. In a discussion of the most appropriate scheme of periodization to adopt for modern Irish literature, Breandán Ó Buachalla proposed the following divisions: 1560–1660, 1660–1730 and 1730–1860.[49] He regarded the transition around 1730 as marking a generational shift which occurred as a cohort of authors whose outlook had been formed in the seventeenth century passed away, and cited Seán Ó Neachtain (*c.*1640–1729), Séamas Dall Mac Cuarta (*c.*1647–1733), Pádraig Mac a Liondain (*c.*1665–1733) and Aogán Ó Rathaille (*c.*1670–1729) as examples. If a little more latitude is allowed in relation to dates, Ó Buachalla's list can be expanded to include such significant figures as Seán Ó Gadhra (1648–*c.*1720), Conchúr Ó Briain (1650–1720), Liam an Dúna Mac Cairteáin (*c.*1668–1724) and Eoghan Ó Caoimh (1656–1726). Ó Buachalla further argues that the post-1730 period witnessed a decline of the aristocratic ethos that dominated literature in the earlier period, and suggests that the new generation of writers who reached maturity in the eighteenth century wrote for an audience that was both larger and more socially diverse than that of their predecessors.[50] The changing tone and content of the literature was accompanied by an important change in form as scribes increasingly associated poems with the airs of popular tunes, a practice that was unknown in the seventeenth century but which began to appear in the manuscripts in the 1720–40 period.[51]

---

48 For a discussion of English and Latin manuscript translations, see Cunningham, *The world of Geoffrey Keating*, pp 182–92.   49 Breandán Ó Buachalla, 'Canóin na creille: an file ar leaba a bháis' in Máirín Ní Dhonnchadha (eag.), *Nualéamha: gnéithe de chultúr, stair agus polaitíocht na hÉireann c.1600–c.1900* (Baile Átha Cliath, 1996), p. 153.   50 Ibid., pp 160–1.   51 Breandán Ó Buachalla, 'Ceol na filíochta', *Studia Hibernica*, 32 (2002–3), 112.

If this view is correct – and I find the evidence persuasive – it can be said that Irish literary culture underwent a process of popularization in the early eighteenth century. It would seem reasonable to associate the greatly increased rate of manuscript production with these changes. I would further suggest that this process of popularization was accompanied by a decline in interest in the learned prose works of earlier centuries as the attention of both the scribes and their clients was drawn to the vigorous literature of their own period, a literature which increased in volume and variety as the eighteenth century progressed. The reduced attention paid by the scribes to Keating's history after 1725, and their growing interest in the more accessible, polemical and portable 'Tuireamh na hÉireann', can be seen as two aspects of the same process of popularization – with the focus shifting from prose to verse (including song), and from works that were mainly of scholarly interest to those that appealed to a wider section of the population. Yet the change was quantitative rather than qualitative – a point of inflection rather than a break in the literary tradition – and *Foras feasa* continued to be copied until well into the nineteenth century. As we have seen, the work would be prized by men of letters who took a special interest in Irish antiquities. Keating's text constituted a valuable compendium of historical and mythological tales from which the authors of later works that were more popular in form could draw; in this way, it would exert a continuing influence on Irish views of the past, albeit indirectly.

For members of the Irish-speaking community generally, 'Tuireamh na hÉireann' provided an acceptable substitute for Keating's history, one that could be quickly copied by the literate or committed to memory by the illiterate. It became a living part of popular culture and the number of manuscript copies increased steadily well into the nineteenth century. In contrast, *Foras feasa* became the preserve of men of letters with an historical bent, a group who regarded it as invaluable work of reference. Although some of its more edifying and entertaining passages (such as the account of Brian's victory-in-death at Clontarf) could be abstracted by scribes and read aloud at sociable gatherings of neighbours, Keating's history was known to most by reputation rather than through familiarity with its contents. By the middle of the eighteenth century it had already become a classic in Mark Twain's definition of the term: 'a book which people praise but don't read'.

4

Verisimilitude or subversion? Probing the interaction of English and Irish in selected warrants and macaronic verse in the eighteenth century

LIAM MAC MATHÚNA

INTRODUCTION

It was observed more than twenty years ago by Seosamh Watson in the English synopsis of his paper on 'The two cultures in conflict – native Irish and foreigner in Ulster poetry of the eighteenth century' that 'the poets themselves, despite their protestations, are found to be not above playing to the English-speaking gallery in their compositions'.[1] In the original article he even appropriates the term 'an Ghaeilge nua' (the new Irish), which the poet Art Mac Cumhaigh used in one poem to distinguish the contemporary medium from the earlier dialect of the schools,[2] and apply it to the Irish of the Ulster eighteenth-century poets in general. This Irish was characterized by the influence of English:

> It is recognized that one of the characteristics of that New Irish of Mac Cumhaigh and the poets of his period is that it was responding to the usage of those people [*viz.* the ordinary people], English loanwords and all, and it is recognised that one of the characteristics of the poets as artists in search of an audience in uncertain times was that they were prepared to yield to the demand of a public among whom bilingualism was progressively expanding and compose songs which would illustrate the condition in which things were, even if they showed themselves as preferring to lament those circumstances.[3]

1 Seosamh Watson, 'Coimhlint an dá chultúr – Gaeil agus Gaill i bhfilíocht Chúige Uladh san ochtú haois déag', *Eighteenth-Century Ireland*, 3 (1988), 85–104 at 85. 2 'Cha léir damh do fhreagra gé go gcanann tú an Ghaelig nua' ('Your answer is not clear to me, although you speak the new Irish') in Tomás Ó Fiaich, *Art Mac Cumhaigh: dánta* (Baile Átha Cliath, 1973), p. 82, quoted in Watson, 'Coimhlint an dá chultúr', p. 100. Unless otherwise stated, translations from the Irish are by the author of this essay. Where English features in the original, it is presented with the translation in italics, for the purposes of differentiation. 3 'Aithnítear gur de thréithe na Gaeilge Nua sin Mhic Cumhaigh agus

The assumption that there was no firm barrier, even in Ulster, between the sphere of activity of the native, Irish-speaking population and the English-speaking relative newcomers is consonant with the familiarity with English evidenced by Irish-language sources in general. It is an assessment that carries general validity for the country as a whole. However, it might be complemented by acknowledging more explicitly the composers' awareness of the creative potential of Irish/English code-mixing for their active handling of the subject matter. Code-mixing, that is the employment of English in an ancillary role to Irish in predominantly Irish-language texts, was a significant feature of the interaction between the two communities and their two languages over a period of some three hundred years and has been studied in depth by the author of this paper in *Béarla sa Ghaeilge*.[4] Triggered by the increasing permeation of English in Ireland from the Elizabethan era, Irish/English literary code-mixing remained largely a matter of individual creative choice up to about 1750. However, the phenomenon of code-mixing became more widespread during the eighteenth century, as native Irish society grew increasingly bilingual.

Whereas the focus of *Béarla sa Ghaeilge* was on the dynamics of the English-language impact on Irish compositions, this essay explores evidence in the texts for intimations of inter-community contact. The essay draws in the main on the compositions in the *barántas* or warrant *genre* and macaronic love-songs, complemented by a few religious compositions and brief reference to burlesque prose.

The exercise of English common law in place of the native Brehon system was the cornerstone of the administrative apparatus established in Ireland arising out of the English conquest. One of the leading legal officers of the new order, Sir John Davies, reflecting on the fundamental nature of the enterprise in *A discoverie of the trve causes why Ireland was neuer entirely subdued* (1612), offered the following observation: 'So a barbarous Country must be first broken by a warre, before it will be capeable of good Gouernment; ... For, that J call a Perfect Conquest of a Country, which doth reduce all the people thereof to the Condition of Subiects; and those I cal Subiects, which are gouerned by the ordinary Lawes and Magistrates of the Soueraigne.'[5] The changed circumstances were seen by the victors to require one king, one allegiance and one legal system, if English sovereignty was to be firmly estab-

fhilí a linne go raibh sí ag freagairt d'úsáid na ndaoine sin [*viz.* na gnáthdhaoine], idir iasachtaí Béarla agus eile, agus aithnítear gur de thréithe na bhfilí mar ealaíontóirí ar lorg pobail éisteachta in aimsir neamhsheasmhach go raibh siad sásta géilleadh d'éileamh pobail a raibh an dátheangachas ag leathnú ina measc de réir a chéile agus amhráin a chumadh a léireodh an bhail a bhí ar chúrsaí fiú má ba mhó an fonn a léirigh siad féin [*sic leg.*] a bheith ag mairgnigh faoi na cúrsaí sin': Watson, op. cit., 104.   4 Liam Mac Mathúna, *Béarla sa Ghaeilge: cabhair choigríche: an códmheascadh Gaeilge/Béarla i litríocht na Gaeilge, 1600–1900* (Baile Átha Cliath, 2007).   5 John Davies, *A discoverie of the trve causes why Ireland was neuer entirely subdued* (London, 1612, facsimile reprint Shannon, 1969), pp 5–6.

lished in Ireland.[6] Common law imposed a new system of inheritance and facilitated the transfer of land to new owners. Linguistically, the change is to be found reflected in the 'Seven Irish documents from the Inchiquin archives', covering the years 1576–1621, which Gearóid Mac Niocaill published in 1970.[7] Primarily written in Irish, these documents are essentially framed within common law and contain small but increasing amounts of English, particularly in the final section, where the documents were signed and sealed. However, another more revealing quotation from Davies makes it clear that English was the ordinary medium for administering the legal system in Ireland from the beginning of the seventeenth century onwards and that the Irish had to reconcile themselves to this new reality:

> Moreouer, these ciuil assemblies at Assises and Sessions, haue reclaymed the Irish from their wildenesse, caused them to cut off their Glibs and long Haire, to conuert their Mantles into Cloaks; to conform themselues to the maner of England in al their behauiour and outward formes. And because they find a great inconuenience in mouing their suites by an Interpreter; they do for the most part send their Children to Schools, especially to learne the English language: so as we may conceiue an hope, that the next generation, will in tongue & heart, and every way else, becom English; so as there will bee no difference or distinction, but the Irish Sea betwixt vs. And thus we see a good conversion, & the Irish game turned againe.
>
> For heeretofore, the neglect of the Lawe, made the English degenerate, and become Jrish; and now, on the other side, the execution of the Law, doth make the Irish grow ciuil, and become English.[8]

Indeed, some of the native Irish adapted enthusiastically to the new circumstances and sought to gain important positions for themselves as justices of the peace under the new dispensation, as is observed in an account dated to 1615: 'if any gentleman of the Irishry be of ten pounds revenues or of any manner of fashion or can speak English ... he will use one means or another to be put in the commission of the peace'.[9] Another indication of the nature of the interaction between the two communities is to be found in contemporary state papers, where it is observed: 'it is also very inconvenient that the judges are unacquainted with the Irish language, and cannot understand the witnesses that speak no English, whereby they cannot so well judge the cause.'[10]

6 See the discussion in Raymond Gillespie, *Seventeenth-century Ireland: making Ireland modern* (Dublin, 2006), p. 10.   7 *Analecta Hibernica*, 26 (1970), 45–69.   8 Davies, *A discoverie of the trve causes*, pp 271–2.   9 Quotation from MS Elsmere 1746, f. 21, Henry E. Huntingdon Library, San Marino, California, cited in Gillespie, *Seventeenth-century Ireland*, pp 69, 307.   10 *Calendar of the State Papers relating to Ireland, 1611–14*, pp 376–7, cited in Tony Crowley, *Wars of words: the politics of language in Ireland 1537–2004*

Although fluency and literacy in English may not have been common among the native Irish population in the seventeenth century, one may follow Raymond Gillespie in recognizing that there was widespread appreciation of the import of various kinds of legal documents.[11] The dominance of the foreign-imposed administrative system spurred a number of poets to compose political poems, which referred to the new practices. These poems employed the legal and bureaucratic terminology being used by the authorities to achieve their goals. The poets in question drew on a common store of vocabulary and phraseology to bemoan the powerlessness of Gaelic Ireland, and to vent their anger at the wretched state of the country, as they perceived it. They embraced sharp and bitter utterances associated with the administration of common law process to show that it was not legal niceties, which held sway, but orders and judgments, expressed in the form of phrases, slogans and litanies, which were a travesty of justice and stratagems in a plot to seize land, to dispossess landowners and to extirpate enemies. The work entitled *Five seventeenth-century political poems*, edited by Cecile O'Rahilly, and dating from the mid-seventeenth-century, gives Gaelic perspectives on the legal process and includes almost manic refrains of the implementation of the outcomes. The literary device of code-switching to English conveys well the frenzied nature of an archetypical assault on some of the native Irish:

> Le *execútion* bhíos súil an chéidfhir,
> costas buinte 'na chuinne ag an ndéanach.
> *Transport, transplant*, mo mheabhair ar Bhéarla.
> *Shoot him, kill him, strip, him, tear him,*
> *A Tory, hack him, hang him, rebel,*
>   a rogue, a thief, a priest, a papist.[12]

> (The first man hopes for *execútion*,
> the later wants the means of exaction against him.
> *Transport, transplant*, my mind on English.
> *Shoot him, kill him, strip, him, tear him,*
> *A Tory, hack him, hang him, rebel,*
> a rogue, a thief, a priest, a papist.)

THE WARRANT

Two or three generations later, when the Protestant interest in Ireland had consolidated its control of the kingdom, some of the poets felt free to employ the legal apparatus for rhetorical purposes, facilitating critical commentary on

(Oxford, 2005), p. 41.   11 Gillespie, *Seventeenth-century Ireland*, pp 24–5.   12 Cecily O'Rahilly, *Five seventeenth-century English poems* (Dublin, 1977), p. 90, lines 127–32.

the everyday happenings of their own time. These poets dressed their compositions in the English legal terminology of the country, declaiming warrants
which often began with the word 'Whereas', so beloved of the officials of the
new order. Thus the so-called warrant poems, composed in Munster in the
eighteenth and early nineteenth centuries, reflect a situation where the
common law legal system was accepted as given, and provided a framework
for satire and banter. Some eighty-three works of this kind have been brought
together by Pádraig Ó Fiannachta in *An barántas*.[13] This collection is quite
heterogeneous as it includes works that relate to the *cúirteanna éigse* (poetry
courts) of the poetic confraternity as well as the satiric warrants, the common
thread being the use of legal terminology and framework.[14] As to form, two-
thirds of the warrants consist of a prose preamble and verse, with one-third
containing verse only; four are exclusively in prose.[15] The majority of the
warrants involve censure of a range of thieving and criminal activities and
mockery of pretentiousness. Much of the humour is generated by the contrast
between the baseness of the crime and the solemn and bombastic nature of
the legal utterances with which they are condemned. A second set of contrasts
is frequently in play, namely, that between the high social station in the
native community of the people involved in these poems – the status of the
Catholic priest, for instance – and the petty nature of the crime of which they
stand accused.

A typical satiric warrant includes a summary deposition by the informant
and a statement of the crime committed. The physical characteristics of the
person pursued by a hue-and-cry posse are usually described at length from
head to toe in most unflattering terms, with alliterating strings of adjectives
occasionally exhausting the entire alphabet, letter by letter. The poet calls on the
sheriff and county authorities to search high and low for the culprit, to check
every nook and cranny of the landscape traversed, the abodes entered and the
males and females encountered. No punishment will be too good for the
criminal, once apprehended. The warrant is frequently, but not invariably dated.

With regard to language, it should be noted at the outset that many warrants have no English component whatsoever. 'Whereas' serves to introduce
35 warrants, with its Irish equivalent 'De bhrí' occurring in 11 instances.

13 Pádraig Ó Fiannachta, *An barántas I: réamhrá, téacs, malairtí* (Má Nuad, 1978), p. 11.
The projected second volume, which was to have contained an analysis of language and
metre, as well as an extensive editorial apparatus (see p. 33), has not appeared.   14
Damien Ó Muirí has usefully summarized the import of the principal legal terms, while
Breandán Ó Conchúir has shown how various poetic circles operated: see Damien Ó
Muirí, 'An cúlra dlíthiúil leis an bharántas' in Máirtín Ó Briain and Pádraig Ó Héalaí
(eag.), *Téada dúchais: aistí in ómós don Ollamh Breandán Ó Madagáin* (Indreabhán, 2002),
pp 425–44; Breandán Ó Conchúir, 'Na cúirteanna éigse i gCúige Mumhan' in Pádraigín
Riggs, Breandán Ó Conchúir and Seán Ó Coileáin (eag.), *Saoi na héigse: aistí in ómós do
Sheán Ó Tuama* (Baile Átha Cliath, 2000), pp 55–81.   15 Ó Fiannachta, *An barántas*, pp
13, 25.

Nonetheless, the warrant is the principal literary *genre* in Irish where code-mixing is a standard and staple ingredient. English is already to be found in one of the earliest examples of the type, attributed to Aodhagán Ó Rathaille. Dated 13 September 1717, this calls on the sheriff of county Kerry to capture one of his own officials, Séamas Ua Síobharráin, who had been entrusted with the delivery of a cock, purchased by a priest called Aonghas at the fair of Dingle. The English used in this warrant, whose verse begins '*Whereas* Aeneas fáithchliste', is fairly minimal: it consists of the introductory 'Whereas', 'Whatsoever' and the phrase 'And for so doing'.[16]

Rather more English is to be found in a warrant by Seán Ó Tuama an Ghrinn, which begins:[17]

> *Whereas* cúigear
> tháinig chúghainne
>   le h*information*,
> *Equally sworn*
> *upon oath*
>   *of declaration.*[18]

> (*Whereas* five people
> who came to us
>   with *information*,
> *Equally sworn*
> *upon oath*
>   *of declaration.*)

Unusually, this poem also ends in English:

> *When he is taken*
> *by all means*
>   *show your orders.*[19]

Otherwise, its English content is confined to one verse, in which a Latin phrase is interpolated:

> *Therefore fail not,*
> *in nomine regis,*
>   *don't neglect to*
> *Search the traitor*
> *in all places*
>   *being suspected.*[20]

16 Ibid., pp 124–5. 17 Ibid., pp 127–8. 18 Ibid., p. 127, lines 1–6. 19 Ibid., p. 129, lines 100–2. 20 Ibid., p. 128, lines 85–90.

Of the 83 examples of the *genre* edited by Ó Fiannachta, just one is totally in English (58), while another (56) is composed predominantly in that language. Four are truly macaronic (8, 57 (ii), 66 (i), 66 (ii)) with almost all of their lines divided between English and Irish.[21] In all four cases the pattern is that of English followed by Irish. The minimal prose introduction and two verses from one of these is illustrative of these macaronic warrants:

> Contae Chorcaí le Donnchadh Gógán .i. aon do bhreithiúnaibh na héigse agus d'uaislibh na síochána san gcontae rémhráite.

> *Whereas this day* do réir réim chirt an chalandair,
> *I received information* le héifeacht go dearfa,
> *The warrant I gave, much* le faobhar chum an fhairceallaigh,
> *He's got a supersedeas* le *means* chum é sheachaint air.

> *To all bums and bailiffs* ó Bhéarra don Mhainistir,
> *Constables, gaolers,* is gach éinne dhen aicme sin,
> *Let none take his orders* barántas ná atharach,
> Atá a theideal ar lár óm' láimhse gan dearmad.[22]

This may be translated as follows:

> County Cork by Donnchadh Gógán i.e. one of the judges of poetry and nobles of the peace in the aforesaid county.

> *Whereas this day* according to the course of justice of the calendar,
> *I received information* with import positively,
> *The warrant I gave, much* with energy after the lump (of a man)
> *He's got a supersedeas* with means to avoid it against him.

> *To all bums and bailiffs* from Beare to Mainistir,
> *Constables, gaolers,* and everyone of that class,
> *Let none take his orders* warrant or alternative,
> His title is wanting from my hand without mistake.

As one enters the nineteenth century the warrants display some intriguing extensions in the use of English. For instance, Clíona, a fairy-woman from the Gaelic otherworld, speaks in English and is responded to in that language in an 1813 warrant beginning '*Whereas* do tháinig / inné dom láthair / gan aon dabhta' (47) on the stealing of an English grammar from one Seán Ó hEithir:

> D'éirigh Clíona
>   do bhí ina suí
>   is do labhair go múinte,

21 Nos. 57 and 66 (i) share many similarities.   22 Ibid., pp 205–6.

Is d'fhiafraigh scéala
díomsa i mBéarla:
  who are you sir?

Or what made you so late
to come this way
  you are not in humour?
Do labhair léithi
go róshéimh
  agus is ea dúras:

I am no stranger
nor neither a ranger
  but I come from Doolagh.
That my book was stolen
from me felonious
  from the schoolhouse.
And if I could get
the vile transgressor
  I would ill-use him.
And if I could make him known
he would pay sore
  for his misdoing.[23]

The first two stanzas may be translated as follows:

Clíona stood up
Who had been sitting
  and she spoke politely,
And she asked for news
Of me in English:
  who are you sir?

Or what made you so late
to come this way
  you are not in humour?
I spoke to her
most easily,
  and what I said was:

In time, the expectation had also grown that the poet should be expert in English as well as Irish, as one sees in a warrant from 1819, where Diarmaid

---

23 Ibid., pp 160–6, lines 229–52. It may be observed that this particular warrant contains a higher than usual number of English words and loans, including *handbasket, peeler, hall-door, fairplay, sleais, scoop, silence, scheme.*

Ó Riain charges Tadhg mac Finghín Mheic Cárthaigh, described as 'Hiberno-
waterlouse', with being a wandering school-master who was 'ruining,
deforming and insulting English and Irish'.[24] In another warrant, dated 1832,
the poet calls upon six priests and fourteen acquaintances to join in the hunt
for the culprit. The surnames of each of the six priests is given in anglicized
form, whereas all the others have both Irish first names and surnames. The
names of each of the priests bears the title *Dochtúir*. The priests' surnames
are 'Collins, Fitzgerald, Foley, Conway, Downes, Moore'.[25]

Interestingly, this practice by the Catholic clergy of anglicizing their
names was noted over a hundred years earlier by John Dunton in *Teague
land; or, a merry ramble to the wild Irish (1698)*, who met 'one Father Gowan
or Smith as he called himself, *a la mode de Angleterr*'.[26] Dunton's latter
remark seems to be adverting in particular to the form 'Smith', whereas his
cursory observation summarizes the main strategies that were utilized in
anglicizing nomenclature. Assuming an original Irish surname 'Mac Gobhann'
[lit. 'son of a smith'], Dunton's 'Gowan' and 'Smith' reflect two approaches.
The first, 'Gowan' settles for a spelling which provides English speakers with
a phonetic approximation of the Irish 'Gobhann/Gabhann', originally the
genitive singular of *gobha* (smith), albeit with the elimination of the prefix
'Mac', which would immediately draw attention to the ethnic origin of the
name-bearer.[27] The second possibility, the translation of the Irish into English
'Smith', represents a further stage on the road to complete anglicization of the
name. Coupled with this comment of John Dunton's, the evidence for anglicizing personal names to be found in the Inchiquin archives and the warrant
poems illustrates well the profound and lasting effect that the common law
system had on the native psyche. In order to be treated officially, Gaelic personal names had to be metamorphosed into anglicized names.[28]

The permeating influence of English to be seen in the warrants testifies to
the interaction of the native Irish and settler communities, and could only
have arisen when there was a high level of contact between them in the
public sphere of jurisprudence and administration. The attempts of the Irish
to enter this new world were not necessarily smooth and unproblematic, as

24 'ag milleadh, ag míchóirú 's ag maslú Béarla agus Gaeilge', ibid., p. 148.   25 Ibid., p.
175.   26 Andrew Carpenter (ed.), *Teague land. or, a merry ramble to the wild Irish (1698)
by John Dunton* (Dublin, 2003), p. 112.   27 See for instance the disparaging reference to
'the septs of *Ose or Max*' made by the Dublin apothecary Thomas Smyth in 1561, cited
in E.C. Quiggin, *Prolegomena to the study of the later Irish bards, 1200–1500* (American
Committee for Irish Studies, [1967], reprinted from *Proceedings of the British Academy*, 5
(1913)), 20.   28 See Liam Mac Mathúna, '"What's in an Irish name?": a study of the personal naming systems of Irish and Irish English' in Hildegard L.C. Tristram (ed.), *The
Celtic Englishes iv* (Potsdam, 2006), pp 64–87. For a discussion of the parallel phenomenon
in relation to place-names, see Liam Mac Mathúna, 'Toponyms across languages: the role
of toponymy in Ireland's language shifts' in Hildegard L.C. Tristram (ed.), *The Celtic
Englishes ii* (Heidelberg, 2000), pp 280–302.

can be seen from John Dunton's wry reproduction of the transfer of the sounds of Irish into the English acquired as a second language. Dunton must not only have had a keen ear but also a very effective system for noting what he heard, for he provides the text of a sermon delivered by a Catholic priest called Fr Laurence at a funeral in Dublin in 1698.[29] At any rate, an extract from his account of this sermon vividly conveys the pronunciation of Hiberno-English, as it was spoken by an educated middle-class native Irish Catholic at the end of the seventeenth century:

> Now, Christians, dere be two sorts of deat according [to] de holly faders, won of de body (fwich is dat I vas now telling you of), de oder of the spirit; and many be de sorts of deat fwich happen to de body. As Saint Augustin hate it, *una wia est witæ, moriendi mille figuræ.* Aldough you have but won way of borning into dis Vorld, dere are a tousand ways and a tousand tricks to sheat you out of it: you dye wid feaver or long shikness, another maybe has a trust with a meddoag or sword in his guts, a turd has long age to kill him (as our deare shister here before you), and many more tings *quæ nunc præscribere longum* – fwich are now to[o] long to rehears.[30]

Somewhat in the same vein, Jonathan Swift drew on the kind of English being spoken in Ireland in the first half of the eighteenth century. His writings imply, however, that Irish had influenced not only the English learned by the native Irish but also that spoken by the descendants of planters as well.[31] The following extract forms part of 'An example of Hibernian eloquence', presented in the form of a letter:

> I was at your Cozen Tom's house in the County of Fermanagh ... His Neighbor Squire Doll is a mere Buddough. I'd give a Cow in Canaught You could see him. He keeps none but Garrauns, and he rides on a Soogaun with nothing for his Bridle but Gadd. In short, he is a mere Spawlpeen, and a perfect Monaghen, and a Munster Crack into the bargain. Without you saw him on Sunday you would take him for a Brogadeer and a Spanel ... We drank Balcan and Whisky out of Maddors. And the devil a Nightgoun had but a Caddow ... I wonder your Cozen does not learn him better manners ... Your cousin desires you will buy him some Cheney Cups. I remember he had a great many; I wonder what is gone with them.[32]

29 Carpenter (ed.), *Teague land*, pp 82–6.   **30** See Carpenter, op. cit., pp 84–5; Alan Bliss, *Spoken English in Ireland, 1600–1740: twenty-seven representative texts assembled and analysed* (Dublin and New Jersey, 1979), p. 135.   **31** See Bliss, op. cit., pp 71–2, where he discusses a similar text, 'A dialogue in Hybernian stile', written *c.*1735.   **32** Cited in William Mahon (ed.), *The history of Éamonn O'Clery* (Indreabhán, 2000), p. 10.

In sum, then, one may note that the warrant *genre* depended for its effect on the legal institutional framework being well known to the poets and their native Irish audience. It was this that formed the source of much of the English to be met with in the warrants. The legal system may well have provided a prime locus of societal interaction between the native Irish and the English settler for much of the seventeenth and early eighteenth centuries. If the instances of code-mixing in the Irish-language sources testify to a certain internalizing of the English language as an ancillary community and creative medium, quotations from Dunton and Swift show that for those whose first language was English, Hiberno-English might be accessible in a way that the Irish language could never be, but it still served as a marker of fundamental ethnic-cum-societal difference. Nonetheless, the development of Hiberno-English is further evidence that the activities of the two communities overlapped in the public sphere.

MACARONIC SONGS

Diarmaid Ó Muirithe's *An t-amhrán macarónach*, published in 1980, provides the most extensive published collection of macaronic or Irish/English dual-language compositions.[33] It contains the texts of some 79 songs, dating from the mid-eighteenth century to the mid-nineteenth century.[34] Divided by Ó Muirithe into a number of categories, the majority of the compositions, 47 examples, are classified under 'Men and Women'. The other categories employed are 'Political Affairs' (7 examples), 'Keens' (3), 'Satire' (4), 'Piety' (4), 'Oral Ditties' (8) and 'Rigmaroles' (6). However, as songs often have more than one theme running through them, rather more than the 47 touch on relations between the sexes.

As a term, 'macaronic' relates to form and not to *genre*. There are many ways in which a song or poem may be macaronic. In the warrant *genre* we have already met with perhaps the most demanding type, where each line combines both languages and metrical features such as assonance and rhyme have to be adroitly applied across them simultaneously. More usually, verses in each language alternate, the content of the second echoing and loosely translating the preceding stanza. Sometimes a pattern is adhered to rigidly, sometimes intermittently.[35]

The dominant theme of the love songs is poet-meets-girl in 'As I roved out one May morning' mode. The motif of the free-moving or journeying

33 Diarmaid Ó Muirithe, *An t-amhrán macarónach* (Baile Átha Cliath, 1980).   34 Ibid., p. 31.   35 Of course, the vagaries of transmission may well have played their part in determining the proportion of the various types of the surviving dual-language compositions, as the works would mainly have circulated orally initially or been distributed in ballad sheets, where the Irish is presented in phonetic English transliteration, which is not always transparent to us today.

poet facilitated these meetings of strangers. In many instances, the maiden is given the initiative in discourse, and in the majority of these cases, she addresses the poet in English. She is often portrayed as being anxious that her clothes should not betray evidence of any encounter, as she needs her parents' blessing before she accepts the poet's entreaty to wed. For instance, in 'Ag taisteal na dtriúch go dubhach im' aonar', the poet Aindrias Mac Craith presents himself as being rebuffed by the fair maiden, who had attracted him, with the following words:

> 'Keep off, I say, you raking rogue,
> Have a care, don't tear my cloak,
> Or I vow and swear I'll break your nose
> If you abuse my gown, Sir!'[36]

In another song the poet tells us that when he saw the girl 'I knew by her gazing she'd play the Hide and Go Seek', and proceeds:

> Do dhruideas féin léi agus d'iarras-sa póigín nó trí,
> *The answer she made, 'Young blade you are making too free',*
> Is é a dúirt mé féin léi gur bheannaigh sí domsa róbhinn,
> *'And I'd like for to teach you to play the Hide and Go Seek'.*

> Do fhreagair an spéirbhean agus dúirt sí gur aerach mo shlí:
> *'I'll tarry a while until more of the world I'll see,*
> Táimse ró-óg, cúig déag an fómhar seo 'imigh dínn,
> *Though I'd like a good dale to play the Hide and Go Seek'.*

> (I moved close to her and asked for a little kiss or three,
> *The answer she made, 'Young blade you are making too free',*
> I said to her that she addressed me most sweetly,
> *'And I'd like for to teach you to play the Hide and Go Seek'.*

> The beauty answered and said that I had a merry way,
> *'I'll tarry a while until more of the world I'll see,*
> I am too young, fifteen this autumn past,
> *Though I'd like a good dale to play the Hide and Go Seek'.*[37])

---

36 Ó Muirithe, *An t-amhrán macarónach*, p. 45.   37 Ó Muirithe, op. cit., p. 70. In 'O'Sullivan's Frolics' the poet had more definite success, albeit with an even younger girl: *"If you be in earnest"*, ar sise,/"Ní leanfad níos mó dem' léann./*My parents do really insist on*/Go bhfuilim ró-óg go léir;/*But I am one-eighth of a century*,/Agus cuiream leis bliain uainn féin,/*And if they don't consent as we wish them*,/Go mbogfam an ród sinn féin."//
'("*If you be in earnest*", says she,/"I won't continue any more with my learning./*My parents do really insist on*/That I am altogether too young;/*But I am one-eighth of a century*,/And let us add a year to that from ourselves,/*And if they don't consent as we wish them*,/That we will move along the road ourselves.")' (Ó Muirithe, op. cit., p. 73).

The outcome remains unclear despite the poet's assurance that he has a fine field of sheep, cattle, a bull and a calf, coupled with the information that his 'mother is old and she hates making butter and cheese'.[38]

One of the most interesting of the macaronic compositions is that beginning 'Do tharlaigh inné orm' by the poet Liam Inglis (1709–78), whose surname was anglicized 'English', for in addition to the bilingual verbal cut and thrust of other such songs, it has echoes of the linguistic misunderstandings to be met with in the prose tales *Pairlement Chloinne Tomáis*[39] and *Stair Éamuinn Uí Chléire*.[40] However, the misunderstandings are almost wilful, the play on the poet's surname and the maiden's eagerness to participate in further Irish-language classes, so-called, set this poem apart. But the poet may have been carried away with the creative exuberance – the intricate repartee may in the end have exhausted his own dexterity, so that he didn't know whether he was coming or going, Irishing or Englishing, so to speak. The poem begins as follows:[41]

> Do tharlaigh inné orm is mé im' aonar sa ród,
> Fánach beag béithe agus éistigh lem' ghlór,
> Ba bhreá deas a béal is ba craorac mar rós,
> Is ba lách deas a claonrosc ag géilleadh don spórt.
>
> Do bheannaigh go tapa is chuir maig ar a beol,
> *'Sir, I am your servant, how far do you go?'*
> 'Béarla níl agam is ní chanaim a shórt,
> Ach Gaeilge liom labhair is freagra gheobhair';
>
> (I happened to meet yesterday, while I was alone on the road,
> A wandering little maid and, listen to my voice,
> Her mouth was nice and fine and red like a rose,
> And her slant eye was nice and pleasant, agreeable to fun.
>
> She greeted me quickly and put a smile on her lips,
> *'Sir, I am your servant, how far do you go?'*
> 'I have no English, and I don't speak that kind,
> But speak Irish to me and you'll get an answer.')

Their meeting continues:

> *'As I hope to be married a word I can't speak*
> *Of that silly language which makes my heart ache.*
> *Therefore I entrust you some pity to show*
> *For I have the colic and I cannot well go'.*

38 Ibid., p. 70.   39 N.J.A. Williams (ed.), *Pairlement Chloinne Tomáis* (Dublin, 1981).   40 Eoghan Ó Neachtain (ed.), *Stair Éamuinn Uí Chléire* ([Dublin], 1918).   41 Ó Muirithe, op. cit., pp 65–6.

'Ná trácht liomsa ar <u>chailligh</u> ní maith liom féin iad,
Oirbheart is easpa is galar is pian;
Do b'fhearr liomsa ainnir a mbeadh lasadh ina ciabh
Is dhá <u>mhama</u> gheala mar shneachta ar shliabh'.

'Don't talk of my <u>mama,</u> but prithee draw near
For I am a poor creature that's raving with fear,
Therefore I beg, sir, some token you'll make
Whereas of <u>English</u> a word I can't speak'.

'Is <u>*English*</u> mo shloinne is ní shéanfad go brách,
A bhruinneall na finne is a chéadshearc thar mhnáibh'.
Do rugas go cluthair is go séimh ar mo ghrá
Is do thit sise is mise in éineacht ar lár.

The latter three stanzas may be translated as follows:

'Don't talk to me of "hags", I don't like them,
Deviousness and want and disease and pain;
I'd prefer a maiden with a shine in her curls
And two bright breasts like snow on the mountain.'

'Don't talk of my mama, but prithee draw near
For I am a poor creature that's raving with fear,
Therefore I beg, sir, some token you'll make
Whereas of English a word I can't speak'.

'English is my surname, and I'll never deny,
O fair maiden and first love above women.'
I grasped my love cosily and gently took
And she and I together fell on the ground.

The song continues (in translation):

'O Lord be quiet sir, what is all that?'
'You don't need, my bright-eyed one, I'll lift without stopping
Your *hoop* and your gown and your petticoat quickly,'
And merrily I taught my treasure her lesson.

'*If that be your Irish,* O youth of my heart,
I vow and declare I'll learn it of thee'.
This is what my sweet little thin-lipped star says:
'Another Irish lesson, if possible, again.'

I set to teach her lively without stopping,
And she understood clearly the works of the writers.

> She enjoyed greatly every verse I read to her,
> And Irish was a hundred times more pleasant to her than English.[42]

Much of the general creative verve of this poem derives from a noteworthy feature of its dual-language composition, namely, the cross-linguistic linking of words in the two languages which echo each other in sound but bear no relation in meaning, namely 'colic' and 'chailligh' [hags], 'mhama' and 'mama' [breast], 'English' and 'English' [Inglis] – 'double entendres' in more senses than one![43] One will recall that the girl's English-language reference to 'colic' was picked up by Inglis as Irish 'cailleach' (the lack of an aspirated 'c' presenting no difficulty), then the poet's reference to the girl's two breasts as 'dhá mhama', was understood by her as referring to her 'mama' or mother (again the mutation in the Irish phrase proved no impediment) and finally 'English' carries two meanings – the language itself and the poet's surname.

The same linking device is to be found in an early eighteenth-century Ulster prose tale called 'Eachtra Áodh Mhic Goireachtaidh'.[44] While the amount of English to be met with in this tale is modest, it is significant in two ways. First, most of it occurs in dialogue, where it is used as a vehicle for sexual allusions, and second the structure of its turn-taking involves links between each piece of conversation, reminiscent of the inter-stanzaic device technically known as *conchlann* in Irish, and as used here by Inglis in macaronic verse. In §23 the following conversation occurs, where the giant/ghost (variously termed in the original *arrachta/ taibhse/geósta/ genie*) addresses Áodh in English, and Áodh responds in Irish. The dialogue proceeds, the ghost's English alternating with Áodh's Irish. Áodh misunderstands the end of each English sentence, and mistakenly feels that he has to defend himself for having sought out the bed of the woman of the house. The following is a comparatively innocuous example of the way the conversation goes:

> 'This is no time to con<u>fess</u>', air an taidhbhse.
> 'Dair Día dúileach', air Áodh, 'ní dearna mise <u>feis</u> léithe aríamh go fóill'.

> ('This is no time to confess', said the ghost.
> 'By the creating God', said Áodh, 'I haven't ever slept with her yet'.)[45]

In this exchange Áodh mistakes the second syllable of English *confess* for the Irish word *feis* 'sleeping'.

42 See also Andrew Carpenter (ed.), *Verse in English from eighteenth-century Ireland* (Cork, 1998), pp 327–8.   43 These words are underlined here to assist the reader to locate them in the text.   44 N.J.A. Williams, 'Eachtra Áodh Mhic Goireachtaidh', *Éigse*, 13:2 (Spring 1970), 111–42.   45 Ibid., p. 126.

The situation is rather different in the song beginning 'Bhíos-sa lá ar thaobh an chnoic', where the ploughman poet is accosted by a fair maid, who addresses him in English, while he responds in Irish:

'Is é dúirt sí liom *'God bless your work'*, is bheannaíos di as Gaelainn.

('She said to me *'God bless your work'*, and I addressed her in Irish.)[46]

The poet subsequently learns the price of her own work:

I'll be at your service, sir, for only sixpence ha'penny'.[47]

He declines the offer, saying that she is the sort that the priests warn about on Sundays, and that he has no intention of going to Hell. Despite the fact that the girl speaks English throughout and the poet Irish, there is no evidence of any misunderstandings arising.

The frequent, indeed regular, use of English by the female party in these macaronic songs, is noteworthy. On the one hand, it suggests that girls, wishing to be upwardly mobile socially may have been to the fore in implementing the language shift from Irish to English. Be this as it may, it would seem also that a second factor was at play, namely that the maiden, the more vulnerable party, was aligning herself with the dominant public sphere, to the extent that her ease with English implicitly relayed the message to the stranger poet that she would be well placed to have recourse to the legal system, should their encounter warrant such action.

One poem where the code-mixing medium permitted opposing messages is 'As I was walking one evening fair' by Donnchadh Ruadh Mac Conmara, set in Newfoundland, which allowed the poet to indulge himself and his bilingual Irish-born audience at the expense of the monolingual English speakers of Newfoundland. For instance, he alternately praises and reviles the power of King George:

> *Come, drink, a health, boys, to Royal George,*
> *Our chief commander* – nár ordaigh Críost,
> Is aitchimis ar Mhuire Mháthair,
> É féin is a ghardaí a leagadh síos.

> (*Come, drink, a health, boys, to Royal George,*
> *Our chief commander* – which Christ never ordained,
> Let us beseech Mary Mother of God,
> To strike down his guards and himself.)[48]

46 Ó Muirithe, *An t-amhrán macarónach*, p. 43. 47 Ibid. 48 Ibid., p. 128.

The gap between the two messages is even greater in regard to the women of Newfoundland:

> *Here you may find a virtuous lady,*
>   *A smiling fair one to please the eye* –
> An paca straipeanna is measa tréithe,
>   Is go mbeiread féin ar bheith as a radharc.
>
> (*Here you may find a virtuous lady,*
>   *A smiling fair one to please the eye* –
> A pack of whores with the worst of traits.
>   And I would be better off to be out of their sight.)[49]

The particular nature of macaronic verse allows for some cross-linguistic comparisons, which seem to have passed unnoticed up to now. For example, the Irish-language place-names of the Irish-medium sections may be paralleled by anglicized versions in the English. Thus, one has 'cuan an Daingin' alongside 'Dingle Bay',[50] and the juxtaposing of 'Kilmurry' and 'Cill Mhuire', 'Cashel' and 'Caiseal', 'Thurles' and 'Dúrlas', 'Charleville' and 'An Ráth',[51] the latter example might have been used to settle the lengthy debate on the contested identification of 'Charleville' with 'Ráth Luirc'. As in the case of personal names, parallel series of Irish-language and anglicized English-language place-names bear testimony to the participation of the native Irish in the public sphere generated by the dominant class, albeit a participation which required them to adhere to the norms of the ascendant polity. This is not to deny that there were deep divisions along the fault-lines of religion as well as language and culture. In the end, as has often been observed, the people's attachment to the Catholic religion was to prove stronger than their attachment to the Irish language, a point appreciated as early as 1729 by that most perceptive observer of societal change, the Dublin-based Tadhg Ó Neachtain.

RELIGION AND LANGUAGE

Ó Neachtain's penetrating analysis of the way his compatriots were adapting to the prevailing realities of Irish life is to be found in *Eólas ar an domhan* (Knowledge about the world), a textbook on world geography, probably written about the year 1721, but certainly before 1729. Ó Neachtain derived much of his information from *A most compleat compendium of geography* by Laurence Eachard (1691) and *Geography anatomized* (1693)[52] by Patrick

---

49 Ibid.   **50** Ibid., p. 112, lines 65, 73, in Donncha Ó Súilleabháin's 'An Móta Glas'.   **51** Ibid., p. 92, lines 8, 16, 22, 30, in 'A new song called the flourishing states of Kilmurry'. **52** Various editions of *A most compleat compendium of geography* by Laurence Eachard or

Gordon, although he added material of his own (or perhaps by his father, Seán). Interestingly, the work is actually presented in the form of a dialogue between Tadhg and his father, both of whom were teachers.[53] Ó Neachtain shows that he was quite aware that a language shift from Irish to English was taking place among the better off native Irish. He states explicitly that the nobility were turning their backs on Irish, but were steadfast in their attachment to the Catholic religion. When broaching the subject he adverts to the traditional attachment of the Gaelic nobles to the Irish language, stressing the regard in which it had been held by all classes since olden times:

Mo-nuar anois ní bhfhuil aon do uaislibh Gaoidhil-fhine nach bhfhuil ag séana a tteanguibh, ag reic a n-ainimionna 7 mórdháil an Ghaodhuil Ghlais 7 fhine an Mhīle ūd do thríall chuguinn ōn Spāinn faoi mhóirscleō cródhacht', filídheacht', 7 foghluim. *Agus* ar bhfhás dóibh bhí meas ar an nGaodhulg, 'bhus 7 [t]hal[l], & is gach ball, mar theanga thíorramhuil líomhtha líonmhar bhríoghmhar ghrinn ghasta bhlasta b*h*inn, 7 sin rē mīltibh bliadhuin ...

As so uile is inmheasta go roibhe sí fo mheas mhór ag an rīgh mar áon ris an sclábhuidh; 7 anois do réir an bhile as airde di, trāth ghearrthar fo a bhun é, is uaithmhíalta troime a leagan go mór nō an rosán bheag bhíos láimh ris a' ttalamh. Do ēirghe an riocht cēadna do uaisle Gaoidhil co maith rena tteangan.[54]

(Alas now there is no one of the nobility of the Gaelic people who is not denying their tongue(s), selling off their names and the pride of Gael Glas and the people of that Míle who journeyed to us from Spain under a great shade of bravery, poetry, and learning. And when they established themselves, Irish was respected, here and yonder, and in every place as a language of the soil, fluent, abundant, lively, precise, swift, tasty, sweet, and that for thousands of years up to now ...

And from all this it may be appreciated that it was held in great esteem by the king as well as the labourer; and now it is as the tallest tree, when it is cut under its base, it is much more dreadful and heavier to fell than the little shrubbery which is close to the ground. The same fate certainly befell the nobility of the Gaels as regards their language.)

Tadhg maintained that the fate of the Irish and the Jews was different, in that the Jews had lost their religion and their native culture, whereas the Irish

Echard (*c*.1670–1730) were published in London in 1691, 1693, 1697, 1700, 1704, 1705 and 1713. Patrick Gordon's *Geography anatomized, or the compleat geographical grammar* first published in London in 1693 ran to 20 editions between then and 1754. **53** See the introduction in Meadhbh Ní Chléirigh (ed.), *Eólas ar an domhan* (Baile Átha Cliath, 1944), pp vii–xi. Tadhg Ó Neachtain was the author. **54** Ní Chléirigh, op. cit., p. 13.

still had their religion: 'Óir d'imigh a gcreideamh 7 a ndúthchas uatha, 7 gī gur imigh a ndūthchas ó c*h*lanna Gaodhuil, tá a gcreideamh ar marthuinn acu.' ('For they lost their religion and their native culture, and although the descendants of Gael lost their native culture, they have still kept their religion alive.')[55]

One of the more arresting instances of the bilingual creativity addresseed in this essay is the dual-language debate in the poem entitled 'Tagra an dá theampall' (The disputation of the two churches) composed by Art Mac Cumhaigh (*c.*1738–73).[56] In this work the Catholic chapel (*Róimhchill*) initiates the altercation in Irish. Every second stanza contains the rejoinder by the Protestant church (a*n teampall gallda*), which is given in English. The first salvo, fired by the Catholic chapel, goes as follows in translation:

> Between Forkhill of the clerics and Faughart of the Gaels, I slept last night in lodgings, and at daybreak I heard a young maid asking questions from afar, from the Roman church; and she enquired of the fine well-built church that she saw ready nearby: 'Was it the Gaels who fixed your walls, or the followers of Luther or the descendants of the *Strongbownians?*'

The Protestant church responds, extolling the English language, British affluence and Protestant ascendancy:

> *In spite of your beads my English shall reign,*
> *Whilst Irish grows daily odious;*
> *England and Wales have riches in heaps,*
> *To flourish away most glorious;*
> *My flock has estates, with land and demesnes,*
> *All riding in state their coaches,*
> *While taxes, arrears, and cesses severe*
> *Upon your Gaedhelian broaches.*

Catholic chapel and Protestant church alternate in subsequent stanzas.[57]

---

55 Ibid., pp 12–13.   56 Énrí Ó Muirgheasa (eag.), *Dánta diadha Uladh* (Baile Átha Cliath, 1936/1969), pp 375–9. See also Tomás Ó Fiaich (eag.), *Art Mac Cumhaigh: dánta* (Baile Átha Cliath, 1973), pp 176–71. The date of composition is discussed on p. 142.   57 It is to be noted that there is a single manuscript exception to the bilingual presentation of the foregoing debate, one in which both protagonists declaim in Irish. Although at first sight this may seem to thwart the creative impact of the work, it is no different to the approach adopted by Brian Friel in *Translations* (London, 1981), where the audience have to ignore linguistic reality and imagine that half the action communicated via English is spoken in Irish. This all-Irish version was chosen by Tomás Ó Fiaich for his anthology of Art Mac Cumhaigh's poems, *Art Mac Cumhaigh*, pp 84–7. The dual-language version of the poem is included, with translation of the Irish stanzas, in Carpenter, *Verse in English*, pp 323–6.

The sermons of Séamus Ó Gallchóir (James Gallagher), who became Catholic bishop of Raphoe (Donegal) in 1725 and subsequently bishop of Kildare in 1737, avoided the fate of most contemporary works in Irish, firstly, by being published at all in 1736, and, secondly, and more significantly by being regularly reprinted. While the sermons, which are based on continental exemplars, are in Irish, the introduction and section headings are in English, and interestingly for our purposes, the author explicitly states why he had recourse to English words in the sermons:

> I have made them in an easy and familiar style and on purpose omit-ted cramp expressions which might be obscure to both the preacher and hearer. Nay, instead of such, I have sometimes made use of words borrowed from the English, which practice and daily conversation have intermixed with our language, choosing with St. Augustine rather to be censured by the critics than not to be understood by the poor and illiterate, for whose use I have designed them.[58]

Like Bishop Gallagher, Fr Muiris Paor (1791–1877) unhesitatingly echoed contemporary language use; he not only included straightforward English words such as 'murdar', 'stage', 'mob', 'sway' but also phonetically adjusted loans such as 'timptáisiun', 'pillóir', 'drúncéir' and 'reibiliúntacht'. Tadhg Ó Dúshláine has shown that Fr Paor even composed new verbs such as 'compordú', 'milsíonn', 'rollaíonn', 'preasálaid', 'síocháineann', and adopted an English proverbial expression: *Inis dom do chuideachta agus neosad duit cé hé tú féin* (Tell me your company and I will tell you who you are).[59]

The following is part of a sermon in which another priest, Fr Pádraig de Bhál *fl.* 1812–33, exhorted his listeners to contribute to a collection to repair the local church in advance of a visit by the bishop. Fr de Bhál had a very clear idea of what needed to be done by way of '*repairs* an tsepeil' [the repairs of the chapel]:

> An lá deanach avi me inso, avi me a tracht air *repairs* an tsepeil 7 an *yard* sin amugh gan bala na fala leish, le morán de vlianta ... cahamaid, gan stad, sraih a leagaint air a bparaisde, 7 *collection* teacrach a yeana, chun an sepeal 7 an *yard* a chur in ordugh, ionus go mbeich seipeal, *yard* slachtvar aguin, le haigh an Easpuig, 7 air vaihe lena ccreiduint féin. Is fada anoish ó creanaig aorad leish a sipeal so, níor rinag aon *collection* le morán do vlianta, ach aon *chollection* avain chun collaiche

58 James Gallagher, *Sixteen Irish sermons in an easy and familiar stile, on useful and neces-sary subjects* (Dublin, 1736), p. iv, cited in Ciarán Mac Murchaidh, 'Oiliúint na cléire san 18ú haois agus an Dochtúir Séamas Ó Gallchóir', *Taighde agus Teagasc*, 1 (2001), 11–25 at 23. 59 These are discussed in Tadhg Ó Dúshláine, 'Gealán dúluachra: seanmóireacht na Gaeilge *c.*1600–1850', *Léachtaí Cholm Cille*, 26 (1996), 83–122 at 99.

7 ornaidigh na haltorach a cheanach, ... insa cceadait, cahamaid balla a yeana leish an *front*, piorudh 7 geata iorain a cheanach, aha na fuinguga le deisiugh 7 *shutters* a chur leoha chun na braoisfai iad, mar do rinad go minic rive seo; 7 ase in uafás ahorm, na go mbriseach aon *vlagard* og nó sean, gan scrupul air a choinsias, *pana* in aon fhuinyog a vaineach le tigh De, 7 na fuil aon *phana* yiav sin na cosanion 2.6., tastion urlár on *sacristy*, *drains* a houirt trid 7 trid a *yard*, chun an altoior 7 aymud na haltorach a havail, an altóir a *feintail*, y lan nihe nach ga trácht orha anoish.[60]

(The last day I was here, I was talking about the repairs of the *chapel* and that *yard* out there without a wall or a fence around it, for many years, ... we will have to, immediately, place a tax on the parish, and take up a gleaning *collection*, to put the chapel and *yard* in order, so that we will have a neat chapel and *yard* for the Bishop, and for our own credit. It is a long time since anything was bought for this chapel, and no *collection* has been made for many years, except one *collection* only to buy cloth and ornaments for the altar, ... In the first place, we will have to build a wall on the *front*, buy a pillar and an iron gate, the windows have to be repaired and *shutters* put on to them so that they won't be broken, as was done often before; and the thing I fear, is that any *blackguard*, young or old, with no scruple on his conscience, would break a *pane* in any window which is part of God's house, and every one of those *panes* costs 2[*s.*] 6[*d.*], the *sacristy* needs a floor, *drains* need to be brought through it and through the *yard*, to the altar and the wood of the altar has to be preserved, the altar has to be *painted*, [and] a lot of things which need not be mentioned now.

The prominence of English loanwords in the Irish-language sermons of Catholic priests and the large number of sermons written in English-based phonetic spellings rather than in standard Irish orthography should not detract from the complexity of the overall position. There were other creative streams at work as well. Sermons were composed under two quite different, and to a certain extent conflicting, linguistic pressures: the desire on the one hand to be understood by the congregation in accessible, everyday language, and, on the other, to reflect the loftiness of the thoughts and teachings pertaining to the sacred and the supernatural. An interesting example of the attempt to attain an appropriate formal register is to be found in a work entitled *Irish sermons with translations*, based on the preaching of Fr John Meany from the Decies, which was published in Dublin in 1835.[61] The following objective was set out in the

---

60 Ibid., 117–18 from the undated sermon entitled 'Deisiú an tséipéil' ['Repairing the church']. 61 *Irish sermons with translations* (Dublin, 1835) was published by John S. Folds. I am grateful to Dr Ciarán Mac Murchaidh for bringing this work to my attention

preface, which accompanied the sermon 'Air charthanacht, nó grádh na c-comharsan' (On charity, or loving one's neighbours):

> it is to the altar and to the clergy we must look for improving the Irish language, and bringing it back to what it was. By degrees this improvement can be effected. The people are delighted when they hear any specimens of a higher style, and they understand it as well as they do the most familiar, or the most common. The present Sermon will not present any great degree of this elevated style, having been, as already mentioned, selected for its plain simplicity, as on that account the most suited to begin with.[62]

A flavour of this work can be got from the sentence 'saidhbhrios agus caithréim agus mórmheas, ní mhairid ach seal' (wealth and triumph and great respect, they only last a while), which is then subjected to insightful discourse analysis:

> The common way of saying this would be, *Ni vairid sai*vrios agus cai*réim agus mór-veas, ach seal;* but the style above adopted, of reciting the nouns first, and throwing the verb with its negative, back to the end of the sentence, adds much to its beauty and force, and makes the style in fact, a little poetic, though at the same time solemn, and particularly suited to the nature of the discourse.[63]

In many other ways the actual production of this volume is at one with other publications in that the title, title page, and preface of *Irish sermons with translations* are all in English and an English translation is provided after the Irish sermons, the Irish text being presented in Gaelic font.

CONTEXT, CONCEPTS AND CONCLUSION

By the eighteenth century much of the rancour associated with the use of English within the Irish textual tradition was yielding to a mixture of pragmatism and literary exploitation, as the Irish were transforming themselves into *lucht an Bhéarla*, the formerly despised 'others' of poets such as Mac Cumhaigh.[64] Code-mixing could serve both to gain the attention of an audience and to keep that attention by deploying a creative dexterity, which at times could achieve linguistic exuberance. The thematic emphasis varied. The warrant, for instance, was explicitly satiric and as a *genre* it parodied the law,

and for making a copy available.   **62** Ibid., pp iv–v.   **63** Ibid., p. v.   **64** See the discussion in Watson, 'Coimhlint an dá chultúr'.

subverting respect for the *status quo*. The cross-linguistic vocabulary echoes common to prose tales and macaronic love-songs show how traditional compositional features could be adapted to represent realistic conversational turn-taking. The handling of place-names and personal names and the monitoring of who speaks which language to whom can tell us much about the stresses and strains, push and pull factors of language shift from the inside.

Bakhtin's observation regarding continental European languages at an earlier period, that 'The macaronic literature of the Middle Ages is likewise an extremely important and interesting document in the struggle and interanimation among languages'[65] would seem to be applicable to Ireland's linguistic experience in the eighteenth century. The linguistic history of the century also confirms Bhabha's judgment that 'the borderline engagements of cultural difference may as often be consensual as conflictual'.[66]

The evidence adduced in this essay is text-based and the analysis has focused on two successful literary fields in which English acquired an ancillary role alongside Irish. The results of the enquiry are at variance with the broad brushstrokes of Daniel Corkery[67] and Joep Leerssen,[68] which paint an over-simplified picture of an apartheid-like organization of Irish life in the eighteenth century in which a single English-only public sphere relegated Irish speakers to non-contiguous Irish-medium private spaces. The linguistic evidence for permeating bilingualism presented in this essay confounds this hypothesis. The *genre* of the warrant shows that the Irish-speaking poets and their community in the southern half of the country were so familiar with the exercise of the common law legal system that they were empowered to use it explicitly, firstly, in a way which lent the requisite verisimilitude to their compositions, and, secondly, in a manner which tended to subvert the power-structure of the overwhelmingly dominant ascendancy polity and the social pretensions of the Catholic clergy within their own community. At least one feature of many macaronic songs, namely the preference of the females depicted therein for English, can be interpreted as an implicit aligning of the more vulnerable party with the public administrative sphere. Of course, the *genre* as a whole bears eloquent testimony to the progress of the language shift from Irish to English, which again can be interpreted as a community decision by the native, Gaelic Irish to insert themselves into the public sphere, the body politic, their assumption being that they would be at least tolerated if they changed their language and culture. The ultimate irony was that, despite the penal laws, they realized that they would not be required to abandon their Roman Catholic religion for Protestantism.

65 M.M. Bakhtin, 'From the prehistory of novelistic discourse' in Michael Holquist (ed.), *The dialogic imagination: four essays by M.M. Bakhtin* (Austin, 1981), pp 41–83 at p. 79. 66 Homi K. Bhabha, *The location of culture* (London and New York, 2005), p. 3.   67 Daniel Corkery, *The hidden Ireland: a study of Gaelic Munster in the eighteenth century* (Dublin 1924/1967).   68 Joep Leerssen, *Hidden Ireland, public sphere* (Galway, 2002).

In addition to the particular areas of concern addressed in this essay, the evidence for social interaction between the Irish-speaking and English-speaking communities would seem to be so all-embracing that it begs the question as to how and why it should have been overlooked or minimized. From the Gaelic perspective, mention may be made of the use of English by Seán and Tadhg Ó Neachtain in Dublin, particularly the dual-language nature of the commonplace entries in a number of Tadhg's manuscripts, where he drew on the Dublin newspapers published in the early part of the eighteenth century, as described by Breandán Ó Buachalla.[69] Studies by Neil Buttimer provide complementary material from elsewhere in later periods.[70] Important volumes by Breandán Ó Conchúir[71] and Meidhbhín Ní Úrdail[72] have shed much light on the interplay of the print-cum-English medium and that of the manuscript-cum-Irish tradition. Alan Harrison has traced Tadhg Ó Neachtain's friendship with Anthony Raymond, a graduate of Trinity College Dublin, by which means the Ó Neachtain circle gained access to works from Trinity's library.[73] Swift's translation of 'Pléaráca na Ruarcach' (O'Rourkes' Revels), attributed to the county Cavan poet, Aodh Mac Gabhráin, whether he received assistance or not, is just one of many instances of the social divide being bridged by music and song.[74] Nor does the evidence for intellectual contact have to be bilingual in nature. On the contrary, Breandán Ó Buachalla's monumental study of the development of Jacobite ideology sources for which are almost exclusively in Irish, shows just how *au fait* with the development of intellectual concepts of governance and authority in western Europe the Irish-speaking intelligentsia were.[75]

69 Breandán Ó Buachalla, 'Seaicibíteachas Thaidhg Uí Neachtain', *Studia Hibernica*, 26 (1991–2), 31–64. See also S.J. Connolly, '"Ag déanamh *commanding*": elite responses to popular culture, 1660–1850' in J.S. Donnelly Jr and Kerby A. Miller (eds), *Irish popular culture, 1650–1850* (Dublin, 1999), pp 1–29, and Liam Mac Mathúna, 'Snapshot or signpost? The role of English in Tadhg Ó Neachtain's early eighteenth-century manuscripts' in Maxim Fomin et al. (eds), *Dimensions and categories of Celticity: studies in literature and culture* (Łódź, 2010), pp 29–46. **70** See for instance C.G. Buttimer, 'An Irish text on the "War of Jenkins' ear"', *Celtica*, 21 (1990), 75–98; *idem*, '*Cogadh Sagsana Nuadh sonn*: reporting the American revolution', *Studia Hibernica*, 28 (1994), 63–101. Citing Buttimer and others, Regina Uí Chollatáin stresses continuity in the historical development of Irish-language journalism and points out that while Irish-language print culture was not as developed as that of Welsh or Scottish Gaelic it certainly did exist. She holds that it is therefore difficult to concur with Leerssen that there was no Irish-language public sphere and also argues that the print culture of the revival provided the public sphere for English speakers through the medium of Irish rather than a 'constituency' for the native Irish speaker: 'Irish-language journalism and print culture in the revival period', paper delivered at the conference on 'Print culture after Union: the impact of 1707 and 1800 on the book in Scotland and Ireland', UCD, 12–13 Dec. 2008. **71** Breandán Ó Conchúir, *Scríobhaithe Chorcaí 1700–1850* (Baile Átha Cliath, 1982). **72** Meidhbhín Ní Úrdail, *The scribe in eighteenth- and nineteenth-century Ireland* (Münster, 2000). **73** Alan Harrison, *Ag cruinniú meala: Anthony Raymond (1675–1726), ministéir Protastúnach, agus léann na Gaeilge i mBaile Átha Cliath* (Baile Átha Cliath, 1988). **74** See C.G. Ó Háinle, 'Neighbors in eighteenth-century Dublin: Jonathan Swift and Seán Ó Neachtain', *Éire-Ireland*, 21:4 (Winter

This is not to deny that there is much of value in the provocative analyses of Leerssen and Corkery before him, as they pit Gael against Gall, or
rather assert that they trod different road networks, one formed of highways,
the other of boreens. The challenge is not to try to impose the straitjacket of
a continental-born and powerful explanatory theory on the particular Irish
circumstances, for periods where there was clearly a major power/cultural/
religious divide and a subaltern population, but rather, informed by such con-
trastive theoretical insights, to seek to develop a conceptual framework which
is responsive to the specific features of the Irish situation. This will necessi-
tate close reading of sources in both Irish and English – reading as often as
not between the lines, as well as the actual lines of the English material in
particular. For surely it was the propensity of the native Irish to be variously,
and sometimes simultaneously, invisible, conformist, subversive and ambiguous, as they struggled to survive, that explains their ultimate ability to de-
anglicize and re-gaelicize (albeit, only partially) the public sphere. Material
developments such as the rotary press and wood-pulp can only be called upon
to explain so much. The public sphere and, indeed, even imagined communities are not static: individuals and groups jostle for power and dominance.
It may have been a case of 'now you see him, now you don't', but the unset-
tling presence of the Gael must have overshadowed everything in the supposedly monoglot English-language public sphere created in Ireland from the
seventeenth century onwards. The dominance of the ascendancy public
sphere is not in question. But the complex nature – and fragility – of this
public sphere still awaits appropriately nuanced analysis.

1986), 106–21, for a discussion of the general cultural context and references.   **75**
Breandán Ó Buachalla, *Aisling ghéar: na Stíobhartaigh agus an t-aos léinn 1603–1788* (Baile
Átha Cliath, 1996).

5

An Ghaelig nua: English, Irish and the south Ulster poets and scribes in the late seventeenth and eighteenth centuries

CHARLES DILLON

The area of south Ulster and north Leinster, coterminous roughly with the Gaelic region of Oirghialla, and with modern day south Armagh, south Down, Louth, Monaghan and north Meath, was characterized as a borderland, or interface between the Gaelic core of central Ulster to the north and west, and the Old English heartland to the south-east throughout the late medieval and early modern period.[1] It can be argued, indeed, that it best lived up to this characterization during the period of the late seventeenth century and throughout the eighteenth century when, as well as experiencing some of the more traumatic events of the Cromwellian and Williamite campaigns, and the growth of important urban centres at Newry and Dundalk, the area was the crucible of an emerging culture of sectarianism, and of Gaelic literary activity in the northern portion of the island. It is a region whose harbours nurtured much of the economic development of south Ulster and north Leinster, but whose mountains sustained a vibrant and sophisticated Gaelic culture – attested by the rich and unique pickings modern day folklore collectors and philologists found there – until the mid-twentieth century.[2]

Editions of the works of late seventeenth- and eighteenth-century Irish poets and song-makers from south Ulster/north Leinster have been compiled by modern scholars from manuscript copies and from the oral tradition, ensuring for them a place in the canon of Irish-language literature.[3] The more eminent of their number also enjoy enduring fame and reputation with the people among whom they once lived; tales and legends abound to this very

---

1 See Raymond Gillespie and Harold O'Sullivan (eds), *Borderlands: essays on the history of the Ulster-Leinster border* (Belfast, 1989).   2 Pádraigín Ní Uallacháin, *A hidden Ulster: people, songs and traditions of Oriel* (Dublin, 2003) contains an exhaustive treatment of this phenomenon.   3 Seán Ó Gallchóir (ed.) *Séamas Dall Mac Cuarta: dánta* (Baile Átha Cliath, 1972); Seosamh Mag Uidhir (ed.) *Pádraig Mac a Liondain: dánta* (Baile Átha Cliath, 1977); Seán de Rís, *Peadar Ó Doirnín: a bheatha agus a shaothar* (Baile Átha Cliath, 1969); Tomás Ó Fiaich (ed.) *Art Mac Cumhaigh: dánta* (Baile Átha Cliath, 1973); Breandán Ó Buachalla, (ed.) *Cathal Buí: amhráin* (Baile Átha Cliath, 1975).

day concerning controversies, courtships and other escapades of these men. A more subtle reading, based on the primary manuscript sources of these texts is overdue, however, as they provide much useful evidence about the linguistic fluctuation and interactive social networks in south Ulster, and, by extension, throughout Ireland, during the late seventeenth and early eighteenth centuries. Account must be taken also of the changing nature of scribal mediation in the reproduction and presentation of texts, when they worked for patrons or, later, in pursuit of personal fame or political agenda; moreover, the nuanced relationship of poets to their patrons, many of whom were not of Gaelic stock, would also bear further attention, and it is my intention that this essay, while seeking to cast light on the linguistic dimension of the interaction between native and newcomer, represents a step in that direction.

I

The south Ulster literary heritage of the seventeenth and eighteenth centuries comprises a rich body of both poetry and prose. For the most part in manuscript form, it was composed, copied and distributed by a learned elite comparable to that which had been the linchpin of the Gaelic order until it succumbed to the relentless aggression of the New English in the sixteenth and early seventeenth centuries. Despite this, a system appears to have remained in existence in this area whereby poets and writers retained the patronage of the remants of the native and elements of the newly established landed class, although this practice weakened as the eighteenth century wore on, and as the number of wealthy Catholic gentry contracted. An early poet, Séamas Dall Mac Cuarta (*c*.1647–1732), and his acquaintance the harper Toirdhealbhach Ó Cearbhalláin (Turlough Carolan, 1670–1738), both benefited from the benevolence of the Old English Cruise and Plunkett families, while there is evidence, in the form of a 211-line lament for Somhairle Mac Dónaill (killed at the Battle of Aughrim, 1691), that Mac Cuarta also enjoyed the patronage of the remnants of the Gaelic Irish landed class – this lament is the earliest extant poem of his *oeuvre*.[4] A contemporary poet and harper, Pádraig Mac a' Liondain (1665–1733) hosted gatherings of musicians and poets in his house in the Fews; such gatherings allowed poets to collaborate and to contend, as is borne out by the many poetic compositions extant from the early eighteenth century which have fellow poets as their subject, either of praise, satire or lament. Mac a' Liondain, for example, composed a poem in praise of the poetic genius of Mac Cuarta, an encomium subsequently lampooned by a younger poet, Peadar Ó Doirnín (*c*.1704–69).[5] Upon hearing of Ó Doirnín's death, his friend Art Mac

---

4 'Is in Eachroim an áir atáid ina gcónaí' in Ó Gallchóir (ed.), *Séamas Dall Mac Cuarta*, pp 63–9.   5 'Moladh Shéamais Mhic Cuarta' in Mag Uidhir (ed.), *Pádraig Mac a*

Cumhaigh (1715–73) composed an elegy of eleven quatrains.[6] Such textual evidence, when set in the context of the substantial volume of Irish manuscript material generated in the area attests to the existence of a sophisticated community of *literati* still attached to the systems and modes of Gaelic Ireland, but reacting to and evolving in the rapidly changing, and increasingly anglophone, society in which they found themselves.

The negative response of poets across Ireland in the late seventeenth and early eighteenth centuries to the anglicization of Irish society and culture was replicated by the poets of south Ulster. Mac Cuarta, for example, lamented the indifference to his craft among the general populace, but, unlike the later Mac Cumhaigh, is less plaintive about the poor reception afforded his art, which is indicative of a further diminution in interest as time wore on. Instead of lamenting times past when his kind were enthusiastically received, the older Mac Cuarta viciously excoriated, even dismissing as sub-human, those who failed to recognize his worth. Mac Cumhaigh, by contrast, is more of a voice in the wilderness, sharing his dreams of halcyon days before the arrival of the foreigners. The contrasting audience for their work and the alienation the poets felt as a result is echoed in some facets of their work, notably the tendency to frame their poems against their own loneliness and solitude. This is particularly manifest in those composed in the *aisling*, or 'vision-poem' *genre*, but it is evident also in the tendency to engage in poetic dialogue with sites and artefacts from the Gaelic heyday – in Ó Doirnín's case with the hill of Tara,[7] and in Mac Cumhaigh's case with Glasdrummond castle, which was formerly the seat of power of the O'Neills of the Fews – and to use them as opportunities for historical and political commentary. In his poem, Mac Cumhaigh addresses Glasdrummond castle as follows:[8]

A aolchloch dhaite bhí i bhfad ag síol Néill gan smúid,
Nó gur básadh in Eachroim gach aicme de na Gaeil, mo chumhaidh, ...
Gur réabadh fá thalamh do bhallaí 'na mbladhaibh dubh.

(Limestone long owned by the spotless family of Niall,
Until all the Gaels died at Aughrim, to my sorrow, ...
Until your walls were razed into pieces to the ground.)

The castle responds, in the next quatrain, that it has given up on the prospect of rescue since its inhabitants are now buried in the nearby churchyard of Creggan, and proceeds to bemoan other Jacobite defeats and the supremacy of the Hanoverians. However, it is the observation on the poet's mode of

Liondain, p. 12. Ó Doirnín's reply is 'Más libh amháin is le mic Dághda': see de Rís, *Peadar Ó Doirnín*, p. 3.   **6** 'Feartlaoi Pheadair Uí Dhoirnín' in de Rís, *Peadar Ó Doirnín*, pp 51–2.   **7** 'Agallamh le Cnoc na Teamhrach': for text see de Rís, *Peadar Ó Doirnín*, pp 6–8.   **8** Ó Fiaich (ed.), *Art Mac Cumhaigh*, p. 82. All translations are by this author.

address – 'go gcanann tú an Ghaelig nua' ('you speak new Gaelic') – that casts the most revealing light upon the cultural and linguistic change in the area. Significantly, the phrase does not allude to the increasing encroachment of English, which is referred to elsewhere by the poet, but rather to the internal changes the Irish language was, to the poet's mind, undergoing; he was evidently conscious of the fact that he was using new literary idioms and forms, different to those employed by his poetic predecessors and, as he perceived it, less authentic and resonant in function and character.

The nature and content of Mac Cumhaigh's dialogues and vision-poems speak of an individual who felt alienated, perhaps even anachronistic, within his own milieu, and the lack of security and certainty that a patron or an appreciative audience must have provided is given expression in such compositions. His sensitivity was doubtlessly informed by the fact that the esteem in which poets and poetry were held had waned considerably since the time of Mac Cuarta. Moreover, this was ongoing, and the anger and resentment that it fostered was given further embittered expression in the contempt that poets directed towards the self-assured, upwardly mobile within their own community, whom they portrayed as social upstarts, bereft of the learning and poetic skills cherished in earlier Gaelic Ireland, but confident and assertive in their dealings with the poets. 'Bodaigh', ('churls') is a term frequently applied to such persons, as in the pair of satires directed by Mac Cumhaigh against the O'Callaghan brothers of Culloville in south Armagh, who had evidently made money in the brewing industry. In these poems Mac Cumhaigh belittles the mode of dress adopted by them and their family for following English rather than the Irish fashion; he derides their gluttonous appetites, their general ignorance, and their lack of appreciation for his poetry, an indifference which appears to have been their only error, and which earned them these satires.[9] No less indicatively, given the traditional rivalry of poets and clergy, and the respect the latter were increasingly afforded, Mac Cumhaigh also alludes in his satire to the propensity of the Catholic clergy to frequent the houses of the brothers and their generous, self-serving hospitality.

Mac Cumhaigh's invocation of hospitality afforded to those ill-deserving of it, and denied to those who, from the poets' perspective, should be feted and hosted, is reminiscent of an earlier satire from the pen of Mac Cuarta, in which the inhabitants of a house near Omeath in county Louth were derided for shunning the poet and his companion. The poet characterizes his detractors as engaging in 'béasa an bhroic' (badger's behaviour), content to scrabble in clay rather than open their ears to the felicity of his verses and his company.[10] The reference is rather cryptic, but suggests that the priority of the general populace was no longer to applaud Mac Cuarta and his poetry, but

9 'Bodaigh na hEorna', ibid., pp 102–4.   10 'Tithe Chorr an Chait' in Ó Gallchóir (ed.), *Séamas Dall Mac Cuarta*, p. 76.

to survive and provide for their own. Mac Cuarta's bitter dismissal of them is revealing of just how difficult the search for patronage had become, how removed from ordinary people the poetic class and their pursuits were, and how resentful the poets were that the quest for wealth and social respectability was being pursued at the expense, they perceived, of traditional conviviality.

This satire by Séamas Dall Mac Cuarta provides one of the most revealing illustrations of a particular innovation that took place within Gaelic poetry during his lifetime, of which he was the foremost exponent. Throughout the late medieval and early modern period, Irish poetry drew on a set of intricate metrical rules, based primarily on the manipulation of syllables within each line coupled to internal rhyme schemes. Excellence in this form of composition was only achieved after years of training and was the preserve of a poetic elite who jealously conserved their craft and among whom innovation was not de rigeur. However, following the disruption of the network of aristocratic patronage that maintained this poetic order, poets began gradually to innovate in order to appeal to a less elitist, less discerning audience, and fewer compositions observing strict, esoteric metrical rules were written from the end of the seventeenth century. Despite this shift in audience reception, Mac Cuarta and others contrived successfully to combine both the older metrics and the popular song metres to new poetic effect, in a form often compared to the English sonnet. Three quatrains were composed in observance of the older metrical formulae, to which were added as conclusion four lines in the looser and more popular *amhrán*, or song metre. While the addition of a concluding verse in song metre to a longer poem was nothing new in the Irish tradition, this self-limiting, sixteen-line form of verse did represent a new departure and considerable skill was needed to make poetic art sit comfortably within the constricted space. Some nineteen poems in this form composed by Mac Cuarta are extant, and the propagation of the 'trí rainn agus amhrán' form in Ulster owes much to his skill in its manipulation.[11]

The epithet 'bodach' is most frequently found in the poetry within the phrase 'bodaigh an Bhéarla' (English-speaking churls), and it is combined with 'clann Liútair' (children of Luther), 'clann Bhullaí' (children of Willy/William) and other such abusive terms to denigrate the settlers, planters, landlords and others whom the poets categorized as oppressors who now occupied lands that the poets deemed the birthright of the Gaelic race. In their protestations at this state of affairs, the poets regularly evoked two distinct ethnicities separated both by creed and tongue, juxtaposing the English 'clann Liútair' etc. with 'Sliocht Ghaeil' (the descendants of the Gael), 'Síol Éireamhoin' (the seed of Éireamhon), 'treibh Mhíleadh' (the tribe of Milesius), and other appellations connotive of the Gaelic and Irish lineage

---

11 Colm Ó Baoill and Cathaoir Ó Dochartaigh (eds), *Trí rainn agus amhrán* (Ceann Drochaid, 2006) contains edited versions of the 103 poems extant in this style.

that stretched back to the origin myth. The new settlers were also often accused of trampling the Catholic faith, harrassing the Catholic clergy, and, although sympathy with the Jacobite cause is less in evidence in eighteenth-century Ulster poetry than in that of Munster, the defeat of the Jacobites is invariably largely presented as the primary cause of the devastating land transferral and the eclipse of the Gaelic aristocracy. The complaint of Mac Cumhaigh's castle is typical:[12]

> Ón lá sin Manchester[13] sé mheasaim go mbéad ar siúl,
> D'fhág Cathal[14] is a bhunadh gan urraim fá na sléibhtibh cúil,
> Muna bhfuasclaidh Paris, Versailles, nó Vénice dúinn
> Ag ardú na mbratach leis an fleur ghlan tséimh de lúce.

> (Since that day in Manchester I hold I am defeated,
> Charles and his followers having been laid low in remote mountains,
> Unless Paris, Versailles or Venice come to our aid
> Raising the flags with the beautiful bright *fleur-de-lys*.)

Mac Cumhaigh, in one of his vision-poems, speaks of the encroachment of the English language into his territory. The lady who addresses him in his reverie, as he lies at Howth harbour, in exile from his own area, tells him:[15]

> Tá mo chroí-se réabtha 'na mhíle céad cuid,
> Agus balsam féin nach bhfóireann mo phian,
> Nuair a chluinim an Ghaelig uilig dá tréigbheáil,
> Agus caismirt Bhéarla i mbeol gach aoin,
> Bhullaigh is Jane ag glacadh léagsaí,
> Ar dhúichibh Éireann na n-órbhall caoin,
> 'S nuair a fhiafraím scéala 'sé freagra gheibhim:
> 'You're a Papist, I know not thee.'

> (My heart is rent in a thousand pieces,
> Even balsam will not soothe my pain,
> When I hear Gaelic completely abandoned
> English chatter in the mouth of everyone,
> William and Jane taking leases,
> In the golden beautiful regions of Ireland,
> And when I ask, the answer I'm given,
> 'You're a Papist, I know not thee.')

12 Ó Fiaich (ed.), *Art Mac Cumhaigh*, p. 83.   13 This may refer to the failure to garner the wholesale support of English Jacobites upon the arrival of the Jacobite force in Manchester on 10 Dec. 1745. The planned advance on London was subsequently abandoned.   14 Charles Edward Stuart, styled Charles III, known as the Young Pretender and Bonnie Prince Charlie (1720–88), was the Jacobite claimant to the English, Scottish and Irish thrones.   15 Ó Fiaich (ed.), *Art Mac Cumhaigh*, pp 111–13.

This one verse encapsulates the poet's despair at the encroachment and, the text suggests, it must be suspected, the increasing dominance of English over the Irish language, and of those of English and Scottish backgrounds and the Protestant religion who were favoured in the leasing policies of landowners throughout the kingdom. It is noteworthy that the poet was in Howth at the time of composition; perhaps a period of time at a remove from home provoked thoughts on the disagreeable social developments to which his *aisling* bears witness in the poem.[16] His evocation of the *aisling*, and her expressed feelings of linguistic isolation, demonstrate the extent to which Mac Cumhaigh felt patrimony and language to be linked. Similarly, the extent to which language, faith and nationhood were linked in his mind is also evident in his poetry, and it finds its most vivid manifestation in his poetic dialogue, between the church and shrine of St Bridget at Faughart, county Louth, long a site of devotion and Catholic worship (and more significant during penal times), and the new Church of Ireland church at nearby Forkhill, erected in 1767, some six years before Mac Cumhaigh's death.[17] The two churches debate heatedly matters of faith and politics, each characterizing the other as being ignorant, in decay, in bondage, and of being based on a whimsical and an ill-conceived theology. The most intriguing aspect of the dialogue, however, is its form; the Catholic Church makes its accusations in Irish and the Protestant church responds in English. The complete text exists in four manuscripts from the nineteenth century; its earliest appearance dates from manuscript 23 L 7, written by Simon Macken in 1782–3, housed now in the Royal Irish Academy.[18] Ó Muirgheasa, in his 1926 edition of Mac Cumhaigh's work suggests that John Short collaborated with Mac Cumhaigh in this composition, contributing the English stanzas, but this may be a nineteenth-century tradition.[19] Mac Cumhaigh was known to have found himself in conflict with his local Catholic clergy, and this bilingual poem displays a measure of objectivity, if not of scepticism, not always manifested by contemporary poets when confessional matters were at issue. To refer to 'false doctrine', 'ignorant papist notions' and 'Luther the great', for example, is near-the-knuckle humour, although the Catholic shrine gives as good as it gets throughout the poem. Whatever inspired him, and even if Ó Muirgheasa is correct in his assumption about Short's involvement, these verses tell us much about poetic composition and its reception; competence in both English and Irish was

16 There is a tradition that Mac Cumhaigh was 'exiled' to Howth after a dispute with a local priest. The reason for the dispute is uncertain: see Ó Fiaich (ed.), *Art Mac Cumhaigh*, pp 34–8.   17 Angelique Day and Patrick McWilliams (eds), *Ordnance Survey memoirs of Ireland vol. 1, parishes of county Armagh 1835–8* (Belfast, 1990), p. 45.   18 M.E. Byrne (ed.), *Catalogue of Irish manuscripts in the Royal Irish Academy*, fasc. 3 (Dublin, n.d.) (hereafter, *RIA Catalogue*), pp 315–9 for a description of the manuscript and its contents.   19 Énrí Ó Muirgheasa (ed.), *Abhráin Airt Mhic Cubhthaigh agus abhráin eile* (Dún Dealgan, 1926), p. 104. For the text of the poem, see pp 7–10.

necessary for any audience in order to process fully and appreciate the import of the poem. Indicatively, of the five manuscript copies of this poem that have survived, one (RIA 24 L 31, dated 1820–3) is entirely in Irish; the English verses attributed to the Protestant church have been translated in this text into Irish, most probably by the scribe Patrick McGahan of Dungooley, Faughart. Evidently, translation activity was not into English alone although McGahan's motives are admittedly unclear; did he translate for a monoglot Irish reader who did not understand the English verses, or to create a single poem in Irish to attribute to Mac Cumhaigh? Whatever the answer, his intervention is further evidence of the growing readiness of scribes to mediate their material as the nineteenth century wore on.

The encroachment of the new language is a motif more commonly encountered in the work of Mac Cumhaigh than of the older Mac Cuarta, and this difference may reflect the shifting language dynamics of the eighteenth century. Mac Cuarta does, however, advert to the increasing presence of English in his home area in one poem in which he addresses a residence to which he has returned, but which has since been inhabited by English-speaking settlers; in response to Mac Cuarta's opening line 'cár ghabh m'fháilte?' (Where has my welcome gone?), the house replies 'What is that you say …? I cannot understand your Gaelic'. Thereafter, the poet translates for the reader in a narrative that presents a discussion between the two sides on the subjects of their differences of religion and language, in which the house asserts the dominance, theologically, economically and militarily of English-speaking Protestants. The poet is instructed to remove himself to 'Inis Eoghain mar labhairtear Gaeilge' (to Inishowen where Irish is spoken) or to 'íochtar Éireann mar a bhfuilid Gael' (to the lower part of Ireland where the Gaels reside) if he wishes to persist in his backward ways.[20] This contention between the poet and the English-speaking Protestant building differs only from Mac Cumhaigh's dialogue between the two churches in that Mac Cuarta completes the narrative in Irish, having established early in the poem that the building's replies are in English, as Irish is not understood. It may be that this is indicative of the fact that the linguistic environment was less securely bilingual at the moment of its composition than it had become a generation later, when Mac Cumhaigh put pen to paper, which fits with an overall picture of a hastening language shift to English during the eighteenth century.

The local poetry of the period certainly demonstrates the insecurity of its composers, their fears for their art, and their disillusionment at the passing of the high culture they revered. It provides invaluable social commentary, and it can, as a result, be assigned to two categories: first, composition for Gaelic or Old English *cognoscenti* in 'shabby-genteel reminders of more prestigious

---

20 Lorcán Ó Muireadhaigh (ed.), *Amhráin Sheumais Mhic Cuarta* (Dún Dealgan, 1925), pp 38–40.

and truly *public* gatherings',[21] such as the laments for fallen Jacobites and the panegyrics for remnants of the O'Neill dynasty in the area, and for members of Old English families such as Cruise, Plunkett etc.; second, poetry which reflects its author's quotidian experiences, as evidenced by their reflections on nature, drinking songs and satires, and their personal, social and political commentary.[22] It is in the latter sphere where are to be found their observations on topics as diverse as matters of state such as Jacobitism and the Austrian War of Succession and the irritating behaviour of local brewers, that conclusions on their perspective on the linguistic landscape of contemporary south Ulster can be drawn. Although it did not overtly espouse the Jacobite cause, the poetry of south Ulster contains oblique references to the support for a Jacobite succession and to its implications at local level, and thus provides the political backdrop against which can be judged the social, religious and linguistic changes which shaped the poets' experience.

II

The implications that there were two competing monolithic cultures – that of the subaltern Gaelic poet, who was the hereditary practitioner of the high art of medieval Irish tradition, occluded now by an encroaching foreign culture to which he is alien – aligns readily with the 'Hidden Ireland' narrative so vividly expressed by Corkery in his treatment of Munster throughout the same period, but it does not apply uniformly if at all to the Ulster experience.[23] Even a cursory reading of the works of the time shows that interlingual and intercultural contact was ongoing, and this is borne out by the number of borrowings from English we find in poems.[24] Moreover, there is textual evidence that the south Ulster poets perceived competence in English as not only a marker of cultural and social otherness but also a sign of erudition; the poet Fearghas Mac Bheatha, in his elegy on Mac a' Liondain referred to his excellence in English,[25] while Peadar Ó Doirnín decried the fact that the woman he loved is with a 'fear gan Bhéarla, dubhghránna, crón' (a man without English, horrible and brown').[26] The implication that a lack of competence in English was indicative of boorishness and want of sophistication is taken further by the same poet in his satire on Muiris Ó Gormáin (Maurice O'Gorman).[27] Ó Doirnín's motivation for the lampoon is unclear,

21 Joep Leerssen, *Hidden Ireland, public sphere* (Galway, 2002), pp 36–7.   22 Tomás Ó Fiaich, 'Filíocht Uladh mar fhoinse don stair shóisialta', *Studia Hibernica*, 11 (1971), 80–129 offers an extensive treatment of the value of Ulster poetry as an historical source.   23 Daniel Corkery, *The hidden Ireland* (Dublin, 1925).   24 See Seosamh Watson, 'Coimhlint an dá chultúr: Gaeil agus Gaill i bhfilíocht chúige Uladh san ochtú haois déag', *Eighteenth-Century Ireland*, 3 (1988), 102 for a list of such borrowings.   25 Mag Uidhir (ed.), *Pádraig Mac a Liondain*, p. 1.   26 Breandán Ó Buachalla (ed.), *Peadar Ó Doirnín: amhráin* (Baile Átha Cliath, 1969), p. 61.   27 Ibid., pp 51–2.

although a nineteenth-century account gives as a reason his ire at O'Gorman having the temerity to set up a hedge school in competition with him, thereby threatening his standing in the locality and endangering his livelihood. The poem is bilingual, and tells of an encounter Ó Gormáin had with a lady on his way to Drogheda and his failed attempt to court her with his comically deficient English. The dialogue of Ó Gormáin and the lady constitutes the only English in the poem, the rest being Ó Gormáin's Irish narrative, and it is his attempts to speak English that provide the basis for the lampoon. On closer examination, however, we can see that Ó Gormáin's imperfect English phrases, as articulated by Ó Doirnín, echo Irish syntax and vocabulary. In this instance, as Mac Mathúna argues, we have an Irish poet wilfully and creatively using English as a medium for his satire; moreover, he is obviously more than competent in the language since he possesses the skill to marry it to his rhyme system without any loss of comic effect.[28] It can readily be imagined the damage that could be done to Ó Gormáin's professional credibility by his puted introduction of himself: 'Me is cristan Moresious Goraman cóir, / I is very school-measther'; but because their full satirical effect is lost upon other than a bilingual audience, it is obvious that the piece was composed with such an audience in mind, which is revealing both of the linguistic capabilities, and of the attitudes to linguistic competence of those in the artistic space that Ó Doirnín and Ó Gormáin inhabited.

Ó Doirnín cannot be categorized simply as a satirist and love-poet. A reading of his corpus reveals a more inflected world view, often at odds with the stereotypical image of the 'hidden Ireland' poet hankering after the high culture of the recent past. Conversely, in this instance, we can see a poet adapting to the new situation in which he found himself, composing poetry bilingually, receiving patronage from the very 'clann Bhullaí' so reviled by Mac Cumhaigh, and, on occasion, composing poetry solely in English. Our view of this complex man has been equally informed and obscured by the biographical sketches prepared in the mid-nineteenth century by Art Mac Bionaid (Arthur Bennett) and Nioclás Ó Cearnaigh (Nicholas Kearney), whose testimony is greatly at odds with respect to key aspects of the life and career of Ó Doirnín.[29] Basic facts such as place and year of birth do not tally. Still more seriously, Ó Buachalla has suggested that Ó Cearnaigh and an associate, Mathew Graham, included poetry of their own composition in their *Louthian bards*, which they ascribed to Ó Doirnín in order to claim him for the emerging nationalist cause in the mid-nineteenth century.[30] This manip-

---

28 Liam Mac Mathúna, *Béarla sa Ghaeilge – cabhair choigríche: an códmheascadh Gaeilge/Béarla i litríocht na Gaeilge, 1600–1900* (Baile Átha Cliath, 2007), p. 204.   29 Breandán Ó Buachalla, 'Peadar Ó Doirnín agus lucht scríte a bheatha', *Studia Hibernica*, 5 (1965), 123–54, carries a detailed treatment of these parties and their accounts of Ó Doirnín and other matters.   30 Unpublished – now Morris MS 7, University College Dublin.

ulation of his body of work has led to a skewed perception of the man and his literary motivations. Based upon the rhetoric and tenor, and the inferior poetic quality of the interpolated compositions, Ó Buachalla has surmised: 'Guth *Young Ireland* agus 'bratachas' an *Nation*, náisiúnachas is rómánsaíocht an 19ú céad is mó atá le brath ... ar an gcnuasach san trí chéile.'[31] (The voice of 'Young Ireland' and the 'flag-waving' of the *Nation*, the nationalism and romanticism of the nineteenth century is the dominant feature of that entire collection.') Yet, there is much in these accounts relating to Ó Doirnín's life that is supported by the poetry he is known to have composed and by other more reliable sources.

Three definite samples of Ó Doirnín's hand survive. There is a fourth which, Pádraig Ó Fiannachta confidently argues, can be ascribed to his pen.[32] However none of the samples contains any of his poetry, or indeed any poetry at all, as they are products of Ó Doirnín's endeavour as a scribe rather than a poet. The three definites are: National Library of Ireland MS G 190, which contains a copy of Keating's famous seventeenth-century history of Ireland, *Foras feasa ar Éirinn*;[33] NUI, Maynooth, MS B 1, which dates from 1747, and which contains from Ó Doirnín's hand two tales, *Comheasgar na gCuradh* and *Eachtradh na gCuradh*, glossed by a later hand as a 'History of the heroes of Ireland called the heroes of the Red Branch';[34] and St Malachy's College, Belfast, MS G, which contains a fragment of the *Táin Bó Cuailgne* [Cattle-raid of Cooley] tale. The piece that Ó Fiannachta ascribes to Ó Doirnín is Laverty MS 12 in Armagh, which is a complete version, neither signed nor dated, of the tale *Oidheadh Chlainne Uisneach*, or the Fate of the Sons of Uisneach. Though it is undated, the paper containing the tale is considerably older in appearance than the latter portion of the bound manuscript, which bears clearly the date 1788, which would place it within two decades of Ó Doirnín's death (1769). The latter half of the Laverty manuscript, incidentally, contains our earliest extant written examples of Ó Doirnín's poetry. None of this content (Ulster cycle, heroic tales, *Foras feasa ar Éirinn*) is out of place in the manuscripts of the period, but it cannot be assumed to have anything definitive to say about the mind and motivations of Ó Doirnín. However, a reference by Bennett and Ó Cearnaigh to Ó Doirnín enjoying the friendship of the Brownlow family of Lurgan points tantalizingly to Ó Doirnín carrying out this scribal work for a patron, and perhaps a Protestant patron at that.[35] It is unfortunate that Ó Cearnaigh is not entirely

---

31 Ó Buachalla (ed.), *Peadar Ó Doirnín*, p. 29.   32 Pádraig Ó Fiannachta, *Clár lámhscríbhinní Gaeilge, leabharlanna na cléire agus mionchnuasaigh*, fasc. 2 (Baile Átha Cliath, 1980), p. 20.   33 *Catalogue of Irish manuscripts in the National Library of Ireland*, fasc. 5 (Dublin, 1979) (hereafter, *NLI Catalogue*), pp 51–2.   34 Pádraig Ó Fiannachta, *Lámhscríbhinní Gaeilge Choláiste Phádraig Má Nuad: clár*, fasc. 4 (Dublin, 1967), pp 110–12.   35 Ó Buachalla, 'Peadar Ó Doirnín agus lucht scríte a bheatha', p. 131; de Rís, *Peadar Ó Doirnín*, p. 69.

to be trusted, although his account is not without value. The Brownlow of whom he speaks, Arthur (1645–1710), was a noted patron of Gaelic letters and a collector of Irish manuscripts. He was the grandson of Sir William Brownlow, who settled in county Armagh during the Plantation of Ulster in 1610, and the issue of the marriage of William's daughter Lettice to Patrick Chamberlain, a member of a long-established Old English family from county Louth. As he had no direct male heirs, William bequeathed his estate at Lurgan to Arthur on condition that he relinquish the name Chamberlain (Irish 'Mac Artúir') and take the name Brownlow (which Arthur duly did, though he did not forsake his Chamberlain origins as his signature is be found followed by 'alias Chamberlain' or 'alias Mac Art').[36] Though his nomination to serve as sheriff of county Louth in 1667, and county Armagh in 1679, and his representation of county Armagh in the Irish parliament, 1692–3, 1695–9 and 1703–11, demonstrated his impeccable establishment credentials, Brownlow's reputation for religious tolerance, and his membership of the Jacobite parliament, 1689, also suggests that he was more open-minded than most of his Protestant *confrères*. This conclusion is given added authority by his enthusiasm for the Irish language, and his antiquarian interest in the collecting of Irish manuscripts. Indeed, the great antiquarian and collector Edward Lhuyd visited Brownlow in Lurgan in 1699 and commented on the manuscripts in his possession; perhaps the most striking being the Book of Armagh. Cunningham and Gillespie have endeavoured to construct the collection of Arthur Brownlow, and have drawn some conclusions as to the motivations of this Ulster settler collector of manuscripts.[37] They emphasize his Old English and Gaelic Irish heritage (his mother, Lettice Brownlow, was the daughter of Sir William Brownlow and Elinor O'Dogherty, daughter of Sir John O'Dogherty of Inishowen) and his interest in his local area as guiding influences. This local influence is clearly in evidence in his acquisition of the Book of Armagh, but it is also identifiable in some of the other manuscripts in his possession. A version of the *Cath Muighe Léana* tells of the victory of Ulstermen, for example; other texts treat of the Ulster dynasty of O'Neills, such as the *Leabhar Eoghanach*, or Book of Eoghan, which is a genealogy of the O'Neills – whom, as Cunningham and Gillespie point out, Brownlow replaced as the dominant influence in north Armagh.[38] He may also have owned a copy of the *Leabhar Chlainne Aodha Buí*, the Book of Clandeboye, which contained material concerning the eastern branch of the O'Neill family. The hand of Brownlow can be identified in some English annotations to the text of the manuscript.[39] Moreover, there is one text by Brownlow among the manuscripts, 27 stanzas of a translation to English from the *Tuireamh Eoghain Rua*, the Elegy for Owen Roe (O'Neill), by Cathal Mac

36 RIA, MS 24 P 33; *RIA Catalogue*, fasc. 24, pp 3005–14.   37 Bernadette Cunningham and Raymond Gillespie, 'An Ulster settler and his manuscripts', *Éigse*, 21 (1986), 27–36. 38 Ibid., p. 32.   39 See note 31.

Ruairí, beginning 'Do chaill Eire a chéile fire', which Brownlow translates as 'Ireland has lost her spouse and only stay'.[40] Brownlow also caused manuscripts to be copied for his collection, and the hand and name of the scribe Pátraic Mac Oghannan appears frequently as, for example, on the copy of 'Cath Mhuighe Léana', copied in 1685, which is dedicated thus: 'arna sgriobhadh do laimh Phatraig Mhic Oghannan da thríath ro-dhearsgnaithe .i. Airtiur Mac Airtiuir alias Brounlowe' (having been written by the hand of Pátraic Mac Oghannan for his most eminent lord, Arthur Chamberlain alias Brounlowe).[41]

It is highly unlikely that Arthur Brownlow made the acquaintance of Peadar Ó Doirnín, given that the latter was still a child at the time of Arthur's death in 1710, but there is evidence, albeit limited, to suggest that he passed on his antiquarian spirit and his ardour for manuscript collection to his son, William Brownlow (1683–1739), whose name appears on a manuscript containing a copy of the *Leabhar Gabhála* (Book of Invasions), some bardic poetry, and some genealogies.[42] Ó Doirnín's skills were certainly availed of since a copy of *Foras feasa ar Éirinn* now in the Royal Irish Academy bears his inscription: 'Airna criochnugha re Peadar O Durnin do chum usaide Shaain Mhic Crolugha … a mbaruntacht … Dhun Dealgna a gCundae Lughmhuighe' (completed by Peadar Ó Durnin for the use of Sean Mac Crolugha … in the barony of Dundalk in county Louth).[43] The question is whether Graham and Ó Cearnaigh are to be believed when they state: 'The gentry also were his friends, and in particular Mr Brownlow of Lurgan. At a visit to Squire Brownlow, who was at electioneering, he composed his 'Independent Man' as an advice to him and his friends'.[44] The poem to which they refer is Ó Doirnín's only extant composition entirely in English, and tells of his intention not to align himself with any movement, but to remain his own man. The earliest extant version, dated 1820–3 (RIA, MS 24 L 31), and in the hand of Patrick McGahan of Faughart, is sandwiched among other works of Ó Doirnín, Mac a' Liondain, Mac Cuarta and Mac Cumhaigh.[45] The Brownlow alluded to must be William (1726–94), the son of William who represented county Armagh in the Irish parliament from 1711 to 1739,

---

40 RIA, MS 24 E 36; *RIA Catalogue*, fasc. 26, pp 3249–53.   41 MS 24 L 36; *RIA Catalogue*, fasc. 3, p. 385. This use of the Irish version of the surname evokes readily the system of patronymics, a feature of Gaelic Irish culture in which lineage was greatly celebrated. The scribe Mac Oghanan may be cognate with the Mac Eoghanáin family linked in the seventeenth century to the townland of Ballymakeonan in the parish of Magheralin, near Lurgan. My thanks to Dr Mícheál Ó Mainnín, Queen's University Belfast, for alerting me to this link. For further information see Kay Muhr, *Placenames of Northern Ireland, vol. 6: north-west Down/Iveagh* (Belfast, 1996), pp 226–7.   42 MS 24 P 13; *RIA Catalogue*, fasc. 24, pp 2975–7.   43 NLI, MS G 190. For a description see *NLI Catalogue*, fasc. 5, p. 52.   44 Quoted in de Rís, *Peadar Ó Doirnín*, p. 69.   45 *RIA Catalogue*, fasc. 20, p. 817. The poem has no title in this version, but was later named 'Independent Man' in Ó Cearnaigh's transcription.

and the grandson of Arthur, who contested a fractious by-election for the constituency of county Armagh in 1753. It would appear that 'Independent Man' was written by Ó Doirnín as a commentary on an appeal for support as the electorate became very divided in the race for the Armagh seat. The story of the by-election has been treated of at length elsewhere;[46] it will suffice for our purposes to say that it became a battleground for competing ideologies in the Dublin parliament with which the rival candidates, William Brownlow and Francis Caulfeild, had become aligned. Brownlow spent huge sums on publicly demonstrating his beneficence to the voting freeholders and his loyalty to the Hanoverian monarchy, because his commitment to the Protestant succession and conscience had been called into question by his opponents who highlighted the fact that Brownlow's mother had converted to Catholicism and his grandfather, Arthur, had sat in the Jacobite parliament of 1689. The combined taint of Popery and Jacobitism could have dealt Brownlow's ambition to represent the county a fatal blow in the fevered atmosphere of 1753 when every vote was needed to secure victory. It is entirely possible, given these circumstances, that an appeal was made to Ó Doirnín to use his literary skills and influence in the south of the county to win support for Brownlow, and to counter the attempts by the Caulfeild campaign to use print to blacken Brownlow's reputation. Two pamphlets in particular, both ascribed to 'a free citizen of Dublin' and addressed to the freeholders of Armagh, sought to invoke traditional Whig principles against Brownlow by adducing the sanctity of parliament, the responsibility of every man to vote by his own conscience, and not to be coerced to vote by his landlord (Brownlow).[47] The following, from the second letter, is typical of the appeal to freeholders to exercise independent judgment:

> Particularly, in the depending case of Elections, nothing further, they cry, is requisite, for the Policy of this free and happy Nation, than that each voter should be naturally endowed, with a *Nose*, whereby, whether he be tenant, or Dependant, or Trader, or Debtor, his Landlord, or Superior, or Customer, or Creditor, may gently tweak him, and guide him to the Line of due Direction ... For my Part, ... I should most heartily rejoice, to see you the first Country Freeholders in *Ireland*, who shall render yourselves eminent, however

46 A full account of the election personalities and issues can be found in Eoin Magennis, 'Patriotism, popery and politics: the Armagh by-election of 1753' in A.J. Hughes and William Nolan (eds), *Armagh: history and society* (Dublin, 2001), pp 485–504. See also C.F. McGleenon, *A very independent county: parliamentary elections and politics in county Armagh, 1750–1800* (Belfast, 2011). 47 *A letter from a free citizen of Dublin to a freeholder in the county of Armagh* (Dublin 1753). This was followed by *A second letter from a free citizen of Dublin, to a freeholder in the county of Armagh* (Dublin, 1753). *Seasonable advice to the freeholders of the county of Armagh, by a brother freeholder* (Dublin, 1753) constitutes the response of the Brownlow camp to the insinuations of the former letters.

singular and blameable, for with-holding your long invaded *Property of Noses*.[48]

The election, which Brownlow won, exposed an easily disturbed sectarian mindset within the county, which sustained a campaign for freeholder independence and the cessation of coercive practices.[49] Ó Doirnín commented on such issues in his 'Independent Man', though it is not clear if he was inspired by contact with Brownlow or his supporters. At first glance, the thrust of the verse might suggest that he sought to keep his distance from the contesting parties, but a more sensitive reading, given the independent stance Brownlow later assumed in parliament, might suggest that it was an endorsement of the young Brownlow, then aged 27, for the independent patriot he became rather than the follower of Primate George Stone, which is how he was regarded at the time:[50]

> Here's a health to all those that at liberty goe,
> That travel the road without a command,
> That drink and that sport, that sit in their clothes
> Whilst taking repose with a glass in their hand,
> I am one of the sort, the track of their sole,
> I love it by Jove, while e'er I stand,
> I'll keep my own Vote, I'll give it to none
> I value no more a Parliament Man …
>
> In heaven's great name, how can they blame
> The poor man, or shame him, in the long run?
> Ambition's their game, what else do they mean,
> But purchase high fame, great power and fun?
> They may swear a big oath that never they'll loath
> The poor dupe that votes for them, 'tis their plan;
> But I'll keep my own vote, I'll give it to none,
> Then what need I care for a Parliament man?[51]

Linguistically and aesthetically, these verses display nothing of the poetic skill of Ó Doirnín's Irish compositions (although they echo his use of the song metre in some of his most celebrated Irish poems), but their relevance derives from their theme rather than their literary merit, as they attest to Ó Doirnín's engagement with the papers and pamphlets, and with issues of voter behaviour that were brought into focus by the contentious Armagh by-election. Buttimer draws from the poem a suggestion that Ó Doirnín's engagement

---

48 *A second letter*, pp 12–13.   **49** Magennis, 'The Armagh by-election', p. 501.   **50** See E.M. Johnston-Liik, *History of the Irish parliament: the House of Commons, 1792–1800* (6 vols, Belfast, 2002), iii, 293–6.   **51** de Rís, *Peadar Ó Doirnín*, pp 45–7.

with English print could have 'encouraged others like this northern bard to resort to English rather than Irish in musing on the events of the day.'[52] There is a social perspective, certainly, in his references to political ambition, and to the disregard for the 'poor dupe' who gives his vote. Elsewhere, he refers to his aversion to war, and to how 'no colour at all shall make me stand'. The following quatrain, and its misspelled reference (in keeping with the metre) to General Lobkowitz of the Austrian army, also demonstrates knowledge of international current affairs:

> What do I care for Holland or Hague,
> Or trouble my mind with packets or news
> From Germany's states to Lobquid's retreat,[53]
> Their taking of Prague, or Spaniard's retreat.

Although somewhat scattered in its focus, moving from kings to clergy to Austrian generals, Ó Doirnín was obviously moved to write because of his unhappiness with the forces he saw at work in society, and the Brownlow election controversy, the self-interested 'Parliament Man' of the first stanza, may well have been the spark.

The ambivalence to matters both local and international, so thoroughly articulated in the 'Parliament Man', is a recurring feature also of Ó Doirnín's Irish compositions. This sets him apart from the other south Ulster poets of the era. Far from decrying the lack of respect for his poetic art and for his learning, for example, he openly admits his mistakes, and acknowledges that he lacks common sense:[54]

> Gé go dtuigim léann níl siolla céille 'gam,
> Mar nach saibhir mé in ór nó i maoin.

> (Although learned, I have not a syllable of sense,
> For I am not wealthy in gold or possessions.)

He speaks of how, were the world to be set to rights, his Gaelic race would forget their learning, but be well off instead. Later in the same poem he tells how, were he wealthy, the clergy would forgive any sin he should commit. From the evidence of his texts, he seems often to have fallen foul of them, largely as a result of his fondness for womanizing and drinking. It is notable that he presents the clergy as part of a privileged caste of society from which

---

52 Neil Buttimer, 'Literature in Irish, 1690–1800: from the Williamite Wars to the Act of Union' in Philip O'Leary and Margaret Kelleher (eds), *The Cambridge history of Irish literature* (2 vols, Cambridge, 2006), i, 340.   53 The reference is presumably to General Lobkowitz (1686–1755), a nobleman from a Bohemian family who commanded a force during various campaigns of the Austrian War of Succession.   54 'Mianta Uí Dhoirnín' in Ó Buachalla (ed.), *Peadar Ó Doirnín*, pp 34–5.

he was alienated, because they hypocritically absolved the sins of the rich, while castigating him for drinking although themselves 'ag fáisceadh a mbéil ar na gloiníbh rum' ('squeezing their glasses of rum to their mouths').[55]

Ó Doirnín was a love poet of considerable skill, and it is in his treatment of this subject we see his finest contributions to literature, but to view him solely in this light is to ignore much that he reveals in his other poems of his attitudes to his situation. He appears to have been fully diglossic, as evidenced by his skilful manipulation of both languages in his satire of Ó Gormáin, and to have been au fait with current events on the evidence of his engagement with the Armagh by-election of 1753. It is more difficult to pin down his attitude to the Jacobite cause, which exercised so many contemporary Irish poets. Ó Cearnaigh, and folk tradition, speak of Ó Doirnín as a firm Jacobite supporter and as a member of the Whiteboy movement. He is reputed to have been a friend of Séamas Mac Murchaidh (James Murphy), a rapparee and folk-hero in the south Armagh and Louth area, and to have written a song about his eventual capture and execution.[56] However, the evidence of his poetry points to an attitude akin to the ambivalence evident in his 'Independent Man' rather than to the ardent Jacobite of tradition. This is the message, certainly, of his poetic commentary on the contention for the Crown, 'Tá bearád i Londain' ('There is a hat in London'), which displays a comic touch, as opposed to the tone of lamentation characteristic of most such interventions, symbolized by the nonsense refrain '*Is iombó!*' which features after each stanza. Yet his latent sympathy for the Stuart Pretender is obvious. Speaking of the crown, he says:[57]

... measann Sir Wully[58] gur cuibhe dá dháid é
is creideann lucht boinéad gur cumadh do Chathal[59] é, is iombó!

(... Sir Willy [Sir William Cumberland] thinks it best suited to his dad, and the bonnet-wearers believe that it was made for Charles, *is iombó!*)

The tone of his 'Independent Man' is reprised in the final stanza where he says:

Mo léan nachar chas siad ar machaire fásaigh
Le chéile, is gan neach acu a bhéarfadh dóibh tarrtháil ...

(What a pity they could not both meet on a desert plain,
Alone together, none to come to their aid ...)

However reserved in tone, this poem manifests considerable awareness on the part of the poet of the background to the battles and protagonists of the

---

55 'Gearán Úí Dhoirnín', ibid., p. 40. 56 Ní Uallacháin, *A hidden Ulster*, pp 245, 348. 57 de Rís, *Peadar Ó Doirnín*, pp 13–14. 58 Prince William Augustus, duke of Cumberland (1721–65), was an army officer, and victor at the decisive Battle of Culloden.

Jacobite rising of 1745–6, which may, as O Buachalla suggested, have facilitated the use of such song forms to disseminate information among an illiterate, but sympathetic, Catholic populace.[60] A surreal poetic dialogue Ó Doirnín
has with a bird, in the mould of Mac Cumhaigh's aforementioned addresses
to the Glasdrummond castle, strikes a more dramatic tone. In the poem, the
high hopes vested in Charles Edward Stuart are analyzed:[61]

> Ní mheasaim gur féidir dó theacht chun na hÉireann
> Le cabhair dár dteampaill naofa,
> … Séarlas leis féin i mbréigriocht is i bpéin
> ag teitheadh sna sléibhtibh uathu.

> (I think he cannot come to Ireland,
> To aid our holy churches,
> … Charles alone, pained and in disguise
> Fleeing from them in the mountains.)

This reading of Ó Doirnín's work, therefore, reveals a complex figure who
does not conform to the monolithic cultural stereotype which has to date
dominated the discourse on Irish poetry and poets of the seventeenth and
eighteenth centuries. Fluidity and change are certainly a feature of his life's
work, as he is to be found engaged in the professional scribal work of copying Irish manuscripts for a patron, which was the norm in former days, as
well as employing the English language creatively for a bilingual audience in
his satire on Muiris Ó Gormáin. That work, and his 'Independent Man', bear
witness to a creativity which transcended the linguistic boundary upon which
many contemporaries focussed, and that Mac Cumhaigh's vision at Howth
and his theological dialogue between the churches of Faughart and Forkhill
can obscure. Where Mac Cumhaigh speaks of Ireland's heart sinking as she
hears the chatter of English, Ó Doirnín's own heart sinks as he realizes he has
been bested in love by an unworthy, unable even to speak English.

III

As indicated above, some distortion of Ó Doirnín's character has arisen from
an over-reliance on the accounts of his life prepared in the nineteenth century
by Graham/Ó Cearnaigh and Bennett. A four-stanza poem attributed to Ó
Doirnín appeared in *The Nation* in 1843, with the explanation that it had been

---

59 See note 14 above.   **60** Breandan Ó Buachalla, *Aisling Ghéar: na Stíobhartaigh agus an
t-aos léinn* (Baile Átha Cliath, 1996), pp 602–3.   **61** 'Agallamh le hÉinín' in de Rís, *Peadar
Ó Doirnín*, pp 10–11.

written by 'O'Dornin, the Bard of Louth, whilst concealed in Donomore Cave, near Dundalk, being then under persecution for teaching the Irish language and singing of the wrong of Ireland'.[62] This piece, probably contributed (if not entirely composed) by Graham and Ó Cearnaigh, who were then preparing their *Louthian Bards*, excited the indignation of another correspondent, most likely Arthur Bennett, who pointed out the inaccuracy of the title 'Bard of Louth', because Ó Doirnín was, to his knowledge, from Munster. Yet, Graham and Ó Cearnaigh attracted the attention of antiquarian interests at the time, eager to know more of the details of Ó Doirnín's life and compositions, and John O'Daly sought to make contact with them through Fr Patrick Lamb of Killeavy. Through his good offices, we have Bennett's account, dated 1844, of Ó Doirnín's relations with the Brownlow family. He evidently came to their attention because of his composition 'Ar Mhala Dhroma Crí' (On the slopes of Drumcree), a song which muses on the early history of Ireland and the various peoples who settled there. Bennett explained:[63]

> The splendid and powerful style of that poem attracted the attention of Honourable Lord Brownlow, ancestor to the present Lord Lurgan, who very kindly requested an interview with O'Dornin and on finding that he was possessed of transcendand talents, unrivalled skill, liberal education, deep penetration, and most insinuating address he took him under his own roof to instruct his rising family, to revise his Irish records and illustrate his library with Irish songs and above all, to enrich his own understanding with the sterling love of Irish literature. This bond of cordiality lasted for a series of years until the election-eering contest of the Brownlows of Lurgan, the Copes of Loughgale, and the Richardsons of Rich-hill, unhinged the ties of fidelity. Our learned author's conduct on that occasion served only to stimulate the malignity of his old employer. His services, like those of many others when he gave all, Brownlow had nothing more to ask for. In order to battle the wintry blasts of persecution he resolved to spend the evening of his days among the companions of his youth, that he might mingle his bones with the ashes of his ancestors ...

In correspondence with O'Daly, Ó Cearnaigh sought to correct some of Bennett's claims about Ó Doirnín, mostly with reference to birthplace and date of birth. Both are in agreement that he was an acquaintance of the Brownlow family, and that he fell into dispute with them over the matter of an election. It is unfortunate that in trying to establish their claim as the authority on Ó Doirnín, and as the true heirs to the literary tradition of the area, both stretched the truth in an attempt to impress. Their romanticized

---

62 Quoted in Ó Buachalla, 'Peadar Ó Doirnín agus lucht scríte a bheatha', p. 123. 63 Ibid., p. 131.

accounts, especially those of Ó Cearnaigh, are in keeping with the spirit of the time, but they are misleading. They are most likely the source of the dubious traditions of Ó Doirnín's involvement with rappareeism and agrarian movements, and of his taking refuge in a cave while singing of the wrong done to Ireland. Such a persona is difficult to reconcile with that of the man in the employ of an MP, enjoying his patronage, and arranging his manuscript collection.

This mid-nineteenth-century retrieval and reappropriation of the eighteenth-century figure of Ó Doirnín chimes with Leerssen's claim that the 'canonicity' of authors like Keating and Ó Rathaille owes much to 'the generation of Mangan, Davis and Ferguson'. Indeed, he views as 'crucial' the 'retroactive nature of the cross-linguistic Irish tradition, the fact that it was established in the English-speaking, modernized nineteenth century in a process of recognizing, retrieving, adopting and canonizing the country's native Gaelic roots and figureheads.'[64] In the fervour to reinforce the nationalist narrative of the mid-nineteenth century, Ó Doirnín the scribe and songmaker, was lost sight of by those like Graham and Ó Cearnaigh, who wished to establish their claim to being the authority on his life and deeds, when he was ill-fitted to the stereotype to which he was required to conform. A more nuanced figure emerges from a closer study of his works, one possessed of a bilingual creativity, and one comfortable in the role of scribe and amanuensis to a settler family in Armagh and other patrons.

Most of the early nineteenth-century manuscript copies of the south Ulster canon of poetry contain translations to English as appendices, or are glossed, introduced or contextualized in English, which indicates that those who made them were fully aware that the landscape of language and literacy in south Ulster had changed profoundly since the originals were generated. They lived and worked now in an intellectual milieu that necessitated the mediation of the texts they were presenting. Their purpose was to position Gaelic literature for posterity, to present it to a new readership, rather than simply to further the tradition, and this is reflected in the amount of textual commentary, contextualization and translation that is a feature of the manuscripts. Indeed, Ó Cearnaigh writes openly in his letters of his labours for old Ireland, and of his scribal work as an element of his patriotism and national duty.[65] Indicatively, his *Louthian bards* was intended for publication in English and he engaged with several antiquarian learned societies in a vain attempt to locate a publisher.

The linguistic landscape had been transformed in the region in the interval between when the eighteenth-century Irish-language poets of the region were in their prime and Bennett and Ó Cearnaigh set out to rescue them from near obscurity. The prolonged nature of the transition can be high-

64 Leerssen, *Hidden Ireland*, pp 20–1.   65 Ó Buachalla, 'Ó Doirnín agus lucht scríte a bheatha', p. 140.

lighted by the fact that there was still enough of a literate Irish reading public in 1800 and again in 1825 to justify the publication in Monaghan by Matthew Kennedy of a set of spiritual meditations and prayers in Irish entitled *The spiritual rose; or, method of saying the rosarie of the most holy name of Jesus and the Blessed Virgin with their litanies, etc, etc.*[66] That the title of Kennedy's work is in English and the text in Irish is emblematic of the fact that linguistic change had penetrated deeply since the heyday of the four poets considered in this essay, but their life and work is no less revealing of this language shift and of the manner in which it was negotiated. It can be concluded with reasonable certainty that Mac Cumhaigh and Ó Doirnín were functionally and creatively bilingual. They had to be so to function in a fast-changing linguistic landscape that echoed to new social realities. Indicatively, language was regarded by Mac Cumhaigh as a marker of race and religion, while Ó Doirnín viewed competence in language as a marker of class and social standing. Both poets were grounded solidly in the tradition of their predecessors Mac Cuarta and Mac a' Liondain (who make but scant reference to linguistic trends and who composed solely in Irish) but the extant poetry of each, in its individual way, captures the evolving patterns of social and linguistic interaction in the second half of the eighteenth century, as English assumed an ever more prominent presence in the lives of all the people.

66 Malachy McKenna (ed.), *The spiritual rose* (Dublin, 2001).

6

The Catholic Church, the Irish mission and the Irish language in the eighteenth century

CIARÁN MAC MURCHAIDH

INTRODUCTION

The relationship of the Catholic Church and the Irish language underwent significant change in the course of the eighteenth century. Both the declining capacity of the Catholic clergy to discharge in Irish the full range of pastoral services required by its people and the creeping bilingualism of the faithful,[1] especially in urban centres and particularly throughout the eastern half of the island, converged to sustain a trend whereby Irish gradually assumed a less central place in the mission of the church. As is the case with the penal laws, their application and their effect, the story of the church's relationship with the Irish language is more complicated than the traditional historiography would suggest. Some forty years ago the historian Maureen Wall observed:

> Today nearly every school child in Ireland will tell you that Daniel O'Connell, the Catholic clergy and the National schools together killed the Irish language. The history text-books in general use in Irish schools list these three causes, rather in the manner of a catechism answer, and they have been widely accepted by the last two generations of our people ... What was completely overlooked was the fact that before the nineteenth century began the Irish language had been banished from parliament, from the courts of law, from town and country government, from the civil service and from the upper levels of commercial life. By 1800 Irish had ceased to be the language habitually spoken in the homes of all those who had already achieved success in the world, or who aspired to improve or even maintain their position politically, socially or economically.[2]

The reasons identified by Wall in the second half of the paragraph quoted constitute a useful listing of the multifarious sociological and sociolinguistic

1 Tony Crowley, *Wars of words: the politics of language in Ireland, 1537–2004* (Oxford, 2005), pp 79, 94–5. 2 Maureen Wall, 'The decline of the Irish language' in Brian Ó Cuív (ed.), *A view of the Irish language* (Dublin, 1969), pp 81–2.

reasons for the deterioration in the place of Irish in civil and religious society and, other than the centrality of print,[3] which it overlooked, it still has purchase today. However, as Ó Ciosáin has noted, the issue of the relationship of the Catholic Church with and its attitude towards the Irish language remains ill understood and inadequately explored. Specifically, the linguistic problem posed a church whose *lingua franca* was Latin and whose officers – priests and bishops – were trained in an environment in which the vernacular – French, Italian, Spanish, Portuguese – was of little use in Ireland, deserve elucidation. At the heart of this problem lay the incapacity of the institutional church to educate and properly to prepare its clergy for ministry in either a monolingual or bilingual environment. The lack of formal structures available in Ireland to provide even a rudimentary knowledge of the Latin language, along with a necessary understanding of the most basic theological principles, were crucial matters for the episcopate. Moreover, the failure to put in place structures in the continental seminaries to equip ordinands with the linguistic skills required to preach in Irish and English, in keeping with the increasingly bilingual character of Irish society, was a serious weakness of the training they received abroad.

Brian Ó Cuív has correctly observed of the Catholic clergy in the eighteenth century that they did not harbour an inimical attitude towards Irish. 'Their concern', he stated, 'was to guide and support the people in the practice of the Catholic faith ... they certainly did not set out to wean them from the Irish language.'[4] It is clear from the available evidence that the clergy saw the protection and promotion of the Catholic faith as their priority and language simply as a means to that end. Moreover, this was in keeping with significant earlier attitudinal developments. Bernadette Cunningham has remarked of seventeenth-century Ireland that 'people's religious affiliation was more a significant indicator of difference than was language'.[5] This is not to overlook the contribution of the Franciscans. Mícheál Mac Craith has demonstrated how the work of the friars at St Anthony's College in Louvain, founded in 1607, led them 'to engage in serious reflection on vernacular languages in general and on Irish in particular' and that their reflections as an *émigré* community also 'led to deeper speculation on the nature of Irish iden-

3 Niall Ó Ciosáin, 'Print in Irish 1570–1900: an exception among the Celtic languages?', *Radharc: a Journal of Irish and Irish-American Studies*, 5–7 (2004–6), 103. For a short, insightful initial exploration of this subject see *idem*, 'Language, print and the Catholic Church in Ireland 1700–1900' in Donald McNamara (ed.), *'Which direction Ireland?'* (Newcastle, 2007), pp 125–36.   4 Brian Ó Cuív, 'Irish language and literature, 1691–1845' in T.W. Moody and W.E. Vaughan (eds), *A new history of Ireland*: iv, *eighteenth-century Ireland 1691–1800* (Oxford, 1986), p. 378.   5 Bernadette Cunningham, 'The culture and ideology of Irish Franciscan historians at Louvain 1607–1650' in Ciaran Brady (ed.), *Ideology and the historians* (Dublin, 1991), pp 29–30; see also *eadem*, *The world of Geoffrey Keating: history, myth and religion in seventeenth-century Ireland* (Dublin, 2000), p. 225.

tity'.[6] However, the evidence extant in church documents, visitation books, reports to the nuncio and to Rome, and allied material leads one to conclude that while the clergy did not purposely seek to neglect the Irish language in the eighteenth century, they did not champion it in the manner of the Franciscans at Louvain in the early seventeenth century. Neither can it be asserted that, as an institution, they perceived it as occupying as strong a place in Irish consciousness in the manner that the Louvain Franciscans aspired.[7] Ó Cuív has remarked that there were 'Catholic churchmen at all levels from archbishop down [to] be found among those involved in literary and scribal activity in Irish throughout this period',[8] but that while this indicated that individual churchmen were disposed to promote the language 'the Catholic Church made little positive contribution'.[9]

A range of evidence will be considered in this chapter which suggests that the generality of the Catholic clergy possessed neither the linguistic skill nor pastoral will to ensure that the language remained central to its evangelizing mission. It is clear that the Catholic hierarchy and the clergy were aware of the gradual increase in the use of English among the Catholic population from the early decades of the eighteenth century. It is also clear that this presented them with a challenge to which they only partly rose. That challenge was to ensure that the clergy had sufficient knowledge of Irish to enable them to function, and specifically to minister, at an acceptable level through the medium of the language for the large sections of the Catholic population who were still monolingual Irish speakers. However, as a growing number of Catholics became bilingual, an increasingly bilingual laity provided many clergy with a reason to forsake any real attempt either to learn Irish or to use it in situations other than the strictly pastoral or catechetical. Thus they unwittingly assisted the creation of a situation by the end of the eighteenth century, when bilingualism was the norm throughout much of the country, and the foundations were in place for the rapid abandonment of the Irish language that occurred from the early decades of the nineteenth century onwards.

I

There is a significant body of evidence with which one can reconstruct the education of the Catholic clergy in the eighteenth century. Given the uniform

---

6 Mícheál Mac Craith, 'Literature in Irish, *c.*1550–1690: from the Elizabethan settlement to the Battle of the Boyne' in Margaret Kelleher and Philip O'Leary (eds), *The Cambridge history of Irish literature* (2 vols, Cambridge, 2006), i, 191.   7 Bernadette Cunningham has shown 'that language largely ceased to be the predominant cultural identifier for the Catholic Irish' in the colonial context that obtained in seventeenth-century Ireland: see 'Loss and gain: attitudes towards the English language in early modern Ireland' in Brian Mac Cuarta (ed.), *Reshaping Ireland 1550–1700: colonization and its consequences* (Dublin, 2011), p. 185. 8 Ó Cuív, 'Irish language and literature, 1691–1845', p. 378.   9 Ibid., p. 380.

criteria laid down by the Council of Trent, and the incapacity of the Church to apply the decrees of the Council in Ireland, it is manifest that the problems associated with priestly formation in the eighteenth century can be ascribed, in large part, to the effects of the penal laws, and specifically those targeted at the Church.[10] The Catholic Church at the beginning of the eighteenth century was a weakened and diminished body. Only eight bishops remained in the country in 1698, a year after the Banishment Act of 1697 came into force. Three left the country before the end of the reign of William III in 1702. Two others were arrested early on in the reign of Anne though one, Maurice Donnellan of Clonfert, was rescued from prison and the other, Patrick Donnelly of Dromore, was acquitted and released. Only Archbishop Edward Comerford of Cashel was left undisturbed, but he was in ill health in the years prior to his death in 1710 and was unable to function as an active prelate.[11] Of those bishops who left the country after 1697, few returned to the home mission and the hierarchy was not restored to full strength until the end of the 1720s when the see of Kilmore, vacant since 1669, was filled. With the passing of the Registration Act of 1704, Catholic secular clergy could remain legally in the country, one per civil parish, if they registered with the local authorities and confined their work to the parish to which they were registered. A total of 1,089 priests registered but they were bound by restrictions. They were unable to have a curate, for instance, or employ a schoolmaster in the locality. As a result, there was no system of primary or secondary school education available to Catholics, although unapproved and unmonitored 'hedge' schools soon emerged. Many of these schools, which were unevenly distributed across the country, provided a basic education, and many student priests, who sought entry to one of the Irish Colleges on the continent, were dependent on 'hedge' schools for instruction.[12]

In the early part of the eighteenth century there was no method of ensuring standards in the 'hedge' schools. However, by the beginning of the reign of George II the intensity with which the laws against Catholics were applied

---

10 For fuller amplification and more recent analyses of the penal laws see S.J. Connolly, 'Religion and history', *Irish Economic and Social History*, 11 (1983), 66–80; L.M. Cullen, 'Catholics under the penal laws', *Eighteenth-Century Ireland* (1986), 23–36; Thomas Bartlett, *The fall and rise of the Irish nation: the Catholic question 1690–1830* (Dublin, 1992), pp 17–29; Anna Heussaff, *Filí agus cléir san ochtú haois déag* (Baile Átha Cliath, 1992), pp 16–49; James Kelly, 'The impact of the penal laws', in James Kelly and Dáire Keogh (eds), *History of the Catholic diocese of Dublin* (Dublin, 2000), pp 144–74; Hugh Fenning, 'A time of reform: from the "penal laws" to the birth of modern nationalism, 1691–1800' in Brendan Bradshaw and Dáire Keogh (eds), *Christianity in Ireland: revisiting the story* (Dublin, 2002), pp 134–43; and John Bergin, Eoin Magennis, et al. (eds), *New perspectives on the penal laws* (Dublin, 2011). 11 J.G. Simms, 'The establishment of Protestant ascendancy, 1691–1714' in Moody and Vaughan (eds), *A new history of Ireland*: iv, *eighteenth-century Ireland 1691–1800*, p. 17; John Brady and Patrick J. Corish, 'The church under the penal code', *A history of Irish Catholicism*, iv (Dublin, 1971), pp 7–9. 12 Antonia McManus, *The Irish hedge school and its books, 1695–1831* (Dublin, 2002), p.13, n30.

had eased, and as early as 1730 the Dublin diocesan statutes 'required every parish priest to have a schoolmaster in his parish to teach Catholic doctrine'.[13] It was only when the government began to establish the Charter Schools in 1733, 'with the avowed purpose of making Protestants of the children of the poor',[14] that the Catholic clergy assumed a more active role in Catholic education. In his 'report on the state of the Irish mission', prepared in 1742, John Kent recommended the establishment of a fund supported by annual donations by each Catholic bishop to cover the costs of Catholic education.[15] Rome approved of this suggestion and a Catholic parish school system gradually emerged across much of the country. It is difficult to establish how effective many of these schools were. Such evidence as exists would suggest that one of their primary functions was to provide children with the basics of the English language, the Catholic faith, and knowledge of the classics. Since a proportion of the schoolmasters were students for the priesthood who had not been ordained, Latin, Greek, English, Religious Education and even Mathematics were often taught.[16] In this way, though provision was erratic and limited, young men aspiring to ordination as Catholic priests could have access to elements of the knowledge required to embark on the theological education provided by Irish Catholic seminaries on the continent. However, this basic preparation could not be assumed. In June 1729, the nuncio at Brussels, Archbishop Giuseppe Spinelli, reported that Bishop Thomas Flynn of Ardagh ordained 'as many as come before him, no matter what condition they are in, so long as they know a few words of Latin and give him some money'.[17] It was noted also that the conditions obtaining in Ireland at the time created difficulties for the church in dealing with cases such as this.

II

The Act of Abjuration of 1709 required registered Catholic clergy to take an oath rejecting the legitimacy of the Stuart king. Most refused to do so. As a

---

13 Ibid., p. 23.   14 Patrick Corish, *The Irish Catholic experience: a historical survey* (Dublin, 1985), p. 126.   15 Hugh Fenning, 'John Kent's report on the state of the Irish mission, 1742', *Archivium Hibernicum*, 28 (1966), 61. An undated letter (but possibly written in 1741) from bishops Michael O'Gara (Tuam), James Gallagher (Kildare), Patrick MacDonagh (Killaloe) and Michael MacDonagh to Pope Benedict XIV related their concerns about the risks to the Catholic faith posed by the Charter Schools: see Cathaldus Giblin, 'Catalogue of material of Irish interest in the collection *Nunziatura di Fiandra* in the Vatican archives, part 6', *Collectanea Hibernica*, 10 (1967), 89.   16 Brady and Corish, 'The church under the penal code', pp 46–7.   17 Cathaldus Giblin, 'Catalogue of material of Irish interest in the collection *Nunziatura di Fiandra* in the Vatican archives, part 5', *Collectanea Hibernica*, 9 (1966), 14. See also James Kelly, 'The Catholic Church in the diocese of Ardagh' in Raymond Gillespie and Gerard Moran (eds), *Longford: essays in county history* (Dublin, 1991), pp 73–4.

result, their legal recognition was incomplete and they were vulnerable to prosecution. Few were actively pursued, but such legislation, and the proclamations that sought to give it effect did, on occasion, make life very difficult for the Catholic clergy and even more so for their ecclesiastical superiors.[18] Following the commencement in 1707 of the appointment of bishops to vacant sees, the work of re-building church structures and coordinating reform commenced in earnest. The appointment of bishops at this time was an intrinsically political matter, as they were normally nominated by James III, the Stuart pretender, and were only formally appointed by the Pope.[19]

Because priestly formation was forbidden in Ireland and the initial education available was not always regarded highly by ecclesiastics,[20] candidates for the priesthood were obliged to study in colleges on the Continent in order to acquire the requisite theological knowledge and pastoral skills. One of the great difficulties with this arrangement was that many clerical students were reluctant to return from France and Rome after ordination to face the challenges of pastoral life in Ireland. This was partly to do with the poverty of the Catholic people and the church, but they were also influenced by the risks involved in ministering in Ireland. These risks were very real into the 1730s and even when they eased after that date concerns persisted. As late as 1762, a document outlining the state of the Irish College in Paris noted that 'at present [there are] 165 students in the college whose names cannot be made public without exposing their families in Ireland to danger'.[21] An addendum to the document, summarized by Swords, amplified the perceived risks:

> The superiors draw attention to the rigours of the penal laws against Catholics who send their children abroad for education. It is necessary for them to preserve the greatest secrecy. Irish students are not known by their real names in foreign universities so as not to expose their relatives in Ireland to persecution and to permit themselves to return to the mission there. Informers are well rewarded.[22]

Because of the costs involved, and the difficulties under which the Irish church mission operated, men were selected for ordination before they completed a formal course of theological or pastoral training, and were sent abroad when they were 24 years of age or older to complete their education, having been secretly ordained in Ireland. Hugh Fenning has described the pattern:

18 James Kelly, 'Sustaining a confessional state: the Irish parliament and Catholicism' in James Kelly, D.W. Hayton and John Bergin (eds), *The eighteenth-century composite state: representative institutions in Ireland and Europe, 1689–1800* (Basingstoke, 2010), pp 54–9. 19 Cathaldus Giblin, 'The Stuart nomination of Irish bishops, 1687–1765', *Irish Eccesiastical Record*, 105 (Jan. 1966), 35–47. 20 Hugh Fenning, 'Clerical recruitment, 1735–1783: documents from Windsor and Rome', *Collectanea Hibernica*, 30 (1972), 1. 21 Liam Swords, 'History of the Irish College, Paris, 1578–1800', *Archivium Hibernicum*, 30 (1980), 105, §408. 22 Swords, 'History of the Irish College', 106, §410.

They received priestly ordination at home and *then* went abroad to
study philosophy and theology without the advantage of a proper classical formation, and at an age when they were no longer amenable to
discipline. Paradoxically these awkward students provided Ireland with
its best priests, for while they were prepared to come back to the life
of toil and hardship they had already experienced, the minority who
had studied abroad from their youth could rarely bring themselves to
face the rigours of the Irish mission.[23]

Younger men who left Ireland to study for the priesthood before ordination
were known as *écoliers* in the Irish College in Paris and usually arrived there
between 16 and 18 years of age.[24] Some were mere boys as young as 12 years
of age,[25] which had a significant impact on their capacity to minister in the
native tongue. Many evidently lost the ability to speak fluently in Irish and,
indeed, in many cases, all sense of their homeland. Patrick MacDonough,
bishop of Killaloe, writing to John Linegar, archbishop of Dublin, in 1748,
cited 'non-use and daily conversation in another language' as the main reasons for the students' loss of their native language.[26] Jean-Baptiste-Michel
Colbert de Villacerf, the Archbishop of Toulouse (1693–1710), was still more
conscious of the problem. Aware that Irish ordinands who 'failed to conserve
the Irish tongue' were of little use on the Irish mission, he sought to take
steps to preclude this happening. Writing in 1700, he observed: 'since ...
once they have been made priests [they] are obliged to go back to Ireland to
preach the Gospel and administer the sacraments, we forbid them to speak
any other languages to each other except their own, apart from Latin'.[27]

It was not unusual for students to spend long periods abroad. Sending students abroad for clerical formation helped the hierarchy to circumvent the
immediate problem of providing priests for the Irish mission, but it created
another significant, and arguably more challenging, pastoral difficulty – the
inability of clergy to function adequately through the Irish language on their

---

23 Hugh Fenning, 'Clerical recruitment', 1. See also Brady and Corish, 'The church under
the penal code', pp 45–6.   24 Swords, 'History of the Irish College', 56, §222; 93, §363.
25 Swords, 'History of the Irish College', 96, §374. Diarmaid Ó Doibhlin has noted a case
in the diocese of Derry where two priests, Thady O'Lunseghan and Cornelius O'Mungan,
were, according to the dates given, thirteen and fifteen years at the time of their ordination, although he suggests that this may have been an error of some sort: see *idem*, 'Penal
days' in Henry Jefferies and Ciarán Devlin (eds), *History of the diocese of Derry from earliest times*, (Dublin, 2000), p. 175.   26 See Liam Chambers, 'Rivalry and reform in the Irish
College, Paris, 1676–1775' in Thomas O'Connor and Mary Ann Lyons (eds), *Irish communities in early-modern Europe* (Dublin, 2006), p. 121.   27 L.W.B. Brockliss and Patrick
Ferté, 'Irish clerics in France in the seventeenth and eighteenth centuries: a statistical
survey', *RIA proc.*, 87C (1987), 566. See also Patrick Ferté, 'The counter-reformation and
Franco-Irish solidarity: Irish clerical refugees at the universities of Toulouse and Cahors
in the seventeenth and eighteenth centuries' in O'Connor and Lyons (eds), *Irish communities in early-modern Europe*, pp 66–7.

return to their dioceses. It was reported in a Dublin newspaper in 1786 that 'when boys are sent abroad [they] have no opportunity of improving themselves for a series of years in that language in which they must afterwards preach, and exhort their congregations'.[28] The bishops of Armagh, Dublin, Kildare, Ferns and Cashel acknowledged this problem in a letter to the Superior General of the Jesuit Order in Rome, Francis Retz, dated 20 February 1731 in which they commended the Jesuits for the manner in which they directed the college at Lisbon because the students acquired knowledge of the vernacular. Lisbon was exceptional in this respect since, according to the bishops, students living abroad tended to forget their Irish.[29] This was particularly true of the boys (the *écoliers*) who travelled as clerical students to Paris to commence their priestly formation.[30] It was less so of the ordained men who left Ireland to complete their theological formation. The authorities in the Irish College, Paris, were keenly aware of the challenge this posed, noting in 1738:

> The priests are mature, arriving in Paris at the age of twenty-four or twenty-five. They come too late to acquire a perfect French accent or to lose their Irish ... The *écoliers* acquire perfect French but lose their Irish, which renders them incapable of serving on the Irish mission. Being obliged to speak Irish in the college is not practicable.[31]

Anxious that this situation should not continue, various attempts were made to address the issue of the promotion of Irish among students destined for the Irish mission. A *mémoire* dated November 1762 relating to the Irish College, Paris, took the form of an appeal against a law passed by the University of Paris that required all students of the humanities and philosophy enjoying burses in the university to attend the Collège des Lisieux. Convinced that this was not in the best interests of those over whom they had responsibility, the memorialists argued that since the Irish College was a seminary rather than a secular college and the priests and clerics in it were destined for the mission in Ireland, it was in the students' interests to continue with their daily exercises which were in the Irish or English language.[32]

It is evident from the records of the continental colleges that the Irish bishops were much activated by the issue of the ability of *écoliers* and priest-

---

28 Cited in David Ryan, 'Catholic preaching in Ireland, 1760–1840' in Raymond Gillespie (ed.), *The remaking of modern Ireland, 1750–1950* (Dublin, 2004), p. 76.   29 Patricia O Connell, *The Irish college at Lisbon* (Dublin, 2001), p. 45; *eadem*, *The Irish college at Santiago de Compostela, 1605–1769* (Dublin, 2007), p. 132.   30 It was alleged that between 1694 and 1734 fewer than twenty-five *écoliers* returned to Ireland to serve as priests: see Cathaldus Giblin, 'The Irish colleges on the continent' in Liam Swords (ed.), *The Irish-French connection, 1578–1978* (Paris, 1978), p. 16, and Swords, 'Collège des Lombards' in *idem* (ed.), *The Irish-French connection, 1578–1978*, p. 54: see also *idem*, 'History of the Irish College', 69–70, §262.   31 Swords, 'History of the Irish College', 69, §262.   32 Ibid., 105–6, §408.

students to use Irish, and that various attempts were made to address the issue. In June 1736, for example, Philipes Joseph Perrotin, *chevalier* St Michel and *garde des registres de finances de France*, remitted the sum of 12,000 livres for the *communauté des clercs et écoliers Irlandois*, Collège des Lombards, provided certain conditions were met. These included:

> (1) to establish a school in the college for the teaching of the Irish language to the students of the other sciences who do not know how to read or write it and to print from time to time catechisms and other little works of piety in Irish, which will be given free to the students and ecclesiastics who return to Ireland, for distribution among those who instruct the young; (2) four prizes, two at 10 l[ivres] each, for those who excel at Irish translation and two at 100 *sols* for best at Irish catechism to be decided by majority vote of masters of the college.[33]

On 26 September 1744, Perrotin changed the details regarding the prize for Irish translation and Irish catechism. The amounts were to be 10 livres for first prize and 100 *sols* for second prize in each case.[34]

This initiative went some way towards ensuring that students in the Irish College in Paris had an incentive to preserve and pursue knowledge of the Irish vernacular, the better to equip them to function in a pastoral environment requiring a sound knowledge of Irish.[35] Yet the problem was ongoing, as was made clear by a priest of the diocese of Kerry who in August 1761 willed a sum of money to enable two students from Kerry to study in the Irish College in Paris. Among the stipulations of the bequest was a requirement that the beneficiaries fraternized with their fellow Irishmen in College in order to preserve their fluency in the Irish language.[36] A further document from the same College, also dating from 1761, providing for a bequest to the *communauté des clercs Irlandois*, stipulated that 100 livres of the bequest should be used for prizes – 60 livres for the best preacher of two Irish sermons, 40 livres for the same in English.[37] Other bequests made to enable students to travel from Ireland to study on the continent also had conditions in relation to the Irish language attached. One such bequest to the Irish College, Paris in March 1764 required that the recipients 'know how to speak Irish ... and that they should take the oath to return to the mission in Cloyne or Ross'.[38]

III

It is clear from these examples that institutions engaged in priestly formation for the Irish mission were acutely aware of the bilingual nature of Irish society.

33 Ibid., 62, §241.   34 Ibid.   35 Ibid.   36 Ibid., 102, §403.   37 Ibid., 103, §404.   38 Ibid., 110, §421.

It certainly tallies with the opinion, expressed by the archbishop of Dublin, Dr John Carpenter, in 1773 that the Irish hierarchy believed it was 'essential that the students of the Irish College in Rome be trained in both native languages'.[39] While it was then a very pressing matter for the ecclesiastical authorities on the Continent and at home, it was not a new concern. As far back as 1650, Cardinal Pier Luigi Carafa (1581–1655), Prefect of the Sacred Congregation of the Tridentine Council, sent a memorial to the Holy See urging that knowledge of their native language should be a mandatory requirement for all students in continental seminaries. The Congregation for the Propagation of the Faith concurred, and decided in the same year 'that for the future a knowledge of Irish vernacular was a pre-requisite for entry into any of the colleges.[40] Interestingly, however, an exception was made for students from those areas in Leinster where Irish was not the vernacular.[41] That stance was not maintained and in 1763 the bishops of Leinster contended that knowledge of Irish 'was a primary pastoral need in their diocese'.[42]

The bishops of Leinster were prompted to offer this observation by the appointment in 1763 of Augustine O'Kelly, an Irish Capuchin from Killinick, county Wexford as superior of the Irish College at Lille. The bishops of Leinster objected to the appointment on the grounds that since O'Kelly did not possess the necessary competence in the Irish language, he was unsuited to oversee the formation and education of clerical students for the dioceses of Leinster. A case was taken in the magistrate's court in Lille and judgment was given in favour of the Capuchin order. The bishops appealed to the supreme court at Douai, which was asked to determine a question of fact – was knowledge of Irish a pastoral necessity for priests in the dioceses of Leinster. As part of the appeal, testimony was submitted by Archbishop Patrick Fitzsimons of Dublin, Eugene Geoghegan, the vicar general of Meath, and Anthony Nowlan, parish priest of Fuldamore [*recte* Tullamore?] by their advocate, M. Vincent, to the effect that the Irish language was not only useful but also necessary. Fitzsimons maintained that even in Dublin confessors could not adequately discharge their pastoral duties unless they were proficient in Irish. Bernard Brady, regent of the Irish Dominicans in Louvain, delivered his testimony in court in Irish and it was translated into French. Anthony Fitzsimons, rector of St Anthony's in Louvain, provided written testimony in Irish and it, too, was translated into French. Hugh MacMahon, president of the Pastoral College, Louvain, and Stephen Taylor, a Dominican of Louvain, supported Fitzsimons' contention. Recalling his days as a student at Lille, Taylor observed that on Tuesdays and Thursdays students spoke only Irish in order to achieve proficiency. Fitzsimons remarked that 'Irish was essential for the instruction of poor Irish Catholics; English was the language

39 Wall, 'The decline of the Irish language', pp 83–4.   40 T.J. Walsh, *The Irish continental movement: the colleges at Bordeaux, Toulouse and Lille* (Dublin, 1973), p. 150.   41 Ibid.   42 Ibid., 159.

of commerce'.[43] Testimony was also heard from the officers and chaplains of Irish regiments in the French service. These were chiefly Clare's regiment at Philipville, Bulkeley's regiment at Rocroi, and Rothe's regiment at Bouchain. Walsh noted that:

> They were unanimous in their opinions: the Irish language was as necessary for a priest in Leinster as in any other part of Ireland. Henry Shee, officer in Clare's regiment, gave personal testimony that he had spent twenty-two months in Lille college: the common language of the students was Irish.[44]

Walsh also recounts that eleven students, who were natives of counties Dublin, Wicklow, Kildare, Meath and Westmeath, all testified in a signed assurance to the court in April 1764 'that proficiency in the Irish language was essential for the discharge of pastoral work in Leinster'.[45]

At the same time, M. O'Faral, advocate for the Capuchins, presented an alternative view of affairs in the dioceses of Leinster. He drew on the written opinions of Francis d'Evreaux (superior of the Irish College, Paris) and David Henegan (prefect of studies at the Irish College, Paris) who attested that English was the vernacular of the province of Leinster and that lectures in theology and scripture were delivered in English in the Irish College, Paris. This opinion was corroborated by a priest of the archdiocese of Dublin, Randolph Mac Donnell, a doctor of the Sorbonne and an examiner at the Irish College, Paris, who claimed that Irish was no longer the mother tongue in Leinster. The views of students were also sought, and in this instance eighteen signed a memorandum supporting MacDonnell's understanding of affairs. Two priests of the diocese of Meath also provided written testimony. They claimed that in Leinster clerical conferences and preaching were always conducted in English, but they acknowledged that 'they would do violence to their consciences if they asserted that a knowledge of Irish was not useful on the Irish mission'.[46] Having heard all the evidence, the court found in favour of the Capuchins and thereby acknowledged that the case for a bilingual superior in the college at Lille was not proven and, by extension, in the eyes of the court, that the requirement for students to have a good working knowledge of Irish while desirable was not essential.

IV

Concern among clergy and laity at the capacity of priests to function through the medium of Irish was acute in various dioceses. When Peter Creagh,

43 Ibid., 159–60.   44 Ibid., 160.   45 Ibid.   46 Ibid., 161.

bishop of Waterford, began a sermon in English in a church in Carrick-on-Suir, county Tipperary, on New Year's Day in 1747, the congregation insisted that he speak in Irish.[47] A priest from the same county mentioned in respect of a bishopric in the diocese of Killaloe did not meet with approval because he was deemed unable to discharge his pastoral duties through the medium of Irish:

> Father Egan, parish priest of Clonmel, ... who has been sought by the bishop of Killaloe as his successor in that diocese, is a man of talent and understanding; ... he preaches well in English, but as he does not know any Irish, he is not capable of instructing the people in the country districts who ... know no other language; this holds true for most of the Irish Catholics; the instructions given to the people by the bishops when they make their visitations and especially on the occasion of the administration of confirmation are most necessary for the preservation of the faith and good conduct of the Irish, whose dislike of the English language and of everything English is one of the means used by providence for the preservation of the Catholic religion among them.[48]

The clergy of the diocese of Kerry succeeded in 1798 in vetoing the appointment of a priest from the diocese of Cork as bishop of their diocese, on, among other grounds, the fact that the individual nominated could not speak Irish.[49]

Use of the Irish language was closely bound up with the capacity to meet the demand for preaching and catechesis through the medium of Irish. The Church's capacity to convey the basic tenets of the Catholic faith was dependent in many locations on the ability of its clergy to preach and catechize through the medium of the Irish language, because the proportion of the laity that could read and write Irish was small.[50] It is also apparent that the need for priests and bishops to be fluent in Irish was related to the ability to preach and to catechize effectively, and not to any commitment to the language *per se*. It was sometimes the case that a priest who was bilingual was deemed appointable to a bishopric for that very reason. Commenting on the appointment of Fr Charles Sughrue as vicar capitular of Ardfert and Aghadoe in 1797, Bishop Francis Moylan of Cork noted approvingly:

> From the knowledge I have of that diocese I am convinced that they could not have made a better choice, as he is truly a gentle man of

47 Hugh Fenning, *The undoing of the friars of Ireland: a study of the novitiate question in the eighteenth century* (Louvain, 1972), p. 38.   **48** Giblin, 'Catalogue of material of Irish interest in the collection *Nunziatura di Fiandra*', part 6, 136.   **49** Wall, 'The decline of the Irish language', p. 84.   **50** Elliott, *The Catholics of Ulster*, p. 181 n68; M.A.G. Ó Tuathaigh, 'An chléir Chaitliceach, an léann dúchais agus an cultúr in Éirinn, *c.*1750–*c.*1850', *Léachtaí Cholm Cille*, 16 (1986), 112–14.

great ecclesiastical abilities, an eminent preacher in English and Irish, zealous in the cause of religion, and esteemed and respected not only by the clergy, but also by the laity of that diocese on account of the integrity of his life and his gentlemanlike manner.[51]

Evidently, bilingualism was regarded as an asset by the clergy and the hierarchy. A successful Catholic bishop or parish priest in the eighteenth century needed not only to be able to serve the needs of the expanding ranks of the English-speaking Catholic middle class but also to attend to the spiritual requirements of that section of the population whose devotional practices were still firmly monolingual. This view is borne out in a collection of sermons in Irish from Ulster dating from the first half of the eighteenth century. The author observed that many of the Catholic people were ignorant of Christian doctrine because of a lack of proper instruction through the medium of Irish:

> Is d'easbhuidh cleachtaigh & staideara air an teagasg Críosdaidhe, agus go sbécialta a gceileamhar agus a gcanamhuin dúchas aar mathara, eadhon san teanguidh Ghaoidheilg, do bheir air na mílte agus air na slóite a bheith ainfhiosach aineólach a bhfóghlaim agus an oideas an Chríosdaidhe.[52]

> (It is the lack of practice and study of Christian instruction, especially in the native speech and dialect of our mothers, i.e., the Irish language, that has left thousands ignorant and unaware of Christian learning and doctrine.)

V

Given the emphasis placed upon students' acquiring a functional knowledge of Irish as part of their pastoral formation it is apparent that the authorities in the continental colleges and the Irish bishops were well aware that some priests failed to meet the pastoral needs of their flocks because they were unable to minister fluently through the medium of the Irish language. The necessity of preserving the Irish language to assist with the inculcation of best devotional practice in Ireland is well demonstrated in the work of Dominican priest, Dominic Brullaughan (or Bradley, also known as An Bráthair Bán), who was based at the Coleraine priory, who wrote a guidebook outlining the duties of the wandering preacher.[53] Brullaughan divided the year's pastoral

---

51 Moylan to Bray, 13 July 1797 in 'Correspondence of Dr Bray, archbishop of Cashel', *Archivium Hibernicum*, 1 (1912), 236.   52 See Cainneach Ó Maonaigh (eag.), *Seanmónta chúige Uladh* (Baile Átha Cliath, 1965), pp 32–3, lines 1094–1098.   53 Dominicus Brullaughan, *Opusculum de missione et missionariis tractans* (Louvain, 1736).

work in two halves: summertime (Easter to October), and wintertime (October to February). His suggestions for the winter programme of pastoral instruction included an exhortation to pray in Irish:

> Teach them how to pray and how to examine their consciences and how to do everything for the glory of God. Conclude with the recitation in the native language of the Litany and other prayers. Bless them and send them away.[54]

The Franciscan priest, Thomas Mahon, who was working in London, wrote to Rome in 1748 with an account of some of the challenges he encountered in his work there. Mahon was involved in the pastoral care of Irish seasonal workers, and was particularly preoccupied with the sacrament of penance. He reported that he would regularly hear ten confessions through the medium of Irish for every one he heard in English. He also reported that he met people 'who had not been [to confession] for years for want of an Irish confessor'.[55] Those circumstances suggest that people who could confess comfortably in Irish only declined to avail of the sacrament until they encountered a priest that had the necessary linguistic skills to hear the confession and absolve them. This is a further indicator that the Church's attempts to address the linguistic deficit through its programmes of formation in the continental colleges did not prove an unqualified success.

The results of a survey conducted by Bishop Nicholas Sweetman of Ferns paint a similar picture. Sweetman made a visitation of his diocese in 1753. Of the 34 parishes that he visited, Sweetman commented on the standard of preaching in 14 of them – mostly at ceremonies of confirmation. On 4 July Michael O'Brien (PP of Bree) 'gave one of ye best, if not ye best, Irish sermon I ever heard'.[56] On 8 July at Newtownbarry, 'Rev Martin Redmond gave a good Irish sermon.' Fr Redmond was attached to the parish of Killann, which Sweetman visited on 10 July, when Fr Redmond preached the same sermon again. It may be that Fr Redmond was a skilled preacher in Irish or that he had a particular sermon that he was happy to repeat, as Sweetman noted that when he visited Fr Bryan Murphy at Rathgarogue on 12 July and Fr James Nowlan at Ross on 13 July, Redmond attended the ceremonies and preached the same sermon on both occasions. Sweetman visited Fr George Kehoe at Dunganstown on 16 July, where Fr James Nowlan 'gave us a good Irish

---

54 Daphne D.C. Pouchin Mould, *The Irish Dominicans* (Dublin, 1957), p. 179.   55 Cathaldus Giblin, 'Ten documents relating to Irish diocesan affairs 1740–84, from Franciscan Library, Killiney', *Collectanea Hibernica*, 20 (1978), 73–5.   56 W.H. Grattan Flood, 'The diocesan manuscripts of Ferns during the rule of Bishop Sweetman (1745–1786)', *Archivium Hibernicum*, 2 (1913), 102–5. Grattan Flood adds the following addendum to his essay: 'It will be observed that a goodly part of the diocese of Ferns was Irish-speaking in 1753, and evidently Bishop Sweetman was himself an Irish speaker. The number of parishes was thirty-two, only three of which had a curate.

exhortation'. On 19 July the bishop was in Ramsgrange where he '…
confirmed and visited, and Rev. Thomas Broders gave a little explanation of ye
Sacrament of Confirmation in Irish.'[57]

In the course of his three-month visitation of diocese of Ferns, Bishop
Sweetman had cause to commend the standard of preaching in English of
only six pastors – Patrick Redmond (Crossabeg), William Doyle (Killurin),
Michael Henrick (Enniscorthy), Bernard Downes (Clongeen) and Andrew
Cassin (Newbawn). Sweetman observed pertinently in the cases of Henrick
and Downes that they 'gave a good English exhortation' although it must be
assumed that the others also preached in English. Sweetman was evidently
proficient enough in Irish to comment positively on the content and delivery
of the sermons he heard in that language, and his report provides clear evidence of the bilingual situation obtaining in his diocese. Signally, what was of
greater concern to him was the fact that in five cases the priest was either not
preaching at all or doing so ineffectively.

Demand for preaching and catechesis through Irish was a recurring feature
of church life, even in Dublin, into the second half of the eighteenth century.
In 1761, the sermon was delivered in Irish at the 7 a.m. mass in the
Dominican chapel in Bridge Street in Dublin. At the 10 a.m. mass in the
same church, however, the sermon was delivered in English.[58] Given this
backdrop, it not surprising to note that the Dominican Order contrived as late
as the 1770s to promote the usage of Irish in the community. Thus when the
prior of the Dominican house at San Clemente, John Thomas Troy, later
archbishop of Dublin, submitted a request to the Pope in 1773 for financial
support to assist with renovation works being carried out in the house, he
informed the Pope *en passant* that if a student preached a sermon in English
he was entitled to an extra dish during dinner. If he preached in Irish, however, he was awarded two extra dishes.[59] It was a rather unusual way of promoting preaching in Irish but it may have been quite effective at the time.

The failure to ensure all Irish clerical students in colleges in Europe were
proficient in Irish was an inevitable consequence of an inadequate and ill-
defined language policy. Its inherent weaknesses are well illustrated in the
case of James Lyons, a priest of the diocese of Elphin who returned to
Ireland from Rome in 1763. Lyons did not mask the fact that he had 'a deficiency in my native language, which for the greater part I forgot in the college'.[60] This suggests that the problem identified by Thomas Mahon in
London with respect to seasonal workers not having access to the sacraments
through the Irish language was symptomatic of a deeper malaise in the Irish
church. It also implies that while priests preparing abroad for the pastoral

57 Ibid., 104.   58 P.J. Corish, *The Catholic community in the seventeenth and eighteenth cen-
turies* (Dublin, 1981), p. 85.   59 Pouchin Mould, *The Irish Dominicans*, p. 173.   60 Hugh
Fenning (ed.), 'The Journey of James Lyons from Rome to Sligo, 1763–1765', *Collectanea
Hibernica*, 11 (1965), 91–110.

mission in Ireland were aware of the need for a proficiency in Irish to discharge their pastoral duties, as Irish was very clearly the people's preferred language of religious and devotional expression, the Church was unable, or unwilling, to remedy that deficiency when and where it occurred.

VI

The case of James Lyons highlights very clearly the 'sink or swim' attitude that prevailed among many of the Irish hierarchy with respect to language proficiency. Lyons, a priest of the diocese of Elphin, entered the Collegio Urbano in Rome to pursue theological studies in 1755 and returned to Ireland in 1763. Alumni of the college were obliged to write annually to the Congregatio de Propaganda Fide with accounts of their work and to report on other matters of interest. Lyons was one of the few to produce more than a perfunctory few lines. His letters are revealing of the difficulties he encountered in relation to Irish when back on Irish soil. The first inkling we have that there was a problem is found in the postscript to a letter dated 18 August 1763, in which Lyons revealed his linguistic limitations:

> Since the cold of Ireland is beginning to trouble me, even in the present month of August, I fear I shall not be able to support the cold of the countryside this winter in my own province of Connaught. I will therefore be obliged to remain in Dublin where I have much to do studying my moral theology, learning my native language (which I forgot in Rome).[61]

Two issues are worthy of note; first, that he adverted to having forgotten his Irish while in Rome, and second, that he sought to regain his lost linguistic skills in Dublin. Whether his concern was more with avoiding the inclement Irish winter in the west of Ireland or genuinely related to having access to tutoring in Irish is not clear, but a fuller picture of his predicament emerges from his correspondence. In January 1764, Lyons wrote again to Rome to seek permission to stay in Dublin:

> There is one thing I most ardently ask of Your Eminence, namely, to let me know whether ... I may remain at Dublin and exercise the mission here for two years. I went at no small expense about ninety miles to see my bishop. He authorized me to return to Dublin, not being able to employ me because of my deficiency in my native language, which for the greater part I forgot in the College.[62]

61 Ibid., 104.   62 Ibid., 106–7.

If the bishop of Elphin, James O'Fallon, authorized Lyons to return to Dublin because he was insufficiently fluent in Irish, it can safely be concluded that knowledge of English alone was insufficient to allow him to minister in his native diocese, even in the town of Sligo, where English had gained a strong foothold by that time.[63] One wonders, however, why the bishop did not encourage him to remain in his home diocese and gradually to reacclimatize himself to his native environment. Perhaps he was not immediately needed. In any event, by January 1765, Lyons was back in his native diocese having been recalled, it appears, by his superiors. His struggle with the language continued, however:

> I am much occupied in learning the Irish language, and I almost despair of ever learning it to perfection. That, and certainly no other, was the reason I wrote to the Sacred Congregation about my stay in Dublin.[64]

It may be that Lyons used the language issue as an excuse. His letters contain frequent references to money and to his need for good quality clothing. It is possible that he had become acclimatized to a better standard of living and quality of life while in Rome and saw Dublin as the closest he would come to such an existence in Ireland. The consistency of his reference to language, specifically his difficulties with Irish, suggests that this was not so. In any event, his difficulties with the Irish language were a key part of his unhappiness and it can safely be assumed that he was not alone in his struggle to attain the proficiency required to serve in the many Irish-speaking parishes of his diocese.

The capacity to use Irish effectively was often desired and more frequently demanded by the church authorities because of the likelihood of English-speaking clergy being cut off, either partly or wholly, from an Irish-speaking congregation. However, aside from attempts to impose some kind of language regime on students studying abroad, and the various literary interventions of Bishop James Gallagher, Bishop John O'Brien, and others, no successful initiative was undertaken to provide systematic support for priests who were struggling with the language. The failure to ensure such support in the eighteenth century ensured continuing challenges for bishops in the early nineteenth century. In 1811, for instance, a young man named William O'Meara, who aspired to join the Franciscan Order in Limerick and who was satisfactory in every other way was deemed unsuitable 'for want of a knowl-

---

63 The town of Sligo was already well anglicized by the 1740s, and education through the medium of English was expensive and much sought-after: see L.M. Cullen, 'Patrons, teachers and literacy in Irish, 1700–1850' in Mary Daly and David Dickson (eds), *The origins of popular literacy in Ireland: language change and educational development, 1700–1920* (Dublin, 1990), p. 29.   64 Ibid., p. 108.

edge of the Irish language, which is necessary for his diocese'.[65] Similarly, Bishop Edward Kiernan of Clogher demanded in 1828 that an otherwise satisfactory candidate for holy orders who did not know Irish 'lay down his shoulders to acquire it.'[66] John Murphy, bishop of Cork (1815–47) claimed that he was unacquainted with the Irish language until he was forty but upon his consecration as 'bishop of Cork ... learned it as 'a duty of conscience ... to be able to examine, in the Irish catechism, those presented to me for confirmation'.[67] Nicholas Archdeacon, who was bishop of Kilfenora and Kilacduagh between 1800 and 1823, grew up 'an utter stranger to the Irish language', yet 'by application and industry, but particularly by secluding himself from his family and boarding himself at the house of a country parish priest who was master of the language, during eighteen months, he learned it radically and now exhorts and catechises with ease.'[68] Archdeacon was the exception rather than the rule, and the approach he adopted would not have been practicable for everyone.

VII

Brian Ó Cuív observed that 'there seems to be no evidence that the Irish hierarchy ever planned collectively to ensure that the clergy would be competent in both Irish and English. There were of course exceptions among the bishops, just as there were many priests who were fluent Irish-speakers and used Irish in carrying out their religious duties, but the trend nationally and locally was to use English in church affairs – in public prayers, sermons, instructions, notices inscriptions church documents, and so on – except in circumstances where Latin would be the normal language.'[69] While Ó Cuív was referring here to the church in the wake of the establishment in 1795 of St Patrick's College, Maynooth, the remark also holds true for the church's activities in the eighteenth century. That it should be so should come as no great surprise. The eighteenth-century church took many decades to come to terms with the effects of the penal laws and did not have a co-ordinated national structure until the last quarter of that century. Moreover, within the diocesan structure sole responsibility for the running of ecclesiastical affairs rested with the bishops and they were not always disposed to collaborative

65 Pádraig Ó Súilleabháin, 'An Dr de Siún, easpag Luimnigh (1796–1813), agus an Ghaeilge', *Studia Hibernica*, 6 (1966), 155–7.   66 Cited in S.J. Connolly, *Priests and people in pre-famine Ireland, 1780–1845* (Dublin, 1982; this edn., 2001), p. 96.   67 Ibid.   68 Cited in Breandán Ó Conchúir, *Scríobhaithe Chorcaí, 1700–1850* (Baile Átha Cliath, 1982), p. 223.   69 Brian Ó Cuív, 'Irish language and literature, 1845–1921' in W.E. Vaughan (ed.), *A new history of Ireland*; v, *Ireland under the Union, 1801–1870* (Oxford, 1996), p. 392; Nicholas M. Wolf, 'The Irish-speaking clergy in the nineteenth century: education, trends, and timing', *New Hibernia Review*, 12:4 (Winter, 2008), 64–5.

endeavour. Given the fact that the Irish language was more an issue of importance and pastoral concern for some bishops than others, and that political developments often assumed a higher priority than pastoral concerns, it is not surprising that the efforts that were made to address the difficulties encountered by priests lacking in the necessary linguistics skills were limited and uncoordinated. Nonetheless, some bishops and priests perceived this as an issue demanding attention and sought in their own way to assist their brethren by producing religious texts in Irish. Chief among these were Bishop Michael O'Reilly (catechism, 1727), Bishop James Gallagher (sermons, 1736), the Carmelite priest Tadhg Ó Conaill (Irish translation of *La Trompette du Ciel*, 1755), Bishop John O'Brien (dictionary, 1768) and John Heely (sermons, *c*.1796), who was a priest of the archdiocese of Armagh.

In their comprehensive review of the literary tradition of the Irish language, J.E. Caerwyn Williams and Máirín Ní Mhuiríosa observed of Bishop James Gallagher's sermons that, except for the *Pious miscellany* of Tadhg Gaelach Ó Súilleabháin, no other book in Irish was as much in demand.[70] The frequency with which the sermons were published is evidence of the high profile this work enjoyed. Between 1736 and 1800, Gallagher's text appeared in print six times (1736, 1752, 1767, 1777, 1795 and 1798).[71] Other religious texts in Irish highlighted the regard in which later authors writing in Irish held Gallagher's work.[72] The following remark, for example, appears on the title page of the Douai bilingual catechism: 'The Doway Catechism in English and Irish for the use of schools, to which is prefixed a method of learning to read the Irish language without a master, for the instruction of such persons as have neglected this useful study in their youth; and it is a most excellent introduction to the reading and understanding of Dr Gallagher's seventeen Irish sermons, so universally read throughout the kingdom of Ireland.' The text also influenced other Catholic preachers, which was one of the aims Gallagher set himself in the English-language preface to the 1736 edition:

> I have compos'd the following discourses for the use of my own fellow labourers principally; and next for such as please to make use of them; that they may preach them to their respective flocks, since my repeated troubles debar me of the comfort of delivering them in person.[73]

---

70 J.E. Caerwyn Williams and Máirín Ní Mhuiríosa, *Traidisiún liteartha na nGael* (Baile Átha Cliath, 1979), pp 276–7. ('Ní raibh aon leabhar Gaeilge eile ann is mó a raibh glaoch air, taobh amuigh de *Pious miscellany* Thaidhg Ghaelaigh Uí Shúilleabháin a cuireadh i gcló den chéaduairi 1805.') See also Niall Ó Ciosáin, 'Printing in Irish and Ó Súilleabháin's *Pious miscellany*' in Gerard Long (ed.), *Books beyond the Pale: aspects of the provincial book trade in Ireland before 1850* (Dublin, 1996), pp 87–99.   71 Ciarán Mac Murchaidh, 'Dr James Gallagher, alumnus Kilmorensis: bishop of Raphoe (1725–37) and Kildare and Leighlin (1737–1751)', *Breifne*, 10:40 (2004), 220–1.   72 Ibid., 222–9.   73 James Gallagher, *Sixteen Irish sermons in an easy and familiar stile* (Dublin, 1736), p. ii.

Two preachers who benefited from a close knowledge of Gallagher's text were Father Tadhg Ó Conaill, a Calced Carmelite, who lived for much of his life in the Carmelite monastery in Kinsale, county Cork and who died in 1779, and Father John Heely from south-east Ulster, a priest of the archdiocese of Armagh who died in 1831. Ó Conaill translated the French religious text *La Trompette du Ciel* ('The Trumpet of Heaven') into Irish.[74] While he translated the original French text quite accurately, he introduced material from Gallagher's sermons into his translation on more than thirty occasions. This usually happened when he encountered a word or phrase in the French text that triggered a remembrance of a similar expression in Gallagher.

Ó Conaill's familiarity with Gallagher's sermons is a strong indication that they were well known to clergy and the wider devotional community across the island of Ireland. In the *First report of the commissioners of education enquiry* of 1825, for example, *Gallagher's Irish Sermons* is listed as a text for religious instruction in schools in counties Donegal, Kildare, Galway and Kerry.[75] Gallagher and Ó Conaill had similar aims. Gallagher wrote in the preface to the 1736 edition of his sermons:

> It may be objected that the generality of our clergy have sermon-books in Latin or French, or other languages, I allow they have, but generally in a stile not so well adapted to our country. But surely they are not the worse to have some in their mother tongue, which may furnish them with thoughts or proper expressions, very often wanting to such as gather their discourses from foreign languages?[76] ... Lest any, then, should be discouraged from making use of this little work, by being strangers to its very elements, I have made choice of letters, which are obvious to all; and in spelling, kept nearer to the present manner of speaking, than to the true and ancient orthography. This seeming difficulty being removed, I hope that as many as can speak or tollerably [*sic*] pronounce the Irish, if furnish'd with any stock of zeal to discharge their duty, will with little pains, soon read and understand the following discourses.[77]

Gallagher evidently felt that the Irish clergy needed assistance and guidance not only with their use of the Irish language but also with the lexicon required to enable them to preach and catechize effectively. It may also be observed that he identified a gap in the competence of the clergy; they could engage with their flock in ordinary everyday conversation but they lacked the

---

74 Cecile O'Rahilly (ed.), *Trompa na bhFlaitheas* (Dublin 1955).   75 McManus, *The Irish hedge school and its books, 1695–1831*, p. 246.   76 Gallagher, *Sixteen Irish sermons*, pp ii–iii.   77 Ibid., pp iv–v. For a detailed discussion of the use by clergy of borrowings from English and phonetic spelling in their Irish-language sermons, see Liam Mac Mathúna, *Béarla sa Ghaeilge* (Baile Átha Cliath, 2007), pp 211–17.

vocabulary and technical skills required to compose adequate sermons. His
intention was that his book of sermons would enable priests to hone their
skills by constant use until they reached a point where they could preach
their own sermons in a competent and confident fashion:

> Take then cheerfully, beloved fellow labourer, this small mess, of
> which I make you a gift; with which you may feed your flock once a
> month, thro' the year, and have some to spare. Nay, rather than they
> should fast, spare not to give them each Sunday a part of the loaf, by
> preaching a point, or even a paragraph; for there are some by their
> length, which can afford to be divided. And by the time your store is
> exhausted, you'll acquire a facility both of expression and invention, to
> serve up fresh dishes of your own dressing.[78]

Andrew Donlevy's bilingual catechism was published in Paris in 1748 and in the
preface he provided the reader with an insight into his purpose in producing
such a work. Noting the unavailability of Irish-language catechisms produced by
the Franciscans in Louvain a century earlier, he identified a pastoral vacuum that
needed to be filled. He was also aware of the need to address the faithful in a
language with which they were familiar. While he does not specifically mention
clergy, one may reasonably conclude that his catechism was conceived with the
intention of assisting priests who did not possess the necessary command of Irish
to preach and teach Catholic doctrine through the medium of Irish:

> The plainest and most obvious Irish is used throughout, preferring,
> with St Augustine, to be censured by grammarians, rather than not to
> be understood by the people. Foreign expressions, except those conse-
> crated to religion, are diligently avoided; and care taken to explain cer-
> tain words not used in some districts of the kingdom by other words
> set down at the bottom of the page. The English part is, perhaps, too
> literal a translation from the Irish. It is for the sake of those who
> understand only the English, or who may be inclined to learn the Irish
> by means of this translation.[79]

Tadhg Ó Conaill, too, conceived of his efforts to provide devotional material
in Irish as following in the footsteps of the Irish Franciscans in Louvain. In
his dedication to Archbishop Butler of Cashel at the beginning of his text Ó
Conaill wrote:

> Dá bhrígh sin, a Thighearna,
> (ar aithris mórnuimhir d'aithreachaibh fíor fhoghlamtha d'Órd

---

78 Gallagher, *Sixteen Irish sermons*, p. v.   79 Aindréas Ó Duinnshléibhe, *An teagasg
Críosduidhe do réir ceasda agus freagartha* (Paris, 1742; this edn., Dublin, 1848), p. xxiii.

naomhtha Naomh Proinsias d'fhág mórán agus do chuir amach do leabhraibh deightheagaisg Críostamhla deighriartha i nGaoidheilge nó i dteangain ár máthar ar reacht Dé do choiméad agus a shlighte do shiubhal ar an modh do theagaisg Críost), an leabhrán beag Fraincise si dá ngoirthear '*La Trompette du Ciel*' nó 'Trompa na bhFlaithios' ... i ndóith go dtiucfadh liom read éigin d'fhágbháil mar chomaoin, do réir mo bheg-dhithchioll, mar chách ar mo dhúthaidh.[80]

(And so, my Lord, (after the fashion of a great number of the most learned fathers of the Order of St Francis, who produced and left behind many efficacious and well-ordered books of Christian teaching in Irish or in our mother tongue on how to observe God's law and to walk in his ways, as Christ showed us) I offer this little French book entitled *La Trompette du Ciel* or 'The Trumpet of Heaven' so that I might do something to serve the people of my native land.)

Two conclusions stand out with respect to this extract: first, that Ó Conaill saw himself as part of a group of clergy who identified, and who sought to address, a need among their fellow priests and the laity for devotional material in Irish, and second, that he saw his work as performing a linguistic and pastoral service for the community in which he resided.

In much the same way, Dr John O'Brien, bishop of Cloyne and Ross, indicated in his correspondence with Propaganda in Rome in 1764, when he sought financial support to aid with the publication of his bilingual *Focalóir Gaoidhilge/Sax-Béarla* that the people under his care expressed their religious devotion in no other language than Irish.[81] Arising out of this, O'Brien endeavoured to impress upon the Roman authorities that the preservation and promotion of the Irish language was synonymous with the preservation and promotion of the Catholic faith:

Another reason which shows the essential connexion between the preservation of Catholicism in this country and the Irish language is that experience has taught us that it is only those ignorant of Irish or those who become fluent in English who abandon the Catholic religion and embrace that of Protestants.[82]

---

80 O'Rahilly, *Trompa na bhFlaitheas*, p. 3.   81 Pádraig Ó Súilleabháin, 'Leabhar urnaithe an ochtú haois déag', *Irish Ecclesiastical Record*, 103 (1965), 301–2. No comprehensive monolingual dictionary in Irish had been attempted since Micheál Ó Cléirigh's *Foclóir no sanasan nua* (Louvain, 1643): see Tomás de Bhaldraithe, 'Foclóirí Gaeilge', *Corpus na Gaeilge 1600–1882: foclóir na Nua-Ghaeilge* (Dublin, 2004), p. 25; Liam Mac Amhlaigh, *Foclóirí agus foclóirithe na Gaeilge* (Baile Átha Cliath, 2008), p. 1.   82 F.M. Jones, 'The Congregation of Propaganda and the publication of Dr O'Brien's Irish Dictionary, 1768', *Irish Ecclesiastical Record*, 77 (1952), 32.

O'Brien further stated his belief that the fate of the Irish language and its future preservation was inextricably linked to the promotion of the Catholic faith and defence of the Catholic people from corruption by adherents of the Anglican church. He implicitly conceded that the major urban centres and bigger towns had become anglicized, but it was also the case that the vast number of the population who lived in rural or less urbanized areas were more likely to be monoglot Irish speakers, who could only be reached through Irish:

> The preservation of the Irish language among the clergy and Catholic population of Ireland is essentially connected with the preservation of the true Faith. The reason is that the majority of the Catholics of Ireland live in the country, in villages and small towns and in general speak only the Irish language which is a dialect of Celtic. As a necessary consequence they learn their Catechism and recite their prayers in Irish; moreover, only in Irish can they make the sacramental confession of their sins. As a result the parochial clergy and other missionary priests must be sufficiently well acquainted with Irish in order to administer the Sacraments, to teach the people Christian doctrine, to instruct them in moral truths and in the truths of the Gospel.[83]

O'Brien was convinced of the importance of the language for the pastoral and cultural mission of the Catholic Church in Ireland. He was bishop of a diocese where the Irish language was still extremely strong and he wished genuinely to be of service to those clergy who laboured in parishes where very few spoke anything other than Irish, in the same manner as James Gallagher. O'Brien certainly communicated to Rome the need for some form of linguistic assistance in order to encourage priests to address shortfalls in their proficiency in Irish:

> The necessity, however, under which our young priests are placed of studying in the Catholic schools on the continent for many years exposes them to the danger of forgetting their mother tongue which is so necessary for them in their work for the preservation of the faith of our poor Catholics. Everyone must see then the benefit that would accrue to the Irish mission from the publication of a good Irish dictionary in which all, or almost all the terms of this language would be correctly explained and in which our missionaries could find the words and explanations which they may have forgotten or perhaps never known.[84]

83 Ibid., 32–3.   84 Ibid., 32.

The missionaries mentioned by O'Brien were clergy with little or no Irish. The dictionary, in all likelihood, was also intended by O'Brien to provide those who had a fluency in Irish with the requisite theological terminology and vocabulary to address such topics. However, in the context of what was being done on a national level to support and promote the Irish language, O'Brien's dictionary was, as Ó Ciosáin has observed, 'not a gesture by the church as an institution in support of Irish ... but ... an attempt by an individual churchman to remedy the neglect of the language by that institution as a whole'.[85]

Armagh priest, John Heely, wrote his sermons in a phonetic script so that clergy unfamiliar with the orthography of written Irish could read and then preach them with ease.[86] The earliest existing manuscript containing his sermons dates from January 1796 to November 1811.[87] Heely drew heavily on Gallagher's work, which is what Gallagher himself intended, as he viewed his sermons as a tool that priests could employ to help them serve the catechetical and homiletic needs of the people.[88]

During the eighteenth century, many bishops laid great emphasis on preaching as a means of teaching the people about their faith and at the same time refuting the doctrines of the reformed faiths. The language was a means of conveying such teaching and, also, as Bishop O'Brien explicitly observed, a bulwark which protected the Catholic Irish-speaking population from proselytizers. Many priests, like John Heely, made their own of Gallagher's work and of other religious material, much of it in French and Latin, in order to assemble a collection of sermon material for their own personal pastoral use. By the fourth quarter of the eighteenth century, however, efforts in the tradition of Gallagher, Donlevy, Ó Conaill and O'Brien were becoming increasingly difficult to sustain, as the linguistic landscape changed inexorably in favour of the English language. Anthony Coyle, a successor of Gallagher's as bishop of Raphoe (1782–1801) and the author of *Collectanea sacra; or, pious miscellany in verse and prose*, which was published in Strabane, county Tyrone in 1780 is a case in point. Coyle wrote *Collectanea sacra* in English (aside from a few short pieces in Irish). The historian, Thomas Wall, in assessing Coyle's work in 1958, was highly critical of this decision, as he felt that Coyle 'had missed the opportunity of rendering service to the cause of the Irish language' as Gallagher and O'Brien before him had done.[89] John J. Silke's assess-

85 Ó Ciosáin, 'Language, print and the Catholic Church in Ireland, 1700–1900', p. 130. 86 Seosamh Ó Labhraí, *Téacs na seanmóirí i lámhscríbhinn MF4 i gColáiste Phádraig, Maigh Nuad leis an Athair John Heely* (unpublished PhD thesis, University of Ulster, Coleraine 1998). 87 The manuscript, MF 4, is in the Russell Library at NUI Maynooth. For a description of its contents see Pádraig Ó Fiannachta, *Lámhscríbhinní Gaeilge Choláiste Phádraig Má Nuad: clár*, fasc. vi (Má Nuad, 1969), pp 110–17. 88 See Ciarán Mac Murchaidh, '"My repeated troubles": Dr James Gallagher (bishop of Raphoe 1725–37) and the impact of the penal laws' in John Bergin, Eoin Magennis et al. (eds), *New perspectives on the penal laws* (Dublin, 2011), pp 149–72 at pp 160–5. 89 Thomas Wall, *The sign of*

ment of Coyle's pragmatic approach is more realistic, as it relates Coyle's actions to the changing times in Ireland and, indeed, to the constantly shifting linguistic environment:

> In the mid-eighteenth century O'Gallagher and Donlevy used [Irish] as a pastoral instrument, while in a later generation Coyle, although his preaching in both Irish and English was marked by erudition and fluency (*mire cum eruditione ac sermonis facilitatae*) and he composed prayers in Irish for his people's use, in his writing he used mainly English ... Anglicization in his diocese had advanced, if unevenly, from the time of O'Gallagher and Donlevy.[90]

Silke observed that Coyle used Irish as well as English in his pastoral work and was known to compose prayers in verse and prose.[91] He has also pointed out that Coyle's pragmatic attitude reflected accurately the linguistic environment in which he ministered: 'The greater part of Raphoe diocese, lying to the north west of Letterkenny, was Irish-speaking. But around Letterkenny, English was gaining the day over Irish, and in dealing with the wider world with which he was familiar, English was his [Coyle's] natural medium'.[92] In that regard Coyle is illustrative of the change of attitude that was evident in the pastoral approaches of many eighteenth-century Catholic bishops and priests. Such a change of attitude can be mapped throughout the course of the century from the Irish-only sermons of Gallagher, through Donlevy's bilingual catechism, to Ó Conaill's Irish-language translation of a French devotional text, O'Brien's Irish–English dictionary, Heely's phonetically rendered sermons and Coyle's English-language devotional miscellany. This mapping illustrates the slow, but steady, change of approach and understanding as a bilingual culture and mind-set percolated through the ranks of the Catholic Church.

CONCLUSION

The eighteenth century was the intermediate period in the shift from a predominantly monolingual to a primarily bilingual environment within the Catholic Church in Ireland. In the early part of the eighteenth century, the focus of the Church's attention was on negotiating a political environment that was intensely inimical to its survival. As the century progressed, and political tensions eased, another pastoral challenge slowly began to develop. While the uneducated and poorer Catholic faithful remained largely mono-

Doctor Hay's head (Dublin, 1958), pp 101–2.   **90** John J. Silke, 'Bishop Coyle's Pious Miscellany', *Eighteenth-Century Ireland: iris an dá chultúr*, 9 (1994), 116–17.   **91** Ibid., 117. **92** Ibid., 119.

lingual Irish speakers, the emerging middle-class Catholic faithful became gradually more bilingual and, as William Smyth has observed, 'the language used in Catholic institutions varied widely – hybridity and complexity ruled'.[93] Education in English was viewed by the lower-class Catholic population as an ever more important means of making social and financial progress, but Irish remained central as a medium, of oral communication and devotional expression.[94]

This was an issue with which the ecclesiastical authorities had to grapple. To do so adequately required that their priests be capable of ministering in increasingly bilingual settings. Addressing this challenge through the education of its clergy was viewed by the bishops as one way of correcting the language deficit. Having to send them abroad to colleges on the Continent for their theological formation, however, retarded rather than aided the achievement of this goal. While efforts were made in the continental colleges to preserve and to promote fluency in the native language, the undertaking was fundamentally flawed because the environment in which such linguistic goals were pursued was far removed from the realities of the Irish pastoral mission. Such an approach was also reliant on the cooperation and good will of the clerics involved, and could only aspire to achieve its desired outcome if the approach adopted was applied with the same efficiency and consistency across all the colleges. This was not the case. Attempts by the ecclesiastical authorities in Ireland to address the situation were similarly doomed for lack of a coordinated, national strategy. It was left to a few churchmen to provide a remedy for the linguistic challenges faced by many priests and this approach, while laudable, did not constitute a successful method of tackling the multifaceted varied nature of the problem as it existed in many Irish dioceses. In fact, the evidence would suggest that the Church authorities took the easier option of allowing the pastoral situation to follow the social trend towards the increasing use of English in the religious as well as the civic spheres.

Ultimately, as an institution, the Catholic Church's approach to Irish in the eighteenth century was at best neutral. Where it sought to address the language deficit, the attempt was frequently erratic and inconsistent. It saw the language as a bulwark against the outside world and against the risk of religious interference but, ironically, it relied on the outside world of the continental colleges to survive. For the greater part of the eighteenth century, it had to send its clerics abroad for their clerical formation, which was not always conducive to good linguistic practice. Of necessity, moreover, it

93 William J. Smyth, *Map-making, landscapes and memory: a geography of colonial and early modern Ireland c.1530–1750* (Cork, 2006), p. 410; Ignatius Murphy, *The diocese of Killaloe in the eighteenth century* (Dublin, 1991), pp 170–3, 203. 94 Smyth, *Map-making, landscapes and memory*, p. 405; Liam Mac Mathúna, 'An Ghaeilge mar theanga phobail i mBaile Átha Cliath' in James Kelly and Uáitéar Mac Gearailt (eds), *Dublin and Dubliners* (Dublin, 1990), pp 157–9.

engaged with the Irish civil authorities though the medium of English, while trying to protect itself against an anglophone established church. The Church did, at times, adopt a more proactive stance in relation to the linguistic formation and proficiency of its clergy, but there was insufficient will within its ranks to ensure that the attempt would succeed. For the Church, language was the medium of its message, and since the message could be conveyed in any medium the faithful comprehended, it followed them in using English and becoming in the process, therefore, part of the anglicized voice that shaped and defined Ireland.

7

Irish Protestants and the Irish language in the eighteenth century

JAMES KELLY

The instinctive suspicion with which Irish Protestants were disposed to regard the Irish language eased palpably in the course of the eighteenth century. The attitudinal amelioration that informed this dispositional change did not extend so far as to prompt *many* among their number openly to view Irish as a useful and advanced living language, and still less to commend its use in official discourse. Nonetheless, there was an identifiable change in outlook between the end of the seventeenth century when parliament was presented with a bill for the 'suppression of the Irish language' and the beginning of the nineteenth when the authorities countenanced the publication of official notices in Irish, and a number of intellectual and antiquarian bodies sought to promote linguistic scholarship.[1] Then, as earlier, sentiment was not uniform or unanimous. There were still those who perceived the extinction of Irish as socially and politically advantageous. The influential conservative ideologue Bishop Richard Woodward of Cloyne (1726–94), who characterized the Irish language in 1787 as an unfortunate 'bar of separation between ... the Irish and the English', expressed a preference then that the state might find a way 'to bring it into entire disuse', while his ideological fellow-traveller, Patrick Duigenan, invoked the traditional cultural prejudice that Irish was the language of an inherently inferior culture when he disparaged Fr Arthur O'Leary in 1786 as the 'friar with the barbarous surname'.[2] Yet the attempt by Henry Flood in 1791 to endow a chair of Irish at Trinity College indicates also that there were others, mostly, though not exclusively, from the ranks of the patriot interest, who were of a more accommodating disposition and empathetic outlook.[3] Their more generous attitude derived in the first

---

1 For a recent survey of 'the politics of language in Ireland' see Tony Crowley, *Wars of words: the politics of language in Ireland, 1537–2004* (Oxford, 2005). 2 Richard Woodward, *The present state of the Church of Ireland* (8th ed., Dublin, 1787), pp 55n, 85–6; Theophilus [pseud. for Patrick Duigenan], *An address to the nobility and gentry of the Church of Ireland* (Dublin, 1786). The quotation is from p. 30 of the third edition Dublin, 1808. 3 James Kelly, 'The last will and testament of Henry Flood: context and text', *Studia Hibernica*, 31 (2000–1), 37–52.

instance from an augmented interest in Irish history and appreciation of the cultural and linguistic merits of the Irish language. But it is improbable that they would have embarked on this intellectual journey in the absence of a complementary change in attitude among elements of the Catholic population. The manifest decline in enthusiasm among elite and respectable Catholics for Jacobitism, the easing in confessional animosity, and the perception, articulated by Henry Grattan in 1782, by Mathew Carey in 1783, and finally, and most influentially, by the United Irishmen in the 1790s, that it was possible to transcend historic religious, cultural and ethnic divisions to forge an Irish 'national' identity were crucial concomitant developments.[4] This process of re-imagining only went so far, however. Grattan's idea of an 'Irish nation' was perceived by a majority of his co-religionists as a hubristic rhetorical flight of fantasy; Carey's precocious scheme 'to unite in the closest bonds of harmony and concord every denomination of Irishman' foundered in the reality of denominational suspicion; while the United Irish organization's more sophisticated plans to achieve the same object imploded amid the heightened sectarianism of the 1798 Rebellion and its aftermath.[5] Moreover, few Protestants sought, and still fewer succeeded, in achieving conversational fluency or literary proficiency in Irish. Though many individuals acted as if this was the case, the Protestant elite as such, and still less those of their number who involved themselves in politics and administration, could not pretend that the Irish language did not exist. The 'more general' recourse to English that Bishop Woodward comfortingly evoked in 1787 may have reflected the linguistic reality that the pendulum of usage had swung decisively in favour of English, but there was no denying the fact that Ireland in the eighteenth and early nineteenth centuries was a bilingual society, and that that this had social, economic, administrative and ideological implications that Irish Protestants simply could not ignore.[6]

I

As the seventeenth century drew to a close, the prevailing attitude of Irish Protestants to the Irish language was hostile and unaccommodating. This may be ascribed in large part to inherited attitudes first given expression in the twelfth century by Giraldus Cambrensis, and reiterated still more vigorously in the sixteenth century, that Irish culture and civilization was not only inferior

---

4 James Kelly, *Henry Grattan* (Dundalk, 1993), p. 3; *idem*, 'Mathew Carey's Irish apprenticeship: editing *The Volunteers Journal*, 1783–4' (unpublished paper, 2011); Nancy Curtin, *The United Irishmen: popular politics in Ulster and Dublin, 1791–1798* (Oxford, 1994), chapters 1 and 2. 5 *Volunteers Journal*, 13 Oct. 1783; James Kelly, *Sir Richard Musgrave: ultra-Protestant ideologue* (Dublin, 2009), passim. 6 Woodward, *The present state of the Church of Ireland*, p. 56.

to its Anglo-Saxon rival but also 'barbarous in all points'; as a result, it was deemed to constitute a barrier in the way of the onward march of civility.[7] The rhetoric of 'civility' yielded to that of 'improvement' in the eighteenth century, but the perception of Irish culture as second rate continued to shape attitudes.[8] The Irish language specifically was perceived in a particularly negative light. Commenting in the record he made of his experiences on a visit to Ireland in 1699, the rector of East Dereham in Norfolk had recourse to the common perception of those schooled in the prevailing theories of the origins of language in the anglophone world when he described 'Irish' as 'the fagg-end of those at Babell'.[9] It was a categorical dismissal, and it was consistent with the prevailing tendency to portray the Irish language as not only 'barren and defective',[10] like the backward and unrefined culture from which it emanated, but also predestined to fill that role because it was one of the less distinguished languages to emerge out of the ultimate repository of human speech – the Tower of Babel.[11] This negative perception was given additional authority by that attitude of reformed religion, for instead of combining the scriptural injunction 'go ye therefore, and teach all nations' with the reformation injunction to employ the vernacular, the Protestant community at large in Ireland concluded that their inability to convert the Irish Catholic population could be both explained and justified by reference to the fact that because the Irish language was not suited to the communication of advanced ideas, it was not an appropriate medium of evangelization. Moreover, there were additional practical obstacles; the necessary human (preachers and ministers with the appropriate linguistic

7 Crowley, *Wars of words*, pp 9–35; Giraldus Cambrensis, *Topography of Ireland* trans J.J. O'Meara (Dundalk, 1951), pp 84–7; D.B. Quinn, *The Elizabethans and the Irish* (Ithaca, NY, 1966); Patricia Palmer, *Language and conquest in early modern Ireland: English renaissance literatures and Elizabethan expansion* (Cambridge, 2001), chapters 3 and 4; Nicholas Canny, *Making Ireland British, 1580–1650* (Oxford, 2001), passim; Colin Kidd, *British identities before nationalism: ethnicity and nationhood in the Atlantic world, 1600–1800* (Cambridge, 1999), p. 157; Journal of a tour by James Verdon, 8 June–Aug. 1699 (BL, Add MS 41769 f. 40). This journal will be published in *Analecta Hibernica*, 43 (2012) 47–67, and I wish to thank Professor Rolf Loeber for bringing it to my attention.   8 Toby Barnard, *Improving Ireland?: projectors, prophets and profiteers, 1641–1786* (Dublin, 2008). 9 Journal of a tour by James Verdon, 8 June–Aug. 1699 (BL, Add MS 41769 f. 40); Toby Barnard, "Protestants and the Irish language, *c*.1675–1725' in *idem*, *Irish Protestant ascents and descents, 1641–1770* (Dublin, 2002), p. 181.   10 The judgment of John Richardson, *A short history of the attempts that have been made to convert the Popish natives of Ireland to the establish'd religion with a proposal for their conversion* (London, 1712), p. 124.   11 Ironically, texts such as *Lebor Gabála Érenn* and *Auraicept na nÉces* took precisely the opposite perspective; they asserted that Irish was one of the most advanced and sophisticated languages, as it comprised the best features of all the confounded languages ordered by God: for a modern commentary see Kidd, *British identities before nationalism: ethnicity and nationhood in the Atlantic world, 1600–1800*, pp 30–3, 59–72; and for Geoffrey Keating's modernization of the thesis about the origins of Irish see Bernadette Cunningham, *The world of Geoffrey Keating: history, myth and religion in seventeenth-century Ireland* (Dublin, 2000), chapter 7.

and homiletic skills) and material (printed texts in Irish) resources were in short supply. More pertinently, the conviction that any attempt to do so through the medium of Irish must impede the necessary policy of anglicization, of which the embrace of English was a priority, also reinforced inherited negative perceptions of Irish as a language.[12]

This was not a view universally shared. It was recognized in certain quarters that because it was 'impracticable to destroy the mother-tongue of any people by the severest methods of conquest', a more constructive strategy might advantageously be pursued.[13] The problem, experience seemed to suggest, was that such schemes as were hatched to evangelize the Irish-speaking population through the medium of the Irish language were destined to fail. This was the experience, certainly, of Bishop William Bedell (1572–1642), whose cultural openness synergized with his religious conviction to promote the translation of the Old Testament in the 1630s, and of Robert Boyle (1627–91), whose energetic intervention paved the way for the publication in 1685 finally of an Irish-language Bible.[14] However, because both initiatives were followed within short order by an outbreak of inter-communal violence that threatened the very survival of the Protestant interest in Ireland, the generality of the largely providentially minded ranks of Irish Protestantism were sceptical that this was the best way to proceed. One of the main difficulties that Boyle's initiative manifested was that an effective programme of evangelization must prove prolonged and costly; this realization was echoed by suggestions that it was necessary also that the 'liturgy, catechism and 39 Articles of the Church of England be printed in the Irish tongue in a Roman character' in order that 'Protestant divines skilled in Irish might be had'.[15] In any event, the accession of James II to the throne in 1685 ensured that the publication of an Irish Bible was not the signal for a lively campaign of evangelization, and that official support would not be forthcoming for any such initiative for the duration of James II's reign. The Glorious Revolution, which brought William of Orange to the throne in 1688, ensured that this interval was not prolonged, but the legacy of political and religious ill feeling generated during James II's reign and, still more, by the expropriation authorized by the Jacobite parliament (1689) and the fighting that followed prompted a hardening of attitudes that was not only inconsistent with a successful programme of evangelization using Irish, but also reinforced the negative dispo-

12 Matthew 28:19 (King James Bible); Barnard, 'Protestants and the Irish language', pp 180–2.   13 'Proposalls for the more effectual subjugation of the Irish to the crowne of England', n.d. (Bodleian Library, Rawlinson A. 238, f. 20 printed in *Analecta Hibernica*, 1 (1930), 73–4).   14 N.J.A. Williams, *I bprionta i leabhar: na Protastúin agus prós na Gaeilge, 1567–1724* (Baile Átha Cliath, 1986), pp 43–56, 72–94; John McCaffrey, 'Venice in Cavan: the career of William Bedell, 1572–1642' in Brendan Scott (ed.), *Culture and society in early modern Breifne/Cavan* (Dublin, 2009), pp 173–87; Barnard, 'Protestants and the Irish language', pp 183–6.   15 As note 13, p. 74.

sition towards the language and ensured it continued to be regarded by Irish Protestants in primarily political terms.[16]

The irony is that James II shared the general antipathy of anglophones to the Irish language. Persuaded that the maintenance of an harmonious Anglo-Irish connection would be facilitated if the language was supplanted, he counselled his son (in the event of his acceding to the Irish throne) that he should support the establishment of 'schools to teach the children of the old natives English' on the grounds that an undertaking of this nature 'would by degrees wear out the Irish language'. Indeed, he added, this 'would be for the advantage of the body of the inhabitants, whether old or new, and would do much to lessen the animosities that are among them'.[17] This was an aspiration that the more prescient of Irish Protestants could endorse, but the generality of Protestant opinion in the 1690s was less understanding and less patient. The immediate security of the Protestant interest in the face of a likely Catholic *revanche* was their priority. As a result, the Irish language did not feature prominently on the agenda of the Protestant representatives who assembled in parliament. However, the inclusion in the 1695 'act to restrain foreign education' of a clause which stated that the permissive attitude adopted towards 'Papists keeping schools or instructing youth in literature is one great reason of many of the natives continuing ignorant of the principles of the true religion, and strangers to the scriptures, and of their neglecting to conform themselves to the laws of this realm, and of their not using the English habit and language' indicated that the prevailing negative disposition towards matters Irish included the Irish language.[18]

This was the import, certainly, of the presentation by James, second viscount Lanesborough (1650–1724) in the House of Lords in September 1697 of a bill for the 'suppression of the Irish language, and encouraging the Irish to learn English'. The object of this measure was to integrate 'the natives of this kingdom into the English government by obliging them not only to learn but [also] to use no other vulgar language besides English'. It is apparent from the support forthcoming for the proposal from some members of the episcopate that Lanesborough was not riding a personal hobby-horse, but the bill failed to progress beyond report stage, and since it was not subsequently reanimated, it can reasonably be concluded that there was insufficient support to countenance such a draconian strategy.[19] Be that as it may, Lanesborough and his allies were not alone of their generation in voicing a negative opinion of the Irish language,

---

16 For James II's reign see J.G. Simms, *Jacobite Ireland, 1685–91* (London, 1965). 17 *Life of James the Second, King of England, collected out of memoirs writ of his own hand, together with the king's advice to his son* ... ed. J.S. Clarke (2 vols, London, 1816), ii, 636; Éamonn Ó Ciardha, *Ireland and the Jacobite cause, 1685–1766: a fatal attachment* (Dublin, 2002), p. 102. 18 7 William III, chap. 4, sec. 9. 19 ILD, bill no. 5147 (accessible at http/www.qub.ac.uk/ild/); Barnard, 'Protestants and the Irish language', pp 187–8.

or in believing that the institutions of the state should play an important part in sustaining an environment that would discourage its use. This attitude was certainly encouraged by the conviction, still widely embraced within the Protestant community, that Irish was not only a linguistically and socially inferior tongue, but also the medium through which those who sought to undermine the Protestant constitution in church and state, and to replace it with a Catholic Jacobite regime, chose to progress their nefarious goals. In practice, the authorities did not possess a sufficiently robust intelligence system or the linguistic capacity required to penetrate the clerical and lay Jacobite networks that existed, but it is notable that their preoccupation with inhibiting recruitment into the Irish regiments in France and with interrupting clerical movement between Ireland and France was matched by their readiness to pursue sanctions against those who sought to articulate their Jacobite loyalties through the medium of Irish. Thus Edward Magennis, a tidewaiter in the employment of the revenue service, was dismissed from his post at Ringsend, near Dublin in 1718, when colleagues informed the commissioners that he had raised a glass and 'drank a health in Irish ... to King James III'. Interestingly, Magennis' words were unintelligible to some of those who were present, but not his host, who was sufficiently disturbed by the sentiments, and by the fact that Magennis compounded his offence by bringing 'a book of seditious songs' to the gathering and by 'his cursing the spawn of Cromwellians and Presbyterians etc', to swear on oath as to what transpired.[20]

Edward Magennis' indiscretion cost him dearly; positions in the revenue were highly prized. Nevertheless, his (and allied) lapses of judgment had less impact in the longer term on Protestant attitudes than the belief that Irish speakers were more likely to engage in crimes against the person, and that the Irish language acted as a brake on commercial development. Though they were not commonplace, the observation in the proclamation offering a reward of £100 for the apprehension of those responsible for the brutal mistreatment of an elderly Quaker couple in King's County in 1725 that the perpetrators 'spoke nothing but Irish to one another' affirmed the former conviction.[21] The connection between the use of Irish and economic backwardness was still less obviously demonstrable, but it did not inhibit its articulation. This was the message, certainly of Gerard Boate's *Naturall history*, which was reprinted in Dublin in 1726 and again in 1755, of Samuel Madden whose resolutions published in 1738 epitomized the improving mentality, and of various works by Walter Harris and Richard Barton, who were members in the 1740s of the lively Physico-Historical Society and warm promoters of 'improvement'.[22]

---

20 Minutes of the revenue commissioners, 21 May 1718 (TNA, CUST1/14 unpaginated). 21 Proclamation, 10 Apr. 1725 in James Kelly and M.A. Lyons (eds), *The proclamations of Ireland, 1660–1820* (5 vols, Dublin, forthcoming), iii, no. 113.   22 Mark Williams, 'History, the interregnum and the exiled Irish' in Mark Williams and Stephen Paul Forrest (eds), *Constructing the past: writing Irish history, 1600–1800* (Woodbridge, 2010), pp 39–41;

Encouraged by such beliefs, and by an instinctive antipathy towards, and lack of understanding of, the language, some landowners sought not only physically to remodel the landscape in accordance with the principles of improvement, but also to re-denominate it.

When 21-year-old John Perceval visited his father's estate at Ballymacow, county Cork in 1731, he recommended replacing 'the long Irish name' by which the place was known with 'a genteeler one'. Viscount Perceval was unenthusiastic, but it is notable that he did not resist the idea provided, he cautioned, 'no inconvenience can follow from it'.[23] Perceval was a benign and engaged landowner, whose commitment to the improvement of his extensive Irish estate was pursued with the object of enhancing the lives and incomes of his tenants as well as his own rent roll. This may account for his conditional response to his son's suggestion, since, as a peer of the realm, he was one of a social elite most of whose members found Irish personal and place-names orthographically and linguistically alien. The extent to which this was so in the half century following the military defeat of Irish Jacobitism is well exemplified by the variants in personal and place-names encountered in proclamations offering rewards for the apprehension of those sought pursuant to the provisions of the 1695 'act for the better suppressing tories, robbers and rapparees'.[24] There one routinely encounters such variants as 'beg' and 'begg' for 'beag'; 'bane' for 'bán'; 'buy' and 'buoy' for 'bui'; 'Bryan' for 'Brian'; 'glass' for 'glas', 'roe' for 'rua', and all manner of variant spellings for non-standardized personal and place-names, which was indicative of the lack of familiarity at official level, and, one might add, interest in acquiring even a working knowledge of Irish.[25] This is not to suggest that mutual incomprehension was the order of the day, or that those in positions of authority were consciously cavalier or entirely contemptuous of Irish and of those for whom it was their medium of expression. In the same proclamations that routinely proffered phonetically variable versions of personal and place names, recognizably anglicized variants of everyday Irish words such as 'skean' (*scian* – a knife) were given the *imprimatur* of official usage, though it is notable that by the time such code-mixing is observable, one can also detect greater regularity in the versions of Irish personal and place-names in official pronouncements.[26]

Barnard, *Improving Ireland?*, pp 35–6; Samuel Madden, *Reflections and resolutions proper for the gentlemen of Ireland* (Dublin, 1738, 1816), p. 78 (1816 ed.); M.J. Powell, *The politics of consumption in eighteenth-century Ireland* (Basingstoke, 2005), p. 80. **23** William Taylor to Lord Perceval and reply, 11 June, 10 July 1731 (BL, Egmont papers, Add. MS 46892 f. 57). **24** 7 William III, chap. 21. **25** Proclamation, 8 Feb. 1715, 15 May 1715, 19 Dec. 1716, 24 Dec. 1717, 10 July 1721, 4 June 1722 in Kelly and Lyons (eds), *The proclamations of Ireland*, iii, George I, nos 13, 42, 49, 56, 86, 93. **26** Proclamation, 10 Apr. 1725, 12 Apr. 1730 in Kelly and Lyons (eds), *The proclamations of Ireland*, iii, George I, no. 113; George II, no. 38.

This is significant, for though the pattern of language usage in official documents is consistent with the general trend,[27] whereby knowledge of English achieved greater currency among the Irish-speaking community than Irish did among English speakers, exchange was not unidirectional. Indeed, in a number of instances – for example, James Annesley, the illegitimate son of Arthur Annesley, fourth Lord Altham, who later sustained a legal claim to the title – children of the elite raised in an Irish-speaking environment achieved oral proficiency in the language, but this was unusual.[28] The generality of Irish Protestants retained a visceral antipathy towards the language in keeping, Revd John Richardson observed in 1712, with 'that national prejudice and aversion, which still remains among too many of the English and Irish nations to one another':

> I know some of the natives of this kingdom, who can speak English, and yet will not, for no other reason but because it is English. The same motive on the other side, induces some to be very earnest for abolishing the Irish language; they have a dislike to the nation, and this unaccountably breeds a dislike to the language, for which no other reason can be given, but that it is Irish.[29]

Richardson was not free of the linguistic prejudices of which he wrote so insightfully. Yet because he prioritized the evangelization of the Catholic population, and because he perceived that the use of Irish was crucial to its success, he was at one with those clergy of the Church of Ireland who, following in the footsteps of William Bedell and Robert Boyle, advocated reaching out to Irish-speaking Catholics in their own tongue.

Though he became the leading Protestant champion of this strategy in the early eighteenth century, Richardson's was not a lone voice. Indeed, the lower house of Convocation resolved on 3 March 1703 that if the Church of Ireland was in earnest when it claimed it aspired to 'the speedy conversion of the Papists of this kingdom', it was necessary that a number of preachers capable of 'preaching in the Irish tongue' were appointed to every diocese.[30] However, the suggestion ventured by the clergy to 'the right reverend the lords archbishops and bishops that they take into their consideration, what number of

27 Reference can be made in this context to the satirical 'proclamation' issued on 24 Dec. 1694 at the 'Councell chamber at Anakelly Bogg' by five tories and their 'adherents' offering a reward for the apprehension of the Lord Chancellor and several privy councillors (Bodleian Library, Rawlinson D921B, f. 98).   28 A. Lang, *The Annesley case* (London, 1912), pp 116, 219, 225; S.J. Connolly, *Religion, law and power: the making of Protestant Ireland, 1660–1760* (Oxford, 1992), p. 131.   29 John Richardson, *A proposal for the conversion of the Popish natives of Ireland to the establish'd religion, with the reasons upon which it is grounded; and an answer to the objections made to it* (Dublin, 1711), pp 25–6.   30 Resolution of the lower house of Convocation, 3 Mar. 1703, printed in Richardson, *A short history*, p. 37.

such preachers will be necessary in every diocese' foundered on the 'practicable' obstacle that there were few clergy with the requisite linguistic skills. As a result, six years were to pass before Convocation re-engaged with the matter. In 1709, prompted by the disruption caused the Catholic Church by the enforcement of the laws against the Catholic clergy arising from an apprehended French invasion, the lower house responded to an approach by the bishops in the upper house by approving a report advocating a major evangelizing initiative through the medium of Irish. Specifically, the clergy recommended the publication in 'the English character' of the Bible and the Book of Common Prayer, and the identification of 'some person ... to prepare a short exposition of the Church catechism, particularly fitted for the instruction of the Popish recusants' that would be printed in a bilingual form. Preachers were still more important, and to this end, the lower house of Convocation recommended that steps were taken to ensure that each diocese was supplied with a number of 'fit persons ... to preach, catechize, and perform divine service in the Irish tongue', and that appropriate measures were taken to ensure that men with these skills were available to work even in those areas where there were 'no beneficed clergymen, nor converted priests'. Conscious of the expenditure that must inevitably be involved, the clergy recommended an appeal to parliament for fiscal support, and to Queen Anne for authorization to establish 'a Corporation capable of receiving and disposing charitable contributions'.[31]

As the idea of appealing for royal support attests, what this scheme lacked in detail it more than made up for in ambition. John Richardson, who was beneficed at Belturbet, county Cavan, was certainly animated by the prospect of serried ranks of clerical graduates schooled in the rudiments of the Irish language taking the gospel into the community.[32] He was determined, moreover, to avail of every opportunity, and while he and others of like mind believed they could take full advantage of the fact that 'the Popish priests in Ireland ... forbore, for the greatest part, to perform any religious office' in the repressive environment then obtaining, by applying 'themselves, in that seasonable juncture, to the conversion of the Irish', another secured 'a font of Irish types in London, in order to print the Bible, liturgy, and such other books in the Irish language, as might be necessary or useful for their conversion'.[33] There were, as this suggests, a host of practical concerns to be negotiated if this strategy to convert Irish-speaking Catholics was to be implemented, which is what made the prospect of securing parliamentary support

31 James Kelly, 'Sustaining a confessional state: the Irish parliament and Catholicism' in D.W. Hayton, James Kelly and John Bergin (eds), *The eighteenth-century composite state: representative institutions in Ireland and Europe, 1689–1800* (Basingstoke, 2010), pp 54–5; Richardson, *A proposal*, pp 39–42. 32 Ibid., pp 42–4. It is noteworthy that this built on a scheme already in operation at Trinity College to equip clergy to minister through Irish. 33 Ibid., pp 44–5.

'so it could be done at the publick charge' so attractive when it was mooted as a possibility.[34] The response of the lord lieutenant (the duke of Ormond), bishops, peers and eminent members of the laity to the idea of establishing a publicly funded 'Society for propagating the true reformed religion, as it is established in the kingdom of Ireland, among the Popish natives thereof' was encouraging, but powerful reservations were soon entered, which frustrated the initiative.[35] John Richardson was convinced that the objections were grounded on a 'wrong view' of the memorial prepared in support of the proposal, but there were enough believers in the merit of a scheme to bring about 'the conversion of the Popish natives' among the Whig interest to elicit a measure for the establishment of 'a sufficient number of charity schools ... for the instruction of the Popish children gratis, in the English tongue and the establish'd religion'. A bill for this purpose was presented to the House of Commons on 7 June 1710, but it was too late in the session for it to be afforded proper consideration and the measure did not proceed even to report stage.[36]

Too much had been achieved for the scheme simply to be forgotten, and when Convocation reassembled, it endeavoured in October 1711 to breath further life into the idea by approving a still-more detailed statement 'for converting ... Papists'. This document built upon the various ideas for evangelizing through the medium of Irish that had been variously proposed in previous years. These included the establishment of a fund for the education and support of Irish speakers and ordinands to assist with the cause of conversion; the publication of the Bible and Book of Common Prayer in Irish; the enforcement of the Popery laws to ensure 'there be no succession of Popish priests' or Catholic education; the establishment of a network of charity schools, and the introduction of a compulsory requirement that all children between the ages of seven and twelve attend school for six months every year.[37] This was a profoundly ambitious plan; the problem was that it could only proceed if it had the backing of parliament and the full church establishment, and the united front suggested by the statements forthcoming from Convocation gave a misleading impression. 'There is such a spirit of jealousy, uncharitableness and dissension ... among Protestants ... that whatever one party proposes, though never so good, will be sure to be opposed by another party', the archdeacon of Armagh, William Hamilton observed.[38] The full extent of the differences were artfully masked, but they were undeniable, and they were well in evidence in the summer of 1711 when the Tory bishop of Killaloe, Thomas Lindsay, presented the House of Lords with the heads of a bill for the union and division of parishes, which included a 'provision for

34 Ibid., pp 45–6.   **35** Ibid., pp 47–54.   **36** Ibid., pp 55–7; ILD, bill no. 2076 (see http/www.qub.ac.uk/ild/).   **37** Richardson, *A short history*, pp 58–63.   **38** Hamilton to Bonnell, 15 Mar. [1711] (NLI, Smythe of Barbavilla papers, MS 41580/9).

erecting free schools to teach Irish children the English tongue'. Conceived of as a counter to the much-publicized scheme, increasingly associated with John Richardson (its most vocal champion), to win over Irish Catholics to Protestantism by using the medium of the Irish language to evangelize, its failure to make it to the statute book belies the symbolic significance of its presentation.[39] It was not the only point of concern; unease within the ranks of Irish Protestants that the object of the expanded network of charity schools might 'be defeated by the obstinacy of Popish recusants', and that the larger social goal of anglicization might thereby be frustrated had prompted the inclusion in the scheme 'for converting the Papists' approved by Convocation on 25 October 1711 of a statement to the effect that the development of a network of charity schools would assist to bring about a situation, whereby 'in time the Irish language may be utterly abolished'.[40] As the reference to this aim in this document indicates, abolition was the optimal linguistic object of the Protestant interest at that moment; the problem was that the proponents of Catholic conversion had devised a suite of very good reasons as to why evangelization through the medium of Irish should take precedence. They had not succeeded as of the end of 1711 in bringing the whole of the Protestant interest with them, but they had advanced the idea a long way, and they had a passionate advocate in John Richardson, who was ready to make his fluent pen available to the promotion and advancement of the cause.

The presence of his signature on the petition seeking Queen Anne's support for a corporation to promote evangelization indicates that John Richardson (*c*.1669–1747) was already acknowledged as one of the leading advocates of evangelization through the medium of Irish prior to his entry into the public sphere as the champion of this cause in 1711 and 1712.[41] Described by the archdeacon of Armagh as 'a worthy good man, ... very well fitted to be employed propagating true religion among the natives of this kingdom', Richardson's enthusiasm struck a chord with those like Hamilton who had already concluded that the policy of repressing Catholics was not only incomplete but also destined to fail in the absence of a concurrent effort 'to show them the errors of their ways'. Perturbed by the realization that 'we suffer so many thousand souls to go on in superstition, ignorance and idolatry', Hamilton highlighted the situation in county Mayo where there were 'not above eleven or twelve Protestant ministers' to tend to '60,000 souls', but the condition of the 'counties of Galway, Clare, Leitrim and Kerry, and many other parts of the kingdom' was no better, he observed dolefully. Anxious that this should not continue, yet aware of the inability of the existing cleri-

39 ILD, bill no. 5210 (see http/www.qub.ac.uk/ild/); D.W. Hayton, 'Bishops as legislators: Marsh and his contemporaries' in Murial McCarthy and Ann Simmons (eds), *Marsh's Library, a mirror on the world: law, learning and libraries, 1650–1750* (Dublin, 2009), p. 85; Barnard, 'Protestants and the Irish language', p. 191. 40 Richardson, *A short history*, p. 60. 41 Ibid., p.53; *DIB, sub nom* John Richardson.

cal complement to reach those of the population who 'can't speak nor do not understand English', he made clear his 'wish [that] Mr Richardson's design may succeed'.[42] He was under no illusion as to the scale of the challenge, and it is significant that he placed the resistance encountered within his own communion ahead of the profound structural weaknesses of the Church of Ireland:

> I don't find that people can be brought to think seriously of the condition of the Papists of this kingdom, and too many of those whose great business is to take care of them, and instruct them, do oppose these methods, without which in my judgement they never will be converted, and there are too many who can't bear any proposals which tend to the increasing their expense in their labours. It is certain that in no part of the kingdom there are sufficient numbers of Protestant ministers, and in those parts where the harvest is greatest the labourers are fewest.[43]

Hamilton's conclusion that the Protestant interest in Ireland was wanting in the zeal required to bring about the religious, and by implication the linguistic, conversion of the native Irish population was informed in the first instance by the lack of unanimity among the high churchmen in Convocation for Richardson's scheme.[44] However, he cannot but have been disappointed also by the fact that Richardson's efforts to provide the necessary literary infrastructure had not had the anticipated galvanic impact.

The publication in Irish in 1711 of a collection of five sermons (one of which was his work) was the first tangible literary expression of Richardson's commitment to make his plan for the conversion of the Irish a reality, but, notable as this was, it was of lesser consequence than the need to win public support.[45] To this end, Richardson published a detailed 'proposal for the conversion of the Popish natives to the establish'd religion', which he pointedly addressed to the membership of both the upper and lower houses of Convocation. In essence an extended articulation of the by now familiar case in favour of a multi-pronged approach to the evangelization of monoglot Catholics through the medium of Irish, whatever assistance the pamphlet provided the cause at Convocation was insufficient, in the absence of a substantial parliamentary appropriation, to secure the support necessary to finance the sustained initiative that he believed necessary.[46] Undaunted, Richardson

42 Hamilton to Bonnell, 4 Feb., 15 Mar. [1711] (NLI, Smythe of Barbavilla papers, MS 41580/9). 43 Hamilton to Bonnell, 15 Mar. [1711] (NLI, Smythe of Barbavilla papers, MS 41580/9). 44 D.W. Hayton, 'High churchmen in the Irish Convocation' in *idem*, *Ruling Ireland, 1685–1742: politics, politicians and parties* (Woodbridge, 2004), pp 148–9. 45 *Seanmora ar na priom phoncibh na chreidimh* (London, 1711). 46 [John Richardson], *A proposal for the conversion of the Popish natives of Ireland to the establish'd religion, with the*

appealed to the wider Anglican community; he took his cause to the Society for Promoting Christian Knowledge in London, which was sufficiently impressed by his scheme, and by the publication in London in 1712 of an extended rationale of his case in support of evangelization through the medium of Irish, to provide the funds for the publication of a bilingual catechism, an Irish-language version of the Book of Common Prayer, and sundry other texts.[47] Unfortunately from his perspective, the fate of his publications mirrored the general fortunes of his initiative; some 6,000 copies each of the Book of Common Prayer and of the Catechism, and 3,000 copies of Richardson's history of the various attempts to convert Irish Catholics that had been pursued since the mid-sixteenth century were printed, but only a small number were sold or distributed; the majority remained in storage – an impermanent and embarrassing monument to an idea that was insufficiently firmly grounded in the political, denominational, and linguistic realities of life in early eighteenth-century Ireland ever to achieve the religious transformation Richardson aspired to bring about.[48]

Though Richardson sought impatiently to rebuff criticism from whatever quarter it came, there were pointers throughout the text of both editions of his proposal for conversion to suggest that it did not take proper cognizance of the problems it must inevitably encounter. Certainly, there were significant language issues that Richardson contrived to assume either did not exist or would never emerge. Thus in response to the argument that 'to print books in Irish, and to send missionaries to preach in that tongue, is to give too much encouragement to the language', he avowed simplistically that he regarded Irish simply as a tool of evangelization: 'I should not be for encouraging the language any farther, than is necessary to promote the conversion of the Irish, and the salvation of their souls'.[49] And in order to allay the apprehensions of those who maintained that the facilitation of Irish in any way must be at the expense of the Protestant interest in Ireland, he countered that it should be conceived of as a strategic, temporary concession that would assist with the longer term project of anglicizing the population:

> To make this use of the language at present is the most effectual way to diminish the use of it hereafter; for if we prevail with them to con-

reasons upon which it is grounded: and answer to the objections made to it (Dublin, 1711); Barnard, 'Protestants and the Irish language', p. 189.   47 Richardson], *A short history ...* [incorporating] *A proposal for the conversion of the Popish natives of Ireland to the establish'd religion, with the reasons upon which it is grounded: and answer to the objections made to it* (2nd ed., London, 1712); John Lewis, *The church catechism explained by way of question and answer ... and render'd into Irish, by John Richardson, minister of Belturbet in Ireland ... Caitecism na heaglaise minighthe, ar mhodh cheiste agus fhreagra* (London, 1712); *Leabhar na nornaightheadh ccomhchoitchoinn agus mhiniostralachda na sscraimeinteadh* (London, 1712); Barnard, 'Protestants and the Irish language', pp 189, 191–2.   48 Barnard, 'Protestants and the Irish language', p. 192.   49 Richardson, *A short history*, p. 109.

form to our Church, their prejudices being thereby in a great measure removed, they will more readily fall in with our customs and language; and being qualified equally with our selves for any office or employment, their interest will soon induce them to speak English.[50]

This was a remarkably candid avowal. Moreover, it was in keeping with Richardson's pragmatic calculation 'that it is much easier for 500 men of letters to acquire so much knowledge in the Irish tongue as to be able to speak and read it, than to teach 500,000 illiterate persons, old and young, English so well, as to be sufficiently edified by our prayers and sermons'.[51] In other words, evangelization through the medium of Irish was a means to an end – an end shared by the majority of the Protestant population of Ireland, who remained as attached as ever to the goal of replacing Irish with English as the vernacular of the population as part of its larger, and ongoing, commitment to the thorough anglicization of the island. Richardson made clear his personal support for this strategy later in the same tract when he articulated his conviction that the medium of instruction in the expanded charity school system would be English, thereby ensuring that the children that were taught in these institutions would be schooled in both the Protestant faith and the English language.[52]

                                                        II

The prominence accorded the politics of language in the extensive list of 'considerations' that John Richardson addressed in both the Irish and English editions of his *Proposal* echoed the disinterest of the Protestant elite in Ireland in the Irish language and Irish antiquities in the thirty years after the battle of the Boyne. Signally, the most important scholarly intervention during these decades was by Edward Lhuyd (d. 1709), who was Welsh, and he had no domestic imitators.[53] Indeed, in keeping with the prevailing belief that the Irish language was a barrier to the beneficial economic, social and political development of the kingdom, Richardson apprehended in 1718 that the Irish parliament might attempt to ban the language. Wiser counsels prevailed, but this was not a signal for a rapid amelioration in attitude. It did not ease the way either for a legislation supporting the teaching of English. A bill presented to the House of Commons on 4 July 1719 'for making a further provision for maintaining schools for teaching the English tongue throughout this kingdom' failed even to make it to the report stage because of the unwillingness of the Church of Ireland clergy to accept the financial and administrative responsi-

50 Ibid., pp 109–10.   51 Ibid., p. 119.   52 Ibid., p.124.   53 Ann de Valera, 'Antiquarianism and historical investigation in Ireland in the eighteenth century' (unpublished MA thesis, UCD, 1978), pp 18–19.

bility.[54] This outcome was not unanticipated, though the emergence in the 1710s of Edward Nicholson, who ministered in county Sligo, as a commentator on educational and linguistic issues, not only hastened the marginalization of John Richardson's ambitious scheme, but also restored the initiative to those who advocated furthering anglicization through the school system.[55] In a communication to the Society for Promoting Christian Knowledge, Nicholson condemned Richardson's 'well meaning project of ... preaching to the Irish natives in their mother tongue ... [as] utterly insignificant (if it does not do us more hurt than good)'. He offered several reasons in support of this conclusion, but the most compelling, because it was informed by his observation that the use of English was expanding, especially among the young, was that it was incompatible with the long-established aspiration of moulding Ireland into a English-speaking Protestant society: 'The promoting [of] that barbarous language (so intimately fraught with cursing and swearing and all vile prophaneness) will but keep up the distinction of their people from ours to make us one people and of one religion, which would have but one language', he avowed.[56] And addressing the objection, frequently entered, that Ireland was being treated differently than Wales, he pointed out that the situation in the two jurisdictions was fundamentally dissimilar:

> 'Tis not alike in Wales, where the Protestants have possession of their own language for the major part, and Popery is not there rampant in the Welch tongue as it is here universally among the natives in the Irish language.[57]

Though he was able to 'speak Irish from my youth and could read it too', Edward Nicholson's conviction that the conversion of Irish-speaking Catholics to Protestantism could best be accomplished if the usage of English was promoted and encouraged was instinctively favoured by a majority of Irish Protestants.[58] They were reinforced in this conviction by the realization that Catholic parents sought increasingly to encourage their children (particularly males) to 'understand and speak English'. Moreover, Nicholson observed optimistically, Catholic parents were disposed for that reason 'cheerfully [to] send their children ... [to] schools [where] they are instructed in the principles of the religion of the Church of England, [and] are taught to read the holy scriptures in the English tongue, and learn every thing which a good Protestant school master instills into the minds of all the children committed to his care'. It was obvious therefore, that English-speaking schools were the appropriate vehicle 'for the instruction of the children of Popish natives in the Protestant religion and the English tongue'.[59]

54 ILD, bill no. 0542 (accessible at http/www.qub.ac.uk/ild/). 55 Barnard, 'Protestants and the Irish language', pp 196–8. 56 'Rawlinson manuscripts, Class C and D', *Analecta Hibernica*, 2 (1931), 27. 57 Ibid. 58 Ibid. 59 Ibid., p. 28; 'Charity schools in Ireland',

Guided by such analyses, attention focussed increasingly, during the reign of George I (1714–27), and the early part of the reign of George II (1727–60), on education as the means whereby anglicization and Protestantization might be forwarded together. Attention concentrated in the first instance on expanding the already impressive charity school network, and belief in its suitability remained strong despite the occasional high-profile sceptic.[60] The most notable example of the latter was the bishop of Down and Dromore, Francis Hutchinson, who printed a bilingual catechism (1722) set in a supposedly easy-to-read phonetic script to assist with the conversion of the Irish-speaking Catholic population of Rathlin Island.[61] Hutchinson's initiative did not produce major results, which dealt a further blow to the credibility of the cause of evangelizing through Irish. Indicatively, the generality of Irish Protestants continued to look positively upon the Society for Promoting Christian Knowledge of London, which adhered to the view that the noble object of 'civilizing the people' of Scotland as well as Ireland could best be advanced by 'extirpating Popery and the Irish language' and by providing funds to assist in its pursuit.[62] However, as time passed, and no visible progress had been made, doubts multiplied, and confidence diminished in the capacity of the charity school system, in which John Richardson, among others, had vested so much hope. There was no going back to the drawing board, however. Instead, attention came increasingly to centre on the conviction that a new school system pursuing a more overtly proselytizing and anglicizing mission was the way forward.

The inauguration in 1733 of a system of Charter Schools, as the new educational network was called, could not have occurred in the absence of the leadership and direction provided by the likes of Bishop Henry Maule of Cork, who had disagreed tactfully with Richardson on the wisdom of pursuing evangelization through the medium of Irish, and Hugh Boulter, the primate, who was eager to establish English ways as normative throughout

n.d., in Sir John Gilbert (ed.), *Calendar of ancient records of Dublin* (19 vols, Dublin, 1889–1944), ix, 496.   **60** D.W. Hayton, 'Did Protestantism fail in early eighteenth-century Ireland? Charity schools and the enterprise of religious and social reformation' in A. Ford, J. McGuire and K. Milne (eds), *As by law established: the Church of Ireland since the Reformation* (Dublin, 1995), pp 166–86; M.G. Jones, *The charity school movement: a study of eighteenth century Puritanism in action* (Cambridge, 1948), passim; David Dickson, *Old world colony: Cork and south Munster, 1630–1830* (Cork, 2005), pp 212–14; Barnard, 'Protestants and the Irish language', pp 196–8.   **61** Andrew Sneddon, *Witchcraft and Whigs: the life of bishop Francis Hutchinson, 1600–1739* (Manchester, 2008), pp 148–76; *idem*, 'Darkness must be expell'd by letting in the light: bishop Francis Hutchinson and the conversion of Irish Catholics by means of the Irish language, 1720–24', *Eighteenth-Century Ireland*, 19 (2004), 37–55.   **62** C.M. Haydon, 'The anti-Catholic activity of the S.P.C.K.', *Recusant History*, 18 (1987), 418–21; Dalrymple to SPCK, 12 Dec. 1724 (TNA, SP54/14/ 34); V.E. Durkacz, *The decline of the Celtic languages: a study of linguistic and cultural conflict in Scotland, Wales and Ireland from the Reformation to the twentieth century* (Edinburgh, c.1983).

society.[63] They were able also to secure the financial backing of parliament, which meant that when this new educational initiative was put on a statutory basis it defined its objects as 'the salvation of souls by rescuing the children of the poor natives from … ignorance, superstition and idolatry…, and to train them up in the pure Protestant faith and worship'.[64] In other words, they officially prioritized evangelization over anglicization, though the decision that English should be the medium of instruction obscured this somewhat, and dovetailed with the weight of opinion in Protestant (and increasingly Catholic) Ireland, which acknowledged that English was not only the language of business, but also the language of civility. This conviction was underlined by the ratification in 1738 of an act that 'all proceedings in courts of justice … shall be in the English language', for though the linguistic targets in this instance were Latin and French rather than Irish, the enactment served further to affirm the linguistic and cultural primacy of English.[65] It also attested to the enduring strength of the conviction within the Protestant interest that Ireland must embrace English if it was to cast off the habits of 'barbarousness' with which the Irish language was firmly identified, and embrace the civility that was emblematical of the improved polity and refined society to which they as an English-speaking people aspired.[66]

Their passionate belief in the superiority of the English, notwithstanding, attitudes to the Irish language among the Protestant interest in Ireland were neither unchanging nor fixedly unaccommodating. Even when sectional suspicion was at its acme in the two decades after the Boyne, there were some among the Protestant interest who sustained an advanced interest in the Irish language. The exceptional enthusiasm manifested by Arthur Brownlow (1645–1711) has been well chronicled, and while this may reasonably be ascribed to his particular lineage, he was not unique in acknowledging that the history of Gaelic Ireland was of more than passing significance to the descendants of settlers.[67] Yet, the hostility that greeted the attempt by Hugh MacCurtin (Aodh Buí Mac Cruitín, *c*.1680–1755) in 1718 to produce a history 'in vindication of the antiquity of Ireland' in answer to 'the many fabulous relations written of the kingdom … these five hundred and odd years past, all by foreign writers', and his singling out of Richard Cox's imposing Protestant reading of Irish history, manifests that there was little mutual respect, even

63 Dickson, *Old world colony*, pp 212–13; Barnard, 'Protestants and the Irish language', pp 199–200. 64 Kenneth Milne, *Irish Charter schools* (Dublin, 1997); *idem*, 'Irish Charter schools', *Irish Journal of Education*, 8 (1974), 3–25; 19 Geo. II, chap. 5. 65 21 Geo. II, chap. 3; 23 Geo. II, chap. 4; 25 Geo. II, chap. 4; 29 Geo. II, chap. 4; 31 Geo. II, chap. 7; 33 Geo. II, chap. 6; 1 Geo. III, chap. 6; 11 Geo. II, chap. 6. 66 Barnard, *Improving Ireland*, passim. 67 Nessa Ní Shéaghdha, *Collectors of Irish manuscripts: motives and methods*, R.I. Best lecture, 1984 (Dublin, 1985), pp 10–11; Bernadette Cunningham and Raymond Gillespie, 'An Ulster settler and his Irish manuscripts', *Éigse*, 21 (1986), 27–36; Breandán Ó Buachalla, 'Arthur Brownlow: a gentlemen more curious than ordinary', *Ulster Local Studies*, 7:2 (1982), 24–8.

among those who specialized in the more arcane and remote aspects of the kingdom's past.[68] Attitudes thawed palpably in the 1720s, though it is difficult to interpret the intentions of the literary coteries surrounding Jonathan Swift, Anthony Raymond and others, and to establish whether the impact of the interaction that clearly took place did more than scratch an itch of curiosity.[69]

However, even if curiosity was the primary motivation, the fact remains that one can point, beginning in the 1720s, to the commencement of a thaw in the suspicion, animosity and negativity with which the majority of Irish Protestants regarded all attempts to proffer a positive impression of pre-Norman Irish history, and of Irish language and culture in the present. Moreover, it embraced several cultural forms. A significant milestone was reached in 1724 when Bishop William Nicholson of Derry published a comprehensive guide, which embraced Irish manuscripts in private hands, to the materials available to those who wished to engage in the study of Irish history.[70] The best-known intervention, because it provided access to native Irish history (and because the underhand manner of its completion continues to intrigue) was the successful orchestration by Dermod O'Connor of an English-language version of Geoffrey Keating's celebrated *Foras feasa ar Éirinn*.[71] Moreover, there were other, less frequently invoked initiatives, which registered in discrete spheres, which were also significant. It is notable, for instance, that the specialist musical publishers, John and William Neal, published a number of 'choice collections' that included Irish music, or that were, as in the case of *A collection of the most celebrated Irish tunes* ..., exclusively of Irish origin.[72] About the same time, a dual-language almanac, purportedly assembled by 'a Protestant clergyman and [a] Popish priest', was also prepared, while, in the political realm, interventions by Edward Synge and Cornelius Nary, and the suggestion that Catholics should present a loyal address to the crown to mark

68 [Hugh MacCurtin,] *A brief discourse in vindication of the antiquity of Ireland, collected out of many authentick Irish histories and chronicles, and out of foreign learned authors* (Dublin, 1717), dedication, preface; Vincent Morley, *An crann os coill: Aodh Buí Mac Cruitín, c.1680–1755* (Baile Atha Cliath, 1995).   69 Alan Harrison, *The Dean's friend: Anthony Raymond* (Dublin, 1999), passim; J.G. Simms, 'Dean Swift and county Armagh', *Seanchas Ard Mhacha*, 5 (1971), 138; M.H. Risk, 'Seán Ó Neachtain: an eighteenth-century Irish writer', *Studia Hibernica*, 15 (1975), 47–60; Nessa Ní Shéaghdha, 'Irish scholars and scribes in eighteenth-century Dublin', *Eighteenth-Century Ireland*, 4 (1989), 41–54; C.G. Ó Háinle, 'Neighbours in eighteenth-century Dublin: Jonathan Swift and Seán Ó Neachtain', *Éire-Ireland*, 21 (1986), 4–19.   70 William Nicolson, *The Irish historical library* (Dublin, 1724). 71 Diarmaid Ó Cathain, 'Dermot O'Connor, translator of Keating', *Eighteenth-Century Ireland*, 2 (1987), 67–87; Cunningham, *The world of Geoffrey Keating*, pp 218–25.   72 *A collection of the most celebrated Irish tunes proper for the violin, German flute or hautboy* ([Dublin, 1724]); *A choice collection of country dances with their proper tunes* ... (Dublin, 1726); Nicholas Carolan (ed.), *John and William Neal, A collection of the most celebrated Irish tunes proper for the violin, German flute or hautboy* ([Dublin, 1724]) (facsimile ed., Dublin, 2010), p. 26; M. Pollard, *A dictionary of members of the Dublin book trade, 1550–1800: based on the records of the Guild of St Luke the Evangelist, Dublin* (London, 2000), pp 426–7.

the accession of George II to the throne, seemed to suggest that anything was possible.[73] This was not the case, of course. It is notable that the grammatical and lexicographical undertakings of the energetic Hugh Mac Curtin were not printed in Ireland. Mac Curtin's *Elements of the Irish language, grammatically explained in English* was published in Louvain in 1728, and that the landmark dictionary he compiled with Conor Begley was published in Paris four years later.[74] This does not mean that copies of both books were not available in Ireland, but the fact that they were not published locally attests to the lack of capacity to generate print in Irish, and, one may assume, since there was no legal prohibition on Irish print *per se*, to the perception of printers that it must involve a financial outlay that prudence discouraged.[75]

Be that as it may, the publication in 1736 of the first of several eighteenth-century editions of James Gallagher's *Irish sermons* attested to the fact that the atmosphere continued to ameliorate.[76] The failure of Ireland to rise in tandem with the Scottish Jacobites in 1745–6, which, had it happened, must have greatly heightened the challenged posed the Hanoverian state in both Britain and Ireland, was also significant since it weakened the casual and causal correlation so long assumed by Irish Protestants between the Irish language, Roman Catholicism and Jacobitism.[77] This facilitated the adoption of an incrementally more relaxed attitude towards the Irish language within the Protestant community in the mid-eighteenth century, symbolized by the announcement in February 1758 that the Revd Anthony Burke, a curate based at Hollywood, county Wicklow, had recently preached the 'first sermon in Irish' at St Patrick's Cathedral 'to a very numerous congregation', and that the practice would continued 'every Saturday during Lent'.[78] Heartened by the positive response of those present, and by the absence of public criticism following the publication of a news reports of the event, other Church of Ireland churches followed suit. Thus the 'very crowded congregation' present in the parish Church of St Audeon on the first Saturday in Advent later the same year was treated to the first of a seasonal series of advent sermons in

73 Carolan (ed.), *John and William Neal, A collection*, pp 2, 51 note 342; Patrick Fagan, *Dublin's turbulent priest: Cornelius Nary, 1658–1738* (Dublin, 1991), pp 113–37; *idem*, *Divided loyalties: the question of the oath for Irish Catholics in the eighteenth century* (Dublin 1997), pp 52–69; Ian McBride, 'Catholic politics in the penal era: Fr Sylvester Lloyd and the Delvin address of 1727' in John Bergin et al. (eds), *New perspectives on the penal laws: Eighteenth-Century Ireland*: special issue no. 1 (Dublin, 2011), pp 115–48. 74 Hugh Mac Curtin, *Elements of the Irish language, grammatically explained in English* (Louvain, 1728); Hugh Mac Curtin and Conor Begley, *The English-Irish dictionary* (Paris, 1732). 75 Lesa Ní Mhunghaile, 'An eighteenth-century Gaelic scholar's private library: Muiris Ó Gormáin's books', *RIA proc.*, 110C (2010), 260. 76 James Gallagher, *Sixteen Irish sermons* (Dublin, 1736); *idem*, *Seventeen Irish sermons* (Dublin, 1752). 77 James Kelly, '"Disappointing the boundless ambition of France": Irish Protestants and the fear of invasion, 1661–1815', *Studia Hibernica*, 37 (2011), 68–70; David Dickson, 'Jacobitism in eighteenth-century Ireland: a Munster perspective', *Eire-Ireland*, 39:3 and 4 (2004), 39–99. 78 *Pue's Occurrences*, 14 Feb. 1758.

Irish by the Revd Edmund Kelly.[79] The Society of Friends did likewise; during the early 1760s, the Sunday afternoon sermon at the Capel Street meetinghouse was also delivered for a time in Irish.[80] It is not apparent, given the absence of further mention of such events, if the initial surge of enthusiasm was long sustained, but whether this was the case or not, their very occurrence was symptomatic of an observable change in attitude towards the Irish language within the Protestant interest. This was corroborated, at the level of the individual, by the admiring description by Charles O'Hara (1715–76) of Nymphsfield, county Sligo, and the MP for Ballynakill, of the Irish-speaking people of Inishmurray. Writing to Edmund Burke in 1762, O'Hara observed warmly:

> They are an unmixed people, their Irish purer than our people speak and many of their stories, I am told, have all the natural beauty so well counterfeited in Fingal.[81] They have ruins very singular and of great antiquity. But the innocent simplicity of their lives is extraordinary. Extremely hospitable to any stranger that goes among them; and miraculously chaste; whatever disputes may arise, are settled among themselves; they were never known to carry a complaint *into the great world*.[82]

The sea-change in attitude to which this comment bears witness was further in evidence in the public sphere, where Irish scholars and scribes, needing to make a living, advertized their services. The advertisement placed by Maurice O'Gorman, a self-styled 'professor' of Irish, in *Faulkner's Dublin Journal* in 1766 has frequently been cited, but what is still more noteworthy is that as well as targeting 'gentlemen' eager to access 'the many valuable chronicles and compositions still preserved amongst us', he was also available for 'the instruction of youth and other as wish for their own cultivation'.[83] And in a further illustration of the fact that attitudes had, and continued to change at an appreciable pace, an anonymous correspondent to the *Dublin Mercury* in 1772 announced that he had opened a school at the sign of St Patrick in High Street, where Irish, Latin, English and accompts were taught by duly 'qualified' instructors. Public pronouncements of this ilk, promulgating the virtue

79 *Pue's Occurrences*, 12 Dec. 1758; John Brady (ed.), *Catholics and Catholicism in the eighteenth-century press* (Maynooth, 1966), p. 95.   **80** *Universal Advertiser*, 4 Oct. 1760; *Public Gazetteer*, 23 May 1761.   **81** A reference to the Ossian controversy sparked by the publication of James MacPherson's (1736–96) forgeries purporting to be Gaelic poetry.   **82** O'Hara to Burke, 10 Aug. 1762 in T.W. Copeland (ed.), *The correspondence of Edmund Burke*, vol. 1, 1744–68 (Cambridge, 1958), p. 146; J.G. Simms, 'County Sligo in the eighteenth century', *RSAI Jnl.*, 91 (1961), 160.   **83** *Faulkner's Dublin Journal*, 5 July 1766. This advertisement is quoted in Thomas Wall, *The sign of Dr Hay's Head* (Dublin, 1958); Ní Shéaghdha, 'Irish scholars and scribes in eighteenth-century Dublin', 51; and Ní Mhunghaile, 'An eighteenth-century Gaelic scribe's private library', 241.

of the programme of instruction offered by private schoolmasters, were not unusual given the rapid expansion in the demand for and provision of private education from the mid-eighteenth century. It was highly unusual, however, for these familiar essays in self-promotion to be prefaced by an observation to the effect that the school was founded:

> To prevent as much as possible the decay of the Irish language, so highly esteemed by all who have knowledge of it, for the natural energy and unborrowed scope of its diction, the sweetness of sound and expression, so much admired by foreigners (though shamefully neglected by the natives of this country).[84]

Though it is likely, given the placement of this item in James Hoey's *Dublin Mercury*, that the master of this school was a Catholic as well as a speaker of Irish, the public articulation (albeit in English) of such positive sentiments, manifested how greatly attitudes towards the Irish language had changed in the space of a generation. There were a variety of reasons for this, but one of the main factors was the palpable easing in the public display of confessional-based antagonism following the failure of Ireland to rise in 1745–6.[85] The effective negation of the possibility of a Jacobite succession by the death in 1766 of James III was also important, not least because it emboldened Catholics from the elite and 'middling sort', many of who had already, or were in the process of forsaking their traditional allegiance to the House of Stuart for that of the House of Hanover. The establishment in 1756 of a Catholic Committee, which pursued a policy of explicit loyalty to the Hanoverian state during the Seven Years War, and afterwards, was also important because it fractured the link that Protestants were disposed to make between the Irish language and disloyalty, thereby paving the way in turn for the acceptance of the argument that a host of the penal laws enacted to secure the Protestant interest against a Catholic *revanche* could be repealed.[86]

A further critical factor in the amelioration of Protestant attitudes was the increasingly active interest taken by elements of the Protestant elite in Irish history and antiquity. Though this could be, and was in many instances, pur-

---

84 *Dublin Mercury*, 11 July 1772. Similar sentiments were expressed in an advertisement for an Irish dictionary published in the same year in another of the Hoey family's news-papers. It maintained 'that of all the dead or living languages, none is more copious and elegant in the expression, or more harmonious and musical in the expression', and cited a correspondent 'who thinks it surprising that the cultivation of so fine a language ... should be neglected' (*Hoey's Publick Journal*, 1 June 1772).   85 Ó Ciardha, *Ireland and the Jacobite cause*, chapter 7; Kelly, 'Irish Protestants and the fear of invasion', 73–4, 78–9; Gerard O'Brien (ed.), *Catholic Ireland in the eighteenth century: collected essays of Maureen Wall* (Dublin, 1989), chapter 7.   86 Thomas Bartlett, *The fall and rise of the Irish nation: the Catholic question, 1690–1830* (Dublin, 1992), chapter 4; O'Brien (ed.), *Collected essays of Maureen Wall*, chapter 7; Kelly, 'Sustaining a confessional state', pp 64–70.

sued without regard to contemporary political and religious debates, the reality, as Joep Leerssen and Clare O'Halloran have persuasively delineated, was that those who were most interested in promoting historical and antiquarian study were also a visible presence within the ranks of the patriot political connexion in parliament.[87] Moreover, though many of their number – and one may specifically instance Henry Flood and Lord Charlemont[88] – blanched at the thought of altering the Protestant constitution in church and state as defined in 1688–9, the practical reality was that the expanding interest in Irish history and antiquity manifest in the second half of the eighteenth century did inform the decision-making of some political figures. What is more interesting, and significant, it that it also exerted an ameliorative influence on the outlook of the Protestant community at large towards the Irish language.

It is not necessary here to rehearse in any detail the rising trajectory in interest in antiquities, in history, or in reconstructing a shared interpretation of the Irish past that can be tracked from the late 1740s.[89] Suffice to observe that there was a palpable quickening in the intellectual pulse, signified by the establishment of the Physico-Historical Society in 1744, the publication of Walter Harris' edition of the works of James Ware (1739–46), of Thomas Wright's *Louthiana* (1748) and John K'eogh's *Vindication of antiquities* (1748).[90] Bodies like the Physico-Historical Society (and its successor, the Medico-Historical Society) devoted little time to linguistic or directly historical issues; they also sustained few, if any contacts with Irish-language scholars. The priority of the Physico-Historical Society was natural history, and it can be anchored in the first instance in the appreciating culture of improvement that, it can plausibly be argued, epitomized the *zeitgeist* of the moment.[91] It was not possible, however, to sustain such an exclusive approach, for though Walter Harris was firmly enmeshed in a fearful Protestant world that responded strongly to the tocsin of seventeenth-century fears, others were less hidebound. It is notable

87 Leerssen, *Mere Irish and fíor-Ghael: studies in the idea of Irish nationality, its development, and literary expression prior to the nineteenth century* (Amsterdam, 1986), pp 385–427; Clare O'Halloran, *Golden ages and barbarous nations: antiquarian debate and cultural politics in Ireland* (Cork, 2004), pp 38, 47 and passim.   88 James Kelly, *Henry Flood: patriots and politics in eighteenth-century Ireland* (Dublin, 1995), pp 94, 196, 304–6, 379–80; *idem*, 'A "genuine" whig and patriot: Lord Charlemont's political career' in Michael McCarthy (ed.), *Lord Charlemont and his circle* (Dublin, 1999), pp 26–7; O'Halloran, *Golden ages and barbarous nations*, p. 45.   89 See de Valera, 'Antiquarianism', chapter 2; Leerssen, *Mere Irish and fíor-Ghael*, pp 372–85.   90 de Valera, 'Antiquarianism', pp 74–89; James Harris, *The whole works of James Ware* (2 vols, Dublin, 1739–46); Thomas Wright, *Louthiana; or, An introduction to the antiquities of Ireland* (Dublin, 1748); John K'eogh, *Vindication of the antiquities of Ireland, and a defence thereof ...* (Dublin, 1748).   91 Eoin Magennis, "A land of milk and honey': the Physico-Historical Society, improvement and the surveys of mid-eighteenth-century Ireland', *RIA proc.*, 102C (2002), 199–217; de Valera, 'Antiquarianism', pp 63–91 passim; Toby Barnard, 'The Dublin Society and other improving societies, 1731–85' in James Kelly and M.J. Powell (eds), *Clubs and societies in eighteenth-century Ireland* (Dublin, 2010), pp 69–75.

that the membership of both the Physico-Historical Society and the Medico-Historical Society was not denominationally exclusive, and that their scholarly enterprises encouraged them not only to access the knowledge contained within Irish-language source (through translation), but also to accept that the history of Gaelic Ireland was a subject of intrinsic interest in its own right and that no self-respecting intellectual could dismiss it as Sir Richard Cox had done when he was writing *Hibernia Anglicana*.[92] This process was assisted by the subtle behind the scenes manipulation of opinion undertaken by Charles O'Conor, whose *Dissertations* on early Ireland, published in 1756, offered a positive reading of early Irish history that Protestant patriots found congenial. Moreover, his personal courtesy, deep learning, and disavowal of Jacobitism made him increasingly attractive to those members of the Protestant interest who were disposed to promote antiquarian, historical and linguistic scholarship.[93] As a result, O'Conor was not only facilitated with admission to Trinity College to view its increasingly impressive collection of Irish-language manuscripts, he was elected to honorary membership of the Antiquities Committee of the Royal Dublin Society. Still more remarkably, so too was John Carpenter, the Catholic archbishop of Dublin, whose scholarly credential were also acknowledged.[94]

The Antiquities Committee of the Royal Dublin Society, which included Lucius O'Brien, the MP for county Clare, and Charles Vallancey, the military engineer, among its members, survived for less than two years, before it disbanded for want of funds. It did not, as a result, fundamentally alter the antiquarian, historical or linguistic landscape. However, it was of enormous symbolic and practical significance as a bridge between the Irish-speaking community of scribes and scholars, which was eager for patrons, and those members of the anglophone elite who required assistance if they were to acquire other than the most superficial knowledge of the country's occluded past. It is noteworthy, for example, that Maurice O'Gorman, who was an important conduit of Irish-language manuscripts between these two linguistic communities, both as a transcriber and as a seller, taught Charles Vallancey Irish, and worked for payment for the Dublin Society of Antiquities. And it is a measure of how increasingly receptive elements of the Anglo-Irish elite became that O'Gorman's 'patrons included some of the most important and influential antiquarians' and collectors of the time.[95]

92 de Valera, 'Antiquarianism', pp 63, 66, 67; Eoin Magennis, 'A "beleaguered Protestant": Walter Harris and the writing of *Fiction Unmasked*', *Eighteenth-Century Ireland*, 13 (1998), 86–111; Richard Cox, *Hibernia Anglicana; or, the history of Ireland, from the conquest thereof by the English, to this present* (London, 1689–90), introductory discourse; Hugh McCurtain, *A brief discourse in vindication of the antiquity of Ireland* (London, 1717), preface.   93 For O'Conor, see Ní Shéaghdha, *Collectors of Irish manuscripts*, pp 11–13; de Valera, 'Antiquarianism', pp 102–10, 118–32; and, especially, O'Halloran, *Golden ages and barbarous nations*, chapter 1 and passim.   94 de Valera, 'Antiquarianism', pp 133, 135ff; Ní Mhunghaile, 'An eighteenth-century Gaelic scribe's library', 242.   95 Ní Mhunghaile, 'An eighteenth-century Gaelic scribe's library', 242, 243, 267, 268 and passim; *DIB*,

One of the key figures in the promotion of inquiry into Irish antiquity, whose endeavour contributed significantly to the revision of received wisdom as to the status and nature of the Irish language was Charles Vallancey. Though his origins were English, Vallancey was possessed of a keen, if essentially *dilettante* interest in antiquity, and he combined enthusiasm with a soldier's resolve and an engineer's capacity to get things done to sustain an impressive scholarly series – *Collectanea de rebus Hibernicis* (1770–86) – devoted to Irish history and antiquity.[96] Vallancey brought the same enthusiasm to bear on his engagement with the Irish language; the problem was that it was not matched by linguistic insight or understanding, with the result that enthusiasm prevailed over good judgment, and he was easily persuaded to elevate superficial similarities into definite connections. His most egregious linguistic error was to conclude that Irish and Phoenician were related, though the impact of his findings, which were presented to a receptive public in his *Essay on the antiquity of the Celtic language* (1772), was empowering. It liberated the Irish language from the enormous condescension with which it had been regarded within the Protestant interest in Ireland for several generations. It could no longer credibly be maintained thereafter that the Irish language etymologically was an inferior tongue, incapable of expressing complex thought, when it could be demonstrated that it derived from one of the most advanced civilizations of the Mediterranean. By extension, those like Charles O'Conor who claimed, based on their study of Irish history and antiquity, that Gaelic Irish culture was as refined and sophisticated as its Anglo–Saxon peer were well justified in so doing.[97]

Though this was not his intention, Vallancey's antiquarian endeavour was replete with political implications for the increasingly vocal patriot interest, which eagerly seized upon any perspective that affirmed the positive impression of Ireland they contrived to promote as they aspired to attain a position of commercial and constitutional equality with Great Britain within a shared empire.[98] It was hardly surprising therefore that Vallancey's linguistic lucubrations and the broader antiquarian enterprise appealed disproportionately to those whose emotional and political sympathies drew them into the patriot fold, though they were not sufficiently emboldened to devise or to promote a language policy based thereon. Nonetheless, the tone and tenor of Irish politics was transformed in the late 1770s as the patriot interest seized upon the

---

sub nom O'Gorman.   **96** *Collectanea de rebus Hibernicis* (4 vols, Dublin, 1770–86); Monica Nevin, 'General Charles Vallancey', *RSAI Jnl.*, 123 (1993), 19–58; O'Halloran, *Golden ages and barbarous nations*, pp 41–56; *eadem*, 'An English orientalist in Ireland: Charles Vallancey (1726–1812)' in Joep Leerssen (ed.), *Forging in the smithy: national identity and representation in Anglo-Irish literary history* (Amsterdam, 1995), pp 161–74.   **97** Charles Vallancey, *Essay on the antiquity of the Celtic language* (Dublin, 1772); O'Halloran, *Golden ages and barbarous nations*, pp 41–56.   **98** James Kelly, 'The politics of patriotism, 1750–91' (forthcoming).

opportunity offered, and the example provided, by the American War of Independence to advance their own agenda of reforms. There was, as a result, a greater receptivity to the advancement of a positive interpretation of the Gaelic past, and, with particular reference to language, a readiness, previously seldom manifest, to acknowledge and, even, to invoke the Irish language in public. This was, it must be acknowledged, peripheral and occasional. Yet it was more than just symbolic; it was significant given the palpable hostility with which the language was long perceived in Protestant Ireland. It is not clear at the same time what the generality of Irish Protestants made of the unrefined phonetic renderings of such *cliché* phrases as 'Nabocklesh' (*recte* 'Na bac leis') and 'Fagh sin' (*recte* 'Fág sin') in unsophisticated caricatures printed in the periodical press, but even if they dismissed them as curiosities of little import (as they reasonably might), the fact that that were issued in an environment that was also responsive to love songs in Irish on the stage, and that accommodated the use of Irish in the names of certain dining clubs, is indicative of the fact that old fears and inherited animosities no longer possessed purchase among elements of the Protestant population.[99]

These developments notwithstanding, the pace of the attitudinal amelioration to which these actions gave expression slowed in the 1780s. The assumption by the newly founded Royal Irish Academy (1785) that the study of Irish antiquity should be a central aspect of its endeavour, and the active manner in which it set about the location and acquisition of Irish-language manuscripts and the employment of skilled amanuenses to prepare copies, illustrates just how firmly enquiry through the medium of the Irish language into Irish antiquity and history had become established in the intellectual realm. Yet, there is little evidence to suggest that this was replicated in the broader public sphere.[1] Indeed, the hostile invocation of Fr Arthur O'Leary's Gaelic background, and Bishop Woodward's characterization of the language as an obstacle in the way of beneficial anglicization, during the bitter 'paper war' sparked off by the Rightboy disturbances in Munster in the mid-1780s demonstrated that there were fixed cultural prejudices that could profitably be invoked at tense, but indicative, moments.[2] The unhappiness of those of a strong conservative disposition, notwithstanding, they were not in a position either to halt or to reverse the now established trend. The most striking lit-

99 Padhraig Higgins, *A nation of politicians: gender, patriotism and political culture in late eighteenth-century Ireland* (London, 2010), pp 94–7; Dickson, *Old world colony*, p. 444; D.A. Fleming, 'Clubs and societies in eighteenth-century Munster' in Kelly and Powell (eds), *Clubs and societies in eighteenth-century Ireland*, p. 440. **1** de Valera, 'Antiquarianism', pp 149–54; R.B. McDowell, 'The main narrative' in T Ó Raifeartaigh (ed.), *The Royal Irish Academy: a bicentennial history* (Dublin, 1985), p. 12. **2** James Kelly, 'The genesis of Protestant ascendancy: the Rightboy disturbances of the 1780s and their impact upon Protestant opinion' in Gerard O'Brien (ed.), *Parliament, politics and people* (Dublin, 1989), pp 93–127; M.B. Buckley, *Life and writings of the Rev. Arthur O'Leary* (Dublin, 1868), pp 300–1.

erary manifestation of this was provided by the warm reception accorded
Charlotte Brooke's *Reliques of Irish poetry*, published in 1789.[3] But, the decision of Henry Flood to bequeath the bulk of his substantial estate to Trinity
College primarily to fund the endowment of a professorship of Irish and to
permit the purchase of books and manuscripts in the Irish language was
arguably still more significant.

Described by Joep Leerssen as 'a remarkable indication of the sympathy
between Irish antiquarianism and patriot political thought', Flood was
prompted to make this gesture by his alienation from members of his family
rather than by the strength of the commitment he had manifested during his
lifetime to what he denominated 'the native Irish or Erse language'. Nevertheless, his decision was significant, and the overwhelmingly positive response
it was afforded in the public prints demonstrated that there were many who
concurred with the judgment of the *Gentleman's Magazine* that his was the
decision 'of a mighty mind and a patriotic heart'.[4] Unfortunately for those
who anticipated that Flood's philanthropy would place the study and teaching of Irish on solid foundations at the educational centre of Protestant
Ireland, Flood's family contested the legality of the will, and their successful
intervention ensured that the imaginative initiative was first frustrated and
then overturned. This took many years to decide.[5] In the meantime interest
in the Irish language did not abate. In keeping with its position as the leading intellectual institution in the kingdom, much was expected of the Royal
Irish Academy. The announcement in 1793 that it would bestow a 'gold
medal for the best essay on the antient Irish language, its present obscurity,
and the means of removing it' was afforded a proper welcome. However, the
Academy was less innovative in practice, and less significant in fact than more
obviously ideological calls to promote the use of what one strong advocate
tellingly denominated 'the mother tongue'.[6]

Though the strongest currents that informed the demand for major political change in Ireland in the 1790s derived from the enlightenment and from
the inspiring example of the French Revolution, there was also a domestic
current which, anticipating nineteenth-century romantic nationalism, sought
to promote a positive, perhaps, even a revivalist attitude towards the Irish
language. The *Cork Gazette*, edited by Denis Driscol (1762–1811), which
became an important radical voice in the Munster region between its foundation in 1791 and its enforced closure in September 1797, was particularly

---

3 See Lesa Ní Mhunghaile (ed.), *Charlotte Brooke's Reliques of Irish poetry* (Dublin, 2009).
4 Kelly, 'The last will and testament of Henry Flood: context and text', 37–41, 47–9. In
addition to the public applause cited in the above article, mention might also be made of
the endorsement by the *Cork Gazette*, 17 Dec. 1791.   5 Kelly, 'The last will and testament of Henry Flood', 41–4.   6 'Remarks on the Irish language', *Anthologia Hibernica*, 1
(Jan. 1793), 10–11; Brady (ed.), *Catholics and catholicism in the eighteenth-century press*, pp
276–7. See also, *Cork Gazette*, 6 Apr. 1793, 22 Feb. 1794.

forthcoming. Thus in February 1794, it availed of the occasion of a toast raised in Irish by the president of the Cork Brogue-makers Club, in which he berated the taxation of 'the absolute necessaries of life', to observe that 'there is no modern language so full and comprehensive as our native one'.[7] Nearly two years later, in January 1796, it welcomed the prospect of the publication by 'a Patriotic Society' of a weekly Irish-language newspaper, targeted at the 'poor peasantry':

> A Patriotic Society have in its contemplation, we hear, to enlighten the minds of the poor peasantry, who cannot read or understand English. They intend to publish every Saturday, a paper of small dimensions, in this city composed in the Irish language, but the characters to be in English, and the words to be spelled, as they are pronounced, by which means the reading will become perfectly easy to any one who can read at all, and understands Irish. This novel work is to contain moral essays, dissertations on agriculture, the rudiments of Geography, historical sketches, lives of great and good men, political essays on such subjects as may concern the people, and many other topics that these friends to the ignorant and rude Irish may conceive conducive to their spiritual and temporal happiness.[8]

The inherently superior attitude manifest in the manner in which this news item was relayed was reinforced later in the same report by the condescending observation that the proposed publication would perform a valuable service by rousing 'our neglected and debased countrymen ... to a sense of their degraded condition, by enlightening their understanding and giving them a relish for VIRTUE and LIBERTY'.[9] Yet because it was anticipated that the venture would reflect well on all 'CORK PATRIOTS', it was embraced within the larger transformative agenda, identified primarily with the United Irishmen, of which Denis Driscol and the *Cork Gazette* were forceful advocates in Munster.[10] Since Driscol was in prison for most of the mid-1790s, his capacity personally to forward a radical programme was limited, but it is significant that he was not alone in his belief that the use of Irish should be encouraged, and that it was the linguistic medium the *soi-disant* radical vanguard had to utilize if they sought to communicate with the substantial Irish-speaking component of the population. W.J. MacNeven spoke Irish, and Thomas Russell, famously, received instruction in the Irish language when he was employed by the Linenhall Library from Patrick Lynch, who later achieved a measure of renown as an author of schools texts (including an introduction to spoken Irish), and as secretary to the Gaelic Hiberno Celtic Society of Ireland.[11] Moreover, both men

7 *Cork Gazette*, 22 Feb. 1794.   8 *Cork Gazette*, 16 Jan. 1796.   9 Ibid.   10 Michael Durey, 'Irish deism and Jefferson's republic: Denis Driscol in Ireland and America, 1793–1810', *Éire-Ireland*, 25:4 (1990), 56–76.   11 *Freeman's Journal*, 25 Oct. 1803; *Ennis*

collaborated in the publication in September 1795 of *Bolg an Tsolair: or Gaelic Magazine*, the first periodical to be published in the Irish language. Consisting of an Irish grammar, Irish vocabulary, prayers and poetry (notably a selection from Charlotte Brooke's *Reliques*), it was calculated that this title might inaugurate a pattern of Irish-language publication and stimulate interest in the language because of its inhersnt 'purity and perfection', but this was not to be.[12] *Bolg an Tsolair* proved ephemeral by comparison with the radical political newspapers – the *Cork Gazette*, the *Belfast Newsletter* and *The Press* – whose disposition to encourage the usage of Irish harkened forward to the revivalist impulses of the nineteenth century.

Moreover, the green shoots of revivalism manifest in the 1790s were not without negative consequences. The interest manifested by those of a radical political perspective in Irish, in its revival and use, was perceived with acute anxiety by those at the conservative end of the political spectrum. They were so alarmed by revolutionary agitation in the 1790s and disturbed by the equation of radicalism and hibernicization that their reflexive inclination to identify the Irish language with sedition was affirmed in the reactionary environment of the early nineteenth century. There was, at the same time, no reversion to the calls for eradication or to the visible official antipathy manifest in the late seventeenth and early eighteenth centuries. Indicatively, when the military authorities produced a revised version of the 'Rules and regulations for the better ordering of his majesty's army' in November 1806, they were translated into Irish and printed as a broadside so that those who were literate in Irish could inform themselves of their content.[13] It may have been, as has been suggested, a calculated attempt to enhance recruitment into the army, but its publication symbolized how far the state had moved. It also amounted to official recognition of the fact that because Ireland was a bilingual society, the Irish language could no longer be ignored by those agencies of the state that aspired to communicate with the population at large.[14]

III

The eighteenth century was a transitional phase in the history of the use of Irish in Ireland. As a consequence of the penetration of English into every

Chronicle, 16, 23 May 1818; Denis Carroll, *The man from God knows where: Thomas Russell, 1767–1803* (Dublin, 1995), pp 85, 89, 113, 179; Diarmuid Breathnach and Máire Ní Mhurchú, *Beathaisnéis* (9 vols, Dublin, 1986–2007), vi, 58–9; Patrick Lynch, *For-oideas ghnaith-Ghaoighilge: introduction to the knowledge of the spoken Irish as now spoken* (Dublin, 1815). **12** Mary Helen Thuente, *The harp restrung: the United Irishmen and the rise of Irish literary nationalism* (Syracuse, 1994), pp 9–10, 94–6. **13** Riaghlacha agus Orduighthe, 1 Nov. 1806 (NLI, LO collection). **14** Patrick Fitzgerald and Brian Lambkin, *Migration in Irish history, 1607–2007* (Basingstoke, 2008), plate 7.

avenue of life, Ireland became an increasingly bilingual society, albeit one in which the linguistic frontier between those who used English as their primary language and those who were primarily Irish speakers was in a state of permanent flux, as the former expanded, and the latter contracted at a variable but, over time, appreciating pace. Moreover, the legal, economic and attitudinal initiative lay firmly with English, with the result that the transition from a position, at the beginning of the eighteenth century, where the use of Irish was equated with sedition, to a position by the beginning of the nineteenth when the authorities were prepared to use Irish print to communicate with the still large number of monoglot Irish speakers was complex and serpentine. Nonetheless, the journey was overwhelmingly in the direction of greater acceptance. Atavistic hostility had by no means disappeared by the beginning of the nineteenth century, but it was palpably less stridently articulated, less assertively promoted, and less widely shared than it had been when John Richardson had advocated the use of Irish as a means of achieving religious conversion and a step *en route* to the melding of the populations of Britain and Ireland and the creation of a common people who subscribed to a cultural and religious sphere that was Protestant and anglophone.[15] A century later, Ireland was, based on language usage, manifestly more anglicized than it had been in the early eighteenth century, but it was also characterized by decreased cultural and linguistic antipathy. Linguistic hostility had not been eradicated; indeed, it was to acquire renewed vigour in the culture wars of the late nineteenth and early twentieth centuries, but it was possible at the beginning of the nineteenth century for Irish Protestants to regard the Irish language, and, even, to engage in linguistic and antiquarian study, in a manner that was inconceivable to the generation after the Battle of the Boyne when the 'wars of words' appositely described the linguistic confrontation then in train.[16]

---

15 For a perspective on thinking on this see Ted McCormack, *William Petty and the ambitions of political arithmetic* (Oxford, 2009).   **16** This phrase derives from Crowley, *Wars of words*.

8

Bilingualism, print culture in Irish and the public sphere, 1700–*c*.1830

LESA NÍ MHUNGHAILE

The eighteenth century in Ireland was characterized by linguistic and cultural change as use of the English language continued to expand throughout the country. Irish remained the language of the majority of the population until well into the nineteenth century, but it is now acknowledged that there was a greater degree of bilingualism than has hitherto been accepted. Niall Ó Ciosáin has noted that between 1750 and 1850, 'Ireland was at all points [...] an intensely bilingual and diglossic society'.[1] Some knowledge of both languages was necessary for commercial transactions and for day-to-day activity on the landed estates. As a result, interaction between the Catholic and Protestant communities was more extensive than posited by Daniel Corkery in his influential *Hidden Ireland* (1924).[2] In an account of his travels in Connacht in the early nineteenth century, Edward Wakefield commented on the ability of the gentry there to communicate in Irish: 'In the province of Connaught the gentry understand Irish, which facilitates their intercourse with the peasantry; they are consequently enabled to become acquainted with their wants, to assist them with advice, and restrain them by admonition'.[3]

By the end of the nineteenth century, the country 'had undergone one of the most rapid and total language shifts in modern European history'.[4] This

The author wishes to thank Dr Úna Nic Éinrí for references, and Dr Eoin Magennis, Professor Mícheál Mac Craith, Dr Vincent Morley and Dr Liam Chambers for their helpful comments. Unless otherwise indicated, translations from the Irish are by the author.
1 Niall Ó Ciosáin, *Print and popular culture in Ireland, 1750–1850* (Basingstoke, 1997), p. 6. See also, *idem*, 'Print and Irish, 1570–1900: an exception among the Celtic languages?', *Radharc: A Journal of Irish and American Studies*, 5–7 (2004–6), 73–106. 2 Daniel Corkery, *The hidden Ireland* (Dublin, 1924); Declan Kiberd, *Idir dhá chultúr* (Dublin, 1993), p. 3. For a discussion of the use of the Irish language in the courts during the eighteenth and early nineteenth centuries, see Lesa Ní Mhunghaile, 'The legal system in Ireland and the Irish language 1700–*c*. 1843' in Michael Brown and Seán Patrick Donlan (eds), *The laws and other legalities of Ireland, 1689–1850* (Aldershot, 2011), pp 325–58. 3 Edward Wakefield, *An account of Ireland, statistical and political* (2 vols, London, 1812), ii, 754, quoted in Nollaig Ó Muraíle, 'Staid na Gaeilge i gConnachta in aimsir Sheáin Mhic Héil' in Áine Ní Cheannain (ed.), *Leon an iarthair: aistí ar Sheán Mac Héil, ardeaspag Thuama 1834–1881* (Dublin, 1983), p. 44. 4 Ó Ciosáin, *Print and popular culture in*

fundamental change can be identified in the Gaelic manuscript tradition, which manifests an increasing engagement with English from the middle of the eighteenth century, evident in the increased embrace of official documentation such as correspondence and material relating to commerce, legal documents and promissory notes, which were invariably in English.[5] The increasing use of anglicized orthography for Irish, a tendency that was to increase as the nineteenth century progressed, is a further indication of the language shift that was taking place, and points towards the acquisition of literacy through English.[6] Writing to the antiquarian James Hardiman in 1826, the Kilkenny scholar Michael Kinchella, who had been employed by Hardiman to collect songs for his *Irish minstrelsy* (London, 1831), noted that he had never written in Irish: 'I never practised writing Irish but I spelt the words as plain as I could'.[7]

The proliferation of macaronic songs as the eighteenth century progressed offers a further instance of the rise in bilingualism.[8] The example afforded by the Munster priest-poet Liam Inglis (*c*.1709–78) 'Do tharla inné orm' and the south-Ulster poet Peadar Ó Doirnín's (*c*.1700–69) 'Suirí Mhuiris Uí Ghormáin' suggests that they were directed at a bilingual audience as comprehension of both Irish and English would have been necessary to appreciate compositions of this nature.[9] A striking twist in this code-mixing is provided by 'As I was walking one evening fair', composed by Donnchadh Rua Mac Conmara (1715–1810) in Newfoundland, which was aimed at both an Irish-speaking and English-speaking audience there. The English and Irish elements of the poem epitomize the linguistic and cultural tension identifiable in Ireland as the poet alternates between the two languages, and contradicts in Irish what he has just stated in English, as illustrated by his praise and censure of the power of King George III. His Irish-born audience, who were bilingual, would have appreciated the poet's intent, whereas Newfoundland monolingual English speakers would not have understood the true nature of the poem.[10] The next stage in

Ireland, p. 6. 5 L.M. Cullen, 'Patrons, teachers and literacy in Irish, 1700–1850' in Mary Daly and David Dickson (eds), *The origins of popular literacy in Ireland: language change and educational development, 1700–1920* (Dublin, 1990), p. 30. The manuscript NLI G473, transcribed by the county Galway scribe Liam Ó hOisín, contains petitions, promissory notes and a copy of a will. Examples of petitions, certificates of exemption from hearth tax, promissory notes and parish summonses to repair roads are found in the following codices, among many others: BL, Egerton 151; RIA 12 E 25, 23 C 30(d), 23 B 2, 12 M 14 and 24 C 33. For an account of this development in county Kilkenny, see Éamonn Ó hÓgáin, 'Scríobhaithe lámhscríbhinní Gaeilge i gCill Chainnigh 1700–1870' in William Nolan and Kevin Whelan (eds), *Kilkenny: history and society* (Dublin, 1990), p. 434. 6 Cullen, 'Patrons, teachers and literacy in Irish', pp 32–3. 7 RIA, MS 23 E 1; Ó hÓgáin, 'Scríobhaithe lámhscríbhinní Gaeilge i gCill Chainnigh', p. 412. 8 For macaronic songs, see Diarmaid Ó Muirithe, *An t-amhrán macarónach* (Dublin, 1980); Liam Mac Mathuna, *Béarla sa Ghaeilge. Cabhair choigríche: an códmheascadh Gaeilge/ Béarla i litríocht na Gaeilge 1600–1900* (Dublin, 2007), pp 183–217. 9 Úna Nic Éinrí, *Canfar an dán* (An Daingean, 2003), pp 90–91; Seán de Rís, *Peadar Ó Doirnín: a bheatha agus a shaothar* (Dublin, 1969), pp 28–9. 10 Mac Mathúna, *Béarla sa Ghaeilge*, pp 194–5; Ó Muirithe,

the process of language shift from Irish to English witnessed poets from a Gaelic background composing in English only. This development can be traced through three generations in county Longford in the compositions of the poet and musician Peadar Rua Ó Conaill (Mac Conaill) (d. *c.*1777) of Cranary, Columbkille, who composed in Irish only, while his grandson George Nugent Reynolds (1770–1807), the noted ballad writer, composed in English only.[11]

The dramatic linguistic change did not pass unobserved by Gaelic poets, who were acutely aware of its implications, and their concern at the situation found expression in their literary compositions.[12] This is particularly evident in an invitation to a convocation to a court of poetry at Croom, county Limerick, issued in 1754 by Seán Ó Tuama 'an Ghrinn' (1707/8–75): 'Óir dá laghad mhaireas anois dár dteangain ghaoisbhriathraigh Ghaeilge gan dul i mbáthadh agus i mórdhearmad trés gach doilíos trénar hionnarbadh í go nuige se, rachaidh go comair chun neamhní muna bhféacham meon dícheallach le cuidiú go caoin caomhchumainn le chéile go toiliúil rena coimeád ar bun'.[13] Later that decade, Liam Inglis was more upbeat. He looked forward both to the restoration of the old order and the Irish language in his poem 'Táid seo sa Teannta'. The poem was composed during the early years of the Seven Years War (1756–63) and referred positively to French victories over Britain. His argument was as much political as linguistic, therefore, as he anticipated that the restoration of the language would come about as a direct consequence of British military losses:

> Ar éigse beidh greann, ar fhoghlaim beid gasta.
> Gaeilge anois labharfar, cé fada le fán.
> An Béarla beidh breall air, gan ansacht gan aiteas.
> Téada arís teannfar, is canfar an dán.[14]

An t-amhrán macarónach, pp 127–8.   11 For Longford's Gaelic literary heritage see, Lesa Ní Mhunghaile, 'The Irish language and Gaelic literary heritage of county Longford in the eighteenth and nineteenth centuries' in Martin Morris and Fergus O'Ferrall (eds), *Longford: history and society* (Dublin, 2010), pp 283–95. For biographical information on Peader Rua Ó Conaill, see Seán Ó Súilleabháin, *Longford authors* (Mullingar, 1978), p. 33. For George Nugent Reynolds, see *ODNB, sub nom*; M.J. Masterson, 'George Nugent Reynolds, A.D. 1767–1802', *Journal of the Ardagh and Clonmacnois Antiquarian Society*, 2:10 (1945), 52–63. Reynolds appeared in Maria Edgeworth's *The Absentee* (1811) as a character merged with Grace Nugent, who featured in Turlough Carolan's song of that name: see Marilyn Butler, 'Edgeworth's Ireland: history, popular culture, and secret codes', *Novel: A Forum on Fiction*, 24:2 (2001), 285.   12 It should be noted, however, that from the end of the fifteenth century literature in the English language became a source of inspiration for Gaelic authors and it also served as a means of mediating continental literature: Mac Mathúna, *Béarla sa Ghaeilge*, pp 1–11.   13 Trans: 'For, however little that now survives of our wise-worded language, Irish, which has not been eroded and forgotten through every sorrow by which it has been destroyed until now, [the little that remains] will quickly be annihilated unless a diligent attitude sees to it that we all willingly band together to keep it alive': Pádraig Ó Fiannachta, *An Barántas I: réamhrá, téacs, malairtí* (Má Nuad, 1978), pp 36–7.   14 Nic Éinrí, *Canfar an dán*, p. 142. Trans: 'Poets

By 1780, however, when the Gaelic poet, scribe and schoolmaster Tomás Ó Míocháin (*c*.1730–1804), from Ennis, county Clare, was lamenting the demise of the language in the county in a poem entitled 'To Mr Lloyd, on his concise description of North Munster', he did so through the medium of English:

> Pure Wit and Parts eclips'd and disrespect'd,
> Our native Tongue most shamefully reject'd;
> A Tongue primitive florid and Sublime,
> Of nervous Force in either Prose or Rhime.[15]

The poem was one of his two poetic contributions in English to Seon Lloyd's *A short tour; or, an impartial and accurate description of the county of Clare* (1780), the earliest example of a local guide book produced in Ireland.[16] Aimed at an affluent English-speaking audience, the fact that the poem has affinities, both thematically and stylistically, with Laurence Whyte's poem 'The parting cup, or, the humours of deoch an doruis', a critique of the Westmeath landed gentry, suggests that Ó Míocháin was familiar with Whyte's poem or was indirectly influenced by it through the work of Oliver Goldsmith.[17] This in turn provides a further indication of the growing level of bilingualism among the Gaelic-speaking population as the eighteenth century progressed, particularly those of the Catholic middling sort to which Ó Míocháin belonged, many of whom were actively involved in propagating and preserving the Gaelic literary tradition. This group has been characterized by Vincent Morley as 'a middle stratum of comfortable tenant farmers, craftsmen, schoolteachers, publicans, shopkeepers and priests, a stratum which was increasingly literate in English and which maintained a vigorous oral and manuscript-based literature in Irish'.[18] The increasing anglicization of this socio-economic interest was a source of resentment with elements of the native population, a fact evidenced by two satires composed by the northern poet Art Mac Cumhaigh (*c*.1738–73) entitled 'Bodaigh na hEorna', directed

will be in good humour, in learning they will be clever./ The Irish language, long in decline, will now be spoken./ The English language will be in a miserable condition, unloved and joyless./ Strings will again be tuned and the poem will be sung'. **15** John Lloyd, *A short tour, or, an impartial and accurate description of the county of Clare* (Ennis, 1780, repr. 1893; Whitegate, county Clare, 1986), p. iii. **16** For Ó Míocháin see, Diarmaid Ó Muirithe, *Tomás Ó Míocháin: filíocht* (Baile Átha Cliath, 1988); Brian Ó Dálaigh, 'Tomás Ó Míocháin and the Ennis School of Gaelic poetry *c*.1730–1804', *Dál gCais*, 11 (1993), 55–73. For Lloyd see, Séamas Mag Fhloinn, 'Seon Lloyd: dánta' (unpublished MA thesis, St Patrick's College, Maynooth, 1989); Eilís Ní Dheá, 'Seón Lloyd (?–*c*.1785)', *The Other Clare*, 24 (2000), 18–22. **17** M.J. Griffin, '"Our native tongue most shamefully rejected": education, print culture and English literature in eighteenth century Ennis' in Matthew Lynch and Patrick Nugent (eds), *Clare: history and society* (Dublin, 2008), p. 161. For Lawrence Whyte, see Patrick Fagan, *A Georgian celebration: Irish poets in the eighteenth century* (Dublin, 1989), pp 32–42. **18** Vincent Morley, *Irish opinion and the American revolution, 1760–1783* (Cambridge, 2002), p. 2.

at the Callaghans of Culloville, county Armagh, and Peadar Ó Doirnín's 'Torlach Cóir Ó hÁmaill', which lambasted the emerging affluent Catholic middle class for rising above their station.[19]

The joint publishing venture of the two Ennis-based Gaelic scholars, Ó Míocháin and Lloyd, provides an insight into the capacity of Gaelic scribes and scholars to adapt to the bilingual reality of their time. These men composed verse in English and utilized the English print media to advance their careers, but continued to transcribe manuscripts and to compose poetry in Irish. The example they offer is, in fact, one of a number of known instances of contact between the native *literati* and the world of print in the English language during the eighteenth and early nineteenth centuries. Seon Lloyd, for example, visited the Cork printer Donchadh Ó Donchú in 1775, possibly with a view to publishing a work.[20] Crucially, Ó Míocháin's ability to comment in English on such contentious issues as excessive taxation gave him entry into the anglophone public sphere, as evidenced by the following verse:

> And now, alas! we see it quite distress'd,
> By Taxes weak'ned and it's Trade repress'd!
> The tenant wreck'd, unable to pay Rent,
> The needy Landlord driving for Content;
> Some gen'rous Souls, that would distress assuage,
> Of Means bereft, or, in the Debtor's Cage …[21]

The articulation by Ó Míocháin of such sentiments in English suggests that Joep Leerssen's observation that Gaelic Ireland was 'a culture without a public sphere' because it was cut-off from the world of print requires modification.[22] Lerssen's concept of the public sphere is modelled on that of Jürgen Habermas' *Strukturwandel der Öffentlichkeit* (Darmstadt, 1962) and Benedict Anderson's *Imagined communities* (London, 1991). But can one apply Habermas' model to an Irish-speaking or bilingual eighteenth-century Ireland

---

19 Kevin Whelan, 'An underground gentry? Catholic middlemen in eighteenth-century Ireland', *Eighteenth-Century Ireland/ Iris an dá chultúr*, 10 (1995), 14; A.J. Hughes, 'Gaelic poets and scribes of the south Armagh hinterland in the eighteenth and nineteenth centuries' in A.J. Hughes and William Nolan (eds), *Armagh: history and society* (Dublin, 2001), pp 544–5; Tomás Ó Fiaich, *Art Mac Cumhaigh: dánta* (2nd ed., Baile Átha Cliath, 1981), pp 102–4; Breandán Ó Buachalla (ed.), *Peadar Ó Doirnín: amhráin* (Baile Átha Cliath, 1969), pp 55–6.   20 *Irish Book Lover*, 30:3 (1947), 49–50. Lloyd composed the poem 'Dursan liom mo scaradh fris' on taking his leave of Ó Donchú. Mag Fhloinn, 'Seon Lloyd: dánta', pp 58–9.   21 Lloyd, *A short tour*, p. iii.   22 Joep Leerssen, *Hidden Ireland, public sphere* (Galway, 2002), p. 36. Since its first publication, Habermas' model has been criticized from a number of quarters. Early modern historians, for example, have demonstrated that an active political public sphere was already taking shape in the seventeenth century in a number of countries. For a summary of recent international research see Andreas Gestrich, 'The public sphere and the Habermas debate', *German History*, 24:3 (2006), 413–30.

and how does one define its public sphere? To attempt to address this question, recent scholarship on the public sphere in early modern and modern
Europe needs to be brought to bear on the subject. Students of Habermas'
work now posit the concept of a plurality of public spheres, and speak in
terms of 'competing publics', 'alternative public spheres', and 'counterpublics'
in contra-distinction to Habermas' narrowly defined model, which was
restricted to the bourgeoisie.[23] In a study of early seventeenth-century Prussia,
Esther-Beate Körber has argued that three 'partial publics' existed: those ori-
entated around power (*Macht*), learning (*Bildung*), and information (*Information*); while Andreas Gestrich's categories for early eighteenth-century
Germany encompass those of the worlds of sovereigns and diplomats
(*Souveräne und Diplomaten*), the educated bourgeoisie (*gelehrte Bürgertum*), and
common people (*Pöbel*).[24] If one applies the concept of multiple public
spheres to an Irish context, is it valid then to argue, as Murray Pittock has
done, for the existence of three separate public spheres during the eighteenth
century: those of 'Church of Ireland Anglicanism', 'northern Presbyterianism',
and 'the covert world of Catholic culture'?[25] Undoubtedly, a certain amount
of overlapping occurred between the various spheres and engagement between
them was a two-way process, particularly in the world of print. This engagement was assisted by the growing level of interaction that occurred between
the various communities on the island as the century progressed, which
Declan Kiberd has defined as a 'confluence of cultures'.[26] Such contact was
facilitated by cultural intermediaries, identified by Sean Connolly as landown-
ing families of Gaelic descent, middlemen, Gaelic *literati* and Catholic
clergy.[27] Attempts at *rapprochement* were made by individuals from the vari-

23 Geoff Eley, 'Nations, publics and political cultures: placing Habermas in the nineteenth
century' in Craig Calhoun (ed.), *Habermas and the public sphere* (Cambridge, MA, 1992),
p. 306; Kevin Gilmartin, *Print politics: the press and radical opposition in early nineteenth-
century England* (Cambridge, 1996), p. 3. Although he acknowledged the existence of a
'plebian public sphere', Habermas did not develop this aspect in his *Strukturwandel der
Öffentlichkeit*, arguing that it was 'a variant that in a sense was suppressed in the historical process': Jürgen Habermas, *The structural transformation of the public sphere*, trans. T.
Burger and F. Lawrence (Cambridge, MA, 1989), p. xviii. It is important to point out,
however, that in a re-consideration of his *Strukturwandel* thirty years later, Habermas himself accepted the argument in favour of different public spheres: *idem*, 'Further reflections
on the public sphere' in Calhoun (ed.), *Habermas and the public sphere*, pp 424–5.   **24**
Esther-Beate Körber, *Öffentlichkeiten der frühen neuzeit: teilnehmer, formen, institutionen und
entscheidungen öffentlicher kommunikation im herzogtum Preußen von 1525 bis 1618* (Berlin
and New York, 1998); Andreas Gestrich, *Absolutismus und öffentlichkeit: politische kommunikation in Deutschland zu begin des 18 jahrhunderts* (Göttingen, 1994), pp 75–134.   **25**
Murray Pittock, *Scottish and Irish romanticism* (Oxford, 2008), p. 92.   **26** Declan Kiberd,
'Irish literature and Irish history' in Roy Foster (ed.), *The Oxford illustrated history of
Ireland* (Oxford, 1989), pp 252–3. Kiberd maintains that 'if there was no final confluence
of cultures in eighteenth-century Ireland, this was due, more than anything else, to the
emergence of a lethal sectarianism during and after the bloody rising of 1798' (ibid., p.
305).   **27** Sean Connolly, 'Ag déanamh commanding': elite responses to popular culture,

ous communities on the island, and it could be argued that, at the very least, the native Gaelic learned class adopted a pragmatic approach in their dealings with the Protestant elite and 'middling sort'.

II

While it is a fact that the print culture of eighteenth-century Ireland was directed primarily at the Protestant English-speaking population, Joep Leerssen's argument that Gaelic Catholic Ireland lacked access to print culture is untenable. Gaelic scribes and scholars engaged with print culture in English in two ways: first, they read material in English in the form of printed books, newspapers, broadside ballads and chapbooks; and second (as we will see below) they became increasingly involved from the end of the eighteenth century in printing, publishing and subscribing, albeit on a small scale, both in Irish and in English.[28] The importance of the practice of reading aloud in the home, tavern and marketplace as a means of connecting illiterate and semi-literate people to the public sphere must also be highlighted. Roger Chartier, for example, has drawn attention to song merchants as intermediaries through which the printed word was mediated to the illiterate in eighteenth-century France.[29] In Germany, the reading aloud of newspapers played an important role in villages, towns and even at court during the same period.[30] In early nineteenth-century England, professional newsreaders were employed in public houses.[31] It follows then that illiterate or monoglot Irish speakers could access information from printed sources in a number of ways, one of which was through articles that were read aloud. According to local tradition, the county Kerry scribe Seán Ó Braonáin read aloud from the newspaper at the local church every Sunday.[32] The practice is also alluded to in a verse entitled 'What's the news from America? Or, Paddy's Reply' published in the Kilkenny-based *Finn's Leinster Journal* in 1780.[33] It consists of a

---

1660–1850' in J.S. Donnelly Jr, and Kerby Miller (eds), *Irish popular culture, 1650–1850* (Dublin, 1997), p. 16. **28** For broadside ballads in Irish, see Alf Mac Lochlainn, 'Broadside ballads in Irish', *Éigse*, 12 (1967–8), 115–22; Hugh Shields, 'Nineteenth-century Irish song chapbooks and ballad sheets' in Peter Fox (ed.), *Treasures of the library Trinity, College Dublin* (Dublin, 1986), pp 197–204. **29** Roger Chartier, *The cultural uses of print in early modern France*, trans. Lydia G. Cochrane (Princeton, 1987), p. 229. The song merchant sold song booklets after first having sung songs from them, while pointing to corresponding pictures on a canvas with his violin bow. **30** Gestrich has drawn attention to the phenomenon of *Zeitungssinger* or singers of material from newspapers in the marketplace in early eighteenth-century Germany. He has also emphasized the important function the clergy played in forming the public sphere of the *ancien régime* through their sermons and reading aloud from newspapers for their congregations: Gestrich, *Absolutismus und öffentlichkeit*, pp 130–4, 142–4, 151–5. **31** R.K. Webb, *The British working class reader, 1790–1848: literacy and social tension* (London, 1955), pp 33–4. **32** Pádraig de Brún, *Filíocht Sheáin Uí Bhraonáin* (Baile Átha Cliath, 1972), p. 27. **33** *Finn's Leinster*

The County Chronicle (1809) by John Boyne (*c.*1750–1810)

conversation between 'English John' and 'Irish Pat' on the American Revolution in which the Englishman, seeking information on the war from the illiterate Pat, observes: 'All that you know come tell us pray,/ Since you heard the news to day'.[34] A further example from Kilkenny documented in a letter from Rev. Robert Shaw of Tullaroan to William Shaw Mason, indicates that Watty Cox's the *Irish Magazine*, published between 1807 and 1815, was regularly read aloud:

> The writer has often known Cox's magazine to be read to a crowd of villagers on a Sunday evening, while the people swallowed down every word, and imbibed every principle, more deeply instilled by the comments of the reader, while it was lamentable to reflect that on their

Journal, 1 Jan. 1780. I am grateful to Dr Vincent Morley for this reference.   **34** Morley, *Irish opinion*, p. 180.

return home, they should have no book nor tract to take up, which might either counteract the feelings thus excited, or contradict the falsehoods thus propagated; or that even if they had such a work, they could not read it.[35]

The folksong 'Bualadh Ros Mhic Thriúin', probably composed in 1798 after the defeat of the rebels at New Ross, county Wexford, refers to news of Napoleon's success in Italy and defeat of the Austrian forces being read aloud from the paper: 'Thá buaite air mar do chualas insa *news* dá léamh' (He [the Austrian Emperor] is defeated as I heard read from the newspaper).[36]

Printed information could also be transferred through traditional oral forms such as ballads, a phenomenon known as 'bridging'.[37] A case in point is provided by the compositions of the illiterate poet Máire Bhuí Ní Laoghaire (1774–*c.*1849), in particular 'Cath Chéim an Fhiaidh', which displays the influence of Charles Walmesley's *The general history of the Christian church* (1771), published under the pseudonym 'Signor Pastorini'.[38] Known colloquially as Pastorini's prophesies, material from the work was disseminated through the medium of broadside ballads in English that were widely available at fairs, horse races and election meetings by the beginning of the nineteenth century.[39] The degree to which Pastorini's prophesies became firmly entrenched in the native Gaelic psyche, to the extent that an illiterate poet could convey them with ease in verse demonstrates that the influence of print was not necessarily limited to printed matter; it extended into popular oral culture also.[40]

Another weakness in Leerssen's argument derives from his perception of the connection between print culture and the public sphere. This is predicated on the assumption that lack of access to print automatically implies lack of access to the public sphere, which ignores the fact that free debate can also take place orally. Denis Richet has posited that in sixteenth-century Parisian parishes, sermons preached by priests and Franciscan and Dominican friars

35 William Shaw Mason, *A statistical account, or parochial survey of Ireland* (3 vols, Dublin, 1819), iii, 639. 36 Dáithí Ó hÓgáin, *Duanaire Osraíoch: cnuasach d'fhilíocht na ndaoine ó Cho. Chill Chainnigh* (Baile Átha Cliath, 1980), p. 39. Ó hÓgáin suggests that the newspaper in question may have been *Saunders' Newsletter*. 37 Eley, 'Nations, publics and political cultures', p. 300; John Brewer, *Party ideology and popular politics at the accession of George III* (Cambridge, 1976), p. 155; R.S. Schofield, 'The measurement of literacy in pre-industrial England' in Jack Goody (ed.), *Literacy in traditional societies* (Cambridge, 1968), pp 312–13. 38 Donncha Ó Donnchú, *Filíocht Mháire Bhuidhe Ní Laoghaire* (Dublin, 1931), pp 55–8; Meidhbhín Ní Úrdail, 'Máire Bhuí Ní Laoghaire: file an 'rilleadh cainte', *Eighteenth-Century Ireland/Iris an dá chultúr*, 17 (2002), 146–56. 39 Georges-Denis Zimmermann, *Songs of Irish rebellion: political street ballads and rebel songs 1780–1900* (Dublin, 1967), p. 22. 40 For a discussion of Pastorini's prophesies, see Samuel Clark and J.S. Donnelly, *Irish peasants: violence and political unrest, 1780–1914* (Manchester, 1983), pp 102–40; J.S. Donnelly, *Captain Rock: the Irish agrarian rebellion of 1821–24* (Cork, 2009), passim.

played a fundamental role in the transmission of anti-establishment ideas.[41] In seventeenth-century Prussia, information was transmitted via non-print modes such as songs, rumours, comical stories, satirical verse and the ringing of church bells. By these means, the illiterate had the potential to play an active role in the process of information dissemination.[42] The work of Arlette Farge on popular opinion under the Orléans Regency and Louis XV has focused on the different modes of popular expression on the streets of Paris such as rumour, gossip and satire.[43] While in a discussion of late-sixteenth- and seventeenth-century Venice, Fillipo de Vivo has drawn attention to pharmacies and barber shops as locations where political information was exchanged, thus allowing for discussions to occur at different levels of the social hierarchy.[44] In an Irish context, it has been convincingly demonstrated for the eighteenth century that Catholic public opinion was shaped by the oral dissemination of vernacular political verse.[45] Furthermore, sermons delivered in the vernacular (either in Irish or English), particularly in the late eighteenth and early nineteenth centuries, often addressed immediate social and political concerns, although sometimes the preacher's views were 'diametrically opposed' to those of his congregation.[46]

A further problematical dimension of Leerssen's argument derives from his assumption that publication can only take the form of print. Yet Harold Love, in his classic work on seventeenth-century scribal production in England, has defined publication as 'a movement from a private realm of activity to a public realm of consumption'.[47] He has argued that 'the circulation of handwritten texts in seventeenth-century England can properly be understood as a system of publication – that is, of making public and distributing texts that otherwise seem private, hidden, or divorced from the book trade'.[48] In so doing so, he evoked the concept of a 'scribal community' in which manuscripts served as a means of 'bonding groups of like-minded indi-

---

41 Denis Richet, 'Les canaux de la propagation des idées contestataires avant la presse révolutionnaire' in Harvey Chisick, Ilana Zinguer and Ouzi Elyada (eds), *The press in the French Revolution* (Oxford, 1991), pp 19–20.   42 Körber, *Öffentlichkeiten der frühen neuzeit*, pp 298–300.   43 Arlette Farge, *Subversive words: public opinion in eighteenth-century France*, trans. Rosemary Morris (Cambridge, 1994). See also Harvey Chisick, 'Public opinion and political culture in France during the second half of the eighteenth century', *EHR*, 117 (2002), 48–77; J.R. Censer, *The French press in the age of enlightenment* (London, 1994). 44 Fillipo de Vivo, *Information and communication in Venice: rethinking early modern politics* (Oxford, 2007), pp 98–106.   45 Breandán Ó Buachalla, *Aisling ghéar: na Stiobhartaigh agus an t-aos léinn 1603–1788* (Dublin, 1996); Éamonn Ó Ciardha, *Ireland and the Jacobite cause, 1685–1766: a fatal attachment* (Dublin, 2001); Morley, *Irish opinion and the American Revolution*, passim.   46 David Ryan, 'Catholic preaching in Ireland, 1760–1840' in Raymond Gillespie (ed.), *The remaking of modern Ireland, 1750–1950. Beckett prize essays in Irish history, 1999–2000* (Dublin, 2003), p. 94; *idem*, '"That most serious duty": Catholic preaching in Ireland, 1760–1840' (unpublished MA thesis, NUIG, 1998), pp 102–5.   47 Harold Love, *The culture and commerce of texts: scribal publication in seventeenth-century England* (new ed., Oxford, 1998), p. 36.   48 Love, *Culture and commerce of texts*, p. v.

viduals into a community, sect or political faction, with the exchange of texts
in manuscripts serving to nourish a shared set of values and to enrich personal allegiances'.[49] Applying Love's theory to the production and dissemination of manuscripts in Ireland, it can plausibly be argued that Gaelic Ireland
possessed its own public sphere and that this was defined by the existence of
networks of communication and by its Irish-language manuscript culture, particularly the copying and exchange of political verse. There is ample evidence
from scribal colophons that manuscripts were not intended solely for private
consumption, but were produced with an audience in mind and that material
was read aloud from them.[50] It is also important to remember, as Nicholas
Hudson has reminded us, that 'the dominance of print culture […] was neither so sudden nor complete as previous studies have suggested'.[51] In Iceland,
print culture was dominated by the Lutheran church until the nineteenth
century, with the result that secular texts circulated primarily in handwritten
form.[52] Both manuscript and print co-existed until well into the eighteenth
century in a number of European countries, including Ireland, where both
forms interacted. It is likely, for instance, that the manuscripts of Muiris Ó
Gormáin served as exemplars for the development of the Parker type, the
first Gaelic typeface cut and cast in Ireland, while print culture gradually
exerted an influence on manuscript production, as is typified by the substantial corpus of manuscripts produced by the Ó Longáin scribal family of
county Cork.[53] Not only do their manuscripts contain references to the printing process, they also manifest features normative of print such as 'title-pages,
paragraph indentations, running heads, tables of contents, punctuation marks,
indexes and footnotes'.[54] Furthermore, a manuscript compiled in 1792 by the
Revd Laurence Morrissey of Owning, county Kilkenny, of poems composed
by Tadhg Gaelach Ó Súilleabháin, bears a strong resemblance to the first
printed edition of Ó Súilleabháin's *Pious miscellany* (Clonmel, 1802) and both
may have been connected.[55] It should be noted also that the Protestant public
sphere was not exclusively a print culture; institutions of the state such as the
courts and the government still depended on oral and handwritten communi-
cations. Moreover, the lord lieutenant, Earl Fitzwilliam, circulated in excess
of fifty manuscript copies of his letters to Lord Carlisle, which were tran-

49 Ibid., p. 177.   **50** Breandán Ó Conchúir, *Scríobhaithe Chorcaí, 1700–1850* (Baile Átha
Cliath, 1982), p. 228.   **51** Nicholas Hudson, 'Challenging Eisenstein: recent studies in
print culture', *Eighteenth-Century Life*, 26 (2002), 87.   **52** Davíð Ólafsson, 'Wordmongers,
post-medieval scribal culture and the case of Sighvatur Grímsson' (PhD dissertation,
University of St Andrews, 2009), p. 88.   **53** Dermot McGuinne, *Irish type design: a history of printing types in the Irish character* (Dublin, 1992), pp 64–71; see also, Lesa Ní
Mhunghaile (ed.), *Charlotte Brooke's reliques of Irish poetry* (Dublin, 2009), p. xxx.   **54**
Meidhbhín Ní Úrdail, *The scribe in eighteenth- and nineteenth-century Ireland* (Münster,
2000), pp 204–5.   **55** John Rylands Library, Manchester, Irish MS 64. Morrissey subscribed to the 1802 edition of *Pious miscellany*: see Ó Ciosáin, *Print and popular culture*, p.
124.

scribed by clerks employed in Dublin Castle, in a vain attempt to control its circulation.[56] Finally, it is important to remember that there are various ways of looking at public space and that the interaction between oral literature, manuscript culture and print culture formed a continuous three way process in eighteenth-century Ireland, with each form exerting an influence on the other.[57] The remainder of this chapter will focus on the interaction of Gaelic scholars and scribes with print culture in both the Irish and English languages, and it will examine instances of Anglo-Irish scholars who engaged with Irish-language material with a view to publishing it.

III

Newspapers, it has been argued, were 'the single most influential product in terms of the formation of the political culture of the Protestant Ascendancy'.[58] Until 1715, they were published only in the capital, but by the middle of the century the provisional press had grown to the extent that the main regional towns – Waterford, Cork, Limerick and Belfast – also had their own newspapers.[59] Although local in focus, these provided accounts of contemporary politics, both national and international. Initially, newspapers were aimed at a Protestant elite readership, but from 1716 or 1717 onwards they began to cater for a wider audience, 'readers of the lower social strata were starting to subscribe in large numbers and [...] were beginning to make their needs known both as subscribers and as advertisers'.[60] Breandán Ó Buachalla has remarked on the difficulty of establishing the degree to which Irish scholars and scribes came into contact with these journals, but, as they were among the minority who were bilingual and were able to read and write, it is difficult to imagine that those who lived in or near the cities where newspapers were published would not have read them and used them as sources.[61] Certainly by the beginning of the following century, sections of newspapers

---

56 Love, *Culture and commerce of texts*, p. v; James Kelly, 'The state and control of print in eighteenth-century Ireland', *Eighteenth-century Ireland/ Iris an dá chultúr*, 23 (2008), 152; D.A. Fleming and A.P.W. Malcomson (eds), *A volley of execrations: the letters and papers of John FitzGibbon, Earl of Clare, 1772–1802* (Dublin, 2005), pp 223, 225.   **57** Gearóid Denvir has provided a detailed consideration of Gaelic Ireland's access to public space during the nineteenth century in 'Literature in Irish, 1800–1890: from the Act of Union to the Gaelic League' in Philip O'Leary and Margaret Kelleher (eds), *Cambridge history of Irish literature* (2 vols, Cambridge, 2005), i, 544–98.   **58** Martyn Powell, *The politics of consumption in eighteenth-century Ireland* (New York, 2004), p. 93.   **59** Robert Munter, *The history of the Irish newspaper, 1685–1760* (Cambridge, 1967), p. 16.   **60** Munter, *History of the Irish newspaper*, p. 132.   **61** Breandán Ó Buachalla, 'Seacaibíteachas Thaidhg Uí Neachtain', *Studia Hibernica*, 26 (1991–2), 33–4. The Wexford teacher Philip Fitzgibbon copied the song 'Paddy's Triumph' from the *Dublin Evening Post* and translated the first verse into Irish: see Vincent Morley, *Washington i gceannas a ríochta* (Baile Átha Cliath, 2005), pp 52–3.

were bound into Irish-language manuscripts as, for example, a copy of *Chute's Western Herald* from March 1808 is to be found in MS RIA 23 O 67, penned by Seán Ó Braonáin.[62] Coffee houses played an important role in the circulation of these newspapers; so too did alehouses, and, according to Munter, combined they were 'probably more important in the dissemination of newspaper information than the sum of all private subscriptions'.[63] We known, for instance, that some of the courts of poetry – such as that presided over by Seán Ó Tuama at Croom, county Limerick, for the poets of the Maigue valley – were convened in taverns and it is not unrealistic, therefore, to assume that newspapers and their contents was discussed there in the same manner as they were in the coffee-houses.[64]

Evidence for the engagement of native scholars with the contemporary press is provided by the commonplace books of the prominent Gaelic scribe Tadhg Ó Neachtain who, with his father Seán, was at the centre of a coterie of at least twenty-six scribes in early eighteenth-century Dublin. Ó Neachtain was a regular reader of the Dublin newspapers, *Faulkner's Dublin Journal* in particular, as his commonplace books include a large amount of material from that publication relating to contemporary politics. One of those books contains a text in Irish on the War of Jenkins' Ear, a term given to the hostilities between England and Spain, which broke out in 1739.[65] It mentions *an nuaighidheacht* (news) as its source, specifically the *Dublin Gazette*, *Faulkner's Dublin Journal* and *Pue's Occurrences*. Detailed information on the ships involved, 'the name, point of origin, destination, cargo, value or identity of the ship's master' was recorded, but it is important to note that the Irish text omitted the English perspective on the war and showed a distinct bias in favour of Spain.[66] This suggests that the information was compiled for the use of those unable to read accounts of the war in English. Scribes like Tadhg Ó Neachtain performed an important function, therefore, as they mediated between print medium and the illiterate by transcribing and translating material from English-language newspapers, and this material was then further transmitted through the manuscript tradition or disseminated orally.

Further evidence of engagement with newspapers in the English language is found in the detailed accounts of political events in Europe contained in Jacobite verse in the vernacular.[67] Seán Clárach Mac Dónaill's 'Éistidh lem

62 de Brún, *Filíocht Sheáin Uí Bhraonáin*, p. 27; see also, C.G. Buttimer, 'An Irish text on the "War of Jenkins Ear"', *Celtica*, 21 (1990), 90 n.   63 Munter, *History of the Irish newspaper*, p. 81.   64 Breandán Ó Conchúir, 'Na cúirteanna éigse i gcúige Mumhan' in Padraigín Riggs, Breandán Ó Conchúir and Seán Ó Coiléain (eds), *Saoi na héigse: aistí in omós do Sheán Ó Tuama* (Baile Átha Cliath, 2000), pp 61–3; idem, *Scríobhaithe Chorcaí, 1700–1850*, passim. For the Maigue poets, see Risteárd Ó Foghludha, *Éigse na Máighe* (Baile Átha Cliath, 1952); Criostoir O'Flynn, *The Maigue poets/ Filí na Máighe* (Baile Átha Cliath, 1995).   65 For a comprehensive discussion of this text, see Buttimer, 'An Irish text on the "War of Jenkins' Ear"', 75–98.   66 Ibid., 77.   67 These poems were set to popular Jacobite tunes and disseminated to the Irish-speaking population.

ghlórthaibh, a mhórshliocht Miléisius' was presumably based on information gleaned from the *Limerick Journal* in 1744. Tomás Ó Míocháin garnered information on events in the Seven Years War, presumably also from the *Limerick Journal*, which circulated widely in Clare, and compositions by Liam Inglis, such as 'S a Éadhbhaird Aoibhinn Uasail Álainn' celebrating the death of Admiral John Byng, who was tried and executed in 1757 for his failure to relieve Majorca, indicate that he referred to journalistic sources such as the *Cork Journal* for information.[68] There is direct evidence, in fact, in Inglis' poem 'Cois na Bríde' that he read the weekly newspapers: 'S a chara, a rún, do ghlacas niús na Máirte inné'.[69] There is also evidence to suggest that print culture in English influenced Gaelic literary composition. One instance of this phenomenon is found in a poem entitled 'Fógraim, leathaim' from around 1760, which closely resembles the information found in notices contained in the *Cork Evening Post* for the years 1757–60. It was composed in praise of the tailor Uilliam Ó Ceallaigh's skills and appears to have been modelled on the format of newspaper advertisements for goods sourced abroad.[70]

Occasionally the death of Gaelic poets was announced in the press. Possibly the earliest example of reporting of this nature was a notice on the death of Eoghan an Mhéirín Mac Cárthaigh (1691–1756), reported in *Faulkner's Dublin Journal*.[71] Other poets whose deaths were reported in the press included Tadhg Gaelach Ó Súilleabháin (1715–95) and Brian Merriman (c.1749–1805).[72] The publication of death notices in these instances indicates that it was considered to be of interest to newspaper readers. The integration of Catholics into the public sphere from the middle decades of the century onwards to which this attests is still more visible from the increasing readiness with which Catholic Gaelic-speaking schoolmasters utilized the press to advertise their schools and scribal services.[73] The northern scribe and schoolmaster, Muiris Ó Gormáin (d.1794), advertised his services both as a teacher

---

68 Ó Buachalla, 'Seacaibíteachas Thaidhg Uí Neachtain', 33–4; Nic Éinrí, *Canfar an dán*, pp 121–2, 243–5; C.G. Buttimer, 'Gaelic literature and contemporary life in Cork, 1700–1840' in Patrick O'Flanagan and Cornelius Buttimer (eds), *Cork: history and society* (Cork, 1993), p. 590. See also, Éamonn Ó Ciardha, 'A voice from the Jacobite underground: Liam Inglis (1709–1778)' in Gerard Moran (ed.), *Radical Irish priests, 1660–1970* (Dublin, 1998), p. 30. **69** Nic Einrí, *Canfar an dán*, p. 19. English's songs were widely disseminated in the manuscript tradition. **70** C.G. Buttimer, 'A Paul Street poem, c.1760', *Journal of the Cork Historical and Archaeological Society*, 93 (1988), 126–37. **71** This paper was sympathetic to Catholics; Faulkner was described by Charles O'Conor of Belanagare as the first Dublin printer who 'stretched out his hand to the prostrate Christian Catholic, recognizing him as a fellow Christian and a brother, and endeavoured to raise him to the rank of a subject and a freeman'; quoted in Munter, *History of Irish newspaper*, p. 69 from J.T. Gilbert, *A history of the city of Dublin* (3 vols, Dublin, 1861), ii, 37. **72** Cullen, 'Patrons, teachers and literacy in Irish', p. 20, 41n; Risteárd Ó Foghludha, *Eoghan an Mhéirín MacCarthaigh* (Baile Átha Cliath, 1938), p. 9. The death in 1810 of the Waterford poet Donnchadh Rua Mac Conmara was announced in the *Freeman's Journal*. **73** Séamus Ó Casaide, 'Irish professors in the eighteenth century', *Irish Book Lover*, 21:6 (1933), 137–8.

of Irish and translator of Irish-language manuscripts in *Faulkner's Dublin Journal* in 1766.[74] On 1 February 1779, Tomás Ó Míocháin placed a notice in the *Clare Journal* seeking employment for his fellow scribe Seon Lloyd as a tutor. Between then and 1805, he advertised his own mathematical school in the *Clare Journal*, the *Ennis Chronicle* and the *Limerick Journal*.[75] Advertisements placed by the county Clare schoolmaster Patrick Lynch (Pádraig Ó Loingsigh) (1754–1818), who was living in Carrick-on-Suir at the time, in *Finn's Leinster Journal* in 1793 and 1795, and by a Mr O'Hely in Ramsey's *Waterford Chronicle* for 22 October 1796 provide further examples of teachers using print media for this purpose.[76]

Gaelic scribes and poets also had access to a cheap form of publishing, that of broadside ballads and chapbooks. The unconventional use of English and the recourse to the *amhrán* (song) metre rather than English metrical forms indicates that some anonymous verse in English found in such publications from the 1780s was composed by native Irish speakers.[77] William Mahon has suggested that Gaelic scribes in county Galway may have supplied songs to printers in Tuam, Loughrea or Galway city as some of the broadsides produced in the county contain material in phonetic spelling in Irish.[78] The influence of broadside ballads can also be identified in the manuscripts of the well-to-do county Galway farmer, Liam Ó hOisín, who followed the format used in the sheets, 'A new song named', to name songs in his manuscript NLI G473.[79]

There are a number of examples of Gaelic scribes and scholars both subscribing to and owning printed books in English; in some cases their collections were substantial.[80] Tadhg Ó Neachtain's manuscript TCD MS H.4.20, compiled between 1725 and 1737, contains a list of the works he had lent to

74 Lesa Ní Mhunghaile, 'Muiris Ó Gormáin (d. 1794): scoláire idir dhá chultúr' in Mícheál Mac Craith agus Pádraig Ó Héalaí (eds), *Diasa díograise: aistí i gcuimhne ar Mháirtín Ó Briain* (Indreabhán, 2009), pp 221–2.   75 Ó Dálaigh, 'Tomás Ó Míocháin', *Dál gCais*, 11 (1993), 55–73.   76 Séamus Ua Casaide, 'Patrick Lynch, secretary to the Gaelic Society of Dublin', *Journal of the Waterford and South-East of Ireland Archaeological Society*, 15 (1912), 49–50; idem, 'Notes and queries', *ibid.*, 13 (1910), 176.   77 Andrew Carpenter, *Verse in English from eighteenth-century Ireland* (Cork, 1998), pp 8, 387.   78 William Mahon, 'Scríobhaithe lámhscríbhinní Gaeilge i nGaillimh 1700–1900' in Gerard Moran and Raymond Gillespie (eds), *Galway: history and society* (Dublin, 1996), p. 644. For printing in Galway, see E.R. McClintock Dix, 'Galway song books', *Galway Archaeological and Historical Society Journal*, 4 (1905–6), 178–9.   79 Mahon, 'Scríobhaithe lámhscríbhinní Gaeilge i nGaillimh', p. 644.   80 Examples included the Clare poet and scholar Hugh MacCurtin, who loaned a copy of Peter Walsh's *A prospect of the state of Ireland* (London, 1682) to Seon Ó hUaithnín; and the Kerry teacher Tomás Rua Ó Súilleabháin, who owned Thomas Comerford, *The history of Ireland from the earliest account of time, to the invasion of the English under Henry II* (Dublin, 1752) and Sylvester O'Halloran, *A general history of Ireland, from the earliest accounts to the close of the twelfth century* (London, 1778) among many others. See Eoghan Ó hAnluain (eag.), *Seon Ó hUaithnín* (Baile Átha Cliath, 1973), p. 61 and Máire Ní Shúilleabháin (ed.), *Amhráin Thomáis Rua* (Má Nuad, 1985), pp 20–4.

friends and acquaintances.[81] References to works on loan from his collection included: 'the bravery of the Irish';[82] a history of Scotland; a historical work by Clarendon;[83] 'the Irish Survey';[84] and a work he referred to as 'the Turkish spy'.[85] There is also evidence in his manuscripts that he had access to an edition of Thomas Ward's *England's reformation (from the time of King Henry VIII to the end of the Oate's plot* (Hamburg, 1710) as excerpts from the work appear in NLI G132.[86] A copy of this work, the 1742 edition printed in London, was also among the English books owned by Muiris Ó Gormáin, whose catalogues of books in his possession, compiled between 1761 and 1776, constitute a further counter to the view that the Gaelic world was cut off from the world of print. On 1 June 1776 the collection included thirty-eight items in the English language, incorporating a diverse range of subjects. A monetary value was indicated beside many of the items in his catalogues, which suggests that Ó Gormáin was most likely in the business of buying and selling books and manuscripts.[87] In addition to purchasing from booksellers, he attended book auctions as is evident from the purchases he made at the auction of the library of his former patron, Dr John Fergus, on 3 February 1766 in Fergus' home on Abbey Street.[88] The county Limerick Jacobite poet and scribe Aindrias Mac Craith (*c*.1709–*c*.1794), also known as 'an Mangaire Súgach', sourced books in English from the Limerick schoolmaster and Gaelic scholar Richard McElligott. In a letter to the schoolmaster, dated 3 July 1787, Mac Craith wrote: 'I would be greatly obliged to you if you was pleased to send me Manering's Entertainment and The Memorial of a Christian Life by bearer'.[89] In a second letter to McElligott in August of the

81 TCD H.4.20, ff 560, 597–8. 82 *A description of the city of Dublin ... wherein, besides taking notice of every thing remarkable in the city ... is represented the happy situation of Ireland for commerce, the richness and fertility of the soil ... By a citizen of London, who liv'd twenty years in Ireland* (London, 1732). 83 This was either *The history of the rebellion and civil wars in England begun in the year 1641* (Oxford, 1712) or *The history of the rebellion and civil wars in Ireland* (London, 1720). 84 Barnabe Rych, *A short survey of Ireland, truely discovering who it is that hath so armed the hearts of that people with disobedience to their prince* (London, 1609). 85 *Letters written by a Turkish spy, who lived five and forty years undiscovered at Paris: giving an impartial account to the Divan at Constantinople, of the most remarkable transactions of Europe* (1687–94). This was an eight-volume collection of articles allegedly written by an Ottoman spy named Mahmut. The first volume of the work, published in Italian in Paris in 1684, was actually written by a Genoese political refugee, Giovanni Paolo Marana (1642–93). 86 Cornelius Buttimer has demonstrated that the Cork scribe Dáibhí de Barra drew extensively on the work to create the poem 'A n-aimsire Bess do bheith 'na banríoghain aluinn' (Coláiste Cholmáin, Fermoy MS PB 7, f. 77), which deals with the settlement of Protestant ministers in Ireland during the time of Elizabeth I: see Buttimer, 'Gaelic literature and contemporary life in Cork', pp 638–9. 87 RIA 23 H 23 (a), and NLI MS G664. For a detailed consideration of these catalogues see Lesa Ní Mhunghaile, 'Leabharlann phearsanta Mhuiris Uí Ghormáin' in Ruairí Ó hUiginn and Liam Mac Cóil (eds), *Bliainiris*, 8 (Ráth Cairn, 2008), 59–102; *eadem*, 'An eighteenth-century Gaelic scribe's private library: Muiris Ó Gormáin's books', *RIA proc.*, 110C (2010), 239–76. 88 Ó Catháin, 'John Fergus MD, eighteenth-century doctor', p. 140. 89 RIA

same year, Mac Craith thanked his correspondent for the books he had sent and also requested 'a catalogue of such in prose and verse'.[90] It is striking that both men corresponded in English although both were well versed in the Irish language.

A further example of the collecting and reading of books in English is provided by the library of the farmer, miller and Gaelic scholar, Pádraig Ó Néill (1765–1832) from Owning, county Kilkenny, which provides a unique insight into the reading material available in one well-to-do Catholic farmer's house.[91] It contained a large quantity of volumes in the English language, as well as others in Latin, Greek and French, many of which had been in his family for generations. Among the many works in English in his library were the following titles: *The history of the empire of Rome*, *The ancient history of the Egyptians*, *The history of the arts and sciences of the ancients*, *The literary works of southern Europe*, Milton's *Paradise lost*, *Monthly Review, or Literary Journal* and Maria Edgeworth's *Early lessons*.[92] Such was the library's importance, it merited mention in William Shaw Mason's *The parochial survey of Ireland* (1814).[93] Ó Néill continued to collect throughout his life, ordering some of his books from Dublin, and obtaining others from friends and acquaintances. Among those ordered from the capital were Charlotte Brooke's *Reliques of Irish poetry* (1789), Charles O'Conor's *Dissertations on the antient history of Ireland* (1753),[94] the works of Spencer, Campion, Hanmer and John Curry's *An historical and critical review of the civil wars in Ireland* (1775).

Apart from owning printed books, Gaelic scribes and scholars also became actively involved in the process of printing and publishing both in Irish and English towards the end of the eighteenth century. The examples of Ó Míocháin and Lloyd in Ennis have already been mentioned. The county Down Gaelic scholar and schoolmaster Patrick Lynch (*c*.1756–1838) was involved in the production of the first Gaelic journal *Bolg an Tsoláir*, only one edition of which appeared on 1 October 1795. He also translated gospels for Whitley Stokes (1763–1845) – *An soisgeal do réir Lucais, agus gniovarha na Neasbol. The gospel according to St Luke and the Acts of the Apostles* (1799) – which contained the Irish and English texts in parallel columns, and was involved in the production of William Neilson's *An introduction to the Irish language* (1808).[95] The Meath poet Michael Clarke (1750–1847) of White-

24 C 55, ff 354–8a; see also, Máire Comer Bruen and Dáithí Ó hÓgáin, *An mangaire súgach: beatha agus saothar* (Baile Átha Cliath, 1996), p. 246.   90 RIA 24 C 55, f. 350; Breandán Ó Madagáin, *An Ghaeilge i Luimneach, 1700–1900* (Dublin, 1974), p. 36; Bruen and Ó hÓgáin, *An mangaire súgach*, p. 247.   91 For Pádraig Ó Néill, see Eoghan Ó Néill, *Gleann an Óir: ar thóir na staire agus na litríochta in oirthear Mumhan agus i ndeisceart Laighean* (Baile Átha Cliath, 1988); Máire Ní Mhurchú and Diarmuid Breathnach, *Beathaisnéis 1782–1881* (Baile Átha Cliath, 1999), pp 126–7.   92 Ó Néill, *Gleann an Óir*, pp 80–5.   93 Ibid., p. 110.   94 The second edition was published Dublin in 1766 under the title *Dissertations on the history of Ireland*.   95 Brian Mac Giolla Fhinnéin, 'Pádraig Ó Loingsigh: saol agus saothar', *Seanchas Ard Mhacha*, 15:2 (1993), 98–124; Ní Mhurchú and

wood, Nobber, published two books by subscription, *Man's final end* (1824), an English translation of the religious poem in Irish entitled 'Críoch dheighneach an duine' and *Ireland's dirge* (1827), a rendition of Seán Ó Conaill's long seventeenth-century poem, 'Tuireamh na hÉireann'. Both works included the original texts in Irish and were based on English translations of the poems that had already been in circulation in the manuscript tradition.[96]

In the south east of the country, Carrick-on-Suir became the focal point for the publishing activities of literary men and scholars from counties Kilkenny, Tipperary and Waterford.[97] This circle of scholars, which included Pádraig Ó Néill; the inn-keeper and scribe Uilliam Ó Meachair (William Meagher) from Ninemilehouse, county Kilkenny;[98] Patrick Lynch, originally from Quin, county Clare, who had founded a classical academy in Carrick-on-Suir;[99] and the well-to-do farmer Seamas Ó Scoireadh (James Scurry), had as their main aim the preservation and propagation of the Irish language and the explication of Gaelic culture to a wider audience.[1] Apart from being a regular contributor to the *Waterford Mirror*, Ó Néill published two works in Irish in addition to proposals for a further two in English.[2] His first publication, *Oific na hoighe Naomtha Muire, translated into Irish for the use of the Carmelites*, was published by John Stacy in Carrick-on-Suir in 1796. This was followed in 1816 by a journal entitled *Blaithfleasg na milsean, cnuasaighthe*, also printed in Carrick-on-Suir. Although it is stated on the title page that the journal was collected by Uilliam Ó Meachair, it was in fact compiled by Ó Néill. It included a preface in English in which he explained the importance of the Irish language. However, only one edition of the journal appeared, as the promised subscriptions were not forthcoming and Ó Néill lost money on the venture.[3] Around 1819 he drafted a prospectus entitled 'Speedily to be put to press: an English translation of the interesting Irish story of Lomnotane'. The work was to contain fifty pages and retail for a price of 3s. 4d. The following year, Ó Néill compiled a prospectus entitled 'Ceol bin na hEirion. Irish melodies. Speedily will be published'.[4] He had also intended to publish a collection of Gaelic poetry in English translation, apparently

Breathnach, *Beathaisnéis,1782–1881*, pp 57–8. **96** Séamus Mac Gabhann, 'Forging identity: Michael Clarke and the hidden Ireland', *Ríocht na Midhe*, 11:2 (1996), 73–95. **97** For printing in Carrick-on-Suir, see E.R. McClintock Dix, 'Early printing in the south-east of Ireland', *Journal of the Waterford and South East of Ireland Archaeological Society*, 10 (1907), 140–6. **98** Ó hOgáin, 'Scríobhaithe lámhscríbhinní Gaeilge i gCill Chainnigh', p. 421. **99** Ua Casaide, 'Patrick Lynch, secretary to the Gaelic Society of Dublin', pp 47–61. It is also worth noting that Lynch was involved, together with Morton Pitt, a major in the Dorset Militia, and Francis White, a local landowner, in compiling an unofficial census of the twin communities of Carrick Mór and Carrick Beg in 1799: see L.A. Clarkson, 'The demography of Carrick-on-Suir, 1799', *RIA proc.*, 87C (1987), 13–36. **1** Ó Néill, *Gleann an Óir*, pp 105–6; Ó hOgáin, 'Scríobhaithe lámhscríbhinní Gaeilge i gCill Chainnigh', pp 423–6. **2** Ó Néill, *Gleann an Óir*, p. 147. **3** Ibid., p. 112. **4** Ibid., pp 119, 133.

inspired by Charlotte Brooke's *Reliques of Irish poetry*, but he failed in his attempt probably due to insufficient funds. Patrick Lynch was more successful in seeing his works through the press, three of which were published in Carrick-on-Suir by the barber, dramatist and printer, John Stacy: *Paddy's portable chronoscope* (1792); *The Pentaglot preceptor; or, elementary institutes of the English, Latin, Greek, Hebrew, and Irish languages* vol. 1 (1796) and *A plain, easy, and comprehensive grammar of the English tongue* (1805). He may also have been connected to the publication of the periodical *The Carrick Recorder* in 1792.[5] He continued to publish after he moved to Dublin in 1808, where he was an active member of the Gaelic Society and around 1816 he published a proposal seeking subscribers for 'Original Irish poems'. However, this and a number of other projects do not appear to have come to fruition.[6] Seamas Ó Scoireadh published *Cheithre Soleirseadha de'n Eagnuidheacht Chriostuidhe* (Waterford, 1820), an Irish translation of a religious treatise in English, together with an introduction in English on the phonetic and orthographical system of the Irish language. This was followed in 1825 by an Irish translation of a pastoral letter issued by the bishop of Kildare and Leighlin, James Doyle (1786–1834).[7] Further examples of printing in the south-east are provided by Pádraig Denn (1756–1828), the schoolmaster, poet and clerk of Cappoquin chapel, county Waterford, who published a number of devotional works at presses in Cork and Clonmel, including *Leavar beag no rosaries, mar aon leis na liodáin agus le toirvirt suas an anma aig dul deag, etc* (Clonmel, 1818) and *Machtnuig go maith air* (Clonmel, 1819), an English rendition of Richard Challoner's *Think well on it* (London, 1728).[8] He also issued revised editions of Tadhg Gaelach's *Pious miscellany*, printed by different publishers in Cork city in 1821 and 1822, both of which incorporated some of his own pious compositions.[9] Most of the editions published after 1822 appear to have been based on Denn's text.[10]

There is also evidence in the manuscript tradition of projected publications that never saw the light of day. The manuscript penned by the scribe Seosamh Ó Dimusa in 1796 (RIA 24 C 57), possibly in Waterford, appears to

5 Ua Casaide, 'Patrick Lynch, secretary to the Gaelic Society of Dublin', p. 49 n.   6 Séamus Ua Casaide, 'List of works projected or published by Patrick Lynch', *Journal of the Waterford and South East of Ireland Archaeological Society*, 15 (1912), 107–17; McClintock Dix, 'Early printing in the south east of Ireland', 146.   7 J. Doyle, *Pastoral letter addressed to the Roman Catholic clergy of the deanery of Kilcock* (translated into Irish by James Scurry) (Dublin, 1825); Ó hOgáin, 'Scríobhaithe lámhscríbhinní Gaeilge i gCill Chainnigh', pp 424–5.   8 McClintock Dix, 'Early printing in the south-east of Ireland', 225; Ní Mhurchú and Breathnach, *Beathaisnéis 1782–1881*, p. 40.   9 Úna Nic Éinrí, *An cantaire siúlach: Tadhg Gaelach* (An Daingean, 2001), pp 34–7; Séamus Ua Casaide, 'Some editions of O'Sullivan's *Pious miscellany*', *Journal of the Waterford and South East of Ireland Archaeological Society*, 14 (1911), 113–22; Ó Ciosáin, *Print and popular culture*, pp 118–31.   10 Ua Casaide, 'Bibliography of Tadhg Gaolach's *Pious miscellany*', *Journal of the Waterford and South East of Ireland Archaeological Society*, 9 (1906), 69.

have been prepared for publication, while NLI G100, compiled by Mícheál Óg Ó Longáin in Cork, contains the following proposal: 'Ready for the Press/And to be published as soon as a competent number of subscribers can be obtained. /The History of the Irish Language / .../ The Combat of Cuchululin with his son Conlaoch / .../ The Dialogue between Death and the Patient/ ...'[11]

IV

The concern demonstrated by native scribes and scholars with the preservation of their language and literary heritage coincided with an upsurge of interest in antiquarian matters and popular culture among the upper classes throughout Europe during the latter half of the eighteenth century.[12] In Ireland, the study of Gaelic antiquities and history became a fashionable pursuit among members of the Protestant elite, and it was closely linked to an emerging awareness of their Irish identity.[13] As pointed out earlier, some members of the Protestant elite may have been able to converse in Irish but the majority of Protestant antiquarians never succeeded in learning to read or write Irish, relying instead on translations. Many appear to have had little interest in learning the modern spoken language as their main aim was to gain access to the contents of ancient documents to assist their research on historical matters. A small number did, however, attempt to learn to read the ancient codices, with varying degrees of success. They were assisted in their endeavours by Gaelic scholars and scribes, who were employed to copy documents and to provide accompanying translations, and the period witnessed the transfer of native Gaelic learning to the elite through these intermediaries. Tomás Ó Míocháin and his circle of literary acquaintances in Ennis perceived themselves as participants in the same antiquarian movement. In a convocation to a court of poetry he issued in 1780, directed at 'an beagán atá re léamh agus litir-ealaí inár measc' (the few among us who are literate and skilled in letters), he referred to the antiquarian activities taking place in Dublin.[14] The court was convened in the house of the draper Traolach Ó Briain, under the authority of Uilliam Mac Gearailt, an attorney at law in the town, to promote the learning of Irish, the composition of poetry, and the sharing of manuscripts. The fact that the poem 'Sláinte ó chroí agus míle fáilte', composed by Seon Lloyd in honour of the occasion, was also ascribed

---

11 Nessa Ní Shéaghdha, *Catalogue of Irish manuscripts in the National Library of Ireland*, fasc. 3 (Dublin, 1976), p. 87.   12 See Peter Burke, *Popular culture in early modern Europe* (rev. edn, Aldershot, 1994).   13 Clare O'Halloran, *Golden ages and barbarous nations: antiquarian debate and cultural politics in Ireland, c.1750–1800* (Cork, 2004).   14 Brian Ó Cuív, 'Rialacha do chúirt éigse i gcontae an Chláir', *Éigse*, 11 (1965–6), 216; Ó Muirithe, *Tomás Ó Míocháin*, pp 33–4.

the title 'Failte Sheoin Lloyd roimh na Antiquarians chum Innis Chlúon-Ramad' (Seon Lloyd welcomes the antiquarians to Ennis) in the manuscript tradition offers further evidence of the influence of the antiquarian movement on the native tradition.[15]

At the centre of the movement in Dublin was the Royal Irish Academy, established in 1785 with, among other functions, the purpose of promoting the study of Gaelic antiquities. A predominantly Protestant body that included some of the most influential men in the country, it provided a forum where those described by Oliver MacDonagh as the 'new Catholic intelligentsia' and 'Anglo-Irish liberals' could find common ground in their research into Ireland's distant past.[16] The 1780s proved to be the highpoint of this co-operation, culminating in two influential works which sought to illuminate the Gaelic world for English-speaking readers: Joseph Cooper Walker's *Historical memoirs of the Irish bards* (Dublin and London, 1786), an account of Irish poets, poetry and music from the earliest times down to the eighteenth century, including a number of poems in Irish together with translations in English, and Charlotte Brooke's *Reliques of Irish poetry* (Dublin, 1789), which was the first substantial collection of Irish poetry translated into English. Both works had distinct political undertones; both were influenced by the patriot politics of the decade, and were an attempt by elements of the Protestant elite to address their ambiguous position, being neither fully English nor fully Irish, and to improve their uneasy relationship with England through the means of literature. In the preface to their works, both authors expressed their Irish identity. Walker, for example, opened his work as follows: 'I trust I am offering to my countrymen an acceptable present: the gift has novelty, at least to recommend it', while Brooke expressed the comparable sentiment: 'I trust I am doing an acceptable service to my country, while I endeavour to rescue from oblivion a few of the invaluable reliques of her ancient genius'.[17] In so doing, Walker and Brooke sought to vindicate the civility of the pre-Christian era in Ireland through the choice of material they included in their respective works. They relied on a network of scholars for assistance and, arguably, neither work would have come to fruition without the assistance of such custodians of native learning as Charles O'Conor, Sylvester O'Halloran, Theophilus O'Flanagan and the scribes Muiris Ó Gormáin and Peadar Ó Conaill of county Clare, all of whom provided access to Gaelic manuscript sources. Not only did such co-operative endeavour provide much needed employment for scribes, it also permitted Gaelic scholars to exert a direct influence on the type of Gaelic material published and, particularly in the case of Brooke's *Reliques*, enabled them to participate in the

15 Mag Fhloinn, 'Seon Lloyd: dánta', p. 94.   16 Oliver MacDonagh, *States of mind: a study of Anglo-Irish conflict, 1789–1980* (London, 1985), pp 1–9.   17 Joseph Cooper Walker, *Historical memoirs of the Irish bards* (London and Dublin, 1786), p. 1; Brooke, *Reliques of Irish poetry* (Dublin, 1789), p. vii.

political discourse surrounding such thorny issues as the vindication of Gaelic civility and the preservation of Gaelic Ireland's literary heritage.

Joseph Cooper Walker's *Historical memoirs* was his first work of scholarship and was completed with the advice and assistance of the Protestant antiquarians William Beauford, Edward Ledwich, Thomas Percy and Charles Vallancey, and the Catholics Charles O'Conor, Sylvester O'Halloran and Theophilus O'Flanagan, who acted as his advisors on the Irish language.[18] The work offers an interesting insight into the delicate balancing act performed by Walker as he sought to tread a middle ground between the conflicting interpretations of Ireland's pre-Christian past that were coloured by the political allegiances of his various correspondents. To complicate matters further, there were divisions and disagreements within both camps, making Walker's success in placating everyone all the more remarkable. Clare O'Halloran has alluded to the 'ambivalent primitivism' of the work; this can probably be ascribed to the fact that it was a collaborative effort by a number of scholars, few of whom would have subscribed to primitivist theory.[19]

Walker's network of informants extended throughout the country. Some of these were approached on his behalf by a third party – for example Aindrias Mac Craith. Contact was established through Richard McElligott – one of a number of scholars in Limerick city at that time involved in promoting and propagating the Irish language and Irish antiquities that included Sylvester O'Halloran, Ralph Ouseley and the Chevalier Thomas O'Gorman. McElligott wrote to Mac Craith on Walker's behalf, seeking biographical information on the ancient bards. As the *Historical memoirs* had appeared the previous year, Walker may have been seeking information for the second revised edition. Mac Craith appears to have been overwhelmed by the volume of information requested of him and in a letter dated July 1787, he apologized for having been unable to provide all of it, implying that such an undertaking was impossible:

> tho had I wrote I know would not answer you or Mr Ferrar's expectation or half Mr Walker's queries to his satisfaction, nor was it reasonable to expect it, or that any man could do so for how is it possible that any man in the kingdom could give a particular true, or satisfactory account of the birth, names, lives, death, parentage, personal description, or places of residence of our ancient bards, of their works, performances, or different compositions in prose or verse, or on what particular instruments they performed their church or other music.[20]

18 For Walker, see Lesa Uí Fhathaigh (Ní Mhunghaile), 'Joseph Cooper Walker (1761–1810): beatha agus saothar' (unpublished PhD thesis, NUIG, 2001); O'Halloran, *Golden ages*, pp 113–17. 19 O'Halloran, *Golden ages*, pp 113–14. 20 RIA 24 C 55, ff 354–358a; Bruen and Ó hÓgáin, *An mangaire súgach*, p. 244. The Mr Ferrar mentioned was John Ferrar, author of *The history of Limerick* (Limerick, 1767): see Jennifer Moore, 'John

This was a tall order indeed, and typical of Walker's youthful enthusiasm to bombard his correspondents with an array of questions. Mac Craith did, however, recommend a lengthy list of sources for consultation that included the *Leabhar Gabhála*, *Annals of Innisfallen*, and Keating's *History of Ireland*.

Charlotte Brooke's *Reliques of Irish poetry* appears to have been a concerted effort by a number of scholars closely linked to the Royal Irish Academy to reject English representations of Irish barbarity and to promote a political agenda that argued for equal status within the British Empire. The project was first suggested to her by two members of the Academy, Judge Robert Hellen, second justice of the Court of Common Pleas in Ireland, and Dominick Trant, King's Advocate of the High Court of Admiralty in the Kingdom of Ireland, and copies of texts from manuscript sources were provided by Sylvester O'Halloran, Theophilus O'Flanagan and Muiris Ó Gormáin.[21] O'Halloran wrote the introductory essay to the poem 'Conloch' included in the volume, and Charles O'Conor provided advice on the accuracy of the translations. Both Charles Vallancey and William Beauford also offered advice on translations and texts but their knowledge of the Irish language was limited, to say the least. Brooke's primary aim was to foster mutual respect and understanding between Ireland and Britain and to encourage better relations between the native Irish and the Protestant ascendancy. Drawing on the familial trope, she likened the muses of both countries to sisters, the Irish muse being the elder and called for a 'cordial union' between them: 'The British muse is not yet informed that she has an elder sister in this isle; let us then introduce them to each other! Together let them walk abroad from their bowers, sweet ambassadresses of cordial union between two countries that seem formed by nature to be joined by every bond of interest, and of amity'.[22] Utilizing the metaphor of the blending of blood, she argued that her class was in no way inferior to its counterparts across the water: 'Let them tell her, that the portion of her blood which flows in our veins is rather ennobled than disgraced by the mingling tides that descend from our heroic ancestors'.[23] Here she echoed Walker, who expressed a similar sentiment the previous year in *Historical essay on the dress of the ancient and modern Irish* (1788): 'Mingling their blood with ours, that brave people have conciliated our affections'.[24] Both authors in turn echoed Sylvester

Ferrar, 1742–1804: printer, author and public man' in John Hinks, Catherine Armstrong and Matthew Day (eds), *Periodicals and publishers: the newspaper and journal trade, 1740–1914* (London, 2009), pp 45–73.   **21** For Robert Hellen, see *Gentleman's Magazine*, 63 (1793), 769; F. Elrington Ball, *The judges in Ireland, 1221–1921* (repr., 2 vols, Dublin, 1993), ii, 218–19. For Dominick Trant, see James Kelly, *'That damn'd thing called honour': duelling in Ireland 1570–1860* (Cork, 1995), pp 145–7; M.J. Bric, 'Priests, parsons and politics: the Rightboy protest in county Cork, 1785–1788', *Past and Present*, 100 (1983), 100–23. Trant was author of *Considerations on the present disturbances in the province of Munster* (Dublin, 1787). **22** Brooke, *Reliques*, pp vii–viii. **23** Ibid., p. viii. **24** Joseph Cooper Walker's *Historical essay on the dress of the ancient and modern Irish* (Dublin, 1788), pp v–vi.

O'Halloran who, seventeen years earlier, had sought to downplay the differences between the Gael and the Old English:

> For, though unhappily for this antient kingdom, *unnatural* distinctions have but too long been kept up by artful and designing enemies, to the almost entire ruin of the whole; yet are we in fact, but *one* people, and as unmixt a race as any in Europe. There is not at this day a Milesian, or descendant of Strongbow, whose bloods are not so intimately blended, that it would be impossible to determine which should preponderate.[25]

In order to emphasize the civility of the ancient Irish, Brooke argued that they had reached a stage of civilization when the rest of Europe was still in a state of barbarism: 'The productions of our Irish bards exhibit a glow of cultivated genius, – a spirit of elevated heroism, – sentiments of pure honor, – instances of disinterested patriotism, and manners of a degree of refinement, totally astonishing, at a period when the rest of Europe was nearly sunk in barbarism!'[26] As proof of this, she drew attention to the poem 'Magnus the Great', arguing that although the poem was most likely written in the Middle Ages, this did not detract from the fact that despite suffering invasion and civil unrest, the Irish had remained a civilized people:

> The ancient Irish have been repeatedly stigmatised with the name of barbarians. Their souls, their manners, and their language, were thought alike incapable of any degree of refinement ... and were we less barbarians, when torn with civil broils, and foreign invasions, than when we were a conquering and flourishing people?[27]

Turning next to members of her own privileged class, Brooke sought to convince them that, in common with the native Irish, they had a rich literary heritage that stretched back to pre-Christian times. She argued that they had every reason to be proud of their 'ancestors' the 'Irish bards': 'and is not all this very honorable to our countrymen? Will they not be benefited, – will they not be gratified, at the lustre reflected on them by ancestors so very different from what modern prejudice has been studious to represent them?'[28]

While Walker and Brooke's engagement with the Gaelic-speaking world may not have been typical of the elite of which they were members, their publications had an important impact on the manner in which the pre-Christian Gaelic past was perceived by members of the Protestant community, and it played a key role in the process of identity formation taking place within their community at that time. The 1798 insurrection had a detrimen-

25 Sylvester O'Halloran, *An introduction to the study of the history and antiquities of Ireland* (Dublin, 1772), p. i.   26 Brooke, *Reliques*, p. vii.   27 Ibid., p. 62.   28 Ibid., p. vii.

tal effect on inquiry into Gaelic antiquity because in its aftermath research into this subject was equated with pro-Gaelic and therefore anti-English sentiment. Antiquarian research became politicized and as Luke Gibbons has noted, it was turned into a battleground between warring political factions.[29] Even Joseph Cooper Walker, who was once such an enthusiast, turned his attention to Italian antiquities. Nevertheless, the publication of *Historical memoirs* and *Reliques of Irish poetry* marked an important stage in the evolving relations between members of the Protestant and Catholic intelligentsia. The co-operation that surrounded the projects enabled native scholars and scribes to enter the public sphere, albeit indirectly, as the providers of the source material that vindicated Gaelic civility and enhanced the esteem in which the Gaelic literary heritage was held. Furthermore, the involvement in publishing of so many of those discussed demonstrates that far from being a hermeneutically sealed world disconnected from the world of print, the Catholic Gaelic-speaking community engaged actively with the English-speaking public sphere throughout the eighteenth century. This engagement was to intensify in the course of the nineteenth century.

29 Luke Gibbons, 'From Ossian to O'Carolan: the bard as separatist symbol' in Fiona Stafford and Howard Gaskill (eds), *From Gaelic to romantic: Ossianic translations* (Amsterdam and Atlanta, 1998), p. 242.

9

A journey from manuscript to print – the transmission of an elegy by Piaras Feiritéar

DEIRDRE NIC MHATHÚNA

This chapter will examine the transmission of 'Mo thraochadh is mo shaoth lém ló thu'[1] – an elegy composed by Piaras Feiritéar (Pierce Ferriter), poet and military leader from the Dingle Peninsula, county Kerry, who flourished between c.1600 and c.1652. The path taken by the poem from its composition in Irish and transmission by manuscript through to its first appearance in print – in English – will be traced in order to illustrate the interaction of the literary and cultural forces that shaped Irish linguistic and literary history from the seventeenth century through to the mid-nineteenth century. The manner in which this was pursued is illustrative of the accommodations, compromises, and, by modern standards, questionable practices involved in making Irish-language texts accessible to a primarily anglophone readership, but it also attests to the extent of the language shift that had taken place in the interval between its composition and its first printing. The survival of Piaras Feiritéar's poetry through the seventeenth, eighteenth and early nineteenth centuries attests to the enduring character of the manuscript tradition in Irish, and of the quality of his compositions. However, once English had superseded Irish as the vernacular of the majority of the population, which was becoming the case by the mid-nineteenth century, translation and its publication in print was increasingly significant if Irish literature was to remain accessible. This generated its own challenges as the edition of 'Mo thraochadh is mo shaoth lém ló thu' produced by its nineteenth-century editor, Thomas Crofton Croker, illustrates.

Piaras Feiritéar was of Anglo-Norman descent. His ancestors are believed to have settled in west Kerry in the early thirteenth century. A member of the minor gentry, he was a military figure of some consequence. He led local Catholic forces in county Kerry during the Confederate wars, playing an active role in the siege of Tralee castle in 1642. Feiritéar was hanged by Cromwellian forces in Killarney c.1652 following the surrender of Ross Castle.[2] He is a central figure in the oral and literary traditions of the Dingle

1 Translation: 'You are [the cause of] my lifelong exhaustion and distress'.   2 Paul MacCotter, 'The Ferriters of Kerry', *Journal of the Kerry Archaeological and Historical*

Deirdre Nic Mhathúna

Peninsula. His status and that of his family is also reflected in the many placenames in the area that bear his name or surname. In addition to his activities as a soldier, Feiritéar was an accomplished poet. Approximately ten of his poems survive, mainly in eighteenth- and nineteenth-century manuscripts. Feiritéar composed in the syllabic metre of the bardic schools and also in the newer accentual verse. His poetry is revealing of his links to the many social and ethnic strands that constituted Irish society in the seventeenth century, as his corpus includes praise-poems to members of such Anglo-Norman families as the Fitzgeralds and the Husseys, and an elegy on a member of the Gaelic O'Brien family. Significantly, Feiritéar also composed a poem in praise of Margaret Russell, a young daughter of the fourth earl of Bedford.[3]

The individual eulogized in 'Mo thraochadh is mo shaoth lém ló thu' is addressed in the first stanza of the poem as 'a Chiarraígh' ('O Kerryman') and as 'a Mhuiris mhic an Ridire ó *Florence*' ('O Maurice, son of the Knight from Florence'), which indicates that he was a member of the Fitzgerald branch which held the title of knight of Kerry.[4] The reference to 't'fheart tar lear i bhFlóndras' ('your grave across the sea in Flanders') and later descriptions of a military funeral clearly indicate a connection with the Spanish army in Flanders. Feiritéar's subject can be identified as the fourth son of William Fitzgerald, 11th knight of Kerry (d. 1640),[5] and may be the Captain Maurice

Society, 2nd series, 2 (2003), 57; Mary Hickson, *Ireland in the seventeenth century or the Irish massacres of 1641–2, their causes and results* (2 vols, London, 1884), ii, 111; John Caball, 'The Siege of Tralee, 1642', *Irish Sword*, 2 (1954–6), 315–17. For brief biographies of Feiritéar, see Máirtín Ó Murchú, 'Feiritéar, Piaras', *ODNB, sub nom.*; and Marc Caball, 'Feiritéar, Piaras (Ferriter, Pierce)', *DIB, sub nom.* **3** The following published works contain editions of Feiritéar's poetry: Pádraig Ua Duinnín (ed.), *Dánta Phiarais Feiritéir* (Baile Átha Cliath, 1903 [edited in English], 2nd edn, 1934 [edited in Irish]); T.F. O'Rahilly, 'A poem by Piaras Feiritéar', *Ériu*, 13 (1942), 113–18; Pádraig de Brún et al. (eds), *Nua-dhuanaire*, 1 (Baile Átha Cliath, 1971). The circumstances of Feiritéar's likely acquaintance with the earl of Bedford through his connection with Richard Boyle, first earl of Cork, are thoroughly investigated in Máire Mhac an tSaoi, *Cérbh í Meg Russell?* (Indreabhán, 2009). For a summary in English, see Máire Mhac an tSaoi, 'Who was Meg Russell?', *The Recorder – The Journal of the American Irish Historical Society*, 13:1 (2000), 62–9. I wish to thank Prof. Ken Nilsen, St Francis Xavier University, Antigonish, Nova Scotia, for drawing my attention to the latter article. **4** It was traditionally understood that the Fitzgerald family originated in Florence, Italy: see C.P. Meehan, *The rise, increase, and exit of the Geraldines, earls of Desmond, and persecution after their fall: translated from the Latin of Dominic O'Daly, O.P., with memoir and notes* (Dublin, [c.1878]), pp 33–4. The long-standing connection between the Fitzgeralds and the Gherardini family of Florence is further discussed in Diarmaid Ó Catháin, 'Some reflexes of Latin learning and of the Renaissance in Ireland, c.1450– c.1600' in Jason Harris and Keith Sidwell (eds), *Making Ireland Roman: Irish neo-Latin writers and the republic of letters* (Cork, 2009), pp 14–35. **5** Charles Mosley (ed.), *Burke's peerage, baronetage and knightage; clan chiefs, Scottish feudal barons*, 107th edn (2 vols, Wilmington, DE, 2003), i, 1436. Various possibilities regarding the identification of Muiris Mac Gearailt are set out in T. Crofton Croker, *The keen of the south of Ireland: as illustrative of Irish political and domestic history, manners, music, and superstitions* (London, 1844), p. 12; Mary Agnes

Fitzgerald documented in Spanish military records until 1641.[6] Two other elegies composed on Muiris Mac Gearailt's death are extant.[7]

The poem 'Mo thraochadh is mo shaoth lém ló thu' is of particular significance within Feiritéar's corpus of poetry for a number of reasons. Firstly, the earliest extant manuscript copy dates to the beginning of the eighteenth century, and is the earliest known copy of any of Feiritéar's poems. Secondly, evidence suggests the elegy was popular with scribes as more copies of this poem survive than of any other poem now recognized as part of Feiritéar's *oeuvre*. Thirdly, at fifty-six stanzas, it is the longest poem in the extant corpus of Feiritéar's poetry. In addition, 'Mo thraochadh is mo shaoth lém ló thu' was the first of Feiritéar's poems to appear in print, albeit in translation.

Ten manuscript copies of 'Mo thraochadh is mo shaoth lém ló thu' are extant. They are, in chronological order: RIA MS 23 M 34; NUIM Murphy MS 95; NUIM MS B 11; TCD MS 1391; RIA MS 23 E 16; RIA MS 23 C 19; NUIM Murphy MS 7; Irish Jesuit Archives MS 8; RIA MS 24 A 6 and RIA MS 12 O 7. The earliest of these, RIA MS 23 M 34, is an acephalous copy penned by Eoghan Ó Caoimh (1656–1726) at some point between 1684 and 1707, and more than likely nearer the latter date.[8] While the incomplete nature of this copy and the poor condition of the surviving text mean that it is of limited value as a basis for an edition of the poem, it is an important contribution to our knowledge of its transmission. The earliest complete copy of the poem, NUIM Murphy MS 95, was penned by Seán Ó Murchú na Ráithíneach (1700–62) for Seán Builléad of Carrignavar, county Cork, in 1754 or 1755.[9]

Textual evidence suggests the extant copies of the poem can be divided into two distinct groups based on the order in which the verses occur. The first group consists of RIA MS 23 M 34, NUIM Murphy MS 95, RIA MS 23 E 16, RIA MS 23 C 19, NUIM Murphy MS 7, and RIA MS 12 O 7, the second of NUIM MS B 11, TCD MS 1391, Irish Jesuit Archives MS 8, and RIA MS 24 A 6. While two distinct variations of the poem have been transmitted, the variation in the order of the verses has little impact on the sense or style of the poem.

Hickson, *Selections from old Kerry records* [2nd series], (London, 1874), pp 224–6; Ua Duinnín, *Dánta Phiarais Feiritéir* (1934 ed.), p. 131.   6 Gráinne Henry, *The Irish military community in Spanish Flanders, 1586–1621* (Dublin, 1992), p. 181, n. 59.   7 These are 'A bháis, ar mharbhais Muiris?' ('O Death, did you slay Muiris?') composed by Diarmaid Ó Dálaigh and 'Bean chaite cheardcha an ghaisgidh' ('The exhausted woman of the warrior's forge') by Muiris Óg Ó Gearáin. Both are found in RIA MS 23 L 17, at pp 36–7 and 128–9 respectively. For further details on this manuscript, see T.F. O'Rahilly et al., *Catalogue of Irish manuscripts in the Royal Irish Academy* (Dublin, 1926–70) pp 19–26.   8 O'Rahilly et al., *Catalogue of Irish manuscripts in the Royal Irish Academy*, pp 63–4, 72. For information on Eoghan Ó Caoimh, see Breandán Ó Conchúir, *Scríobhaithe Chorcaí, 1700–1850* (Baile Átha Cliath, 1982), pp 33–6.   9 Pádraig Ó Fiannachta, *Lámhscríbhinní Gaeilge Choláiste Phádraig, Má Nuad*, fasc. 3 (Má Nuad, 1966), pp 103, 105. For information on Seán Ó Murchú na Ráithíneach, see Ó Conchúir, *Scríobhaithe Chorcaí*, pp 167–72.

The publication in 1844 of Thomas Crofton Croker's *The keen of the south of Ireland* was a significant milestone in the transmission of the poetry of Piaras Feiritéar.[10] Croker published eighteen compositions, which he designated 'specimens of the keen', in translation, accompanied by a lengthy preface contextualizing the material for a readership unfamiliar with the tradition of keening. Seán Ó Tuama has credited *The keen of the south of Ireland* with providing vital evidence regarding the prevalence of keening in counties Cork and Kerry in the nineteenth century.[11] It remains an important source and reference work for studies of the *genre*.[12]

'Mo thraochadh is mo shaoth lém ló thu' was entitled 'Keen on Maurice Fitzgerald, Knight of Kerry' in Croker's anthology.[13] A slightly abridged version of Croker's text had previously been included by Lady Henrietta Chatterton in *Rambles in the south of Ireland*, which was published in London in 1839.[14] However, the publication of *The keen of the south of Ireland* marked the first occasion a poem by Feiritéar appeared in print in its entirety, albeit in the form of an English translation. A short introduction, which includes a pedigree of the knights of Kerry provided by Sir William Betham, accompanied the poem.

Several seminal collections of Irish-language poetry were published in the half century prior to the publication of *The keen of the south of Ireland*. Croker was fully aware of this emerging tradition; he personally possessed copies of Charlotte Brooke's *Reliques of Irish poetry* (1789) and James Hardiman's *Irish minstrelsy* (1831).[15] Croker held the editor of *Reliques of Irish poetry* in high esteem, referring to her as 'the accomplished Miss Brooke'.[16] Referring to the inclusion by Brooke of the original Irish texts in *Reliques of Irish poetry*, he observed approvingly that 'to prevent doubt, the originals are given, with

10 T. Crofton Croker, *The keen of the south of Ireland: as illustrative of Irish political and domestic history, manners, music, and superstitions* (London, 1844).   11 Seán Ó Tuama, *Caoineadh Airt Uí Laoghaire* (Baile Átha Cliath, 1961), pp 21–2.   12 See, for example, Seán Ó Coileáin, 'The Irish lament: an oral genre', *Studia Hibernica*, 24 (1988), 97–117; L.M. Cullen, 'The contemporary and later politics of "Caoineadh Airt Uí Laoire"', *Eighteenth-Century Ireland / Iris an Dá Chultúr*, 8 (1993), 7–38; Breandán Ó Buachalla, *An caoine agus an chaointeoireacht* (Baile Átha Cliath, 1998).   13 It would appear that Muiris Mac Gearailt (Maurice Fitzgerald) never held the title of Knight, however.   14 Lady Chatterton, *Rambles in the south of Ireland during the year 1838* (2 vols, London, 1839), i, 250–62.   15 Miss [Charlotte] Brooke, *Reliques of Irish poetry: consisting of heroic poems, odes, elegies, and songs, translated into English verse: with notes explanatory and historical; and the originals in the Irish character, to which is subjoined an Irish tale* (Dublin, 1789); James Hardiman, *Irish minstrelsy or bardic remains of Ireland with English poetical translations* (2 vols, London, 1831). These are listed as items no. 211 and 392, respectively, in *Catalogue of the greater part of the library of the late Thomas Crofton Croker* (London, 1854). Also listed are John O'Daly, *Poets and poetry of Munster, a selection of Irish songs, with the original music* (Dublin, 1850) [item 621] and John O'Daly, *Reliques of Irish Jacobite poetry*, parts 1 & 2 [listed under item 634; no further details given]. The last of these was first published in Dublin in 1844, the same year as *The keen of the south of Ireland*.   16 Croker, *The keen*, p. 38.

translations, elegantly versified, and literal in the extreme.'[17] Croker did not provide the original Irish-language texts in his own publication, nor did he offer a reason for not including them. In two instances, however, he printed verses in Irish in a script based on English orthography.[18] One of these verses is introduced in the preface to 'Keen on Young Drinan' as follows: 'For the amusement of the English reader, the sixth verse ... is here written according to the sound on the ear.'[19] Croker's claim that 'it will be however sufficient to enable the Irish scholar to recognize the closeness of the translation' is consistent with his view, previously expressed with regard to *Reliques of Irish poetry*, that the provision of the original text would serve to promote the fidelity of the translation.[20] This concurs with the assessment offered by Lesa Ní Mhunghaile of Brooke's possible motives for including the original Irish texts:

> It is likely that her desire to offer authentic texts motivated Charlotte to publish the originals in the Gaelic typeface because very few, if indeed any, of her readers would have been able to comprehend the Irish characters or understand the Irish. Her aim, therefore, was to prove the existence of her source material rather than expect it to be read.[21]

Croker informs us that 'the original is in an Irish MS. volume (p. 65), belonging to Dr Lee of Hartwell, lent to me by Lieutenant Hall, of the 17th Foot, and in which the author is stated to have been Pierce Ferriter.'[22] This manuscript was also the source for 'Keen on John Fitzgerald'.[23] In his introduction to the latter poem, Croker reproduced the following note by Lee, which, we are told, was contained in the manuscript:

> John Lee, Colworth. These poems were written for me from old MSS. during the winter of 1806 and 1807, at Cork, by the favour and assistance of Mr. Flyn, a learned grocer of that town, who introduced me to an old schoolmaster well skilled in ancient Irish history and mythology.[24]

On first consideration, it would appear that the manuscript referred to is that now known as NUIM MS B 11, since 'Mo thraochadh is mo shaoth lém ló thu' is also found at page 65 of that manuscript.[25] NUIM MS B 11 was writ-

---

17 Croker, *Researches in the south of Ireland*, p. 336.   18 Such a script was usually associated in pre-Famine Ireland with printing within the Catholic tradition: see Niall Ó Cíosáin, 'Print in Irish, 1570–1900: an exception among the Celtic Languages?', *Radharc*, 5/7 (2004–6), 73–106.   19 Croker, *The keen*, pp 95–6. The other example is on p. xi. Several lines of verse in the Irish language appear within a quote from 'Lloyd in his *Archaeologia Britannica*' on p. x.   20 Ibid., p. 96.   21 Lesa Ní Mhunghaile (ed.), *Charlotte Brooke's Reliques of Irish poetry* (Dublin, 2009), p. xxx.   22 Croker, *The keen*, p. 12.   23 Ibid., pp 43–52.   24 Ibid., p. 43.   25 For a description of this manuscript and its contents, see Pádraig Ó Fiannachta, *Lámhscríbhinní Gaeilge Choláiste Phádraig, Má*

ten by Éamann Ó Mathúna (d. 1822), Donncha (Bán) Ó Floinn (*c*.1760–1830) and his son, Donncha Óg Ó Floinn (*c*.1802–84).[26] The first two of these individuals certainly fit Lee's description of 'an old schoolmaster well skilled in ancient Irish history and mythology' and a 'learned grocer'. Indeed, Ó Floinn referred to Ó Mathúna as 'Oide léinn i gCaisleán Uí Liatháin' ('a master of learning in Castlelyons').[27] The transcription of 'Mo thraochadh is mo shaoth lém ló thu' in NUIM MS B 11 was Ó Mathúna's work.[28] However, if NUIM MS B 11 was the manuscript to which Croker was referring, it does not appear that the copy of 'Mo thraochadh is mo shaoth lém ló thu' in that manuscript provided the basis for the translation published in *The keen of the south of Ireland*.

RIA MS 12 O 7 contains poems, textual and linguistic notes by the scribe David Murphy and letters he wrote to Croker. 'Mo thraochadh is mo shaoth lém ló thu' is found at pp 449–65, preceded by a translation of the text entitled 'My weariness and dullness thou art for ever' (pp 439–48). Directly following Murphy's transcription of the original poem is a copy of an elegy on Seaghan Mac Gearailt (John Fitzgerald), which begins 'Mo dhíth, mo dheacair, mo mhairg ar chéadaibh'. As mentioned above, a translation of this elegy was included by Croker in *The keen of the south of Ireland*.[29] Both of these elegies are also found in RIA MS 23 E 16, a collection of loose leaves penned by Mícheál Óg Ó Longáin and gathered together by the scribe in 1809.[30] Ó Longáin was also a close associate of Ó Floinn.[31] This manuscript was sometime in the possession of Sir William Betham as evidenced by the presence of his bookplate on the inside of the front cover. The text of 'Mo thraochadh is mo shaoth lém ló thu' as found in RIA MS 23 E 16 is close to that of RIA MS 12 O 7. The order of verses in these two manuscripts is identical, and significantly different to that in NUIM MS B 11. The evidence suggests that RIA MS 23 E 16, or a manuscript closely related to it, was used by Murphy as his exemplar.

The text of 'Mo thraochadh is mo shaoth lém ló thu' in RIA MS 12 O 7 and the preceding English translation are found in a portion of the manuscript which contains material once in Croker's possession that was subsequently acquired by his fellow antiquarian John Windele (1801–65).[32] A titlepage with the words 'correspondence & Irish transcriptions of David Murphy with Thomas Crofton Croker' accompanies this latter section, followed by an

Nuad, fasc. 6 (Má Nuad, 1969), pp 87–94.   **26** Ó Fiannachta, *Lámhscríbhinní Gaeilge Choláiste Phádraig, Má Nuad*, fasc. 6, p. 87. For further information on Donncha (Bán) Ó Floinn, Donncha Óg Ó Floinn and Ó Mathúna, see Ó Conchúir, *Scríobhaithe Chorcaí*, pp 69–77, 77–8 and 159 respectively.   **27** Ó Conchúir, *Scríobhaithe Chorcaí*, p. 159.   **28** Ó Fiannachta, *Lámhscríbhinní Gaeilge Choláiste Phádraig, Má Nuad*, fasc. 6, pp 87, 91.   **29** The first line of the elegy on Seaghan Mac Gearailt may be translated as 'My loss, my sorrow, my woe shared by hundreds'.   **30** O'Rahilly et al., *Catalogue of Irish manuscripts in the Royal Irish Academy*, pp 1370–400.   **31** Ó Conchúir, *Scríobhaithe Chorcaí*, p. 73.   **32** O'Rahilly et al., *Catalogue of Irish manuscripts in the Royal Irish Academy*, pp 3470–9.

intriguing note signed by Windele: 'N.B. Croker was enabled to pass as an Irish scholar by means of this Murphy. Jnᵒ Windele'.³³ As both title and note are in the same hand, it would appear that these were added when Windele acquired the manuscript. Notwithstanding the criticism implicit in Windele's observation, his statement serves to draw attention to an issue that is central to any assessment of Croker's research involving Irish-language sources, namely, his level of proficiency in Irish. Opinions vary as to whether it was of a sufficient standard to allow him to translate complex texts, as claimed in *The keen of the south of Ireland*. His contemporary, Lady Chatterton, and the twentieth-century folklorist Richard Dorson have both accepted without question Croker's assertion that he translated the Irish material.³⁴ Others have been more circumspect in their appraisal of his ability in the Irish language, with W.J. Mc Cormack and Neil C. Hultin both concluding that he had a certain level of competence, but that he was by no means an expert.³⁵ B.G. MacCarthy is still more critical; she has asserted that 'there is strong evidence to support the view that of the Irish language he never had more than a smattering.'³⁶ This conclusion is supported by Séamus Ua Casaide's echo of Windele's assertion that Murphy's role was more central to Croker's endeavour than that of amanuensis; he observed that Croker 'was assisted in the Irish part of his literary work by an Irish scholar named David Murphy.'³⁷ The processes at play in the production of the translated texts published by Croker will be investigated below, as will the nature of Murphy's contribution.

Thomas Crofton Croker (1798–1854), the son of an army major, was born in Cork city into a family described as 'Protestant, well connected, and respectable.'³⁸ Significantly, his maternal great-grandfather, Revd Charles Bunworth (*c*.1704–72), rector of Buttevant, county Cork, is said to have held the position of 'umpire or president' at *cúirteanna éigse* (poetic courts) at Bruree, county Limerick between 1730 and 1750.³⁹ Employed by the British

33 This note is inaccurately reproduced in O'Rahilly et al., *Catalogue of Irish manuscripts in the Royal Irish Academy*, p. 3476. 34 Chatterton, *Rambles in the south of Ireland*, p. 250; Richard M. Dorson, 'The first group of British folklorists', *Journal of American Folklore*, 68:267 (Jan.–Mar., 1955), 4. 35 W.J. Mc Cormack, 'Croker, Thomas Crofton (1798–1854)', *ODNB*, *sub nom.*; Neil C. Hultin, 'Mrs. Harrington, Mrs. Leary, Mr. Croker and the "Irish Howl"', *Éire/Ireland*, 20 (Winter 1985), 47, n.15. 36 B.G. MacCarthy, 'Thomas Crofton Croker 1798–1854', *Studies*, 32 (1943), 542. 37 Séamus Ua Casaide, 'Birthplace of Tadhg Gaedhlach', *Journal of the Waterford and South-East of Ireland Archaeological Society* (Jan.–Mar. 1915), 27. 38 Maureen Murphy, 'Croker, Thomas Crofton', *DIB*, *sub nom.* 39 *Catalogue of the greater part of the library of the late Thomas Crofton Croker*, p. 16. For biographical and contextual information regarding Bunworth, see Diarmaid Ó Catháin, 'Revd Charles Bunworth of Buttevant: patron of harpers and poets', *Journal of the Cork Historical and Archaeological Society*, 102 (1997), 111–20. I am grateful to Diarmaid Ó Catháin for bringing this article to my attention and for also suggesting other important lines of enquiry: see footnotes 4 and 80. For a comprehensive study of the *cúirteanna éigse* in Munster, see Breandán Ó Conchúir, 'Na cúirteanna éigse i

Admiralty from 1818, Croker spent most of his adult life living near London.[40] Nonetheless, the customs and traditions of the people of his native Cork and the surrounding countryside, which first caught his attention while in his teens, proved a source of lifelong fascination. Croker's interest prompted him to offer numerous contributions on the subject to *Fraser's Magazine* and to produce publications such as *Researches in the south of Ireland* (1824) and *Fairy legends and traditions of the south of Ireland* (1825).[41] A number of Croker's friends contributed significantly to the latter work, when, shortly before publication, he lost the manuscript he had prepared. *Fairy legends* was first published anonymously; the second edition was accompanied by Croker's name only. Croker's fame was largely built on the success of *Fairy legends*, which was highly praised by Walter Scott and Wilhelm Grimm, among others, though the lack of recognition afforded his collaborators was a source of unease to many contemporary and subsequent generations of scholars.[42]

Croker makes some allusion in *The keen of the south of Ireland* to his knowledge of Irish which suggested that he was proficient in the language. When recounting a trip to Gougane Barra, county Cork, in 1813, he explains that he was required to ask for assistance in order to understand a song which was rousing much interest among those present: 'as I was *then* ignorant of the Irish language, and anxious to know the meaning of what had elicited so much popular approbation, I applied to an old woman near whom I sat, for an explanation or translation, which she readily gave me ...'.[43] The suggestion is, of course, that the editor no longer required such assistance at the time of writing. One of Croker's principal sources for the keens he published was a woman called Mrs Harrington, whom he first met in 1818. Described by Croker as 'a true representative of the expiring race of Bardic Ireland', Mrs Harrington provided him with English translations.[44] The readiness with which she performed this task was much admired by Croker: 'Her memory was, indeed, extraordinary; and the clearness, quickness, and eloquence, with which she translated from the Irish into the English, though unable to read or write, was almost incredible.'[45] Croker's description of the process of his transcription and subsequent publication of material from Mrs Harrington

gCúige Mumhan' in Pádraigín Riggs et al. (eds), *Saoi na héigse* (Baile Átha Cliath, 2000), pp 55–81.   40 Murphy, 'Croker, Thomas Crofton'.   41 T. Crofton Croker, *Researches in the south of Ireland, illustrative of the scenery, architectural remains and the manners and superstitions of the peasantry with an appendix containing a private narrative of the rebellion of 1798* (London, 1824); [idem,] *Fairy legends and traditions of the south of Ireland* (London, 1825). 42 Dorson, 'The first group of British folklorists', pp 1–2, MacCarthy, 'Thomas Crofton Croker 1798–1854', pp 547–54. For a related discussion of Croker's approach to the editing of Joseph Holt's memoirs, see Ruan O'Donnell and Bob Reece, '"A Clean Beast": Crofton Croker's fairy tale of General Holt', *Eighteenth-Century Ireland / Iris an Dá Chultúr*, 7 (1992), 7–42.   43 Croker, *The keen*, p. xx (my emphasis).   44 Ibid., p. xxiv. 45 Ibid.

seeks to emphasize the veracity of his source material: 'From the keens which I took down after this woman's recitation, literal translations of four were published in *Researches in the south of Ireland*.'[46] One would infer that since Croker required English translations from Mrs Harrington, it was these that he transcribed, and not the Irish originals. Several of these translations were later published in *The keen of the south of Ireland*. During a visit to Ireland in 1825, Croker learned that Mrs Harrington had died several years previously. Hearing that a keening woman named Mrs Leary had surpassed all others at Mrs Harrington's wake, he sought her out and finally made her acquaintance in 1829.[47] Mrs Leary, too, provided him with many keens and introduced him to 'an old man named Murray, who styled himself "a land surveyor and Philomath", who had some knowledge of the Irish language.'[48] Murray, in turn, provided Croker with the 'Keen on Mr Hugh Power'.[49] Croker did not seek to conceal his dependence on others for these texts: 'from these oral sources and from three or four manuscripts, for the communication of which the editor is indebted to Dr Lee of Hartwell, to Lucius O'Brien, Bart., and to Sir William Betham, the present selection of specimens of the keen of the south of Ireland has been made'.[50] Despite the distinction he drew here between oral and manuscript sources, Croker does not discuss any differences in the type of material contained in those sources. In presenting all his material as 'specimens of the keen' no distinction is made between those compositions which can properly be termed keens and which were principally transmitted through oral culture, and the more formal elegies composed in the accentual *caoineadh* metre that are found in manuscript sources. It is to this latter category that 'Mo thraochadh is mo shaoth lém ló thu' belongs.

In addition to the information provided on the sources used in its preparation, contributions by others are also acknowledged in *The keen of the south of Ireland*. Perhaps mindful of the controversy which surrounded *Fairy legends*, a clear attempt is made to show who is responsible for particular aspects of *The keen of the south of Ireland*. The title-page asserts that the material was 'collected, edited, and chiefly translated by T. Crofton Croker'. Significantly, a second heading accompanying each keen attributes the translation to an individual. Of the eighteen texts contained in *The keen*, fifteen, including the 'Keen on Maurice Fitzgerald', were 'translated from the Irish by the editor', two were translated by 'Mr Callanan' and one was 'versified by a lady, and communicated to the editor by Mr Maurice O'Connell.'[51] Referring to the latter composition, Croker acknowledged that 'a literal translation, which the editor obtained in 1818 from Mrs Harrington, was printed by him in *Researches in the south of Ireland*'.[52] Indeed, many of the texts had previously appeared in other publications, specifically *Researches in the south of Ireland*

---

46 Ibid., p. xxv.　47 Ibid., p. xxv–xxvi.　48 Ibid., p. xxvi.　49 Ibid., p. 66.　50 Ibid., pp xxvi–vii.　51 Ibid., p. 77.　52 Ibid.

and *Fraser's Magazine*, and this information, too, is usually given in the introduction to each text. Additionally, in his main introduction, Croker acknowledges the 'many marks of polite attention which he has received from several
parties to whom he had occasion to apply for information, especially from the
right hon. the Knight of Kerry and the Knight of Glin.'[53]

In 1829, when Croker was about to return to England following a visit to
his mother's house in Cork, he encouraged Mrs Leary to compose a keen on
his imminent departure. Croker writes that after some persuasion, his

> proposition, which was accompanied by a couple of shillings, pro-
> duced, almost without a moment's consideration, ... verses in Irish,
> which the editor took down as recited, and has since translated with
> the greatest fidelity.[54]

We are also informed that the verses, which are included in *The keen of the
south of Ireland*, were first published in *Fraser's Magazine*.[55] Described by
B.G. MacCarthy as having been published with 'guileless egoism',[56] both the
text of this 'keen' and the contextual information given by Croker as to the
circumstances that gave rise to its composition are revealing of his *modus
operandi*. Croker's earlier statement that he transcribed material as it was
being recited is corroborated by Mrs Leary's words, as the following extract
attests:

> Of hearing your voice, too,
> I never would weary,
> When you'd say, 'Here's a shilling
> For you, Mrs. Leary.
> Come sit here beside me,
> A keen I delight in;
> While you sing one, I'll take it
> down from you in writing'.[57]

Mrs Leary's appearance the evening before Croker was due to return to
England prompted a companion to enquire if she was his nurse, to which
Croker responded 'No, not my nurse, but a far more extraordinary woman in
her way – a keener.'[58] It transpires that Croker's companion was not far off
the mark, however, as Croker's nurse did indeed provide material for *The
keen of the south of Ireland*. Referring to 'Keen on Young Drinan', Croker
states that 'The original was obtained from the editor's nurse, in April
1829'.[59] The fact that Croker maintained contact into adulthood with the

53 Ibid., p. lviii. 54 Ibid., p. 102. 55 Ibid., pp 102–3. 56 MacCarthy, 'Thomas
Crofton Croker 1798–1854', p. 544. 57 Croker, *The keen*, p. 102. 58 Ibid., p. 101. 59
Ibid., p. 95.

Irish-speaking woman who had been his wet-nurse in infancy is evidence of the close ties that sometimes existed between members of different social and linguistic strata in nineteenth-century Ireland.

Although David Murphy's is not credited as a translator nor among those whose assistance is acknowledged by Croker, his name occurs in a different context, namely as the author of a poem conveyed to Croker and accompanied by the statement 'translated from the Irish by the editor'. Murphy is effusive in his praise of 'the well fed scholar, of the cheerful face' and credits him with drawing long overdue attention to Irish poetry:

> To Crofton Croker
>
> O well fed scholar, of the cheerful face,
> How neat your hand to plane and polish verse is!
> To English turning, with a silken grace,
> The branchy Irish, that so sweet and terse is.
>
> Early and late, once proudly sung the bard,
> The glowing strains his busy brain created;
> And surely on such honied fame 'twas hard
> That none his valued stores should have translated.
>
> But Erin's long neglected minstrelsy,
> Thy skill will save – nor shall it be neglected;
> A merry champion has it found in thee,
> Who seeks to make our country's name respected.
>
> Ceangal.
> Go on! and prosper, make a glorious gleaning,
> I pray the Fays may aid you in your keening.[60]

Letters in RIA MS 12 O 7 reveal much about the nature of the work carried out by Murphy and suggest that he performed an important function as a bridge to the Irish tradition in the years during which Croker was preparing *The keen of the south of Ireland*. A native of Kinsale, county Cork, David Murphy was employed as an Irish scripture reader in London.[61] While biographical information is limited, some valuable details can be gleaned from his surviving letters to Croker. He was living in London during the earlier years of their correspondence – three separate addresses in that city are given at various dates. The letters date from 17 July 1833 to 27 September 1841, by which time Murphy had emigrated to Canada. He was a member of the Irish

---

60 Ibid., p. lix. Two copies of a draft English translation of this poem in David Murphy's hand are found at RIA 12 O 7, p. 575 [*recte* 574c] and 574e.   61 Pádraig de Brún, *Scriptural instruction in the vernacular – the Irish Society and its teachers, 1818–1827* (Dublin, 2009), p. 38, n. 2.

Society for Promoting the Education of the Native Irish through the Medium
of their Own Language, a society founded in Dublin in 1818 to provide scriptural instruction through Irish.[62] Murphy published a book of Irish hymns
entitled *Laoithe Chruit Ársa na hÉireann* in 1835.[63] He was also involved in
the preparation of an English-Irish dictionary, a prospectus for which is
inserted within the leaves of RIA MS 12 O 7.[64] He was greatly concerned
with the preservation of Irish-language material, but his efforts 'in regard of
forming a little Society, to enable us to get up an Irish Library' were
thwarted by the Irish Society on the grounds that 'it would injure the cause
we are advocating in bringing people to read the holy scriptures.'[65]

It is interesting to note that while the principal language of his correspondence with Croker is English, Murphy occasionally included short
phrases in Irish. One letter ends with the words 'A shaoí/ do shearbh-
fóghantuígh gnáthach / Daibhí Ó Murchadha' (Dear scholar/ Your humble
servant, David Murphy).[66] A lengthy letter written by Murphy after he had
emigrated from England to Canada is much warmer in tone than the earlier
correspondence, which was at times rather perfunctory. The letter ends with
the following bilingual wish:

> I must conclude by biding [*sic*] you slán iomlán acht ní go bráth, ta
> muingí[n] – agam go bh-feicfidh me arís tu le cúngnamh Dé me
> bheith slán 7 tusa mar an gcéadna. And Sir believe me to be your ever
> grateful and most humble servant David Murphy.[67]

62 For an in-depth study of the Irish Society, see de Brún, *Scriptural instruction in the vernacular.*   63 D.O.M., *Laoithe chruit ársa na hÉireann* (London, 1835). The copy of this
title in TCD library is inscribed by 'the author, David Murphy'. Murphy asks Croker's
assistance in promoting such an undertaking in Murphy to Croker, Aug. 1834 (RIA MS
12 O 7, p. 551). Murphy also contributed to Norman McLeod, *The psalms of David in the
Irish language, now for the first time rendered into metre, for the use of the native Irish*
(London, 1836) and published a religious tract entitled 'Is ceart dona boicht an Biobla
leigheadh': see de Brún, *Scriptural instruction in the vernacular*, pp 37–8 and Ua Casaide,
'Birthplace of Tadhg Gaedhlach', p. 27.   64 The prospectus is bound between the leaves
of Murphy to Croker, 22 Apr. 1839 (RIA 12 O 7, pp 568a–568d). It clearly states the
proselytizing aim of the endeavour. Recognizing 'the use and importance of the Irish language as a vehicle of instruction to the native peasantry of the country, it is proposed to
publish an *English-Irish Dictionary*, in a full and complete form, to facilitate the study and
acquirement of that language.' A '*standard pronunciation* of the Irish language' would be
included. Prospective subscribers are invited to direct enquiries to Rev Henry Hamilton
Beamish or Mr David Murphy, Irish Scripture Reader, West-Street Chapel.' These are
undoubtedly the 'Irishman, who has spoken it [Irish], as his *mother-tongue*, from his *youth*;
and who has made the deep study of it the principal occupation of years' and the
'*Clergyman* of the *Church of England*' described as responsible for the Irish and English
sections of the dictionary, respectively.   65 Murphy to Croker, 8 Nov. 1833 (RIA MS 12
O 7, p. 542a).   66 Murphy to Croker, Aug. 1834 (RIA MS 12 O 7, p. 551).   67 Murphy
to Croker, 27 Sep. 1841 (RIA MS 12 O 7, p. 574). The Irish portion of Murphy's saluta-
tion may be translated as 'a complete farewell but not forever, I am confident I will see
you again; God willing I shall remain well and you likewise.'

The extent of Murphy's collaboration with Croker is apparent from their surviving correspondence. In one letter, Murphy refers to 'lines composed for the Duke of Wellington' for which 'I have given a litteral [*sic*] translation. I am sure you will put it in good rhyme, if you think it any good.'[68] In the light of this observation, it is also likely that Murphy's translation of 'Mo thraochadh is mo shaoth lém ló thu' was also created as a 'crib' to be reworked by Croker.[69] The number of emendations made to the English text, and the rather inelegant hand, suggest Murphy was translating directly from an Irish exemplar as he worked. Several words are glossed and in some instances the Irish word is given. In contrast, his transcription of the original poem is in a careful, regular hand and contains only a small number of corrections. In addition to the occasional glosses that accompanied Murphy's translation, a more extensive discussion of several words is appended to a letter dated 7 November 1835. Included here is a discussion of the adjective 'bómhar' (abounding in cattle) where Murphy says he benefited from the knowledge of 'one Maurice O Connor a poor Irish man living near the spot' who could 'tell many stories about the Kerry mountains and was very well versed in the keens'.[70] Murphy's letters display an astute understanding of the aims of translation and of the relationship between text and audience. After requesting Croker's honest opinion of other English translations he had prepared, he adds 'if you think the translation unnecessary, I would get them done without, as the intent is to serve the Irish speaking people'.[71]

A close examination of the translation of 'Mo thraochadh is mo shaoth lém ló thu' published in *The keen of the south of Ireland* and that penned by Murphy in RIA MS 12 O 7 reveals much about the process involved in the preparation of Croker's published text. The translated text in RIA MS 12 O 7 is preceded by the colophon 'Pierce Ferriter composed, on the death of Maurice Fitzgerald the Knight of Kerry, who died in Flanders'.[72] A comparison of the first verse in the two versions casts considerable light on the aims of each writer:

> Mo thraochadh is mo shaoth lém ló thu
> a Chiarraígh id chianluí i gcomhrainn,

---

68 Murphy to Croker, 17 July 1833 (RIA MS 12 O 7, p. 523).   69 Charlotte Brooke may have similarly been provided with literal translations in English of Irish poems: Ní Mhunghaile (ed.), *Charlotte Brooke's Reliques of Irish Poetry*, pp xxv–xxvi.   70 Murphy to Croker, 7 Nov. 1835 (RIA MS 12 O 7, p. 559).   71 Murphy to Croker, 11 June 1835 (RIA MS 12 O 7, p. 555). Niall Ó Ciosáin has observed that it was not necessary for Catholic catechisms and other devotional works published in Irish in the early nineteenth century and directed at a lay readership to contain translations: 'the title page was frequently in English (though this was by no means a universal feature), but the text was entirely in Irish ...; none included translations, since the readers did not need them.': Ó Ciosáin, 'Print in Irish, 1570–1900: an exception among the Celtic languages?', p. 83.   72 The words 'son of Gerald' which preceded 'Fitzgerald' have been crossed out. The surname 'Mac Gearailt' (Fitzgerald) is literally translated as 'son of Gerald.'

mo chreach t'fheart tar lear i bhFlóndras,
a Mhuiris mhic an Ridire ó *Florence*.   Edition, verse 1

My weariness and dullness thou art for ever.
Oh! Kerryonian your remote lying in a coffin,
My distress your grave beyond the seas in Flanders
Thou Maurice son of the Knight from Florence   Murphy, verse 1

My woe and my dullness
For ever and ever;
O Chieftain of Kerry!
Is that death should us sever.
That in Flanders you're coffined
Far away from my sight
O Maurice! brave son
Of the Florentine Knight.   Croker, *The keen*, verse 1[73]

Murphy's text is a literal rendering of the original Irish text, while Croker's
text is similar in meaning, but metrically more ambitious. The third verse
displays Croker's reliance on Murphy's literal translation:

M'úidh leat is mo shúil go mór riot,
's an chinniúin do chiorrú na comhairle,
mar do rug an cnoc luch mar thoirrcheas
's na seacht mbliana i ndiachair thórmaigh.   Edition, verse 3

Abroad and I expecting thee impatient
About the destiny that shorten'd the council
As the Hill brought forth a mouse for pregnance
And the seven years after springing.   Murphy, verse 3

That heart which with dreams
Of the future throbbed high
As it saw the proud council
In humbleness lie;
Now resembles the hill
Which for seven long years
Swell'd up, when a small mouse
Its offspring appears.   Croker, *The keen*, verse 3

73 'Edition' denotes quotations from an edition of 'Mo thraochadh is mo shaoth lém ló
thu' in Deirdre Nic Mhathúna, 'Filíocht Phiarais Feiritéar: cnuasach dánta' (unpublished
PhD thesis, UCC, 2 vols, 2008). The edition, based primarily on NUIM MS Murphy 95,
is currently being prepared for publication. The quatrain references are identical with
those of Ua Duinnín's 1934 edition of the poem (see note 3 above). 'Murphy' refers to the
translation of the poem by David Murphy in RIA MS 12 O 7 while 'Croker, *The keen*'
refers to the text published by Croker in *The keen of the south of Ireland*.

Murphy's rendering of 'comhairle' as 'council' in his translation in RIA 12 O 7 prompted Croker to interpret this as a reference to 'The parliament of England', as detailed in his corresponding footnote, thereby overlooking 'counsel', an alternative meaning of 'comhairle'. In the eighth verse, however, it is Croker's translation that most closely matches the literal meaning of the original. The fourth line of this verse in the original – 'ní chaoinid mná sí an sórd san' ('fairy women do not keen the likes of them') – has been incorrectly translated by Murphy:

Insa Daingean níor chaigil an ceólghol
gur ghlac eagla ceannaithe an chnósda;
dá n-eagla féin níor bhaol dóibhsean:
ní chaoinid mná sí an sórd san.   Edition, verse 8

In Dingle the lamentation did not cease
Till busy Merchants got afraid,
Hiding themselves, tho they need not fear.
Such as this is not a Banshee's Wailing   Murphy, verse 8

At Dingle the merchants
In terror forsook
Their ships and their business;
They trembled and shook.
Some fled to concealment,
The fools – thus to fly!
For no trader a Banshee
Will utter a cry.   Croker, *The keen*, verse 8

That Croker consulted an alternative source in relation to this verse is clear from the accompanying footnote, where he states 'This is the verse quoted by Dr O'Brien in his Irish dictionary, to show that the banshee is solely a spiritual aristocratic appendage.'[74] O'Brien's dictionary, first published in Paris in 1768, is referred to on several occasion in Croker's footnotes.[75] Several other footnotes are clearly dependent on notes added by Murphy to his translated text, or are based on his literal translations. In none of these instances is Murphy's contribution acknowledged.[76]

In the twelfth verse, Croker's version displays his considerable skill in rendering the literal translation in rhyme while retaining the meaning:

---

74 Croker, *The keen*, p. 18. The verse is referred to in O'Brien's dictionary *sv* síth-bhrog: see [John O'Brien], *Focalóir Gaoidhilge-Sax-Bhéarla; or, an Irish-English dictionary* (Paris, 1768), pp 437–8. The entry is quoted extensively in Croker, *The keen*, p. 15.   75 Ibid., pp 15, 16, 17, 18, 19.   76 Examples include notes on the following: 'Glen Fogra' (p. 16), 'Carah Mona' (p. 17) and 'Kinalmeaky' (p. 17). Page numbers refer to Croker, *The keen*.

Gidh eadh, a ghleacaí, a chaptaoin chródha,
tig do dhamain in aisling shróllchuilt,
ionam féin do shaoth gur thomhaiseas
t'éagsa tar éag *Caesair* Rómha.   Edition, verse 12

But Oh Wrestler! Oh! valiant Captain
Thy news cometh in a silken dream
In due time you measured enough,
Your death exceeded Caesar's of Rome   Murphy, verse 12

But O skilful wrestler! –
O captain most brave! –
Whose death comes to me
As a dream of the grave,
Had the time but arrived
When your skill could be seen,
Further spread would your fame
Than proud Cæsar's have been.   Croker, *The keen*, verse 12

The text in *The keen of the south of Ireland* departs from the structure of
Murphy's translated text and consequently from that of the original poem
with the inclusion of an additional verse after the fifteenth verse in the original. Why Croker included the following lines is a mystery:

But oh! there's one lady,
Whose soul-rending cries
Ascend from this cold earth
And pierce into the skies;
She knew thee–she valued
Thy seraph-like mind;
She knew, that no purer
On earth could she find.   Croker, *The keen*, verse 16

Nor did Croker always remain close to the content of Murphy's text, as is
evident from the following:

Tug do ghaisge dhuit gairm is glóire,
tug fá ndeara in armaibh h'óirneadh,
tug gradam dhuit do ghlacadh dho ar dhóidghil
King Philip 's níor mhisdede a mhórdhacht.   Edition, verse 22

Thy valour gave thee shouting and glory
Thou art the cause of ornamented weapons.
Gave grandeur to take them in your white fist
King Phillip and his magnitude was no harm.   Murphy, verse 22

> Thy valour shed round thee
> A halo of glory;
> And the deeds of your sharp sword
> Will long live in story.
> King Philip's own white hand
> That weapon presented,
> In a case set with blue stones,
> And royally scented.   Croker, *The keen*, verse 23

In the twenty-fourth verse, Murphy inaccurately translates the term 'uain na bóchna' as 'lamb of the sea', but gives the correct translation of 'uain' in the accompanying gloss: 'or froth'. Croker correctly interprets the meaning and employs the phrase 'foam of the brine' in his version. In the same verse, Croker's version does not advert to the red and white hues competing for attention in the dead man's cheeks, but stresses that both are present:[77]

> Cia agár fhágbhais h'áille is t'óige,
> an cneas ar snua uain na bóchna,
> an leaca ar lí ghrís an óiglil
> 's an dearc ar dhath na leag lóghmhar?   Edition, verse 24

> To whom did you leave your youth and beauty?
> The skin equal to the lamb of the sea
> The cheek mixed with embers and young lily.
> And the eyes dyed like precious stones   Murphy, verse 24

> In whom now is found
> Youthful beauty like thine?
> The skin that resembles
> The foam of the brine;
> The cheek whose red blaze
> With the snow doth unite,
> And the diamond-like eyes
> That flash fire's varied light.   Croker, *The keen*, verse 25

In the twenty-sixth and twenty-seventh verses, Croker once again fleshes out Murphy's rather bare translation:

> An rí ramhar, an chealtair chomhardach,
> an teanga mhall ar gheall gur chomhaill,

---

77 For a discussion of the use of this metaphor and similar contrasting imagery in poems by Piaras Feiritéar, see Deirdre Nic Mhathúna, 'In praise of two Margarets: two laudatory poems by Piaras Feiritéar', *Proceedings of the Harvard Celtic Colloquium*, 26 & 27 (2010), 146–59. See Seán Ó Tuama, *An grá in amhráin na ndaoine* (Baile Átha Cliath, 1960) for further examples of the motif of the lily and the rose.

an troigh thréan 's an taobh mar shróll geal,
an ionga chaol 's an béal mar phórpair.

Do chleasaíocht i marcaíocht mhóireach
do staraíocht sheanscríofa sheólta
pionnsa go n-ionnlas n-eólais
ó finit píce go bóidcin.   Edition, verses 26–7

The thick arm and the body in proportion
The slow tongue amidst jaws of the fellow members.
The forcible foot and the side like white satin,
The slender nail and mouth like rubie.

Your artfulness riding a strong steed.
Your happy Pedigree correctly written
Sweetly penned in knowledge
From the beginning to the end.   Murphy, verses 26–7

Thine the broad chest of power
And the sinewy arm;
The tongue slow to move
In dissension or harm;
The vigorous foot,
And the white satin skin,
The lip like the ruby,
The nail clear and thin.

Without equal in skill
On the back of a steed,
With a pedigree blazoned,
Which few could exceed,
Correctly recorded,
And carefully penned,
And full of proud knowledge
From beginning to end.   Croker, *The keen*, verses 27–8

The twenty-ninth verse shows how Croker elaborated on a metaphor contained in the original and in Murphy's translation:

Cia bhus oidhre dod shaidhbhreas seóide?
Cia dhearscnas an dán id dheoidhse,
gan bheith é led mhéaraibh pósda
cleite gé is tu ag déanamh cló ris?   Edition, verse 29

Who shall be Heir to your rich jewels
Who will complete the poem since your [sic] gone

> Oh! that it's not to your fingers married
> A goose quil [sic] and you with it printing   Murphy, verse 29

> Who now shall inherit
> Thy rich jewel's store?
> Who thy poem complete
> Now that thou art no more?
> Alas! that a goose-quill
> Was not thy hand's bride,
> To keep thee composing
> Sweet verse by her side.   Croker, *The keen*, verse 30

In the final verse, the text published in *The keen of the south of Ireland* contains little more than an echo of Murphy's translation. This is due, no doubt, to the meaning of much of Murphy's verse being obscure:

> Do shaoth rom thraoch is rom thoirsigh,
> rom shaoth do thraochadh is do thósdal,
> féithle na féile 's a fóir thu,
> mo thraochadh is mo shaoth lém ló thu.   Edition, verse 56

> Thy trouble with my subduing and with my pursuit
> With my disorder, thy weakness and thy arrogance
> Phelix of the hospitality and affording relief
> My loss and tribulation you are during my days Murphy, verse 56

> Subdued is my spirit
> The grave ends my career,
> It's muteness will cover
> My pride, once so dear!
> Oh! Phœnix of glory
> Whose far spreading rays,
> With destruction's red glare,
> Light up my last days.   Croker, *The keen*, verse 57

Feiritéar's elegy contains several lines that lend the poem a personal tone. The ninth verse contains one such example where the poet refers to his native area: 'Bean tsí i nDún Chaoin ag brónghol / 's bean dúchais *mo Dhún an Óirse*' (A fairy woman in Dún Chaoin crying sorrowfully / and the native woman of *my own* Dún an Óir[78]). This biographical dimension is absent from both Murphy's translation and Croker's version:

> The Beanshee of Dun Caoin bemoaning
> And the native woman of Dún an Óir   Murphy, verse 9, ll 1–2

78 My emphasis.

> The banshee of Dunqueen
> In sweet song did deplore,
> To the spirit that watches
> On dark Dun-an-Oir.   Croker, *The keen*, verse 9, ll 1–4

In the forty-fifth verse, a reference by the poet to himself is retained by Murphy in his translation, but omitted by Croker.

> Gidh eadh dob éagóir, a ghrian eóil nóna,
> nách tu is airde chaoinfinn d'Fhódla,
> nách é is dísle chaoinfeadh dóibh tu,
> do Phéaras budh phéarla id phóirdhearc.   Edition, verse 45

> But it was unjust, oh! sunbeam of evening
> Are not you highest I would keen of Fodla
> Is not he the most loyal would lament you for them
> Thy Pierce who was a pearl in thy offspring.   Murphy, verse 45

> Oh! sun-beam of evening
> Gone down in the west,
> Your refulgence has sunk
> In the wild waves to rest.
> And storm clouds are up
> In the grey twilight sky
> And the wind is abroad-
> Tho' as yet with a sigh.   Croker, *The keen*, verse 46

A significant feature of Croker's treatment of the text is his elaboration or, indeed, introduction of several references to elements of Irish tradition not present in Murphy's translation or in the original. In the following instance, Croker develops the reference to the 'dead willow' of Murphy's text and writes of the 'mute harp.' Croker acknowledges that this interpretation is rather free by stating in a footnote: 'The original, literally rendered, is, "Who can give a voice so sweetly to a dead willow?"':[79]

> Cia chuirfeas mar do chuiris i mbeó-riocht
> ag innsin h'intleachta is t'eólais,
> ag tabhairt teangan di is anma a dóithin
> saileach mharbh nár bhalbh cé feódhadh?   Edition, verse 30

> Who will put as you did enliven
> Telling your ingenuity and knowlege [sic]
> Giving her tongue and life enough
> A dead Willow which was not dumb fading.   Murphy, verse 30

79 Croker, *The keen*, p. 27.

> Say, who with thy art now
> Can knowledge advance,
> Ingeniously breaking
> With rivals a lance?
> Who can fill a small pen
> With the tongue of command,
> Or wake the mute harp
> With so skilful a hand.   Croker, *The keen*, verse 31

Although no musical instrument is mentioned in Murphy's translation of verse thirty-five, the harp makes a further appearance in the corresponding verse of Croker's text:

> Do hadhlaiceadh thu in aghaidh mo thóichim,
> íslíodh píce chum dóibe,
> an drum budh glonnmhar glórach
> anocht balbh ód mharbh, ina thómas.   Edition, verse 35

> You were buried against your going
> And a pike shall pretend to make mortar
> They who were noisy and loathsome
> In a dumb manner
> from measuring thy death.   Murphy, verse 35

> And now that you're laid
> In the silence of death,
> Still they fondly prolong
> Their last musical breath;
> Like the string of a harp
> That keeps vibrating on,
> Though the hand that has waked it
> For ever is gone. –   Croker, *The keen*, verse 36

The corresponding translated verses have little in common. Murphy's translation contains several inaccuracies. The second line should read 'and a pike was lowered towards the earth'. Croker has omitted any reference to the pike. In the third line, Murphy has evidently misinterpreted the meaning of 'drum' (Eng. *drum*) as 'drem, dream', Eng. 'band', 'company'.[80] Although Murphy has no reference to a musical instrument here, Croker includes a metaphor based on the sound of the harp. The verse in question is one of a series, which

80 Indeed, the Irish text of the poem, penned by Murphy in RIA MS 12 O 7, reads 'drong', a synonym of 'drem, dream'. The word occurs as 'drom'/'drum' in all other manuscript witnesses, including RIA MS 23 E 16, the manuscript likely to have served as Murphy's exemplar.

describes the funeral service held for Muiris Mac Gearailt. The details presented have been judged accurate. The verses caught the attention of a military
historian who showed that elements of modern military funeral observance
could be traced back to those portrayed in Feiritéar's elegy, and in an account
of the funeral of Bishop William Bedell of Kilmore, in 1642.[81] The absence of
the drum from the translation published by Croker, coupled with the mention
of the harp, alters the tone of the verse and detracts considerably from the
authenticity of the historical detail contained within Feiritéar's elegy. One can
only speculate as to why Croker introduced repeated references to the harp, but
it probably echoes the contemporary identification of the harp with Irishness,
which suggests, in turn, that he did not perceive the original to be sufficiently
Irish. A further attempt by Croker to enhance the authenticity of the text, as
it were, occurs in the twenty-first verse:[82]

> Dá silleadh sin t'inneall is t'ógchruth,
> do chreidfeadh Vēnus éirghe Adōnis;
> dá bhfaicfeadh tu it arm dófhulaing
> Vulcān dod ghabháil mar ghleóMhars.   Edition, verse 21

> If she shed abundant and youthlike,
> Venus would believe the rising of Adonis
> If you'd be seen with your unsufferable weapon
> Vulcan awailing thee like Gleomars   Murphy, verse 21

> Tho' Venus did fondly
> Adonis adore,
> Yet the daughters of Erin
> They loved thee still more.
> Through the green wood he followed
> His game without fear;
> But you rushed on the red field
> 'Mid gun, pike, and spear.   Croker, *The keen*, verse 22

The references to 'the daughters of Erin' and to the 'pike' in Croker's version
do not occur in Murphy's translation or in the original text, and are far
removed from references to the classical figures of Venus, Adonis, Vulcan and
Mars present in the original and retained in Murphy's translation. Only the
first two of these figures appear in Croker's version. Such alterations obscure
the classical dimension of these verses, and consequently restricted readers'

81 C. D., 'Two 17th century Irish military funerals', *Irish Sword*, 6 (1963–4), 117.   82 For
a related discussion of the manifestation of cultural forces in translations of 'Caoineadh
Airt Uí Laoghaire', see Ríona Ní Fhrighil, '"Knight of the generous heart": Caoineadh
Airt Uí Laoghaire agus stair a aistrithe' in Charlie Dillon and Ríona Ní Fhrighil (eds),
Aistriú Éireann (Béal Feirste, 2008), pp 49–67.

appreciation of the literary horizons of seventeenth-century Irish poetry. Croker's intervention here is not consistent with an attempt he made elsewhere to alert his readers to a widespread familiarity with classical literature among the general Irish population.[83]

It is clear that Thomas Crofton Croker's assertion that the 'Keen on Maurice Fitzgerald' was 'translated from the Irish by the editor' would not be regarded today as an accurate reflection of the process that shaped its production. The account provided here of the central role played by the Irish scribe David Murphy in the formation of the translated text enhances and amplifies our appreciation of the interface between manuscript and print cultures in the mid-nineteenth century, and of the dependence of English-speaking authors interested in engaging with Irish language and literature upon scribes and others anchored in that world. Croker clearly thought highly of Murphy's expertise in the Irish language, describing him elsewhere as 'an ingenious Irish scholar'.[84] Despite this approbation, Murphy's role as translator is not documented in *The keen of the south of Ireland*. Croker's action was not unique. A further revealing, and related, example of mid-nineteenth-century attitudes to acknowledging contributions to literary works is provided by the publication of 'A lamentation for the death of Sir Maurice Fitzgerald Knight of Kerry (an abridged translation from the Irish of Pierce Ferriter)'. Two years after the publication of Croker's *The keen of the south of Ireland*, this six-verse poem appeared in *The Nation* above the initials 'J.C.M.'.[85] It can be assumed that these initials refer to the poet and translator James Clarence Mangan who was a contributor to the newspaper at the time of the poem's publication.[86] No source is cited for the material, but it is likely that Mangan's text is a reworked versification of that previously published by Croker. A transcription of Mangan's text is found among a collection of translations of Irish poetry in RIA MS 3 C 28, which serves as a reminder that the transfer of material between manuscript and print was not a one-way process.[87]

---

83 'Amongst the peasantry, classical learning is not uncommon; and a tattered Ovid or Virgil may be found even in the hands of common labourers': T. Crofton Croker, *Researches in the south of Ireland* (London, 1824), p. 326.   84 T. Crofton Croker, *The historical songs of Ireland: illustrative of the revolutionary struggle between James II and William III* (London, 1841), p. 2.   85 *The Nation*, 29 Aug. 1846, p. 9.   86 Sean Ryder, 'James Clarence Mangan', *DIB*, sub nom.   87 The manuscript appears to have been transcribed by John Windele, to whom it belonged in 1847: T.F. O'Rahilly et al., *Catalogue of Irish manuscripts in the Royal Irish Academy* (Dublin, 1926–70) pp 3052–4. Mangan's role in another publication provides an interesting parallel to Croker's representation of himself as translator. In the third edition of John O'Daly, *The poets and poetry of Munster* (Dublin, 1883), Mangan is solely credited with providing 'poetical translations'. C.P. Meehan, the editor of the edition in question notes, however, that 'The late Mr. O'Daly turned the Gaelic songs in this volume into literal English prose, and Mangan transfused the spirit of their authors as no other could': see Proinsias Ó Drisceoil, *Seán Ó Dálaigh: éigse agus iomarbhá* (Corcaigh, 2007), p. 197.

The lack of transparency regarding the process of its production notwithstanding, the translation of 'Mo thraochadh is mo shaoth lém ló thu' published by Thomas Crofton Croker was a significant juncture in the transmission of the poetry of Piaras Feiritéar. *The keen of the south of Ireland* served to transmit in print material that had previously only been available within the manuscript tradition. Murphy's role as translator was central to the task. Nonetheless, while Croker and Murphy were important mediators in this process, it must be borne in mind that their role was limited to the transmission of a translation of Feiritéar's elegy to an anglophone audience. It fell to Pádraig Ua Duinnín to make the surviving corpus of Feiritéar's poems available in print in the Irish language half a century later. With the publication of *Dánta Phiarais Feiritéir* in 1903, Feiritéar's poetry was seen into print in the original language of composition, a full 250 years after the poet's demise.

10

Pious miscellanies and spiritual songs: devotional publishing and reading in Irish and Scottish Gaelic, 1760–1900

NIALL Ó CIOSÁIN

We were not long ago in the towns of Inverness and of Galway: in the former we found the printing of the Gaelic going on with enterprise and success; we saw sundry booksellers' shops, in whose well furnished windows we noticed well printed Gaelic books, on all subjects, and more especially on religious; we saw, not only original Gaelic works for sale, but also well executed translations of many of the most valuable treatises in English theology; and what was best of all, Bibles and Testaments, cheap and in abundance. On the contrary, in Galway, a much larger town, amidst a population of, we believe, 40,000 – the greater part speaking Irish – no Irish printing-office – no shop where an Irish work, religious or miscellaneous, could be produced – nothing that evinced that the Irish were at all inclined to read their own language.[1]

The boundaries between languages in eighteenth- and nineteenth-century Europe were not only geographic or social, but also corresponded to domains of usage, particularly in bilingual or diglossic societies and communities. One of the most potent boundaries in terms of utility and prestige concerns writing and reading. Typically the dominant or official language is the language of writing and print, and consequently that of reading also. However, the contrast was rarely between a subordinate language that was purely oral and a dominant one with extensive written and printed usage, and most subordinate languages had some written and even printed forms. The extent of these forms could vary, as the above description of two languages, which were otherwise very similar in their social and legal status, suggests. This chapter explores the contrast between publishing and reading in Irish and Scottish Gaelic, taking the most frequently printed genre in the two languages as a case study.

The contrast between Inverness and Galway was drawn by a correspondent of the *Christian Examiner and Church of Ireland magazine* in 1832. Such

1 *The Christian Examiner and Church of Ireland Magazine*, 1 (1832), 627.

comparisons between Irish on the one hand and Gaelic or Welsh on the other were common throughout the nineteenth century. This was particularly true of evangelical Protestant commentators such as the *Christian Examiner* writer, who attributed Irish unrest, and the rebellion of 1798 above all, to religious causes, to 'superstition' or 'popery', or both. Their solution was to catechize the population, to distribute Bibles and other religious matter and to teach people to read them. Some of these commentators devoted their energies to publishing in Irish. In their view, the Protestant Reformation had failed in Ireland in the sixteenth and seventeenth centuries largely because it departed from the principle of access to scripture in the vernacular. They contrasted the delay in translating the Bible into Irish, and the paucity of its eventual dissemination, with the rapid translation and circulation of the scriptures in Welsh. Thus, Ireland remained largely Catholic, troublesome and alienated, while Wales became Protestant and was integrated successfully into the British state.[2]

The same contrast was made between Irish and Scottish Gaelic, although literacy and reading in Gaelic were less widespread than in Welsh. As Whitley Stokes, who himself published an Irish-language edition of St Luke's Gospel in 1799, put it:

> It will be said that very few indeed can read Irish; but this must have been the case of every language, before printed books were in common circulation. It must have been so in the highlands of Scotland, Wales and the Isle of Man, where the Bible has been published in the native dialects and extensively circulated.[3]

The relationship between the different Celtic language areas was not just a matter of comparative analysis. There was also a good deal of movement of people and ideas. Scottish Gaelic circulating schools in the later eighteenth century were modelled on those of Wales, while Welsh and Gaelic-speaking clergy toured Ireland and, in the case of some of the Gaelic speakers, even preached to Irish-speaking congregations in Gaelic.

This comparative context, while apparent to contemporaries, is largely missing from modern studies of the history of language use, language shift and literacy in the respective regions. The major exception to this is Victor Durkacz's *Decline of the Celtic languages*, published in 1983, which traced in detail the interaction between the different Celtic language areas at the level of popular education and literacy. Durkacz's explanatory approach was threefold: he focussed first on mass literacy as a force for language mainten-

2 An example is Christopher Anderson, *Memorial on behalf of the native Irish, with a view to their improvement in moral and religious knowledge, through the medium of their own language* (London, 1815).   3 Whitley Stokes, *Projects for reestablishing the internal peace and tranquillity of Ireland* (Dublin, 1799), pp 45–6.

ance, then on the role of schooling in creating mass literacy, and finally on the role of religion, particularly evangelical religion, in creating those schools. Wales had a major religious revival in the eighteenth century, in which nonconformist groups such as Methodists and Baptists created mass literacy in Welsh. In the Scottish Highlands, the evangelical revival of the early nineteenth century greatly increased schooling and publishing in Gaelic. In Ireland, Durkacz suggested that the publication of an Irish-language Bible by the British and Foreign Bible Society in 1811 was 'a decision of fundamental consequence for the future of Irish literacy'. By extension, therefore, although Durkacz did not explicitly say so, the failure of evangelical Protestantism in the early nineteenth century crusade referred to earlier, underlay the failure to achieve mass literacy in Irish and the subsequent rapid decline in Irish speaking.[4]

Durkacz is broadly correct in emphasizing religious factors in language loyalty, as opposed to the almost exclusive concentration on economic and political processes in most of the historiography of language shift in Ireland. The very different chronological patterns of language use and survival in Wales, Scotland and Ireland, along with the striking contrasts in the history of publishing and reading in the three languages, correspond much more closely to differences in religious regimes than to levels of economic or political integration into the United Kingdom.[5] However, Durkacz's overwhelming concentration on evangelical Protestantism led him seriously to misinterpret the Irish case. Remarkably, the Catholic Church, to which the vast majority of Irish speakers belonged, is almost invisible in his presentation. To write, for example, that 'the only Irish religious publications of the eighteenth century were John Richardson's *Liturgy* of 1712 and several catechisms published in the Irish colleges on the Continent' ignores the most frequently printed Irish-language text of the century, the sermons of Bishop James Gallagher, which ran to two editions and four reprints in the eighteenth century, all printed in Dublin, as well as the growing number of catechisms published in Ireland from the 1760s onwards.[6] A Catholic missionary drive had just as much

4 Victor Edward Durkacz, *The decline of the Celtic languages: a study of linguistic and cultural conflict in Scotland, Wales and Ireland from the Reformation to the twentieth century* (Edinburgh, 1983), p. 119. 5 The standard expression of the economic and political explanation in the Irish case is Maureen Wall, 'The decline of the Irish language' in Brian Ó Cuív (ed.), *A view of the Irish language* (Dublin, 1969), pp 81–90; for criticism of this line of explanation, see Niall Ó Ciosáin, 'Gaelic culture and language shift' in Laurence Geary and Margaret Kelleher (eds), *Nineteenth-century Ireland: a guide to recent research* (Dublin, 2005), pp 136–52 and *idem*, 'Language, print and the Catholic Church in Ireland, 1700–1900' in Donald McNamara (ed.), *Which direction Ireland?* (Newcastle, 2007), pp 125–38. 6 Durkacz, *The decline of the Celtic languages*, p. 75; there is a listing of the of editions and reprints of Gallagher's *Sermons* in Ciarán MacMurchaidh, 'Seanmóirí an Easpaig Séamas Ó Gallchóir: eagráin, aistriúcháin agus aidhmeanna' in Damien MacManus et al. (eds), *Féilscríbhinn do Chathal Ó Háinle* (forthcoming), which corrects the partial list

potential to create mass literacy in a non-official language as did evangelical Protestantism. This is clearly demonstrated by the case of Breton, the principal Celtic language not considered by Durkacz. A series of Jesuit missions in the seventeenth century – as dramatic and emotional in their own way as Protestant revivals – produced a printed devotional literature in Breton, and consequently a readership for secular works as well. The number of books published in Breton in the eighteenth century was substantially more than that published in Scottish Gaelic. In the nineteenth century, while the amounts were roughly equal, printed Breton texts were far more varied than Gaelic texts, which remained overwhelmingly religious.[7]

Taking all churches into consideration, therefore, an argument similar to Durkacz's is persuasive. Literacy in a language which is not the language of the state or the language of trade and commerce is rooted in religious usage, and its extent is largely determined by the attitudes and actions of institutional churches. Moreover, since literacy which was devotional in origin was used to read secular texts also, the extent of a reading public for all kinds of texts in non-official languages was also largely determined by the extent of the initial impetus given to it by institutional churches. In all Celtic languages, the central corpus of printed production remained predominantly devotional, and the act of reading was likewise frequently a devotional act.

What this analysis suggests, therefore, is that a study of reading in any one of these languages can most fruitfully be located in the religious sphere and in a comparative manner between languages, as both Durkacz and the writer for the *Christian Examiner* suggest. This essay attempts to explore some of the characteristics of the reading of print in Irish during the nineteenth century by examining the format and content of the most popular devotional printed book in that language, and by comparing it to its two counterparts in Scottish Gaelic. It will focus as far as possible on the appearance of the books and on their publishing history, but their content will also be taken into consideration. The three titles in order of first publication are *Laoidhe spioradail* by Dugald Buchanan (1767), the *Pious miscellany* of Timothy O'Sullivan, or Tadhg Gaelach Ó Súilleabháin (1802), and *Dain spioradail* by Peter Grant (1815).

The three books are examples of one of the most widespread genres in popular printed books in early modern and modern Europe, the collection of canticles or devotional songs. These collections were produced by all denominations from the Reformation onwards as instruments of reform of popular belief and practice, being intended for domestic as well as church

in Pól Breathnach (ed.), *Seanmóiri Mhuighe Nuadhat* vol. 4 (1911); Michael Tynan: *Catholic instruction in Ireland, 1720–1950: the O'Reilly/Donlevy catechetical tradition* (Dublin, 1985), chapter 5 'The Irish texts'.   7 Michel Lagrée, 'La littérature religieuse dans la production Bretonne imprimée: aspects quantitatifs', in *idem* (ed.), *Les parlers de la foi: religion et langues régionales* (Rennes, 1995), pp 85–94.

use, and the more popular collections were reprinted for decades and even centuries. Many of these collections shared a strategy of infiltrating previous popular secular song, and of producing new devotional words for the melodies of the secular songs they intended to displace. There were of course denominational differences. In Protestant areas, and particularly in Calvinist ones, vernacular translations of the Psalms were among the most widely used collections. This was certainly true of Gaelic Scotland, where a translation was commissioned by the Synod of Argyll and a selection of fifty first printed in 1659. The full psalter was published in 1694, and it had 24 editions during the eighteenth century. In Catholic collections, by contrast, psalm texts were uncommon, and sometimes even deliberately avoided.[8]

It is of course true that the most probable use made of such devotional song collections was that their contents would be memorized, so that their incorporation into domestic religious practice did not involve continuous reading. However, this can be said of many, if not most, of the texts of popular printed literature before the later nineteenth century. Their format was close to that of oral literature, and was suitable for reading (or singing) aloud and, consequently, for memorization and performance independently of a printed text. Nevertheless, the sustained demand for these printed books, in the case the devotional song collections, suggests that new readers were being catered for, and that a readership, in the strict sense of the word, existed for them as long as they were being reprinted, and perhaps longer.[9]

THE BOOKS

The earliest of the three books to be published was *Laoidhe spioradail* by Dugald Buchanan (1716–68), which first appeared in Edinburgh in 1767. It had 9 editions by 1800, and a further 31 editions during the nineteenth century. It contains eight poems, songs or hymns, on subjects such as death and the last judgment. Buchanan was a schoolmaster with the Scottish Society for Promoting Christian Knowledge for many years, and oversaw the translation and publication of the first Gaelic New Testament which appeared in 1767, the same year as the *Laoidhe spioradail*.

Thirty-five years after the appearance of Buchanan's collection, the *Pious miscellany* of Timothy O'Sullivan, or Tadhg Gaelach Ó Súilleabháin (*c*.1715–

---

8 Jean Queniart, 'Contenus et pratiques du livre de cantiques dans la France Catholique' in Hans Erich Bödeker et al. (eds), *Le livre religieux et ses pratiques* (Göttingen, 1991), pp 252–65; on the Gaelic psalms, see Donald Meek, 'Gaelic and the churches' in Colin MacLean and Kenneth Veitch (eds), *Scottish life and society: a compendium of Scottish ethnology: religion* (Edinburgh, 2006), pp 363–78, particularly pp 369–70; on Catholic avoidance of psalm texts, Denise Launay, *La musique religieuse en France du Concile de Trente à 1804* (Paris, 1993), p. 88.   9 Niall Ó Ciosáin, *Print and popular culture in Ireland, 1750–1850* (Basingstoke, 1997), pp 186–91.

95), was published in Clonmel, county Tipperary. It had 18 editions by 1850, and 4 more by 1880. It is a good deal longer than Buchanan's collection, with 25 poems or songs altogether.[10]

The last and longest of the three collections was that of Peter Grant or Pàdraig Grannd nan Òran (1783–1867), whose *Dain spioradail* was first printed in Inverness in 1815 and had 22 editions during the nineteenth century. Grant was an itinerant Baptist missionary who became the pastor of a congregation in Spey in 1826. He was the only one of the three authors to follow the progress of their work in print, since Buchanan died within a year of the publication of *Laoidhe spioradail*, and Ó Súilleabháin in 1795, before the *Pious miscellany* appeared, and he added new songs and new prefaces to later editions. The 1815 edition had 13 songs, the 1827 had 18, while all editions printed after 1835 contained 39 hymns or songs altogether.

In terms of content, the three collections can be situated on a spectrum of chronology, length and scope. Buchanan's is the earliest of the three, the shortest and also the most restricted in scope. His *Laoidhe* are principally meditations on the glory of God, on the last judgment, sin and the transience of life. Ó Súilleabháin's has a series of poems on similar themes to Buchanan's – death, sin and the last judgment – but added to this are songs or hymns on more social issues, with exhortations against drinking, swearing and loose behaviour in general, as well as songs on specifically Catholic themes, such as three hymns to the Virgin Mary and two in praise of the rosary. Grant's is the latest and longest, deals like Buchanan with sin and death, like Ó Súilleabháin with social behaviour, and also with recent issues such as the international missionary organizations of the early nineteenth century, in 'Orain na Missionaries'. In summary, we might say that Buchanan is personal, Ó Súilleabháin personal and social, and Grant personal, social and international.

Stylistically, a distinction can be drawn between Buchanan on the one hand, and Ó Súilleabháin and Grant on the other. The latter two are far closer to the poetical traditions of Irish and Gaelic respectively, indeed can be said to emerge from them, while the former represents more of an introduction of elements of English-language poetry and hymnody into Gaelic. As Donald Meek has shown, some of the hymns in Buchanan's collection were modelled on those of well-known hymn writers in eighteenth-century England such as Isaac Watts (1674–1748), and in fact could be considered translations and paraphrases of them.[11] One of them, 'Fulangas Chriosd', 'The suffering of Christ', uses common or ballad metre, which was unknown in Gaelic verse, but which was introduced from English by the translations in the Gaelic Psalter

---

10 Most editions after 1820 also included additional poetry in Irish by Patrick Denn, the editor of those editions.   11 Donald Meek, 'Ath-sgrudadh: Dughall Bochanan', *Gairm: an raitheachan Gaidhlig*, 147 (1989), 269–80; *idem*, 'Ath-sgrudadh: Dughall Bochanan: 2', *Gairm*, 148 (1989), 319–31.

referred to above. If we regard the Psalter as an attempt to introduce new elements into Gaelic culture, then Buchanan's books was following closely in its footsteps. Indeed, some of the editions of the *Laoidhe* use as their epigraph the same biblical quotation, an exhortation to praise God in song, as had appeared on some editions of the Psalter.[12]

Ó Súilleabháin's *Pious miscellany*, by contrast, emerges from contemporary literary culture in Irish. His poems, both sacred and secular, were copied into manuscripts in Munster from the 1760s onwards, decades before the first edition of the printed book. They formed part of a substantial corpus of poetry in Irish which was being composed and circulated in manuscript throughout the eighteenth century, and they are in fact the only example of a successful transition from manuscript to print of texts from that tradition. The songs in the *Pious miscellany* display all the formal characteristics of this poetry, being composed in stressed verse with intricate patterns of internal assonance and highly ornamental vocabulary.[13]

Like Ó Súilleabháin, Peter Grant's songs use a variety of metres, some of them close to those of eighteenth-century secular songs in Gaelic. Donald Meek describes the best-known of them, 'Glòir an Uan' 'The Glory of the Lamb' as follows: 'Despite its transcendent theme, the style of the hymn is that of a traditional Gaelic panegyric song, praising the triumphant hero, but doing so in biblical rather than secular terms.'[14] Moreover, the metre and tune of this particular hymn were based on a song by Duncan Ban McIntyre, one of the most prominent Gaelic poets of the eighteenth century. This was 'Màiri Bhàn Og', 'Fair Young Mary', which would have been familiar to many of Grant's readers. Grant, in other words, was using the forms of secular Gaelic culture as a vehicle through which to infuse that culture with evangelical religious values. Meek views Grant's relationship to Gaelic culture as paradoxical, since evangelicals like him were hostile to so many of its manifestations.[15] Such accommodation was, as noted above, a standard strategy in church campaigns against popular culture, albeit more common in Catholic areas than in Calvinist ones. Most editions of the *Pious miscellany*, for example, suggest secular melodies for its songs, such as 'The Flowers of Edinburgh' which was frequently used by secular ballad composers of the period. To my mind, what is even more striking in Grant's songs is the

---

12 Col. 3:16, from the cover of *Sailm Dhaibhidh a meadar dhana gaoidheilg, do reir na heabhra* ... (Glasgow, 1724): 'Ar dteagasg agus ar munadh dhaoibh a chèile à Salmaibh, agus a bhfonnaibh molta Dé, agus a gcainticaibh spioradalta ag deanamh ciùil don Tighearna le gràs ann bhur gcroidheadhaibh', 'Teaching and admonishing one another in psalms and hymns and spiritual songs, singing with grace in your hearts to the Lord': Buchanan, *Laoidhean*, 1773 and 1775 edns.   13 Úna Nic Éinrí, *An cantaire siúlach: Tadhg Gaelach* (An Daingean, 2001); Ó Ciosáin, *Print and popular culture*, pp 134–50.   14 Donald Meek, '"The glory of the lamb": the Gaelic hymns of Peter Grant' in D.W. Bebbington (ed.), *The gospel in the world: international Baptist studies* (Carlisle, 2002), pp 129–64.   15 Meek, 'The glory of the lamb', pp 131, 151–4.

repeated emphasis on the virtue and glory of the Lamb. As well as 'Glòir an Uan', there is a song called 'Eifeachd a'm fuil an Uain', 'The power of the blood of the Lamb', while 'An Deagh Shaighdear', 'The Good Soldier', is described as fighting 'Fo ard bhratach an Uain' 'Under the high banner of the Lamb', and the songs constantly emphasize 'fuil an Uain' 'the blood of the Lamb' and 'gras an Uain' 'the grace of the Lamb'. Indeed of the 39 songs, 32 mention the Lamb and another mentions lambs metaphorically, meaning the faithful, while only 6 do not. Given that Grant's readers belonged to a society which was being traumatically uprooted, evicted and resettled, in order to make way for large-scale sheep farming in the 'Clearances', this emphasis is savagely ironic.

READERS AND PRINTERS

While the three books belong to the same *genre* and have certain similarities in content as a result, when we look at the presentation of the books in print, at the type of reader which is implied by that presentation, and at the publishing history of the three books, a very clear difference emerges between the two Scottish books on the one hand and Ó Súilleabháin's on the other.

The first and most striking difference is in the linguistic presentation of the texts. In all editions during the nineteenth century, the cover and title page of the *Pious miscellany* are in English: 'Timothy O'Sullivan's, commonly called Tadhg Gaolach's, *Pious miscellany*, recommended to all devout Catholics as a work of great merit'. They all contain a two-page 'Instructions for reading this miscellany', also in English, which explains some of the conventions of Irish orthography, such as the initial mutations of words. Some editions also include a few English-language hymns. There are, however, very few translations or explanations of Irish words, even though Ó Súilleabháin's vocabulary is quite ornate and far from straightforward. The readership for this book, therefore, is implicitly bilingual, and as the reading instructions make clear, the assumed reader is an Irish-speaker who has learned to read English and wishes to transfer that skill to Irish. Thus, one of the later editions, that produced by John O'Daly in 1858, explains the choice of roman letters rather than the celtic lettering of the manuscripts and some printed books, on the grounds that 'every peasant who speaks Irish and reads English can master the work in its present form'.

The collections of Buchanan and Grant, by contrast, normally had title pages in Gaelic only, and never had instructions for reading. The implied or inscribed reader has a literacy in Gaelic, which is assumed to be independent of his or her literacy in English. It is true that editions of Peter Grant from the fifth (1837) onwards have a preface in English by Grant himself explaining the appearance of new poems, and editions of Buchanan after the

Map 1: Locations of two or more subscribers to the *Pious miscellany* (1802)

1840s have two title pages, one in each language. However, the the song texts remain in Gaelic only, and none has instructions for reading.

This difference reflects two related aspects of print culture in the two languages – partly, the potential existence of monoglot readers, but above all the existence of a settled form of language and presentation in print. O'Daly's comment above was made to justify his choice of roman rather than celtic letters, and such choices regarding type, orthography and forms of language had to be made by all printers of material in Irish during the eighteenth and nineteenth centuries, since no norm for a popular readership existed. Texts were printed in both roman and celtic typography and in a wide range of orthographic forms, from the elaborate learned norms of the older manuscript tradition to a completely phonetic rendering using the forms of English.

Buchanan and Grant, on the other hand, worked within a print culture which had strong normative texts, or which was acquiring them. The metrical psalter had established the precedent of a religious song book in Gaelic, while the translations of the Bible, the Old Testament in 1767 and the New in 1801, contributed to the consolidation of norms of printed language. The effect of the latter on Gaelic readers may be illustrated in terms of content rather than appearance. Buchanan does not have a great deal of biblical reference, and he focusses on the New Testament, particularly on the passion of Christ, referring explicitly to the Old Testament only three times (twice to

Map 2: Some subscribers to Turner, *Comhchruinneacha* (1813)

Adam and Eve and once to manna). Grant, by comparison, has a wide range
of Old Testament references, partly because he could assume a greater
biblical knowledge among his readership by 1815.

The greater strength of a norm of printed language in Gaelic as opposed
to Irish can also be inferred from the geography of readerships in the two
languages. The space within which the *Pious miscellany* circulated, the market
which it served, was the eastern part of the province of Munster, that is,
county Waterford, east county Cork, south county Tipperary and east county
Limerick, along with south county Kilkenny. The first edition of 1802 was
published by subscription, with a list of over two hundred names, all located
within this area (Map 1). All pre-Famine editions were printed in Clonmel,
Cork and Limerick, in whose hinterland this area was, rather than in Dublin,
which would have served a more national market. Buchanan's *Laoidhe
spioradail*, by contrast, was usually published in Edinburgh and Glasgow,
which served a wider market (there were two editions in Perth, two in
Inverness and one in Elgin). Grant's *Dain* was initially published, like the
Pious miscellany, locally or regionally, and of the first 10 editions, 5 were
printed in Inverness and 3 in Elgin, both close to Strathspey where Grant
ministered. After 1850, however, all editons were published in Glasgow or
Edinburgh, as were all editions of Buchanan. It is not possible to illustrate
precisely the geography of readership of Buchanan and Grant, since neither
was published by subscription. We can, however, form some impression by

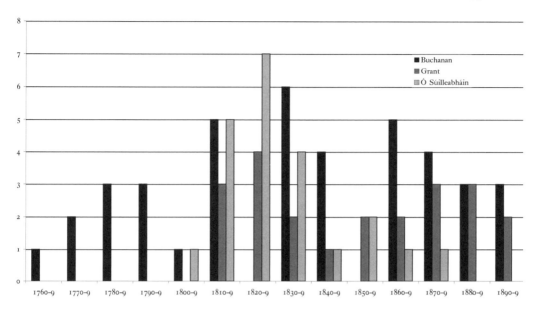

Fig 1: Editions of Buchanan, *Laoidhe spioradail*, Grant, *Dain spioradail*, and
Ó Súilleabháin, *Pious miscellany*, 1760-1900

examining the extensive subscription lists of some collections of Gaelic secular
poetry published in the same period, such as the 1790 edition of the songs of
Duncan Ban MacIntyre or an anthology published by Patrick Turner in
1813.[16] These illustrate the wider market implied by publication in the larger
cities (see Map 2, which shows some of the subscribers to Turner's book).
Finally, the readership of Buchanan and Grant was not confined to Scotland.
Editions of both books were published in Montreal in 1836, presumably sold
to Highland settlers, some in Ontario but mostly in the maritime provinces
of Nova Scotia and Prince Edward Island, where publishing in Gaelic
continued throughout the second half of the century.[17] By contrast, despite
rising levels of migration from Irish-speaking areas to both Canada and the
United States, no book in Irish was published in North America during the
nineteenth century.

The chronology of publication of the *Pious miscellany* might at first sight
suggest the beginning of a transition to a similar national readership. Having
been published entirely in Munster before 1850, there were Dublin editions

16 *Orain Ghaidhealach le Donnchadh Macantsaoir* (Edinburgh, 1790); Padruig Tuirneir
(ed.), *Comhchruinneacha do dh'ain taghta Ghaidhealach* (Edinburgh, 1813).   17 Charles
Dunn, *The Highland settler: a portrait of the Scottish Gael in Nova Scotia* (Toronto, 1953),
chapter 6, 'Gaelic in print'.

in 1858 and 1868. However, the story these editions tell is quite different to
that of the Scottish collections. The chronology of printing of the three books
is the second major difference between them. All three gained immediate
success and a sustained reprinting for decades. In the thirty years following
their respective first publications, there were 8 editions of Buchanan, 14 of Ó
Súilleabháin and 11 of Grant. In the second half of the nineteenth century,
however, there were only 4 editions of Ó Súilleabháin, and none at all after
about 1880. Buchanan and Grant, by contrast, remain in print, with 13
editions of the former and twelve of the latter, and both continued being
reprinted into the twentieth century:

In this respect, these texts are emblematic of the contrast between the
overall print cultures of Gaelic and Irish. The high point of production of
Gaelic printed books was the second half of the nineteenth century, a feature
it has in common with Welsh and Breton. Printing in Irish peaked between
1800 and 1845, and collapsed thereafter. Its revival after about 1890 was
essentially a revivalist project, directed at learners of the language outside
Irish-speaking areas rather than at speakers of the language within them. The
reasons for this contrast are beyond the scope of this contribution, but relate,
in my view, to the promotion and support of Celtic languages by institutional
Christian churches in Wales, Scotland and Brittany as opposed to the neglect
or even outright hostility of the Catholic Church in Ireland to Irish.[18]

These processes can be illustrated by contrasting the appearance of the
later editions of Ó Súilleabháin with those of Buchanan and Grant. The
printed format of the Scottish texts after 1850 shows a remarkable degree of
stability. Successive editions were identical, which indicates that they were
reproduced from the same stereotype plates, since those plates can be
observed to decay slightly from edition to edition. The 1872 and 1885
editions of Buchanan were produced from the same set of plates, as were the
1867, 1875, 1884, 1889, 1893 and 1903 editions of Grant. This suggests a
market for both books that was substantial and extremely stable in its expec-
tations, both in terms of content and typography. Moreover, they established
or consolidated a print *genre*, inspiring a long series of sacred song collections
throughout the nineteenth century. Buchanan's title, *Laoidhe spioradail*, for
example, was used for seven collections published in the first half of the nineteenth century. One of these, by Daniel Grant, a Baptist like his namesake
Peter, had on its cover the same biblical exhortation to song that appears on
the cover of some editions of Buchanan and of the Psalms. It had editions in
1842 and 1862.

---

18 Ó Ciosáin, 'Language, print and the Catholic Church'. This aspect of the language shift
was clear to writers of the early twentieth century, some of whom had first-hand
experience of Catholic Church attitudes to Irish: see, for example, T.F. O'Rahilly, *Irish
dialects past and present* (Dublin, 1932), pp 10–12.

16   Caḃg Ʒaolach O'Súilliobáin.

caRḃaLL ṁuiRe.

AIR.—"*Carolan's Devotion.*"

IS cṗéiċ-laʒ mo ċeallcaiṗ a ʒ-cannclaḃ na ʒ-cáṗ,
Am ṗṗṗéaċaḃ le ṗṗlanncaiḃ 'ṗmc aiṗ ḃ́ṗannṗaḃ
   aʒ an m-báṗ,
Ṁo ḃ́ṗéaʒa, mo ḃlannḃaṗ, 'ṗmo ċlampaṗ ʒan ṗṗáṗ,
Do ṗ́ċiḃ miṗc a ḃ-cṗcaḃlaiḃ neaṁ-ṁeaḃṗaċ am páṗ.
     a ṗ́éilcean na n-ainʒiollaiḃ,
     Ná h-éimiʒ mc ċaṗmuinn,
     Ʒo ḃaonaċcaċ, caṗċanaċ,
     Leḃ' ḃeanaiʒccaċc do ʒnáċ :—
Lá anḃaoṗéa, lá'n ḃíoʒalca, lá'n éiṗliʒ, lá'n ṗʒeṁile,
Lá'n ḃaoṗéa, lá'n ḃaoʒail, lá'n ḃ́inṗe, lá'n ḃ́ṗáċ,
Lá ṗaoṗṗaṗ na ṗaoíċe ʒo ṗíoṗ-ċeaṗc éuʒ ʒ́ṗáḃ,
Dá nʒéaṗ-ċuman IOSa na caoiḃe ʒan cṗáʒ.

Níl éiṗeaċc aim annṗaċc ná ceannṗaċc aim ċáil,
Aʒ cṗéineaċc an íompċaiṗ iṗ ṗallṗa le ṗáʒail;
An ṗaoʒal-ṗo ní ʒaḃan liom cia ṁeall me maṗ ċáċ,
'Sʒuṗ ṗ́éanaṗ lem' ċam-ċoiṗ mo ṗ́ṗionṗa ṗa páiṗc.
     a ċaoṁ-ċ́ainḃcal ċaḃaṗéaċ,
     Na cléiṗe ná capcuiṗniʒ,
     Mo ṗaoéaṗ, mo ċaiénioṁ ḃuic,
     a ḃanalcṗa na nʒ́ṗáṗ ;—
Do cṗ́éiċe, do ʒníoṁaṗéa, do naoṁéaċc, do ṁíslṗeaċc,
Do léiʒeancaċc, do aoiṗḃeaċc, ḃá aoiḃinne acáiḃ;
Dá ḃ-ṗéaḃṗainn ʒo bínn-ʒlic, ʒo bṗíoʒṁaṗ, ʒo bláiċ,
Do ḃéanṗainṗi a ʒ-caoin-ċuṗ a ʒ-cṗíċ ḃuic le ʒ́ṗáḃ.

Mo léan-ʒuiṗc mo laḃaṗéa éuʒ cancaṗ am ċneáḃa,
Ʒo léiṗ-ʒonca am lóḃa-ṗa a ḃ-cónnċaċa pláʒ,

Fig 2: *Pious miscellany*, 1868 edition

The publishing history of the *Pious miscellany* after 1850 tells a very different story. An edition was printed in 1858 by John O'Daly, a publisher and scholar of Irish, who was from from county Kilkenny and worked in Dublin.[19] O'Daly was familiar with Ó Súilleabháin's book from his youth, and in his preface he mentions that his father knew the poet. This edition resembled closely the pre-Famine editions, and O'Daly was clearly targeting the same market. The preface, in English, envisaged the readers as 'the peasantry, to whom, in Munster particularly, its contents are as familiar as household words'. O'Daly adopted the convention of having an English-language title page, and also used the roman type of previous printed editions rather than the Gaelic script of the manuscripts from which the poems were originally taken. 'Some may ask', he wrote, 'why we have adopted Roman instead of Irish characters? Our answer is simply this, that if we did adopt the Irish, those for whom the work is intended would not be able to use it, being entirely unacquainted with that character...'. However, when O'Daly produced another edition in 1868, it had completely changed in appearance. It was printed in a Gaelic typeface that imitated the manuscripts from which the poems were originally taken (Fig. 2). O'Daly also added explanatory notes to the poems, clarifying meanings and names. The previous printed versions had very few notes, and these explained religious terms.

O'Daly's 1868 notes, by contrast, were more ethnographic. One song to the rosary has as a suggested melody 'An Spailpín Fánach', which O'Daly glossed as follows: 'The term spailpín signifies a person who travels about the country looking for hire among the farmers at the potato-digging season; and fanagh means wandering.' O'Daly was clearly aiming this edition at a new audience, one much less familiar with the culture from which the songs emerged. The Munster peasantry would not have needed such explanations, or to have words like 'casúr', a hammer, or 'péist', a worm or serpent, translated for them, and would, by O'Daly's own admission ten years earlier, have struggled with the typeface. He also changed the content of the book, dropping some long devotional poems which had been added to most pre-Famine editions, but which were by the editor of those editions, Patrick Denn, rather than by Ó Súilleabháin. More significantly, he added a number of secular poems by Ó Súilleabháin himself and other eighteenth-century Munster poets. In effect, this 1868 edition is a secular and antiquarian publication as much as, perhaps even more than, a devotional one. Editions of Ó Súilleabháin after 1880 were exclusively scholarly and pedagogic, unlike those of Buchanan and Grant, which, as we saw, continued in the same popular format until the early twentieth century at least.[20]

19 For O'Daly, see Proinsias Ó Drisceoil, *Seán Ó Dálaigh: éigse agus iomarbhá* (Cork, 2007), particularly pp 173–8.   20 Pádraig Ua Duinnín (ed.), *Amhráin Thaidhg Ghaedhealaigh Uí Shúilleabháin* (Dublin, 1903); Risteárd Ó Foghludha (ed.), *Tadhg Gaelach: ath-eagar ar a dhuanta diadha agus ar a chuid amhrán maille re mórán nuadh-eolais*

The publication history of the *Pious miscellany*, therefore, is one of different formats implying different styles of reading or use. The oldest versions of the poems were in manuscript, written in Gaelic script, mixed in with poetry by others, both sacred and secular, in a context that was mainly literary. When Ó Súilleabháin's sacred poems were gathered together in a single printed volume, published initially with support from some Catholic clergy and using the roman typeface familiar from catechisms and other printed religious books in Irish, their context of reception became a predominantly devotional one, and the *genre* to which they belonged was that of the printed hymn book. When, in the 1868 edition, O'Daly changed the typography and added some secular poems from the same manuscripts in which Ó Súilleabháin's were first copied, he partly reversed the process, returning the poems to a literary, but by now largely antiquarian, context.

The instability of the appearance and material form of Ó Súilleabháin's poetry and, by extension, the instability of its audience, contrasts strongly with the continuity of those of Buchanan and Grant. This difference can be further illustrated by the relationship of these books to a manuscript tradition. The songs of both Buchanan and Grant appeared in print first, and did not have any substantial manuscript transmission, either before or after publication. By contrast, some of Ó Súilleabháin's poems not only circulated in manuscript for decades before the printed book, but were frequently copied from the printed book back into manuscript during the early nineteenth century.[21] By contrast, MacKechnie's catalogue of Scottish Gaelic manuscripts lists only 7 copies of poems by Buchanan, in 4 different manuscripts, mostly small notebooks of uncertain provenance, and no copies of any poems by Grant.[22] The weakness of print culture in Irish was partly counterbalanced by continuing manuscript activity, whereas the strength and stability of Gaelic print culture in Scotland went with a far weaker manuscript sphere.

CONCLUSION

A comparison of these three texts reveals a number of suggestive contrasts between the print cultures of Irish and Scottish Gaelic, between the cultures of the two languages more broadly, and between their different relationships to English-language print culture. What emerges most strikingly is the strength, stability and homogeneity of Gaelic print culture as opposed to that of Irish. Buchanan's *Laoidhe* and Grant's *Dain* were regularly reprinted throughout the later nineteenth century and into the twentieth, in stereotype editions, which suggests substantial print runs, and in an almost identical

ar a bheatha (Dublin, 1929). **21** Nic Énrí, *An cantaire siúlach*, pp 120–3. **22** John MacKechnie, *Catalogue of Gaelic manuscripts in selected libraries in Great Britain and Ireland* (2 vols, Boston, 1973).

format, which suggests a very stable readership. Printing of the *Pious miscel-lany*, by contrast, collapsed after 1860, and re-emerged in an entirely differ-ent format, which removed it from the purely religious sphere and placed it more in the realm of cultural nationalism and language revival, a domain that was less in evidence for Gaelic in Scotland.

More broadly, this contrast demonstrates that there was a different rela-tionship between language and religion in the two areas. The waves of evan-gelical religion that swept the Highlands and Islands during the nineteenth century were largely in Gaelic, and when the more evangelical Free Church of Scotland seceded from the Church of Scotland in the 1840s, one of its principal bases was in the Gaelic-speaking parishes. In Ireland, by contrast, in the same period, the Catholic equivalent of an evangelical revival (the so-called 'Devotional Revolution') was very much an anglicizing and romanizing process, and it produced next to no devotional publishing in Irish, even though Irish-speaking Catholics were numbered in the hundreds of thou-sands. In sum, the situation of the Catholic Church in Ireland was similar to that of the Free Church, and indeed that of the Non-Conformist churches in Wales or the Catholic Church in Brittany, that is, a non-established church with mass membership, whose political orientation was partly in opposition to the central state. Unlike all those churches, however, it has never had a lin-guistic politics centred on the devotional use of a non-official vernacular. In present-day Scotland, as Charles Withers has put it, 'the future of the Gaelic language is still bound up with the fate of the Free Church'.[23] That has not been true of Irish and the Catholic Church in Ireland since at least the middle of the nineteenth century.

---

23 Charles Withers, *Gaelic in Scotland, 1698–1981: the geographical history of a language* (Edinburgh, 1984), p. 246.

Index